THE CHANGING SYSTEM
OF INDUSTRIAL RELATIONS
IN GREAT BRITAIN

THE

CHANGING SYSTEM OF

INDUSTRIAL RELATIONS

IN

GREAT BRITAIN

A Completely Rewritten Version of
The System of Industrial Relations
in
Great Britain

HUGH ARMSTRONG CLEGG
Professor of Industrial Relations
University of Warwick

BASIL BLACKWELL
OXFORD

© 1979 BASIL BLACKWELL

British Library Cataloguing in Publication Data

Phototypeset in V.I.P. Bembo by
Western Printing Services Ltd, Bristol

Printed in Great Britain by
Billing and Sons, London, Guildford
and Worcester

British Library Cataloguing in Publication Data

Clegg, Hugh Armstrong
    The changing system of industrial relations in Great Britain.
    1. Industrial relations – Great Britain
    I. Title   II. Clegg, Hugh Armstrong. System of industrial relations in Great Britain

    331'.0941   HD8391

    ISBN 0 631 11091 7
    ISBN 0 631 11101 8 Pbk

CONTENTS

TABLES AND FIGURES

PREFACE

The original *System of Industrial Relations in Great Britain* was published twenty-five years ago in 1954. Consisting of six separate contributions edited by the late Allan Flanders and myself, it went through five reprints before it was replaced in 1970 by a new book, with the same title, written by myself. Apart from reprints, there were new editions of this version in 1972 and 1976 in which the final chapter was rewritten to take account of new developments, among them the Industrial Relations Act 1971 and the Employment Protection Act 1975. The preface to the 1976 edition already noted the need for a 'thorough recasting' of the whole book which was to take another 'two years or more'. This is the recast version, and it seems appropriate to indicate the accelerating rate of change in British industrial relations in its title—*The Changing System of Industrial Relations in Great Britain*.

New laws and their interpretation are only one of the elements of change. There have been three distinct incomes policies since 1970, two of which were revised periodically while they were in operation. Less dramatic than these instances of government intervention, but possibly more important in the long run, have been alterations in the structures of employers' organizations, management and trade unions, and in their relationships with each other. Ten years ago the foremost change was the growth of workplace bargaining and shop steward organization. Since then there have been further important developments in the workplace, but, in addition, the reactions to changes in the workplace from the other parties to industrial relations, which began to take shape in the sixties, have now produced substantial reorganization. Meanwhile industrial relations research has continued to produce results which not only add to our knowledge of the subject but also prompt reassessment of what was once thought to be firmly established.

The 1970 version began with chapters on shop stewards, trade unions, employers' associations and management, followed by chapters dealing with structures and subjects of industry bargaining and of workplace bargaining. As part of the recasting, structures and subjects of collective bargaining have been treated within the chapters dealing with the parties to collective bargaining. This has made for economy of exposition, and also draws attention to the close interrelationships between employer, managerial and union organizations and the structures through which they bargain with each other. Many features of British industrial relations are explained by reference to these interrelationships, and contrasts are identified between three major sectors of employment—the public sector, manufacturing and private services. An increased emphasis on analysis should also be evident elsewhere in the book, notably in the chapters on 'The Process of Bargaining' and 'Theories and Definitions' which had no counterparts in the previous version. Nevertheless considerable weight is still placed on historical explanation, and in particular the origins of shop steward organization are examined more fully than before.

Over the winter 1977–8 Industrial Facts and Forecasting Limited conducted a major survey of industrial relations in British manufacturing industry on behalf of the Social Science Research Council's Industrial Relations Research Unit at the University of Warwick. Preliminary results became available before the manuscript went to the publisher. No reference is made to them where they confirm earlier surveys, but several new findings are noted at appropriate points in the text. The survey is described simply as the 'Warwick survey' in the text and the index, but it is now expected that a book will be published by Blackwell later in 1979, entitled *The Changing Contours of British Industrial Relations*. Otherwise abbreviated references are made to works cited in the text and footnotes, and full bibliographical identification is given in the 'Index of References'.

The manuscript was sent to the publisher at the end of September 1978. No additions or amendments have been made to take account of events since then.

The description of my post is currently correct and will still be correct when the book is due to be published, but I shall retire from the chair of industrial relations at Warwick at the end of September 1979, although I hope to retain an association with the University after that.

My thanks are due to my colleagues William Brown, Linda Dickens, Paul Edwards, Joe England, Richard Hyman, Robert Price, Keith Sisson, Michael Terry and Brian Weekes, each of whom read one or more chapters in draft and gave expert advice and comment; and to Annemarie Flanders and Jenny Penfold who typed successive versions with skill, patience and tolerance of my whims.

Hugh Clegg

Chapter 1

INTRODUCTION

THE SUBJECT

What is industrial relations? Among other things, it deals with negotiations between unions and employers, with strikes, and with government intervention in strikes and negotiations; but that is not enough to define an academic subject. The answer which is assumed in this book is that it is the study of the rules governing employment, together with the ways in which the rules are made and changed, interpreted and administered. Put more briefly, it is the study of job regulation. This definition is not universally accepted, but the reader may find it easier to make his own judgements about the matter at the end of the book rather than at the beginning. The debate, along with the discussion of different approaches to the subject, is therefore left to the last chapter which can be read first by those who choose to do so.

The rules governing employment, and the ways in which they are made and interpreted, cannot be understood apart from the organizations that take part in the process. Industrial relations therefore includes the study of trade unions, management, employers' associations and the public bodies concerned with the regulation of employment. Each of these organizations has its own sources of authority, and wherever there are separate sources of authority there is the risk of conflict. When organizations are in conflict, they may apply pressure to persuade each other to make concessions. The most notable form of pressure in industrial relations is the strike, although there are other forms of 'industrial action' as well. Industrial relations therefore includes the study of industrial conflict and the use of industrial action.

The rules themselves are of two main types. There are the rules that settle such issues as pay, the length of the working day, over-

time, holidays, and the way in which a job should be done and the
time it should take. These are called *substantive* rules. Then there are
the rules that settle the ways in which the substantive rules are made,
and the ways in which they can be challenged, changed, interpreted
and applied. These are *procedural* rules.

One way of making employment rules is by *collective bargain-*
ing—jointly by trade unions and employers, or managers. At one
time the words were confined to bargaining between trade unions
and employers' associations, but now bargaining between unions
and the managers of individual plants and companies is also
included. Another method is for the rules to be laid down unilaterally by employers or managers, which may be called *employer regula-*
tion or *managerial regulation* (the difference between them does not
matter at this stage). Subjects on which employers or managers
make the rules are often described as 'managerial functions', or
matters of 'managerial prerogative'. Trade unions also make rules
concerning the jobs of their members and try to enforce them
on employers. This method may be called *trade union regulation*.
A fourth method is *statutory regulation*. The state prescribes legal
rules governing aspects of employment generally or for particular
classes of undertaking, with statutory arrangements for their enforcement.

A fifth method contrasts with the other four because it is, properly
speaking, not a method of making rules, but a method through
which rules emerge. It is *custom* or 'custom and practice' as it is
commonly called in British industrial relations. A custom does not
have force because anyone specifically prescribed it, but because
it has come to be accepted. Consequently there is no prescriptive
way of changing a custom. Where managers have not given specific
consent to a custom, they may argue that its subject-matter falls
within the area of managerial prerogative, and that they are entitled
to alter it unilaterally. On the other hand, where trade unionists
find a custom advantageous, they usually argue that it should be
changed only with their consent, in other words by a collective
agreement.

Another distinction can be drawn between collective bargaining
and *joint consultation*, which is a halfway house between joint regulation and employer or managerial regulation. Managers discuss issues
with representatives of their employees, setting out their problems
and proposals, and listening to what the representatives have to say,

but the final responsibility for the decisions remains with management.

All these distinctions have value for industrial relations analysis. The behaviour of British trade unions today cannot be properly understood unless it is appreciated that unilateral trade union regulation was the predominant method of operation for skilled unions through most of the nineteenth century, and was only gradually overtaken by collective bargaining. The erosion of employer and managerial regulation by custom and practice continues to shape industrial relations today. A dramatic increase in statutory regulation has been one of the outstanding features of the last ten years. The distinction between collective bargaining and joint consultation is essential to an understanding of the development of managerial and trade union ideas in Britain since the First World War, and to explain changes in public policy on industrial relations.

Nevertheless, the distinctions have their limitations. To insist upon them may prevent an appreciation of the processes of industrial relations as a whole. They concentrate attention upon different ways of *making* employment rules, and the making of rules is not necessarily the most important element in industrial relations, and certainly not the most time-consuming. Rules have to be administered and many hours of the time of managers, union officers and shop stewards are spent on administering the rules governing employment for every one that they spend in making them. It is not entirely true to say that rules are only as good as the way in which they are applied, but it certainly is true that industrial relations can differ radically from one plant to another even though both operate under the same or closely similar sets of rules. In addition, the manner of administration moulds the rules. To an extent, and over time to a considerable extent, the power to administer the rules is also the power to amend and extend the rules. Administration, however, does not usually emphasize distinctions between different types of regulation. Problems and disputes arise in the plant, and are settled in the plant by managers and shop stewards dealing with whatever happen to be the relevant rules. The process cannot be divided into the administration of agreements, the administration of custom, the administration of unilateral rules, the administration of statutory rules and so on; to attempt to do so for the purpose of analysis may confuse rather than clarify.

It is, however, not only in the administration of rules that distinctions between different methods of making the rules show their limitations. The origins of the rules are not always distinct. William Brown gives the example of 'a generous allowance' by a foreman

> to one man for a minor favour [which] is liable to set a precedent which will be pressed for by others in the same situation and, eventually, generalised into a local [custom and practice] rule. What started out as a minor individual reward from within the range of the foreman's discretion can easily come to stretch at and then break through his discretionary limits, establishing new transactional rules in the process.[1]

In this instance an exercise of managerial prerogative on a matter assumed to be within the scope of managerial regulation led to the emergence of a custom. In recent years it has become fairly common for procedural agreements to include *status quo* clauses stating that where workers object to a proposed change in an established practice, the practice is to continue to operate until the dispute has been dealt with through the procedure. This arrangement gives the status of an agreement to a custom. To take a further example, the Social Security Pensions Act 1975, which requires companies to consult with recognized unions over occupational pensions schemes, has led to widespread bargaining over these schemes. Their terms also have to comply with the provisions of the Act. The resultant schemes are both collective agreements and statutory rules. This example also demonstrates that what begins as consultation may end as bargaining.

Accordingly, in this book collective bargaining is not generally given the narrow meaning that is appropriate in some contexts. Collective bargaining is treated as the whole range of dealings between employers and managers, on the one hand, and trade unions, shop stewards and union members, on the other, over the making, interpretation and administration of employment rules, and the 'intra-organizational bargaining' that goes on within either side over the approaches and responses that they make to each other. It also includes bargaining between the two sides over the application of statutory controls.

---

[1] *Piecework Bargaining*, p. 99. A 'transitional rule . . . is a pattern of behaviour governed by a reciprocity relationship between two parties which both parties regard as legitimate' (*ibid.*, p. 84).

If further justification is needed for this use of words, it is that, in comparison with the past and with some other countries today, the joint regulation of employment by employers and managers on the one hand, and by trade unions and shop stewards on the other is central to British industrial relations. It so overshadows the other methods of regulation with which it is intertwined that the process of industrial relations is essentially a process of collective bargaining.

THREE SECTORS OF EMPLOYMENT

At many points in the following chapters, reference is made to differences in patterns of industrial relations among three sectors of employment—the public sector, manufacturing, and the private services. They are not very far apart in overall size. In round figures, the public sector accounts for about 7.0 million employees, manufacturing for about 7.25 million, and the private services for about 8.25 million. The main constituents of the public sector are: central government services; local, educational and health services; and the nationalized industries. The great majority of manufacturing employees work in food manufacture, chemicals, metal manufacture, textiles, clothing, paper and printing, and above all in the engineering group of industries, which accounts for about 40 per cent of manufacturing employment. The main private services are: distribution; hotels and catering; and insurance, banking, finance and business services. For the purpose of this book, construction and agriculture have been included along with them. There are, in addition, a large number of smaller services that nevertheless employ considerable numbers of workers. Over two million employees work in what are classified as 'miscellaneous services'.

Employing units in the public service are generally large. Most civil servants are employed by the crown. The Post Office is a single employer, the National Coal Board is another, and the British Steel Corporation a third. Most employees in the local, education and health services are employed by local, education and health 'authorities', each accounting for several thousand employees or more.

Precise figures are available for the manufacturing sector. The report of the 1972 Census of Production shows that just short of 45 per cent of the total employment was in companies with more than five thousand employees.[2] Manufacturing, therefore, comes in an intermediate position between the public sector and the private services where the average size of employing unit is generally small. Although there are no overall figures for the private services, there are a number of substantial indicators. By far the largest of the private services is retail distribution. In 1971 there were about 352,000 enterprises[3] and about two million employees in retailing. The average size of employing units was therefore about six workers. Figures for construction are available for 1974, when there were rather more than 94,000 undertakings[4] and about 1.3 million employees, giving an average of about 14 workers to a firm.

The significance of these figures for industrial relations is, among many other things, that small firms can usually manage with relatively few rules, on the basis of personal dealings between the employer and individual workers, whereas large firms have to operate through rules. Moreover, in large firms individual employees on their own cannot expect to have much influence in seeking to change rules which they find unsatisfactory or unjust. There is, therefore, greater pressure to form and to join unions in large firms than in small firms.

The validity of this hypothesis is borne out by the figures of what is called trade union *density*. In 1974 the proportion of public sector employees who were trade union members was about 83 per cent. In manufacturing the proportion of trade unionists was about 62 per cent. In private services, as they are defined in this book, trade union density was about 20 per cent.[5]

However, the individual employer is not always the main unit for rulemaking in industrial relations. Many of the most important industrial relations rules in the public sector apply throughout an industry or service, whether it has only one employer or a number of them. Local government, the health service and the education service are the three largest examples. In manufacturing there are also industry-wide rules settled between employers' associations and the unions, but their scope and significance is generally much less than in the public sector. The most important level of rulemaking in manu-

---

[2] PA 1002.118, *Business Monitor*, 1977.
[3] *Census of Distribution*, 1971, SD23, table 39.
[4] PA 500.9, *Business Monitor*, 1974.
[5] These figures are based on the work of Price and Bain, 'Trade Union Growth Revisited'.

facturing is neither the industry nor the company, but the plant. Nevertheless, this statement does not invalidate the comparison just drawn between manufacturing and the private services. In 1974 almost a third of manufacturing employees (32.2 per cent) worked in plants with one thousand or more employees,[6] and the average size of plant was about seventy workers.[7] Thus, in terms of employment, the average manufacturing *plant* was several times larger than the average *company* in retail distribution or construction.

Many other differences between the three sectors will be noted in subsequent chapters.

THE PLAN OF THE BOOK

Logic does not dictate any particular starting point for a textbook of industrial relations. However, in Britain at the present time there is something to be said for beginning with workplace bargaining and trade union organization in the workplace, for they are uniquely important in contemporary Britain compared with the past or with countries overseas. Chapter 2, therefore, deals with these topics, starting with manufacturing industry—where workplace bargaining has developed furthest.

The structure of collective bargaining outside the plant has been strongly influenced by the organization of employers' associations and the shape of employing units. This is the subject of Chapter 3, together with the response of employers and their associations to the growth of workplace bargaining. The evolution of collective bargaining since the war has also been influenced by changes in the structure and style of management within the plant, and by the practice of a number of managerial techniques designed to give managers greater control over the organization of work. These topics are covered in Chapter 4. Chapter 5 returns to the unions, dealing with their structure and methods of government outside the plant, and showing how they have responded to changes in collective bargaining.

---

[6] *Annual Abstract of Statistics*, 1977, table 6.17.

[7] In 1974 there were 59,691 manufacturing plants with over ten employees, and in all they employed 7,439,000 workers. It was estimated that there were about 50,000 plants with ten employees or less, accounting for approximately 250,000 employees in all. There were therefore roughly 110,000 plants and 7.7 million employees. (*ibid.*)

With the structure of bargaining and the parties to bargaining sketched out, Chapter 6 turns to the process of bargaining, proceeding through a discussion of its styles and values to the topic of power in collective bargaining. It therefore leads on to the subject of Chapter 7, which is the pattern of strikes and other forms of industrial action in postwar Britain and the reasons for them.

Chapter 8 turns to the state, beginning with the traditional voluntarism of the law relating to industrial relations, and then describing the growth of political intervention through successive incomes policies and attempts to reform collective bargaining and trade unions by legislation. Incomes policies and their effects on industrial relations are further analysed in Chapter 9; and Chapter 10 introduces the more important of recent laws affecting industrial relations, especially the Employment Protection Act, exploring their preliminary results.

Finally, by discussing different theories and definitions of industrial relations, Chapter 11 fulfils the commitment given at the beginning of this introduction.

Chapter 2

SHOP STEWARDS AND WORKPLACE BARGAINING

PAY NEGOTIATIONS IN MANUFACTURING

The pay of manual workers in the great majority of manufacturing plants of any size—say with more than a hundred employees—is settled largely or entirely by collective bargaining between unions on the one hand and managers or employers' associations on the other. Bargaining may take place at several levels. Unions and employers' associations may make pay agreements for a whole industry, or for an industry within a particular district or region. Multi-plant companies (or 'groups') can make company agreements with the unions, or, where their plants are assigned to divisions, they may allow each division to make its own agreements. Alternatively, bargaining may take place at the plant. More often than not, issues relating to pay are settled at more than one level.

In 1975 W. W. Daniel estimated the importance of these various levels of pay settlement by a sample survey of 254 plants with over two hundred employees drawn from the whole range of manufacturing industries. All but twelve of them recognized trade unions. In answer to a question concerning the levels of collective bargaining that directly affected 'adjustments in rates' or formed 'the basis of subsequent negotiations' in their plants, 13 per cent of the management respondents mentioned three or more levels, 39 per cent mentioned two, and 42 per cent mentioned only one. The level most frequently mentioned was the plant (72 per cent), with the industry next (49 per cent), and the company or division, which were taken together, coming third (34 per cent). Another question asked for the most important level of bargaining over pay. The answers, summarized in Table 1, show that the plant is by a considerable margin the most important level overall, and by far the most important in engineering and metalworking; with the company or division level a little ahead of the industry.[1]

The limitation of the survey to plants with more than two hundred employees probably led to underestimation of the importance of industry bargaining over pay. Small plants are less likely than larger plants to devise their own pay structures and more likely to apply the increases negotiated in industry agreements without much further bargaining in the plant. The survey gives an indication of this tendency, for 22 per cent of the plants with 201–500 employees gave the industry as the most important level, compared with only 14 per cent of those employing more than five hundred. But since almost 70 per cent of British manufacturing employees work in plants that employ two hundred workers or more,[2] the bias is not likely to make very much difference to the overall relative importance of the several levels of bargaining.

These figures demonstrate the importance of workplace bargaining over pay in manufacturing, but they do not indicate who does the bargaining on the union side. In some instances it is conducted by a full-time trade union officer coming in from outside. A study of the hosiery industry found that although 'plant bargaining over piece rates' was 'not limited by an industry agreement. . . nevertheless the officers were in control, and were called in to handle negotiations at an early stage, even in the larger plants, on the principle that "we pay them to do the talking".'[3] But Daniel's survey showed that this practice is exceptional. He found that

> union representatives at plant level tend to operate independently of their official trade union organisations. In only 10 per cent of the cases was the leader of the union negotiating team a full-time officer of the union. . . . Indeed in most cases . . . a full-time officer was not even consulted in the preparation of the claim. . . . The role of the full-time officer was to be brought in when there was deadlock.[4]

These findings are supported by the evidence of a number of other surveys and case studies which will be mentioned in the following pages.

All this refers only to manual workers. Less is known about

[1] *Wage Determination in Industry*, pp. 25–30.　　[2] *Bullock Report*, p. 14.
[3] Boraston *et al.*, *Workplace and Union*, pp. 122–3.
[4] W. W. Daniel, *The Next Stage of Incomes Policy*, pp. 11–12.

Table 1

Relative Importance of Levels of Bargaining over Pay in Manufacturing

Level	All Industries	Engineering	Metal-working	Chemicals	Food, Drink Tobacco	Other
Industry	17	7	15	26	33	28
Company/ Division	20	15	12	32	27	26
Region/ District	2	4	–	–	–	4
Plant	55	71	73	37	33	31
Other	1	1	–	–	–	2
Can't say	4	2	–	5	7	7
	100	100	100	100	100	100
Base: all plants where unions recognized	(241)	(105)	(33)	(19)	(30)	(54)

collective bargaining among white collar workers, but some generalizations can nevertheless be made with fair confidence. There is probably much less collective bargaining among white collar than among manual workers. It is reasonable to assume that the extent of union membership is some indication of the coverage of collective bargaining, and in 1974 only 32 per cent of white collar employees in manufacturing were unionized, compared with 73 per cent of manual employees.[5] It is certain that white collar pay is less affected by industry agreements than is the pay of manual workers. Most employers' associations in manufacturing do not negotiate with unions representing white collar employees; and although the largest of them, the Engineering Employers' Federation, recognizes the unions, it no longer negotiates minimum salary scales as it once did, but leaves the settlement of salaries to the companies and the plants. It is probable that the company or the division is the most important level of white collar bargaining. In 1974 the Commission on Industrial Relations reported that

> although in some multi-plant companies we found that manual workers' minimum pay and conditions are negotiated at industry

[5] Price and Bain, 'Union Growth Revisited'.

or group level, in most cases actual pay is settled at the plant. On the other hand, non-manual workers' pay and conditions are generally decided at the level of the group, often on a company-wide basis.[6]

Even where white collar pay is settled in the plant, as is not unusual in engineering, the shop stewards probably take a less prominent part than manual shop stewards in the settlement of their members' pay. One of the few studies of white collar bargaining in the plant reported that 'the leadership is often assumed by the full-time officials' who 'tend to be involved not merely in the actual making of decisions, but also more frequently in the definition of problems. On the shop-floor, in contrast, the conveners tend to play a more central role in decisions and are also more able to control the involvement of full-time officials in the formulation of problems.'[7] However, only just over a quarter of manufacturing employees hold white collar jobs, so that the pattern of bargaining among manual workers is of greater significance.

The plant is therefore the most important level of bargaining over pay in manufacturing, and plant bargaining is in most instances in the hands of shop stewards. But it was not always so, and things are different overseas. How, then, has plant bargaining by shop stewards come to predominate in Britain?

THE RISE OF PLANT BARGAINING

In 1968 the Donovan Commission marshalled statistics 'to show that over the last thirty years there has been a decline in the extent to which industry-wide agreements determine actual pay.' They took the difference between wage rates for a standard working week and average weekly earnings in 1938 and compared it with the difference between the two in 1967. In 1938 the average engineering rates[8] were

---

[6] *Industrial Relations in Multi-Plant Undertakings*, p. 15.

[7] Batstone *et al.*, *Shop Stewards in Action*, p. 211. 'Convener' is an alternative to 'senior shop steward', although in some instances both titles are used in the same plant where there are, say, departmental senior stewards and a plant convener.

[8] At that time an engineering worker's pay consisted of two parts—a district rate and a national bonus. Increases and decreases came through alterations of the national bonus, but district rates differed, so there was no single industry rate. In 1947 differences in district rates were removed and industry rates were introduced.

£3.36 for fitters and £2.52 for labourers, whereas average earnings for men were £3.68. In 1967 the fitter's rate was £11.08 and the labourer's was £9.37, but average earnings for men had risen to £21.39 in the general engineering and electrical goods sections of the industry and to £24.42 in vehicle manufacture.[9]

However, these and similar figures for other industries do not prove that plant bargaining had come to play a major part in pay determination by 1967. In conditions of labour shortage such as prevailed almost continuously from 1940 to 1967, many employers are ready to make pay concessions of their own accord in order to retain workers. With one or two setbacks, such as the one occasioned by demobilization and the switch to peacetime production in 1945–6, earnings rose faster than wage rates continuously from 1938 to 1968 in industries in which shop stewards appeared to have some power, in industries in which they appeared to be weak, and also in industries in which there was little trade union organization at any level. The evidence that workplace bargaining played a considerable part in settling the constituents of pay other than industry rates comes from sample surveys and case studies, many of them conducted by the Donovan Commission and the National Board for Prices and Incomes during the latter half of the sixties. Surveys established that shop stewards operated in an overwhelming majority of manufacturing plants which employed more than 150 workers and recognized trade unions. Over half of these stewards regularly discussed and settled with management one or more aspects of their members' pay, and most of the remainder did so sometimes.[10] The case studies give an indication of how they went about it.

Payment by results was a major issue of workplace bargaining in many plants. According to Ministry of Labour figures for 1961, 42 per cent of wage-earners in manufacturing were paid by results. The report of the National Board for Prices and Incomes on *Payment by Results Systems* showed that, although one or two industries, includ-

[9] *Report*, pp. 14–15.
[10] In 1966 the Government Social Survey conducted a series of surveys of workplace industrial relations for the Donovan Commission whose results appeared in *Workplace Industrial Relations* published in 1968, henceforth quoted as *Workplace Industrial Relations 1966*. Subsequently the same body, now called the Social Survey Division of the Office of Population Censuses and Surveys, carried out two similar inquiries: *Workplace Industrial Relations 1972* and *Workplace Industrial Relations 1973*, published in 1973 and 1975. The surveys were not confined to manufacturing but were heavily biased towards it.

ing cotton textiles and footwear, made some attempt to control payment by results by industry agreements, elsewhere the measuring of performance and its relationship to monetary rewards were left to the individual undertakings so long as a minimum level of earnings was achieved. The construction of a system of payment by results was therefore a matter for plant bargaining; and there were also many opportunities for bargaining over payment by results after its introduction.

When new products were introduced, values had to be settled for the new jobs involved in making them. When car workers were paid by results a new model led to the negotiation of hundreds or even thousands of new values. Even where the product remained substantially the same there was usually provision for re-evaluation where the equipment, the material or the methods of production were improved, presenting further opportunities for bargaining.

In addition to periodic increases in the basic rate, there was almost invariably an upward 'drift' in earnings under any system of payment by results, and it was unequally distributed. The faster the drift, the wider the range of variation. Workers left behind demanded that their jobs be reviewed. Machine breakdowns, shortages of parts, defective materials and other hindrances to production prevented workers achieving their expected earnings and led to negotiations for 'allowances'.

As a result of their case studies, the National Board for Prices and Incomes found that these opportunities were in many instances exploited, especially among male workers—and the proportion of men paid by results had increased substantially since 1938.[11] They reported that in 'the factories we studied where the labour force is predominantly male there has often been a readiness to argue and fight for quite small gains.'[12] They also noted the 'significant amount of valuable time' spent on bargaining over payment by results 'by workers, shop stewards, foremen and management' in the 'constant time-consuming process of shop-floor haggling.'[13]

Bargaining over payment by results led to bargaining by timeworkers in the same plant to catch up with rising piecework

[11] For all industries covered, including other industries besides manufacturing, the proportion of male wage-earners paid by results rose from 18 per cent in 1938 to 30 per cent in 1961 (*Ministry of Labour Gazette*, September 1961).

[12] *Payment by Results Systems*, p. 19.

[13] *Ibid.*, pp. 24, 29.

earnings. In some plants, managers tried to find means of relating their pay to output as well, but in others there was

> no pretence that bonuses are linked to output, and the result has been a medley of lieu bonuses, special bonuses, dubiously entitled merit payments, and 'out of office' supplements. . . . In yet another firm, the various groups of indirect workers periodically submitted separate claims for time rate increases. These claims came in waves: usually the toolroom workers and electricians led, and were then followed by the others.[14]

Rising piecework earnings also provided targets for pay claims in plants which employed only timeworkers. But timeworkers did not need that inducement to negotiate pay increases for themselves. The main trades employed in the construction of ships (as opposed to the finishing trades) substituted lieu rates for piecerates long before the war. These rates were fixed job by job, and it was not uncommon for further adjustments to be made during the course of the job. Workers made 'wage claims at a point when management greatly requires their particular skill.'[15] Similarly in printing, and particularly in newspaper printing, the highly developed system of chapel bargaining—with a separate chapel for each department—dealt mainly with the negotiation of various timerates, including 'merit money', 'house rates' and 'machine extras'.[16]

One of the most common subjects of workplace bargaining among men in timeworking plants is overtime, which has increased rapidly in postwar Britain. In April 1947 the difference between the weighted average of agreed 'normal hours' and hours recorded as worked by men was about an hour a week. By April 1966 periodic negotiations had reduced average normal hours from 45.3 to 40.3 a week but hours worked had altered little so that the difference had increased fairly steadily to about six hours; and since the average hours worked includes workers who were absent for part of the week, average overtime was probably between seven and eight hours a man. This overtime was unequally distributed between industries, with some averaging well over ten hours a week; and

[14] *Ibid.*, p. 30.

[15] G. C. Cameron, 'Post-war Strikes in the North-East Shipbuilding and Ship-repairing Industry'.

[16] National Board for Prices and Incomes, *Wages, Costs and Prices in the Printing Industry*, p. 5.

'within industries overtime is highest in the lowest-paid occupations and among those workers not on incentive schemes.'[17]

The Donovan Commission's surveys found that the level and distribution of overtime were two of the most common issues discussed and settled between shop stewards and managers; and their research director reported that a series of case studies had discovered that

> in all the workplace situations studied, grievances had arisen over the uneven distribution of overtime. . . . In one of the engineering firms . . ., a position had been reached in the recent past in which stewards, in effect, were accepted by management as having the right to grant or withhold overtime.[18]

In his study of the Esso refinery at Fawley, Allan Flanders noted that, 'although decisions about the working of overtime nominally remained with supervision, the stewards . . . came effectively to control its distribution.'[19]

Not long afterwards, in his evidence to the Donovan Commission, Flanders wrote his famous description of British workplace bargaining as 'largely informal, largely fragmented and largely autonomous'.[20] It was largely informal because pay and other issues were usually settled by understandings or customs rather than written and openly acknowledged agreements; largely fragmented because piecework values were bargained job by job, and because timeworkers negotiated piecemeal, trade by trade in the shipyards, chapel by chapel in printing, and section by section over the distribution of overtime at Fawley (although some shop stewards' committees tried to co-ordinate piecework and sectional claims); and largely autonomous because on the union side it was commonly in the hands of shop stewards with little control from the unions outside the plant. However, signs of change were already visible when those words were written, and before long the overall trend was obviously in a different direction. Workplace bargaining remained the centre of attention and its autonomy was even strengthened; but considerable formalization has been introduced into workplace bargaining in many plants, and there has been a widespread shift away from

[17] E. G. Whybrew, *Overtime Working in Britain*, pp. 11, 63.
[18] W. E. J. McCarthy, *The Role of Shop Stewards in British Industrial Relations*, p. 12.
[19] *The Fawley Productivity Agreements*, p. 63.
[20] *Selected Written Evidence*, p. 552.

fragmentation to plant-wide and even company agreements over pay.

The new trend became evident in the spread of productivity bargaining. The pioneer was Fawley where the original agreements were signed in 1960. Their essence was a series of changes in working practices and the deployment of labour which allowed the refinery to operate with much reduced levels of overtime. Workers were compensated for loss of overtime earnings by substantial increases in their hourly rates of pay. Most of Fawley's imitators over the next few years also aimed to raise low levels of productivity associated with high levels of overtime, but some of them included in their agreements the termination of systems of payment by results which, they believed, had lost their incentive effects and were impeding the effective deployment of labour. Towards the end of the sixties the replacement of payment by results systems by 'measured daywork' became the chief feature in the reform of payment systems, with the additional objectives of reducing 'wage drift' and cutting down the large number of strikes associated with piecework bargaining.

Fawley was not federated to an employers' association so that the negotiation of hourly rates of pay in the plant involved no new principle. The difference was that the new rates constituted a much larger part of total pay than before. But for many federated firms the negotiation of a productivity agreement entailed the settlement of hourly rates in the plant for the first time. Previously they had relied on industry rates of pay supplemented by fragmented plant bargaining over piecerates, lieu rates, merit rates, various bonuses, overtime, and so on.

Although full-time union officers played a considerable part in the negotiation of some of the original agreements, in most of them 'the main burden at almost all stages of the move to plant bargaining fell upon chief lay officials', and 'in the operation of factory agreements it was again the lay official rather than the full-time officer who played the major part.'[21] The general outcome therefore was a considerable enhancement of the authority of conveners or senior stewards and of the central shop stewards' committee in the plant, for they henceforth controlled negotiations over pay about which the individual steward could now do little by himself. This was true both of federated plants and non-federated plants like Fawley. Man-

---

[21] Department of Employment, *The Reform of Collective Bargaining at Plant and Company Level*, p. 84.

agers found that they could not negotiate reduction of overtime or the elimination of payment by results except with the stewards who controlled these matters.

Productivity agreements and measured daywork do not, however, account for the whole of the shift to plant-wide bargaining. Some plants chose to rationalize systems of payment by results rather than go over to timerates.[22] This rationalization usually involved increasing control over the assessment of values by improved 'work study', and reducing the proportion of piecework earnings to total earnings. The latter change involved negotiating a general increase in hourly rates within the plant.

Another factor, and perhaps the most important of them all, is job evaluation—a device 'to determine the relationship between jobs and to establish a systematic structure of wage rates for them.'[23] In 1967 the National Board for Prices and Incomes found that job evaluation had been applied to about a quarter of the labour force and was 'increasing rapidly'.[24] This figure includes workers covered by many productivity and measured daywork agreements which provided for the new hourly rates to be settled by job evaluation, but also many other workers as well. In any case, because job evaluation is carried out at plant or company level in Britain, its introduction involved a departure from industry rates and in most instances the formal negotiation of the new rates with shop stewards.

It is possible to balance a plant or company pay structure on top of rates negotiated in industry agreements, with the consequence that periodic increases are provided by industry negotiations. But this is an awkward arrangement where, as is often the case, the grades in the plant pay structure cut across the industry agreement; and even where the two sets of grades are matched, the differentials may not be the same, so that the application of industry increases may distort the plant pay structure. With the spread of plant-wide bargaining, therefore, industry pay agreements have tended to become 'safety nets' with no direct application to plants and companies which negotiate their own pay structure, unless the industry rates begin to overtake some of the rates settled in plant negotiations.[25]

[22] There is some controversy over whether payment for measured daywork should be classified as timerated or not. Payment is by time but—nominally at least—for the performance of a given task in that time. Here it is treated as timerated.
[23] Trades Union Congress, *An Outline of Job Evaluation and Merit Rating*, p. 1.
[24] *Job Evaluation*, p. 10.
[25] Brown and Terry, 'The Changing Nature of National Wage Agreements'.

This account of the development of plant bargaining still leaves one important question unanswered: how was it that shop stewards were able to get control of fragmented bargaining in the beginning? It is necessary to look further back in their history to provide the answer.

THE ORIGINS OF SHOP STEWARDS

The printing industry's shop steward—the 'father of the chapel'—can be traced back long before the earliest trade unions.[26] At that time the chapel was an independent association of printing craftsmen—compositors or pressmen—in a single shop. Its functions were to make rules for the protection of its members, to organize social events, and to look after its members when in need. So firmly were the chapels established that, when the unions were formed, the chapels were incorporated into their branches, a branch being a federation of chapels with the chapel fathers now responsible for the observation of union rules in their shops in addition to their other duties.

It is, however, in the Amalgamated Society of Engineers that the history of shop stewards is best documented. The Engineers were a craft union, and the power of a craft union depends on limiting membership of the union to qualified workers—normally those who have completed an apprenticeship—and protecting certain jobs as the prerogative of the craft. The Engineers entrusted the formulation of the craft rules to their district committees who were also empowered to decide the terms on which their members would accept employment, including rates of pay and hours of work. For collective bargaining was relatively rare in the craft trades until the last decades of the nineteenth century. When the district committee decided that it was time for an increase in pay or a reduction in the working day, they circularized their decision to the local employers, just as the employers posted notices in their workplaces if they decided on a reduction in pay. Unless one side gave way there would then be a strike or a lockout. As time passed some district committees began to see an advantage in discussing proposed changes in pay and hours of work with the employers, but they regarded themselves as the sole arbiters on craft practices. Such matters were not the business of the employers.

[26] J. Moxon, *Mechanick Exercises*, p. 356.

The enforcement of the craft rules therefore rested on the vigilance of the district committees. Some of them began to appoint a delegate in each shop to help them. He was elected by his fellow-members in the shop and known as a shop steward. His duties were to check that all qualified employees were in the union, to see that the craft rules were observed, and to report infringements to the committee. The employers were well aware of his existence. In 1897 one of their leaders, Colonel Dyer, complained that

> in every shop and in every department there have been for years, what are known as 'shop stewards', members of the ASE, whose duty it is see that the rules, written and unwritten, of their society are carried out, and he is a brave employer who dares say 'nay' to their demands.[27]

During the eighteen-nineties a conflict developed with the recently-founded federation of local engineering employers' association over the 'machine question'. New machinery had simplified and given greater precision to the cutting and shaping of metal. Where craftsmen were no longer needed to do the job, the employers wanted to put less skilled men to work the machines at lower rates of pay. The federation threw down the gauntlet in 1897 with a national lockout in reply to a union attempt to impose the eight-hour day in London by circularizing the London firms in the traditional manner. Eventually a settlement was reached in February 1898. The union was forced to admit that 'employers are responsible for the work turned out by their machine tools, and shall have full discretion to appoint the men they consider suitable to work them.' The men were to be paid 'according to their ability as workmen'.

The agreement also settled a number of other issues in the employers' favour. The closed shop was outlawed and union members were committed to work peaceably with non-unionists; apart from a monthly limit, all restrictions on overtime were to cease; and there was to be no limit on the number of apprentices. There was also a clause on piecework. As the new machines made jobs more repetitive, engineering production became more suited to piecework, and the employers hankered after the higher productivity that piecework might be expected to bring. Piecework had already been introduced

---

[27] *Cassier's Magazine*, November 1897, quoted in B. C. M. Weekes, *The Amalgamated Society of Engineers, 1880–1914.*

into some shops but the district committees sought to prevent its extension. The agreement therefore gave the right to work piecework 'to all members of the Federation and to all their Union workmen', with 'prices to be paid for piecework' to be fixed 'by mutual arrangement between the employer and the workman or workmen who perform the work'.

Finally, the agreement ordained that 'general alterations in the rates of wages in any district or districts will be negotiated' between the local employers' association and union representatives, and set out a procedure for dealing with unresolved local disputes. They were to be referred to a conference between 'the Executive Board of the Federation and the central authority of the Trade Union', and until after that there was to be no stoppage of work.

The unforeseen consequence of the agreement was a widening of the scope for shop steward action. There was no longer anything that the district committees could officially do when a shop steward reported an infringement on craft rules. Had a committee disputed the employers' right to put less skilled workers on to a machine, or to employ non-unionists, or to work overtime, the dispute would have had to go 'into procedure' where the employers would have pointed triumphantly to the relevant clause in the agreement. But things were different in the shop. There the shop steward could hint to his employer that his fellow-workers might be very unhappy if he went ahead with his intention to exercise his rights. For his part, having considered the consequences of upsetting his skilled men, the employer might decide to play safe; or he might learn from experience that it was not worth his while to challenge them.

The district committees could no longer object to piecework, which began to spread rapidly; nor could they negotiate piecerates. But in the plants 'special "Workshop Committees" or "Piece-work Committees" sprang up for the purpose, among others, of considering all [piecework] prices before any man was allowed to accept them.'[28] As a result of the 1898 agreement the shop steward had become both the guardian of the craft rules and a workplace negotiator.

So successful was the shop stewards' defence of their craft that the government had to intervene during the First World War to achieve what the employers had failed to accomplish in spite of their victory in 1898. Recruitment to the forces and the demand for munitions led

[28] G. D. H. Cole, *Workshop Organisation*, p. 15.

to an acute shortage of skilled engineering workers. After negotiations with the unions, the government acquired powers under the Munitions Act 1915 to enforce 'dilution'—the replacement of skilled men by less skilled workers, including women. Even then little was done until the government appointed dilution commissioners who negotiated with the shop stewards, factory by factory, the terms on which the men would accept dilution.

The Engineers were the pioneers in developing new forms of workplace organization because it was their jobs that were primarily threatened by the new machinery and wartime dilution. But the practice of electing shop stewards spread to other engineering and shipbuilding craft unions as well, including the Boilermakers and the Ironfounders. As unionization spread among the less skilled workers under the impetus of the 'new unionism' of 1889, they too felt the need for workplace representatives to negotiate in the plant—although not, of course, to defend craft rules. In the Northeast the National Amalgamated Union of Labour appointed shop stewards from the start, and relied heavily upon them.[29] In other 'new unions' the job was done by dues collectors. In 1889 the Gasworkers' collecting stewards enforced a closed shop at the South Metropolitan gasworks,[30] and in 1914 an organizer of the Workers' Union wrote:

> Upon the collector rests the responsibility of advice in the first instance, in those emergency difficulties which occasionally spring up even in the best shops; and upon him frequently falls the duty of acting as spokesman for the others, in discussion with Foreman or Works Manager.[31]

Under the impetus of war, shop steward organization spread throughout the engineering and shipbuilding industries and to other manufacturing industries as well. It is significant that, when government influence and a major strike in Coventry persuaded the engineering employers to negotiate an agreement in December 1917 acknowledging the status of shop stewards as workplace negotiators and establishing an official procedure for them to raise grievances in the plant, it was signed by the other engineering unions, skilled and

---

[29] H. A. Clegg, *General Union in a Changing Society*, pp. 28–9.
[30] Clegg, Fox and Thompson, *A History of British Trade Unions Since 1889*, Vol. 1, pp. 58–9.
[31] *The Workers' Union Record*, January 1914.

unskilled, and not by the Engineers who accepted a modified document two years later.

For most of the interwar years the unions were in retreat, and workshop organization fell back too. Shop stewards did not disappear, at least where the unions retained substantial membership, and they continued to take up their members' grievances; but they found it politic to maintain a low profile, and to avoid the aggressive actions, or militant responses to management action, which had helped to provoke major unofficial strikes during the war, and another engineering lockout in 1922. The 1922 settlement was a further reassertion of managerial prerogatives, although a good deal less sweeping than in the 1898 agreement, but there is no reason to suppose that it inhibited trade union action in the workplace any more than had the 1898 settlement. Workplace activity was held back by the economic depression, and when the rearmament programme brought renewed prosperity to engineering several years before the Second World War, the shop stewards began to feel their feet again. By this time trade union amalgamations had made the Transport and General Workers' Union and the General and Municipal Workers' Union the two largest unions in engineering after the Engineers, and both of them had substantial membership in many other manufacturing industries. Meanwhile technological progress had increased the demand for maintenance fitters in all manufacturing industries. The Engineers and the two general unions therefore constituted channels through which developments in workplace organization in engineering could spread to other industries.

The question with which this section began is therefore answered. Shop stewards gained control of the fragmented bargaining over pay which developed in the workplace, as earnings began to pull away from wage rates after 1939, because they were already in control of such workplace bargaining as there was in engineering, and in some other areas of manufacturing as well.

However, bargaining over pay was not the shop steward's original function, and even after 1939 it was not necessarily his main function. After 1898 the regulation of piecework became an increasingly important job for the Engineers' shop stewards, but their first duty in both pieceworking and timeworking shops was to protect the rules of their craft now that the trade unions outside were debarred from doing so. Since the First World War craft rules have lost some of their importance because of technological change and the increased unionization of other workers. The Engineers long ago ceased to be an exclusively craft union, and probably less than a third of their current members are craftsmen. But the development and defence of craft rules is only one example of the regulation of work by workers and their trade unions. Other workers achieve similar objectives by different rules. In order to understand the work of shop stewards today it is therefore necessary to examine their part in the regulation of work at the workplace as well as their part in pay negotiations.

CUSTOM AND THE REGULATION OF WORK

In the last official survey of plant industrial relations, *Workplace Industrial Relations 1973*, which dealt mainly but not exclusively with manufacturing, senior managers who said that they dealt with shop stewards were asked whether they had personally settled a number of issues with their shop stewards—and senior managers are unlikely to exaggerate the number of issues handled by shop stewards. There were twenty-eight issues in all. Eight of them were classified as wage issues, and only one of these—'promotion or upgrading'—was mentioned by more than two-fifths of the senior managers, although 'bonus payments other than piecework' and 'job evaluation' came close to that figure. Of the remaining twenty issues, eight were mentioned by more than half of the managers. They were: general conditions in the workplace, safety, transfers from one job to another, overtime, dismissals, other disciplinary action, the introduction of new machinery or jobs, and health. Another nine issues were mentioned by between half and two-fifths of the managers: suspension, allocation of work, quality of work, stopping and starting times, breaks in working hours, holidays, manning of machines, taking on new labour, and redundancy. Most of these issues deal directly or indirectly with the organization of work. Disciplinary matters, for instance, cover what workers may and may not do in the workplace and on the job; and safety issues affect the design of the job and the equipment. One reason for the relatively low score of pay issues is that each of them can be the subject of negotiation with stewards only in plants which use the relevant pay system. For instance, piecework prices are only negotiated where piecework is used, and job evaluation is a matter for discussion with shop stewards only where job evaluation has been introduced, or has been proposed. Transfers, new jobs, safety, health, and discipline, on the other hand, are potential issues for negotiation in every plant.

Twenty years earlier the same question might have got different answers. The formalization of collective bargaining in the workplace has brought senior managers into negotiations with shop stewards to a much greater extent than was then common. At that time many of these aspects of work might have been discussed between foremen and shop stewards in a twilight zone about which senior managers were ignorant or preferred not to know too much. Perhaps the best example of this twilight zone is an issue which is not specifically mentioned as a topic of workplace bargaining in the survey—the closed shop. When W. E. J. McCarthy brought out his book on *The Closed Shop in Britain* in 1964, many managers and trade union leaders were surprised by his estimate that about two trade union members out of five had no choice but to belong to a trade union if they wanted to keep their jobs.[32] They expected the proportion to be much smaller because they knew that formal agreements on the subject were confined to a few areas of employment such as coalmining, docks, and co-operative societies. McCarthy's surveys revealed that, although less than three-quarters of a million trade unionists were covered by agreements of this kind, more than three million trade unionists worked in situations where a closed shop was sustained by workplace arrangements, either because a closed shop had been informally recognized, or simply because the workers concerned would not work with non-unionists.

Many of these three million trade unionists might have said that the closed shop—they would probably have preferred the euphemism '100 per cent trade unionism'—was 'custom and practice' at their places of work, thus drawing attention to the enormous significance of custom in British industrial relations, going back to the beginnings of trade unionism and beyond.

It is often supposed that nineteenth-century employers were autocrats who ran their businesses as they pleased until trade unions forced them to accept some restrictions on their power. In fact they were restricted by custom. In most instances custom settled the rate of pay and the hours of work which an employee in a given occupation and district expected to receive, along with the way in which his work would be arranged and carried out. In many instances trade

[32] *The Closed Shop in Britain*, pp. 30–4.

unions came into being as the protectors of custom. Perhaps the most imposing union in the first half of the century was the Operative Builders' Union which flourished from 1831 to 1833 and was the only union ever to have brought together all the building crafts in Britain into a single organization. In 1833 the union launched an unsuccessful campaign against the new system of 'general contracting'. Previously customers had dealt separately with master craftsmen from the various building trades, but with the industrial revolution had come the master builder who tendered for the erection of the whole building. According to G. D. H. Cole, the workers' objection to the new system was 'partly because it tended to deprive them of the chance of becoming masters, and partly because the "general contractor" was apt to be intolerant of the traditional rules and customs of the various trades, which the small masters, being themselves mostly apprenticed craftsmen not far removed in status from skilled workmen, were accustomed to observe.'[33]

Custom was not static. It developed to suit the needs of employees and employers. Trade unions sought not only to protect custom, but also to develop it to give greater security to their members, the skilled men who formed the great majority of trade unionists through most of the nineteenth century. The Engineers, the printing unions, and other craft societies perfected their rules on apprenticeship and the work reserved for craftsmen. In other trades where there was no apprenticeship, such as iron and steel and cotton spinning, the unions systematized the rules governing the size of each team and the promotion ladder from labourer to the top man; and the top men ran the unions. No difference was made between the customs which survived from pre-union days and the rules which they themselves decided upon, and in some instances wrote into their union rulebooks. Both were interchangeably the rules or customs of the trade. So long as they were upheld there was a reasonable chance for skilled men to secure work at acceptable rates of pay and under tolerable conditions. Without them their pay, their jobs, and their future were at risk.

The main danger to the customs upheld by the unions was technological progress. The history of trade unions in the first half of the nineteenth century is littered with the ruins of trade unions wrecked by the introduction of new machinery. The millwrights were des-

[33] *Attempts at General Union*, pp. 104–5.

troyed by the lathe. The powerloom broke the unions of handloom weavers in cotton and wool manufacture. The powerful societies of hand-mule cotton spinners were undermined by the self-acting mule. But after the dust had settled, new customs evolved around the new jobs; and, sooner or later, new unions—such as the Engineers—were formed to mould and protect these customs, only to meet new challenges from the advance of technology.

The development of collective bargaining brought a distinction between the rules contained in collective agreements and customary rules. The employers were specifically committed to uphold the agreements. Their obligation to custom was less clear. Indeed the 1898 settlement unequivocally established the right of engineering employers to override the customs of the Engineers. Few other employers' associations attempted to define managerial prerogative with the precision of the 1898 settlement, and most of their agreements were mainly concerned to regulate pay, hours of work, overtime, shifts, and later holidays. They contained few rules on selection, promotion, manning, transfers, and other aspects of work. Consequently for them as for the engineering employers these matters came within a twilight zone. Individual employers were left to deal with them as they pleased within their own plants, and union action to regulate them had therefore to be taken in the plant, generally by workplace representatives. Inter-war unemployment did not put an end to union regulation of work, but pushed it further back into dark corners, and brought greater variety in the rules from one plant to another. Strongly organized plants might keep many of their practices intact, whereas elsewhere customs withered or were drastically pruned.

Custom and practice in postwar British industrial relations has been most fully studied by William Brown in his investigation into payment by results. He showed that managers and foremen play a part in the origin of new customs by 'a process whereby managerial error or omission establishes a practice that workers see as legitimate to defend.'[34] One example was the intervention of a senior manager in a dispute which he settled by allowing average earnings to be paid where a worker was unable to make his normal piecework earnings through no fault of his own. The manager, 'unaware of the prevailing custom', had helped to create a new one.[35] Another example

---

[34] William Brown, 'A Consideration of "Custom and Practice"'.
[35] William Brown, *Piecework Bargaining*, pp. 96–7.

concerns the control of 'feeds and speeds' which determine the rate of output from machine tools. Where operators regulate their own feeds and speeds they are able to slow down when jobs are being studied to settle the rate of pay, and speed up at other times to increase earnings. In this instance a foreman locked the regulator of a machine worked by 'a man he considered to be a regular offender at speeding up. The whole factory came to a standstill with an immediate strike and the foreman was forced to remove the lock.' Operator control of the machines was thereby 'strengthened into a [customary] rule'.[36]

Even when sanctioned by overt acceptance, however, customs do not always have the authority of a signed agreement. In one instance managers decided to acquiesce in the workers' practice of blacking piecework jobs for which an acceptable job value had not been settled by not asking workers on subsequent shifts to touch those jobs. 'When a new works manager arrived he tried to reverse the practice, so precipitating a series of strikes.' He 'refused to credit any legitimacy to what he considered a scandalous practice'.[37]

Brown found wide differences from one engineering plant to the next in the customs governing piecework. A major reason for this was the rate of what he called 'custom and practice drift' whereby the customs shifted towards greater leniency to workers who wanted to increase their individual or sectional earnings. Paradoxically a rapid rate of this kind was not necessarily welcome to strong shop steward organizations. On the contrary, such organizations saw that their strength depended on unity among their members which would be fostered by a steady general upward movement in earnings and not by the inconsistencies which would follow the exploitation by individuals and groups of every opportunity to push up earnings and take advantage of managers. Strong shop steward organizations might therefore not be averse to a degree of managerial control over piecework systems—so long as they shared in the control.[38]

Consequently

an integrated shop steward body develops a predilection for explicit negotiation with management. In doing this it can engage in the creation of fresh rules of job regulation in a deliberate,

---

[36] *Ibid.*, p. 113.   [37] *Ibid.*, pp. 103–4.
[38] *Ibid.*, Chapters 5 and 6.

intentional way and can deploy its sanctions economically and with maximum effect.[39]

This objective of shop stewards has received a great deal of help from the development of productivity bargaining. For productivity agreements involve the admission by managers that they cannot effectively regulate the processes of production without the consent of their workers and that they therefore propose to enter into 'explicit negotiation' with the shop stewards on the rules governing work. Many of them also give explicit recognition to shop steward organization in the plant.

A further move towards the explicit negotiation of working practices is the spread of what are known as *status quo* clauses in collective agreements. The most important of them is contained in the engineering agreement of 1976. It states that

> in the event of any difference arising which cannot immediately be disposed of, then whatever practice or agreement existed prior to the difference shall continue to operate pending a settlement or until the procedure has been exhausted.

This means that wherever workers object to managerial interference with a practice, or custom, managers must comply with the custom while they try to negotiate a change. The clause therefore gives to customs the same status as to explicit agreements in the plant.

The development of formal and explicit agreements and procedures in the plant has not put an end to custom. Many plants have been relatively unaffected by the trend, and most of the others negotiate formally over only some issues. Even where formalization is most extensive, jobs cannot be completely specified, and customs are needed to amplify agreements. Some issues widely subject to workplace bargaining are not usually governed by collective agreements because most unions and shop stewards prefer to avoid responsibility for them. In 1975 a Department of Employment study reported that 'trade unions only rarely participated in the formulation of the [disciplinary] rules of an establishment. They might challenge a particular rule, seeking perhaps to have it modified or rescinded. They were in general unwilling to join with management in determining the rules. Managers equally were in general opposed

[39] *Ibid.*, p. 151.

to having rule-making made the subject of negotiation and joint determination, though some managers saw advantage in inviting union comment on a consultative basis when drawing up or revising works rules.'[40]

It is probably also exceptional for unions to be involved in settling the procedure through which disciplinary decisions are taken. Since a statutory procedure for appeal against unfair dismissal was instituted in 1971, employers have shown more concern than before to establish formal disciplinary procedures because the tribunals consider the manner of a dismissal to be one of the criteria of fairness. In a survey of the effects of the 1971 Act it was found that almost two-thirds of a sample of large companies

> had formal procedures for discipline and dismissal. But of these procedures only four in ten had either been negotiated with unions or were operated with their informal agreement. . . . Of the medium-sized firms just over half . . . had written procedures. But only just over a third . . . claimed these had been formally negotiated with unions or else were operated with the unions' informal agreement.[41]

Even where the unions have given formal or informal assent to the structure of the disciplinary procedure, the decisions are with rare exceptions reserved for managers. The procedure merely states which managers can take certain disciplinary decisions, the higher managers to whom employees may appeal against disciplinary decisions, how cases are to be heard, and what formalities are to be observed. There are, however, a few companies in which decisions are taken by a joint panel.[42]

If unions do not normally share in making the rules, or in settling the procedures, or in taking disciplinary decisions, how is it that disciplinary cases form a major part of the shop steward's job? What do shop stewards do about discipline? Fifteen years ago a survey carried out by McCarthy and Coker found that shop stewards in all the plants they examined 'communicated to their members management concern over the breach of rules and orders and warned of intentions to "tighten up" on discipline'. They did not inform on

---

[40] Norman Singleton, *Industrial Relations Procedures*, p. 39.
[41] Weekes *et al.*, *Industrial Relations and the Limits of Law*, pp. 21–2.
[42] Norman Singleton, *op. cit.*, p. 41.

individuals who broke rules, but many of them gave private warnings of 'the consequences of continuing to break particular rules and orders'. In every plant shop stewards 'acted as spokesmen for those facing disciplinary charges', aiming 'to secure removal or reduction of the sanctions proposed. . . . In general, shop steward efforts to reduce or eliminate penalties were based on the establishment and acceptance of various precedents.'[43]

THE PUBLIC SECTOR

The outstanding characteristic of industrial relations in the public sector is that 90 per cent or more of public employees are subject to agreements which lay down standard conditions of service and rates of pay for a whole service or nationalized industry. It might be supposed that in these circumstances there would be relatively little workplace bargaining and workplace organization in the public sector. However, although the structure and functions of trade union organizations in public sector establishments differ from those of shop steward organizations in manufacturing, many of them exercise wide responsibilities and exhibit considerable strength.

Current workplace organization in the civil service, the Post Office, and the railways goes back to the Whitley reports issued by a government committee in 1917–18 on the structure of industrial relations after the war. These reports recommended that joint industrial councils should be set up in all well-organized industries to deal not only with the settlement of pay and conditions of employment, but also with 'the better utilisation of the practical knowledge and experience of the work people'. This should be done by securing 'co-operation in the centre between national organisations', and by joint works committees in the plants.[44] The latter were not to interfere with 'questions such as rates of wages and hours of work' but 'to establish and maintain a system of co-operation in . . . workplace matters'.[45]

Many joint industrial councils were set up in the private sector, but most of them concentrated on collective bargaining and gave little attention to their wider functions or to setting up works committees.

---

[43] McCarthy, *The Role of Shop Stewards in British Industrial Relations*, pp. 12–13.
[44] *Interim Report on Joint Standing Industrial Councils*, pp. 4–5.
[45] *Supplementary Report on Works Councils*.

Meanwhile the civil service unions, whose right to bargain on behalf of their members had not yet been explicitly recognized, argued that the Whitley principles, which the government had approved for private industry, should apply to the public sector as well. After some prevarication the government gave way. For the first time the civil service, which then included the Post Office, enjoyed fully recognized arrangements for collective bargaining, which became known as the Whitley system. They included provision for local Whitley committees in individual establishments. Soon afterwards a similar system was set up on the railways when, at the request of the unions, the Act of 1921, which amalgamated the railway companies into four undertakings, also gave statutory force to their arrangements for collective bargaining which included 'local departmental committees'.

Unlike many unions in manufacturing, the civil service and railway unions did not object to constitutions for these local committees which allowed workers to vote and to stand for election regardless of union membership. Instead they made sure that their members, and in many instances their branch officers, dominated the workers' side. In the civil service and the Post Office, many union branches covered a single establishment each, so that branch secretaries and chairmen held the major offices on the workers' sides of the committees. As time passed, the meetings of the committees did little more than ratify the arrangements which these officers had made with the management since the last meeting. Branch and workplace business became inseparable.

What was there for them to do? It must be remembered that workplace surveys have established that the negotiation of pay is not the most widespread subject of workplace bargaining in manufacturing. General conditions in the workplace, health and safety, discipline, transfers, the introduction of new machinery and jobs, and overtime are some of the most common issues handled by manufacturing shop stewards, and these are all issues which arise in the public sector, many of them probably as frequently as they do in manufacturing. Moreover, standardized rates of pay in the public sector do not prevent workplace negotiators from exercising control over their members' earnings. Overtime is worked by many manual employees and a fair number of white collar employees in the public sector, and the volume and distribution of overtime are in many instances negotiated in the workplace there just as they are in manufacturing. According to the surveys, promotion and grading are almost at the top of the list of pay issues settled between shop stewards and managers. They are probably more important in the civil service, the Post Office, and the railways than in most manufacturing industries, since most long-service employees in these services hope to pass through one or more promotions to higher grades, and the subject is therefore a matter of intense interest. The rostering of duties is another issue of widespread concern in the Post Office and the railways where many employees work variable hours or shifts.

In one large civil service establishment the business handled by the branch officers was found to vary 'enormously, from dismissals to holiday rostering, but probably most of their time was spent on the organisation of work, the allocation of jobs and overtime, and handling individual cases on behalf of their members'.[46] The scheduling of duties for train staff on the railways can provide another example. Their duties may begin and end at any hour of the day or night. They often travel long distances to pick up a train, or between jobs, or to return to depot; and they may work two or three trains in a single turn of duty. At each depot the drivers are grouped into 'links', as are second men (formerly firemen) and guards; and each man works his way through the roster of duties prescribed for his link which may take fifteen or twenty weeks or more to complete. Payment varies considerably from one duty to another according to the overtime and mileage payments involved. The construction of the rosters, which is done annually, may take the local departmental committees many weeks. They have to consider the effective use of available manpower; to smooth out extreme fluctuations in earnings; and to provide a gradual increase in earnings, or reduction in awkward turns, or both, from one link to the next. For men progress from one link to another by seniority, and drivers in particular expect to reap rewards for long service as they pass from link to link.

Nationalization in 1948 made little difference to workplace organization in the railways. Like the railways, gas and electricity supply had fairly centralized systems of collective bargaining and road passenger transport had three agreements, one for London Transport's road services, one for local authority undertakings and one for the 'company' undertakings (which have all been taken into public ownership since then). In gas, electricity, and road passenger

[46] Boraston *et al.*, *Workplace and Union*, p. 139.

transport, therefore, the issues settled in workplace bargaining were generally much the same as in the Post Office or the railways. Coalmining, however, had a highly fragmented system of collective bargaining which continued for some years after nationalization. It was only in 1955 that the Coal Board and the union agreed a national wage structure for timeworkers, and another eleven years passed before the national powerloading agreement put an end to piecework on the coalface. This agreement radically changed the job of the workplace negotiator. Previously his main job had been the settlement of disputes over piecework prices and allowances. Now he

> argued the case of men who wanted to be regraded to a higher rate of pay, or moved to another job or shift; dealt with disciplinary cases; investigated accidents; checked on safety, dust and lighting; advised the injured and the sick on their entitlements; and helped his members with domestic problems—housing, debts, divorce and so on.[47]

Since its second nationalization in 1967 the steel industry has standardized its agreements on hours of work, overtime, shifts and holidays, but it still retains some of the most fragmented arrangements for pay settlement to be found in Britain today. White collar salaries are negotiated separately by the various divisions of the Steel Corporation, and the pay of manual workers, which in most instances includes a tonnage bonus, is settled by negotiations in the plant in which each department has considerable freedom to make its own settlement.

The structure of workplace organization in coalmining, road passenger transport and steel has many similarities with that of the civil service and the Post Office. The National Union of Mineworkers normally has a separate branch for each colliery. The senior officers of the branch are the chairman, the secretary and the delegate who represents the branch at the meetings of the area council. One of the three—the practice varies from one area to another—is the branch's chief negotiator, and is allowed to give the whole of his working time to union business. The branches of the Transport and General Workers in the bus industry are garage (or depot) branches, or cover several garages or depots in a single town or city, with the branch

<hr>

[47] *Ibid.*, pp. 129–30.

secretary taking the lead in workplace negotiations. Generally each department in a steelworks has its own separate union branch, whether of the Iron and Steel Trades Confederation, the Blastfurnacemen or the Transport and General Workers' Union, with the branch secretary as its negotiator. The maintenance craftsmen have their own shop stewards.

By contrast, workplace organization in gas supply, electricity supply, and the industrial civil service has a structure much closer to that of manufacturing. The four main unions in the three services—along with several others in the industrial civil service—are the four main unions in manufacturing: the two general unions, the Engineers, and the Electricians; and their members elect their shop stewards in the plant to handle workplace bargaining. The integration of union branch, workplace representation and workplace committee membership is not so close as it is in the civil service and the Post Office. In electricity supply, for example, works committees are elected by and from all manual workers to handle the application of industry agreements relating to them, and there are also local advisory committees to consult over wider issues which include the works committee members along with white collar representatives. Shop steward constituencies do not coincide with works committee constituencies and it is not uncommon for workers who are not stewards to be elected to committees while some stewards are excluded. But in practice the stewards appear to be in control of workplace bargaining.

Until recently things were different in local government, health and educational services which account for over two-thirds of public employment. There workplace organization was the exception. Among the manual employees of local and education authorities and hospitals 'collective bargaining . . . remained very much in the hands of the union's officials'.[48] Local government and hospital officers were happier dealing with professionals like themselves rather than with representatives elected by and from their manual employees; and the workers appeared content. Of course full-time officers could not deal with every detail of every case by themselves. They relied on the branch secretaries whose job it was to prepare case papers for the full-time officers. Among white collar employees the branch secretaries of the National and Local Government Officers' Association and the National Union of Teachers often dealt directly with the

[48] H. A. Clegg, *General Union*, p. 198.

employing authorities, but the branch covered the whole of a local authority or a group of schools, and the branch secretary came into a particular department or school as an outside union representative, not as a workplace negotiator. The rigid hierarchical administration of the hospitals was especially inimical to workplace organization, and there was little enough trade unionism of any kind among nurses.

The turning-point was a report of the National Board for Prices and Incomes in 1967 which recommended incentive payments for manual employees in local government and hospitals.[49] The report was accepted by the authorities and the unions, and gradually its application got under way. Both services were determined that incentive payments should be centrally controlled, with vetting by national joint committees and careful work study on the spot. Union representatives had to be involved in the work study and preparation of each scheme, and neither full-time officers nor branch secretaries could carry this volume of work by themselves. Both the unions and the authorities therefore recognized the need for workplace organization. A general agreement recognized shop stewards in local government in 1969 and the health service followed two years later. The largest of the unions, the National Union of Public Employees, authorized the election of shop stewards for the first time in 1970. Because of its wide interests in manufacturing, the other major union, the General and Municipal Workers, had adopted rules on shop stewards twenty years earlier, but they had not so far been generally applied in local government and the hospitals. Both unions had therefore to set about finding potential stewards, securing their election, giving them an understanding of their duties, and providing them with continuing support.

By 1974 seventy per cent of male manual local authority employees were paid under incentive schemes, and shop steward representation was the norm. But incentives were not the only influence at work. Women, who form the majority of the labour force in both local authorities and hospitals, have been little affected by incentive schemes. Plenty of other issues, however, had awaited the establishment of shop stewards. The extreme rigidity of the hospital Whitley system was a special source of grievance. The improvisation of strike committees in the local authority strike in 1970 encouraged

---

[49] *Pay and Conditions of Manual Workers in Local Authorities, the National Health Service, Gas and Water Supply.*

workplace organization; and, although it was on a smaller scale, the strike of manual workers in the hospitals three years later had even more dramatic effects. Hospital managers had to negotiate with shop stewards over the organization of emergency services and the return to work. For many of them these were their first dealings with shop stewards, but not their last.

Rather more tentative steps towards workplace organization have been taken by the National Union of Teachers. School representatives have been appointed to serve as links between the branch and the teachers in the schools. Some of them take up grievances and problems as they arise in the schools, although others do no more than report them to the branch officers. In 1974 the union's annual conference launched a campaign for the negotiation of procedure agreements with the local education authorities to give formal recognition to school representatives and to accord them facilities to carry out their duties; and it has met with considerable success. In the National and Local Government Officers Association a few large branches have arranged for the election of shop stewards and authorized them to take up departmental issues; and the question of introducing a shop steward system generally is under debate.

The structure of workplace organization in local, education and hospital services is generally more akin to that of the civil service than to manufacturing industry. Among teachers and local government officers, workplace representatives are part of the branch organization and report to the branch secretary. Among manual employees the situation is more complicated, but many branches cover employees of an authority, or of a hospital, or of a department within it, so that the branch secretary can fulfil the role of senior steward. In many instances the branches appoint the stewards. In a survey of shop stewards in the General and Municipal Workers it was found that, where shop stewards faced problems too big for them, 48 per cent of those in manufacturing would turn to a senior steward and 19 per cent to a branch official, whereas in the public sector (including gas and electricity) 13 per cent would turn to a senior steward and 43 per cent to a branch official. The authors attributed the difference partly to the dispersion of the workforce in small sections in many public services, for example in local government, hindering the development of strong workplace organization.[50]

[50] Brown *et al.*, 'Factors Shaping Shop Steward Organisation in Britain'.

The four main differences in workplace organization between manufacturing and the public sector, therefore, are its recent origin among the majority of public sector trade unionists; its conscious development from the top in many public services; the absence of plant-wide pay bargaining in the public sector; and the close link between the branch and workplace organization in much of the public sector—so close that in many instances the branch is the workplace organization. In some ways, however, the differences between the two sectors are diminishing. Workplace organization is now general in both sectors; whereas the Whitley system in the civil service, Post Office and railways was always accepted as legitimate, shop stewards were not formally recognized in much of manufacturing until fairly recently, but now recognition is common in both sectors; and the extension of bargaining over work organization in both sectors has meant that the scope of workplace organization in the two sectors is not so different as it used to be.

THE PRIVATE SERVICES

Workplace organization and bargaining in the private services are very different from both manufacturing and the public sector. Most private services have some form of industry regulation which specifies minimum requirements on a narrow range of issues and leaves the rest to individual employers, whose discretion is not usually fettered by workplace bargaining because no workplace organization exists, or because whatever organization there is lacks the strength to bargain. In many private services, including retail distribution, hotels and catering, hairdressing and laundries, industry-wide regulation is provided by a wages council. These councils are statutory bodies appointed by the Secretary of State for Employment. They consist of equal numbers of employer and union representatives nominated by their organizations along with three independents, one of whom is chairman; and their decisions are enforceable in the courts.

However, there are a few exceptional services whose workplace organizations deserve some attention. Trade unionism in the building industry is remarkably weak considering the unions can trace their history back to the beginning of the nineteenth century, if not further, and collective bargaining at industry level originated before the First World War. Their overall membership is only about 25 per cent of the labour force. Casual employment hinders their efforts to recruit and retain members, and the rapid growth of self-employment among building workers since the war has made their job still more difficult. Nevertheless both workplace organizations and workplace bargaining can be found, especially on big sites. In 1947 the employers' federation and the unions agreed to the introduction of payments by results on building sites, and in 1964 they granted official recognition to shop stewards, although there had been stewards on building sites long before that. Shop stewards' organizations of considerable strength may emerge on major sites, bargaining over site bonuses and the organization of work with little reference to unions off the site. Some of them have attained notoriety.[51] But even the strongest site organization is disbanded when the job is finished, and a new start has to be made elsewhere. Because of this, building workers who are willing to take the initiative in setting up site organization easily acquire reputations as 'trouble-makers' and experience difficulty in finding jobs. One or two national firms have signed company agreements with the unions that provide, among other things, for the selection and recognition of shop stewards on new sites; but such agreements are rare.

Road haulage is exceptional in that its system of collective bargaining is based on regional agreements. After several attempts to develop voluntary collective bargaining at industry level had failed, the unions developed the practice of negotiating regional agreements with groups of 'assenting hauliers'. These spread to cover the country, and made it possible for the Road Haulage Wages Council to be abolished in 1978. Because most haulage firms are small and there is no effective employers' association, the task of policing these agreements falls mainly on shop stewards in the firms and on district committees of stewards drawn from the firms in the area.

In two other services, docks[52] and shipping, official union organization at the workplace is a recent innovation despite a long history of almost universal trade union membership and of industry bargaining. Casual employment was held to prevent workplace organization on the docks because a man elected steward one day might be off

---

[51] *Report of a Court of Inquiry into trade disputes at the Barbican and Horseferry Road construction sites in London.*

[52] Employment in the docks is partly private and partly public, but it is included among private services in this book.

to another ship or quay the next. Full-time union officers were therefore responsible for dealing with all grievances and problems. Although the ratio of full-time officers to union members was far higher on the docks than elsewhere, their job proved impossible, and in practice the 'ganger', whom managers and foremen held responsible for the work of the gang, became the gang's 'representative in the first stage of any negotiations with management on a dispute concerning members of the gang and their work'.[53] The influence of the famous unofficial 'liaison committees' on the docks in the fifties and sixties rested on the authority of the gangers as unofficial stewards.

The implementation of the Devlin Committee's recommendations for decasualization in 1967 included setting up a system of shop stewards throughout the docks. The stewards were elected by the whole labour force of a firm or a department so that they owed allegiance to no particular gang. The problem of contact with ships and quays remained, and was resolved by 'duty' (full-time) stewards. Initially all stewards in London were full-time, and there was roughly one steward to a hundred dockers.

For the next three years the stewards were mainly occupied with piecework bargaining and with practices affecting piecework earnings. In London they were responsible for the emergence of a new custom of equalizing earnings in which 'the stewards clearly led rather than followed the men. . . . Any gang which had high earnings was to be placed on low-paying cargoes until its earnings came into line with the average, and vice versa. This entirely negated the principle of payment by results.'[54] Nevertheless the dockers 'were extremely well disposed to the new steward system.'[55]

In 1970 the second stage of the Devlin reforms abolished piecework in London and many other ports. Once the consequences of the change had been absorbed the workload of the stewards dropped sharply. Thereafter the job of stewards in the Port of London Authority—the major employer in London—was to take up 'individual grievances with managers on lateness, absence from work, rotas and working conditions', and to attend 'monthly meetings with the docks manager and see him as issues arise.' They could also 'object to a particular manning arrangement, and they have authority to check productivity records.'[56]

---

[53] *Devlin Report*, pp. 10–11.   [54] Stephen Hill, *The Dockers*, p. 124.
[55] *Ibid.*, p. 135.   [56] Michael Mellish, *The Docks after Devlin*, p. 92.

Any form of workplace representation would have received no support from the men who led the National Union of Seamen before 1960, but thereafter a new generation of leaders began to show an interest in introducing elected representatives to deal with problems while a ship is at sea. The employers and the officers' associations felt that 'a "shop steward" would be quite inappropriate at sea, operating as he must in a closely knit community in which it was essential that the system of authority was preserved'.[57] In 1963 the industry's negotiating body, the National Maritime Board, agreed to a procedure for dealing with grievances on board ship, but left it to individuals to take up their own cases. In 1965 they set up a series of experiments with elected 'liaison representatives' on selected foreign-going ships, and two years later they extended the scheme generally. Representatives are elected before their vessels sail, and at least half of those eligible must vote. The union provide courses to train representatives, and by 1970 there were representatives on about a quarter of British ships. However, representatives have no authority and no agreed workplace rules to apply, and the officers' associations continue to oppose any challenge to their members' authority. By 1975 the proportion of ships with representatives was down to one in eight. The union's assistant general secretary commented that the scheme 'emasculates a shop stewards' movement. Now you can't have a shop stewards' movement and call it a liaison scheme.'[58]

THE STRUCTURE OF WORKPLACE ORGANIZATION

It has so far been assumed that there is no difficulty in defining a shop steward. In fact there are several difficulties. Most trade unions which rely to a considerable extent upon shop stewards have arrangements for granting them credentials, and accredited shop stewards must come within any definition. But the most extensive survey of shop stewards conducted in Britain, by the Commission on Industrial Relations,[59] also included a large but unspecified

---

[57] *Pearson Report*, p. 29.

[58] Union General Meeting, May 1976, *Report of Proceedings*, pp. 112–13. I am indebted to Mr James McConville for this quotation and for information on the scheme.

[59] *Industrial Relations at Establishment Level: A Statistical Survey*.

number of unaccredited shop stewards, who were treated as shop
stewards by their employers but not officially recognized by their
unions outside the workplace. The survey also discovered a large
number of 'non-union' representatives, some of whose duties over-
lapped with those of shop stewards. It took no account of another
large number of 'spokesmen'—union members who act as representatives of groups of workers without being recognized as shop
stewards by either unions or their managers. The existence of this
form of representation was identified in the *Workplace Industrial
Relations* surveys, which found that about half the managers received
some representations on behalf of groups of workers by others than
shop stewards; and that a third of the employees who were represented by shop stewards said they also had a spokesman.[60]

There is also the problem of the union branches which are themselves workplace organizations as in the civil service, the Post Office,
coalmining, and the steel industry. Are the branch secretaries and
chairmen to be counted as shop stewards? In large branches of this
kind the task of workplace representation and negotiation is often
shared with some or all of the branch committee members. Should
the committee members who share in this work be accounted shop
stewards?

Given these difficulties, any attempt to quantify shop steward
behaviour is bound to be imprecise. But the evidence concurs fairly
well in putting the average number of trade unionists to a steward at
about fifty. The Commission on Industrial Relations suggested that
the average for manufacturing was lower—nearer thirty; and William Brown and his colleagues found a median figure of thirty-nine,
their average of fifty being influenced by a relatively small number of
large constituencies.[61]

The shop steward is sometimes presented as the representative of a
primary work group—a group of employees whose jobs bring them
into such close contact that they form a cohesive social unit. But the
title 'shop steward' indicates that this situation is unusual. A shop is
not usually a primary group, and few primary groups, if any,
number anything like fifty. One study of a sample of nineteen
stewards found a median number of five primary groups to a
steward. 'One steward represented ten different primary groups
and another nine and, excluding those, the mean average was

[60] *Workplace Industrial Relations 1973*, pp. 52–3.
[61] Brown *et al.*, 'Factors Shaping Shop Steward Organisation in Britain'.

three.'[62] The interests of these groups may differ so that it is not surprising that some of them have their own spokesmen, in addition to the shop steward.

Nevertheless shop stewards are in close contact with their constituents. Most trade unionists see their shop stewards every day. The members also have a considerable share in deciding industrial relations issues. *Workplace Industrial Relations 1973* reported that, in their national sample of employees, 73 per cent of those represented by shop stewards said that a majority of union members decided what action was to be taken over any grievance and claim. More of them complained that their steward did not try hard enough to get his own way than thought he tried too much.[63] In their study of stewards in a large plant, Batstone and his colleagues divided them into 'leaders', and 'populists'—who thought it was their job to put forward the expressed wishes of their members.[64] Populists outnumbered leaders, and even the leaders had to mobilize support for their opinions and actions.[65] However, all this relates to decisions affecting an individual steward and his section. Decisions affecting several sections or the whole plant are necessarily further removed from the shop floor. In the plant studied by Batstone and his colleagues, leader stewards and conveners handled business at these levels, although important issues might be referred to the Joint Shop Stewards' Committee or a mass meeting.

About a quarter of the stewards in the sample surveyed in *Workplace Industrial Relations 1973* had originally been elected in a contested election; and, although their average period of office had been five years, only two-fifths of them had had to face an election since taking office. One reason for the small proportion of contested elections is that more than a third of the stewards had to be persuaded to take the job because no one else wanted it.[66] But these figures do not necessarily demonstrate a lack of democracy. In a group of fifty or so a consensus can easily emerge without the need to hold an election. If a shop steward has lost the confidence of his members, they can make sure that he is aware of their feelings, and he may well resign without waiting for an election. Among the stewards studied by Batstone and his colleagues only 12 per cent of populists had been in office for more than five years, and 30 per cent of leaders. Populists

---

[62] J. F. B. Goodman and T. G. Whittingham, *Shop Stewards in British Industry*, p. 74.
[63] p. 63.   [64] Batstone *et al.*, *op. cit.*, p. 36.
[65] *Ibid.*, Chapter 5.   [66] pp. 18–19.

might be expected to leave office when their members wished them to, but leaders also resigned. 'Some leaders become disillusioned and "fed-up" with "working their guts out" for an ungrateful member-ship.' Others were brought to 'defeat or enforced resignation' by 'major blunders on their part'.[67]

The rapid spread of the check-off—the collection of union dues by the employer through deduction from pay, which is now the general rule in Britain[68]—has had an effect on dealings between shop stewards and their members. In the past one of the chief services of stewards to their unions was the collection of subscriptions, whether they were collectors acting as stewards, or stewards taking on the job of collector.[69] Now most shop stewards no longer handle money unless they collect for shop stewards' funds, or run raffles or pools for the same purpose. The check-off has also diminished the need for stewards to recruit new members and conduct card checks to ensure that members remain in good standing. Before the check-off became widespread many union leaders expressed the fear that its introduc-tion would do away with the one occasion on which the steward regularly met his constituents, so that communication would suffer. But there is no evidence that this has happened. *Workplace Industrial Relations 1973* found that 'nearly half of the employees worked together with their steward, so there was no problem meeting him. The rest were able to meet their steward fairly frequently. Most employees thought it was easy to see their steward on union matters whenever they needed to.'[70]

The modest performance of the branch as a means of direct communication with union members is confirmed by low figures of branch attendance.[71] But it does not follow that branches do not have

[67] Batstone *et al.*, *op. cit.*, p. 227.

[68] Brown *et al.*, *op. cit.*, found an incidence of 89 per cent among manual workers in manufacturing.

[69] Until 1969 the Engineers' rules prescribed payment of contributions at branch meetings. Nevertheless in 1959 Clegg *et al.*, *Trade Union Officers* (p. 160) found that 68 per cent of the union's stewards collected contributions. In 1969 the rule was changed to allow branches to appoint collectors and use the check-off.

[70] p. 51.

[71] Probably the most detailed study of branch attendance in British unions was conducted as part of an inquiry into branches of the Engineers and the General and Municipal Workers in 1964. It put average attendance at 9 per cent and 5 per cent respectively, with attendance at the biggest meeting of the year averaging 16 per cent and 13 per cent. Some of these findings and a brief outline of the survey methods are given in W. E. J. McCarthy, *The Role of Shop Stewards in British Industrial Relations*, p. 39.

an indirect part to play in union communications with the members. Shop stewards are much more diligent attenders of branch meetings than their members,[72] and many of them are members of branch committees,[73] so that much of the information that the stewards pass on to their members may come through the branch.

Where the union branch acts as a workplace organization its constitution is defined by union rules. The chairman and secretary are the chief negotiators, the branch meeting and committee are empowered to take decisions which are recorded in branch minutes, and so on. Where the workplace organization is divorced from the branch, its constitution is largely of its own making. The structure of these workplace organizations has been most thoroughly investigated by William Brown and his colleagues in a survey of manual shop stewards in almost 450 unionized plants, mainly in manufacturing and the public sector.[74] They asked whether there was a senior shop steward (or convener); whether the senior steward was elected by the other stewards; whether there were regular meetings of the stewards; whether minutes of these meetings were taken; whether there was an executive committee consisting of only some of the stewards; and whether there was a full-time steward (or senior steward). The answers varied with the size of the plants, but even among plants with less than a hundred manual employees, 29 per cent had senior stewards, 28 per cent held regular meetings of stewards, and 21 per cent had written constitutions. Two of these plants even had full-time stewards. There was also a considerable difference between manufacturing and the public sector. Table 2 summarizes the findings which show that hierarchies have been established in the great majority of workplace organizations of any size, and that their procedures have become formalized in most manufacturing plants with over five hundred manual employees. One of the reasons for the lower scores returned by the public sector in these respects is that in many instances the workforce covered by a single workplace organization was not concentrated in a single site

[72] According to *Workplace Industrial Relations 1966* (p. 25), 28 per cent of shop stewards claimed they had attended every branch meeting in the previous twelve months, and a further 31 per cent that they had attended more than half.

[73] An unpublished survey of nineteen branches of the General and Municipal Workers' Union conducted by the Social Science Research Council's Industrial Relations Research Unit at Warwick University found that the average membership of a branch committee was thirteen and the average number of shop stewards on them was twelve.   [74] Brown *et al., op. cit.*

but dispersed over a considerable area. This was particularly true of local authority employment and gas supply.

Ever since the Donovan report appeared there has been a controversy over the extent to which descriptions of shop steward organization and activity, most of which draw heavily on the experience of the engineering industry, are representative of other British industries. This survey confirms that there is a difference in characteristics of workplace organization between engineering and other manufacturing industries—providing no account is taken of the size of plants. Table 2 shows that, size group for size group, public sector workplace organizations are less articulated and formalized than manufacturing workplace organizations. On the same basis, there is very little difference between engineering and other manufacturing industries. An apparent difference is due to the small average size of plant in manufacturing industries other than engineering, both in the sample and in fact. Sixty-eight per cent of British engineering employees work in plants with over five hundred employees, compared with 40 per cent of employees in the rest of manufacturing.

Size of plant was also found to affect turnover of shop stewards. Only 13 per cent of stewards in plants with less than a hundred manual employees had held office for over four years. The proportion rose with each size group up to five hundred, after which it stabilized at about 45 per cent. Further investigations showed that this finding is more closely associated with the number of stewards than with the size of the workforce—although these two variables are, of course, closely associated. The authors conclude that 'shop steward organisations are below the optimal size for stable membership when they have fewer than approximately 10 members'.

The evidence of *Workplace Industrial Relations 1973* is that most stewards are granted full recognition and considerable facilities by their employers. Although about a third of the stewards in the survey expressed some dissatisfaction with the physical facilities provided for them—accommodation, telephone, typing, and so on[75]—very few of them were dissatisfied with their opportunities to contact their members at the workplace.[76] About three-quarters of the plants had joint committees or councils where managers met workers' representatives, and in the majority of them the workers were represented by shop stewards only.[77] Well over half had their own written procedures for settling grievances and claims in the

[75] p. 26.   [76] p. 25.   [77] p. 37.

Table 2

Characteristics of Workplace Organizations

	N		Senior Steward		Elected by Stewards		Regular Meetings		Minutes Taken		Executive Committee		Written Constitution		Full-time Steward	
	Under 500	500 and over	Under 500	500 and over	Under 500	500 and over	Under 500	500 and over	Under 500	500 and over	Under 500	500 and over	Under 500	500 and over	Under 500	500 and over
Manu-facturing	124	122	70	97	40	66	60	87	53	82	37	81	23	61	19	62
Public Sector	117	38	43	79	17	42	39	72	53	78	27	58	31	45	8	21

plant, and the proportion rose to 70 per cent in plants with five hundred employees or more.[78]

It is tempting to relate this high degree of acceptance of workplace organization by managers with the sophistication of shop steward organization found by Brown and his colleagues. If there is a relationship it would imply that the increase in employer acceptance which has almost certainly taken place over the postwar period may have helped the formalization and articulation of shop steward organization. Brown and his colleagues explored this point, and found in plants with less than five hundred manual employees a history of continuous acceptance by managers and a history of continuous opposition were *both* associated with a relatively low level of workplace organization. A higher level of organization was found where managers had resisted shop stewards in the past, but now accepted them. In plants with five hundred employees or more, management attitudes appeared to make little difference, except that there were far fewer full-time stewards in plants whose managers currently resisted shop steward organization.

Another influence on workplace organization is multi-unionism. A manager, it is often argued, finds it cumbersome to deal with full-time union officers from two or more unions when an issue affects several groups within the plant. It is easier to call together several stewards, and the advantage of dealing with a joint shop stewards' committee, if there is one, is overwhelming. Brown and his colleagues found evidence to confirm that, allowing for the size of the workplace, multi-unionism is 'generally associated with a higher degree of development in most aspects of steward organization'—especially in manufacturing.

A relatively unexplored aspect of workplace organization is the 'combine committee'.[79] This is a committee of representatives from shop stewards' organizations in some or all of the plants of a multi-plant company. The Warwick survey found that 10 per cent of its sample of workplace organizations in multi-plant companies were represented at regular combine committee meetings and another 16 per cent took part in occasional meetings. Combines are also found in the public sector, for example in electricity supply. No provision is made for these committees in union rules or in industry agree-

---

[78] p. 40.
[79] A pioneer investigation was by Shirley Lerner and John Bescoby, 'Shop Steward Combine Committees in the British Engineering Industry'.

ments, and they are rarely accorded recognition by managers except in companies such as Ford and Dunlop which negotiate primarily at company level. Their most universal function is the exchange of information about pay and other conditions of employment, but sometimes they go beyond that to agitate for equalization between plants, or to co-ordinate pay claims. In recent years many of them have been active in redundancies and mergers. Occasionally a combine committee has called a strike. But few of them have an assured and permanent existence. They depend on the enthusiasm of leading shop stewards in one or more plants to service them. They fall apart over issues in which the interests of the plants pull in different directions.

One finding of Brown and his colleagues which confounds much that has been said about women in trade unions is that, although their survey discovered a lower level of shop steward organization and activity where the labour force included women as well as men, the relationship is slight. 'Some predominantly female workforces . . . had steward organizations quite as sophisticated as the average predominantly male ones with comparably sized workforces.'

This brief outline of British shop steward organization suffers from several defects. Firstly, the surveys from which it is drawn give scant coverage to the private services, which account for over a third of total employment, and in which workplace organization is for the most part feeble or absent. The previous pages have therefore given the impression that British workplace organization—although almost certainly the strongest in any major country in the world—is more robust that it is in fact.

Secondly, surveys are not only confined to reporting certain easily observable features of social life, but also present them by means of averages and distributions. Deviance, which is such an important element in social behaviour, goes almost unremarked. One example of deviance cannot correct the fault, but it can illustrate it. Union recognition was secured in one textile mill, employing nine hundred workers, only in 1968. 'The original agreement merely authorised shop stewards to raise grievances, and did not constitute a pay agreement or an undertaking to negotiate.' Next year a brief strike brought a negotiated pay increase, and union membership almost reached five hundred, but even so the full-time officer had to take charge of all dealings with the plant managers. 'Little reliance could be placed on the convener. He was a demoted supervisor who

appeared to have more loyalty to the company than to the union.'
Within six months of the strike union membership began to
decline.[80] This state of affairs is very different for the typical workplace organization in a large manufacturing plant. Descriptions of
workplace organization in the giant chemical company 'ChemCo'
provide further illustrations of shop steward behaviour which does
not match the general description given in this section.[81]

Thirdly, surveys report behaviour at a particular time, and most of
the surveys used here were conducted in the last twelve years. They
cannot give historical depth to an account of workplace organization. The explosion of workplace organization in the public sector
has been noted, but the account of the rise of shop stewards in
manufacturing has rested heavily on engineering, and does not adequately convey the rapid expansion which took place in the sixties
and seventies. Five of the eleven large companies investigated by the
Department of Employment's study of the reform of collective
bargaining—all of them outside engineering—had little trade union
organization or bargaining in the plant until the sixties.[82] Surveys
may show that, once size of plant is taken into account, there is now
little difference in characteristics of workplace organization between
engineering and other manufacturing industries; but there may have
been a wide divergence little more than a decade ago.

Finally, without historical depth surveys cannot offer much of a
guide to the future. In recent years there has been a centralization of
industrial relations policy in many multi-plant companies, and a
spread of company bargaining not only for white collar employees,
but also among manual workers. A continued development of company bargaining must strengthen combine committees. Various
schemes for extending industrial democracy have proposed that new
representative trade union structures should be established to speak
for all trade unionists in such companies.[83] Were one of these to be
adopted, company shop steward organization would be further
strengthened, and that would not only bring important changes in
collective bargaining, but also create new centres of power within
the unions.

[80] Boraston *et al.*, *Workplace and Union*, pp. 73–4.
[81] Nichols and Armstrong, *Workers Divided*, and Nichols and Beynon, *Living with Capitalism*.
[82] Department of Employment, *The Reform of Collective Bargaining at Plant and Company Level*, Appendix 2.
[83] See pp. 438–43.

THE NUMBER OF SHOP STEWARDS

Despite the problems of defining a shop steward, there have been several attempts to estimate their numbers. The first with a claim to be taken seriously was that of the Donovan Commission. They started with a figure derived from returns to the Trades Union Congress by those unions which kept records, and adjusted to allow for unions which did not. This gave a total of 'at least 200,000 stewards in 1959',[84] rising to 225,000 by the time the Donovan Commission was making its calculations. Next they turned to the average number of union members for which, according to their surveys, each steward was responsible—55. They divided total union membership by 55, after allowing for another finding of the surveys—that 20 per cent of trade union members had no steward. This calculation gave a second total—168,000 stewards. The commission then turned their attention to the substantial difference between the two totals. Their surveys had derived their samples from lists supplied by the unions, and the investigators discovered that almost 20 per cent of those listed were no longer shop stewards. Allowing for this the Trades Union Congress total came down to 180,000. It seemed reasonable to split the remaining difference and make the final estimate 175,000.[85]

In 1973 the Commission on Industrial Relations published the results of a much more extensive survey of industrial relations, conducted primarily to assist their inquiry into industrial relations training. Their method was to send postal questionnaires to a sample of plants for the appropriate manager to return. Their findings led them to conclude that 'it seems probable that there were well in excess of 250,000 and perhaps approaching 300,000 shop stewards in 1971', when the survey was carried out.[86]

Why was there such a gap between this estimate and the Donovan Commission's figure for 1966? Firstly there had been a 10 per cent increase in union membership in the interval, and the number of stewards might have been expected at least to keep pace. This would have increased the Donovan figure to over 190,000 for 1971. Secondly, all the available evidence suggests that the number of

[84] Trades Union Congress, *Annual Report*, 1960, p. 128.
[85] W. E. J. McCarthy and S. R. Parker, *Shop Stewards and Workshop Relations*, p. 15.
[86] *Industrial Relations at Establishment Level: A Statistical Survey*, p. 4.

stewards has been increasing faster than union membership in post-war Britain. Between 1947 and 1961 the number of stewards accredited by the Engineers rose by 56 per cent whereas the membership rose by 30 per cent.[87] The figures given by the Trades Union Congress are probably a much better guide to the rate of growth in numbers of shop stewards than to the total number at any particular time. They show an increase of 12.5 per cent between 1959 and 1966 when union membership grew by 5 per cent. Assuming a similar development from 1966 to 1971, the Donovan figure for 1971 becomes well over 200,000. Thirdly, the number of shop stewards probably grew at an unusually rapid rate over those five years, both because of the encouragement given to workplace bargaining in local government, hospitals and education and because of the formalization of workplace bargaining in manufacturing.[88] Fourthly, the Donovan figure did not include unaccredited shop stewards. Taken together these four factors probably account for most of the discrepancy.

Given further growth in union membership and in the coverage of workplace organization since 1971, the total for 1978, calculated by the Donovan method, must be more than 250,000; and on the definition adopted by the Commission on Industrial Relations (i.e. including unaccredited shop stewards) it may be over 300,000.

One per cent of the Donovan Commission's sample of shop stewards were full-time stewards (defined as giving all or most of their working day to their duties as stewards).[89] Taken together with their estimate of the number of stewards this suggests that there were then rather less than two thousand full-time stewards. *Workplace Industrial Relations 1973* gave the proportion of their sample of stewards who devoted thirty hours or more of their time each week to their duties as stewards as 5 per cent.[90] If that is taken as the equivalent of a full-time steward, and the number of stewards at that time is assumed to be 200,000 or more, then the number of full-time stewards in 1973 was ten thousand or more—a staggering rate of increase. But a total of this order or larger for 1976 is implicit in the

---

[87] A. I. Marsh and E. E. Coker, 'Shop Steward Organisation in the Engineering Industry'.

[88] In an as yet unpublished study, M. Barratt Brown and his colleagues at Sheffield University found that the number of shop stewards on the list of the Engineers' Sheffield district committee doubled in 1968–9 'with the introduction of productivity bargaining'.

[89] *Workplace Industrial Relations 1966*, p. 16.   [90] p. 18.

findings of the survey conducted by Brown and his colleagues. 'Taken together with the size distribution of establishments and . . . the density of unionisation', their data implied, 'that there are approximately 5,000 full-time stewards covering manual workers' in manufacturing.[91] It is probably true that full-time stewards are more likely to be found representing manual workers in manufacturing than representing other groups of trade unionists. But since manual workers in manufacturing constitute only 35 per cent of total trade unionists, this figure is entirely consistent with a national total of ten thousand or more full-time shop stewards. Certainly they outnumber full-time union officers whose number was estimated by the Donovan Commission as three thousand,[92] and probably has not increased much faster than the number of union members since then.[93]

THEORIES OF WORKPLACE ORGANIZATION

The opening sections of this chapter offered a historical explanation for the importance of workplace organization in Britain today, especially among manual workers in manufacturing industry. But in addition to seeking to explain the relative importance of workplace organization at different times and places there is a logically prior question to be answered—why workplace organization at all? One possible reply is that it is an inevitable concomitant of an industrial society. Industry brings men and women together to work, they naturally associate in groups, and it is natural that these groups should try to exercise some control over their working conditions.

The docks before the Devlin reforms offer an example. There the gang forced its way through into the regulation of industrial relations even though the union had specifically provided that all bargaining should be reserved for union officers. And this experience is not unique. Before the powerloading agreement ended piecework on the coalface, 'chargemen' often acted as spokesmen for pieceworking groups. These chargemen were chosen by the

---

[91] Brown *et al.*, *op. cit.* A year or so later the Warwick survey, relying on answers from managers, came up with a figure of about 3,500 full-time stewards in manufacturing. The divergence suggests that managers are less likely to admit the presence of full-time shop stewards than are shop stewards themselves; and indicates the order of uncertainty on this topic.

[92] *Report*, p. 188.   [93] Boraston *et al.*, *op. cit.*, p. 191.

pieceworking groups and paid an additional rate by colliery managers who maintained 'that they should assume some responsibility
for production', whereas the officers of the colliery branch had sole
authorization to handle piecework problems on behalf of the men.
Nevertheless, in one colliery, the functions of the chargemen in
practice were

> to allocate stints amongst their particular face groups, to act as
> unofficial checkers of their group's wages, to act as spokesmen
> when grievances occurred and to influence the kind of action to be
> taken over those grievances.[94]

Work group regulation of industrial relations has been found in
even more unlikely places. The most famous investigation ever
conducted into industrial relations on the shop floor was carried out
by a team of Harvard research workers at the non-union Hawthorne
plant of the Western Electric Company in Chicago during the late
nineteen-twenties and early thirties. Part of their work was to
observe a group of men in the 'bank wiring room'. These men
had their own notion of a fair day's work, lower than the firm's
'bogey', which they enforced by ridicule, mild physical violence, and
ostracism. They protected themselves from outside interference by
manipulating their bonus system. They were allowed considerable
discretion in submitting claims for 'daywork allowances' to compensate for delays in production, and their supervisors could be
embarrassed by a large number of claims. 'The men had elaborated,
spontaneously and quite unconsciously', wrote the investigators, 'an
intricate social organisation around their collective beliefs and sentiments', which cut across the 'formal organization' laid down in the
rules and policies of the company.[95]
This and other evidence may be taken to suggest that there is a
tendency to work group regulation in an industrial society, but there
is also plenty of evidence of groups formed at work which do not
attempt to regulate industrial relations,[96] so that a theory of workplace organization must explain why some groups try to control
their working conditions and others do not. There have been no
serious studies of the circumstances in which primary work groups

[94] Scott *et al.*, *Coal and Conflict*, pp. 154–7.
[95] F. J. Roethlisberger and W. J. Dickson, *Management and the Worker*, p. 524.
[96] One example is the group of girls engaged in relay assembly at the Hawthorne
plant who were also observed by the research team.

take to regulating the conditions under which they work. The nearest thing is a study by Leonard Sayles of the part played by different bargaining groups—most of which probably consist of more than one primary group—in trade union workplace activity in manufacturing industry in the United States. He distinguished four types of bargaining group behaviour according to skill and status in the plant and position in the production process. Craft groups were generally quiescent because they received the most favourable treatment, but fully capable of taking effective action if challenged. The next type of group, whose skill and status fell a little below those of craftsmen, he called 'strategic' because they sustained a high level of effective bargaining and union activity. The 'erratic' type was capable of intermittent bouts of activity. Finally the 'apathetic' type came nowhere.[97] It may not be unreasonable to take this typology as some indication of the capacity of different classes of worker to regulate their conditions through primary groups.

The next stage is the shift from primary group regulation to workplace organization. There are instances of workplace organization outside trade unions in the past, such as the early printing chapels, and there also examples today, but most of them are representative committees in non-union plants formed with the support of employers. Trade unions which established workplace branches, like the miners, had workplace organization from the start. Most unions, however, based their branches on residence. They needed a link with the plant, but probably in most instances an informal arrangement was sufficient—or a collector with no formal authority to exercise regulative authority nevertheless filled the need. Subsequently, as workplace bargaining developed, workplace organization might be given formal recognition by the union. If this account is roughly correct, then the printing unions and the Engineers, with their early recognition of workplace organization, were exceptions; and there were also the unions which positively discouraged workplace organization, like the dockers' unions. Until the attitude was reversed in 1967, primary groups continued to supply an unofficial workplace organization in the docks in spite of their unions; and elsewhere primary groups might continue to play a part in workplace regulation within the trade union workplace organization, or even, as with piecework groups in coalmining before the power-loading agreement, outside it.

[97] Leonard Sayles, *Behavior of Industrial Work Groups*, p. 55.

However, the scope for action by a workplace organization is limited unless it is recognized, at least informally, by foremen and managers. Formal recognition may be granted by an industry agreement such as the engineering agreement of 1917 or the local authority and health service agreements of 1969 and 1971. But since the effect of such agreements depends on the spirit in which they are applied, they vary in their impact at the plant, especially in private industry where the employers' associations which sign them have no direct control over managers in the plant. The shipping agreement on liaison representatives has had little effect because of the attitude of masters and other officers on board ship. It is the degree of recognition accorded in the plant which counts, and in many private industries plant recognition was widespread, if usually informal, before the issue had been raised in discussions at industry level. This happened because foremen and managers found that it was the most effective way of handling their industrial relations problems. A question first posed in a survey of personnel managers in 1959, and repeated in a number of surveys of personnel managers, works managers and other managers since then, was whether they preferred to deal with a full-time officer or a shop steward over an issue which either was competent to settle. On every occasion about three-quarters of the answers have favoured the steward.[98] These replies do not imply that managers generally were prepared to grant formal recognition to shop stewards in 1959, or to acknowledge their right to bargain over a wide range of work organization issues; it merely shows that, where they had to talk to a union representative, most of them preferred a shop steward. Contradictions of this kind continued to be a common feature for more than a decade thereafter. Reporting on a survey conducted in the early seventies, Turner and his colleagues noted that, 'as between dealing with full-time union officials, with shop stewards directly, and with conveners of stewards, a clear majority of managements preferred to negotiate or consult with conveners'; but, despite this 'positive preference for the convener system, in only a minority of concerns were conveners formally recognised by the management!'[99]

If both support from the union and recognition by the employer

---

[98] The first survey was reported in Clegg *et al.*, *Trade Union Officers*, p. 175. Similar questions have been posed in the surveys reported in *Workplace Industrial Relations 1966, 1972* and *1973*.

[99] Turner *et al.*, *Management Characteristics and Labour Conflict*, p. 22.

are important to the development of workplace organization, joint action by employer and union can prevent or retard its growth, as was the case until recently in local government and the hospitals. Case studies in hosiery and footwear found that 'when an issue began to cause trouble, the manager sent for the full-time officer. The officer expected to be called in to take charge of negotiations. And also because the workplace representatives lacked the experience and the desire to handle matters for themselves, they were happy to have their officer called in, or to send for him themselves. Workplace representation in hosiery was rudimentary and patchy; the footwear shop presidents occupied a more recognized role, but it was nevertheless modest and subordinate.' Among the reasons for this state of affairs—besides union and employer attitudes—are that both industries are traditional and localized with relatively small plants and highly competitive product markets.[100]

These instances lead on to a third topic—the independence of outside union control shown by many trade union workplace organizations in Britain. The shop presidents in the footwear industry were fully recognized by both their union and their employers. Nevertheless serious workplace issues were handed on to their full-time officers. But this is not the normal state of affairs in manufacturing, as Daniel's evidence demonstrates. Most shop stewards in plants with over two hundred employees handle even their annual pay negotiations on their own, calling in their full-time officer only in case of deadlock. Few public sector workplace organizations enjoy similar scope to negotiate their own pay settlements, but an equally fierce independence of outside control can be found in many of them in handling those issues which can be settled at the plant. In many instances plant managers are only too anxious to avoid reference to senior managers or to 'London' which might be the consequence of bringing in full-time union officers or referring the issue to procedure.[101]

This preference for dealing with shop stewards, discovered by both surveys and case studies, serves as one reason for workplace independence. But critics of trade unions reply that managers have very little option but to deal with workplace organizations, for the unions offer them little alternative. If so it was not until recently a consequence of union policy. Horrified by the development of the shop stewards' movement in the First World War, most British trade

[100] Boraston *et al.*, *op. cit.*, p. 182.　　　[101] *Ibid.*, p. 142.

union leaders frowned on workplace independence until the succession of Hugh Scanlon to the presidency of the Engineers and of Jack Jones to the general secretaryship of the Transport and General Workers in the late sixties. The argument therefore rests on defects in trade union organization. The first is multi-unionism, whose effect on workplace organization has been confirmed by the surveys of Brown and his colleagues; and the second is a shortage of full-time officers. The ratio of officers to members in British unions is of the order of one officer to three or four thousand members. Allowing for national officers and regional administrators, the ratio of 'field officers' to members is certainly no better than one to five thousand. In the Engineers it is one to ten thousand, and some of their district secretaries are responsible for more than twenty thousand members, scattered over hundreds of plants. It is therefore entirely reasonable for employers to point out that many field officers cannot be expected to maintain more than the most superficial contact with their workplace organizations. By contrast, there is only one union each in hosiery and footwear, and the ratio of officers to members in these two unions is a good deal more favourable than the national average.

Nevertheless the argument cannot stop there. Ratios of officers to members vary widely from one union to another, and it has been argued that differences are largely the consequence of the circumstances which each union has faced in the course of its development.[102] A powerful influence in engineering was the 1898 settlement by which the employers sought to exclude union district committees and full-time officers from the plant, so that union members had no protection other than their workplace organizations and these organizations were forced to be self-reliant.

If the exceptional independence of trade union workplace organization in Britain has therefore to be explained by the interaction of employers' attitudes and union structures, there can be little doubt that the structure of management is the primary cause of another exceptional feature—the wide scope accorded to most workplace organizations in sizable manufacturing plants to negotiate their own pay agreements. Although their colleagues in the public sector have an even higher level of trade union membership, and in many instances equally independent and sturdy organizations in the plant, the great majority of them are limited to the application of industry

---

[102] Clegg *et al.*, *Trade Union Officers*, Chapter 11.

pay agreements. This feature of the public sector is due to the centralized systems of management imposed by the Acts of Parliament constituting nationalized industries and public services, and by the control of government departments with their predilection for standardization and their commitment to public accountability. Employers' associations in manufacturing could hardly have been expected to achieve a similar degree of centralization in industrial relations, although several associations in private services come within hailing distance of the performance of the public sector. But individual manufacturing companies might choose to negotiate similar standardized pay agreements covering all their plants. A few have done so, but most of them have allowed the pay of their manual employees to be determined by plant bargaining, at first fragmented, but now often plant-wide.

There are two other exceptional features of British workplace bargaining. The first is the considerable control that many workplace organizations exercise over the arrangement and conduct of work, and the second is the high proportion of workplace strikes that are conducted unofficially—without union authority—and unconstitutionally—without first making full use of the procedures for dealing with claims and grievances. The early sections of this chapter emphasized the continuity of customary regulation of work practices, and the dependence of this regulation on workplace organization. If British workplace bargaining is exceptional in this respect, then part of the reason may be the unique longevity and continuity of British trade unionism. But perhaps it might be expected that workplace organizations with abnormal independence and scope for action in other respects should record outstanding achievements in the control of work arrangements as well. It is equally plausible to argue that workplace organizations, with their unusual responsibilities and bargaining strength, would make more use of the strike than less well-endowed workplace organizations; and, if they could not do so officially and constitutionally, they would act on their own authority. Further discussion of strikes is reserved for Chapter 5.

This account of workplace organization and bargaining has relied for its explanatory variables on union and employer attitudes and structures, and on managerial controls. Little weight has been placed on technology which is often considered to have considerable influence on the character and conduct of industrial relations. Two reasons may be offered. The first is the finding of Brown and his colleagues that, once size of plant is allowed for, the stability and sophistication of workplace organizations vary little across manufacturing industry.[103] It suggests that size is a more important direct influence than technology, although technology, of course, affects size. Secondly, the argument has attempted to account for the exceptional features of British workplace organization and bargaining, and technology is not contained by national frontiers.

Nevertheless explanations in terms of structure have an unduly deterministic appearance. They neglect the never-ending daily activity which is essential to create or maintain any organization. Batstone and his colleagues investigated this activity in the engineering plant in which they classified the stewards as populists and leaders. The more influential leaders formed a 'quasi-elite' in close contact with the three conveners (one for each of the two major manual unions in the plant and one to cover all the smaller manual unions) and with considerable weight in the joint shop stewards' committee. One of their main functions was to mobilize opinion on the shop floor, for contrary to what might have been expected, the manual workers did not display a clear-cut preference for collective approaches to industrial issues. In fact there was widespread ambivalence between collective and individualist approaches both on the shop floor and in the office. The way in which employees worked in teams on the shop floor promoted collective attitudes there, but the leader stewards constantly reinforced these attitudes by encouraging sentiments of solidarity and canvassing collective solutions to current problems; whereas the office representatives were usually ineffective in their attempts to mobilize opinion. The members of the 'quasi-elite' and other leader stewards on the shop floor made use of an intricate network of contacts which linked them to the more influential members of informal groups throughout the plant ('opinion leaders'). Although their emphasis was always on solidarity, this criterion did not dictate a unique course of action in every situation. Solidarity could justify sympathetic action in support of a group with a grievance, but it could be invoked equally well to persuade the aggrieved group to handle their case through procedure so as to avoid the risk that other workers would be laid off by a strike.[104]

---

[103] Their sample did not extend to hosiery and footwear, but included two hosiery plants which confirm the deviant behaviour of workplace organization in that industry.   [104] Batstone *et al.*, *op. cit.*

It is impossible to say how typical this behaviour is among workplace organizations, but if the mobilization of opinion in favour of collective behaviour is a common feature, then the work of Batstone and his colleagues helps to resolve a final problem concerning British workplace organizations in manufacturing: if they are so self-reliant and have such wide scope for independent action, what binds them to their unions?

There are several links. In many instances, including the plant studied by Batstone and his colleagues, there are frequent meetings and telephone contacts between full-time officers and senior stewards. Stewards value the advice of experienced full-time officers. Full-time officers want to keep themselves informed on plant affairs in case they are called on to settle a dispute or to report to headquarters. The stewards may want the full-time officer to intervene at a mass meeting; he may want their support in an election or at a committee meeting. Stewards also hold other jobs in their unions. *Workplace Industrial Relations 1973* found that 23 per cent of their sample of stewards held other offices in their unions, and for senior stewards the proportion was 58 per cent.[105] They serve on branch committees, as branch secretaries, on district and regional committees, on trade group conferences and committees, on the workers' side of negotiating committees, as conference delegates and on national executives. With all these contacts shop stewards and their unions can hardly be said to be 'out of touch' with each other.

On the evidence of Batstone and his colleagues, there is also another link. They show that shop stewards have to mobilize support for collective responses to shop floor issues. But solidarity is not just a matter of shop floor expediency. It is also the central principle of trade unionism, which the national unions claim to embody. Workplace organizations may challenge particular interpretations, but they cannot deny the superior right of their unions to define and apply the principle without cutting away the ground on which they themselves stand. Another link between workplace and union is therefore a traffic in ideas.

[105] p. 18.

Chapter 3

EMPLOYERS AND THE STRUCTURE OF COLLECTIVE BARGAINING OUTSIDE THE PLANT

THE DEVELOPMENT OF EMPLOYERS' ASSOCIATIONS

It is widely assumed, especially within employers' associations themselves, that these associations were founded to protect their members from the growing power of the unions; and because they could not get rid of the unions, they were gradually forced to enter into dealings with them as a means of avoiding industrial conflict. This was a convenient hypothesis through most of the nineteenth century when middle-class opinion generally held that any interference with economic competition was harmful and wrong. It followed that concerted action among employers was wrong; but if combination was forced on them by the unions, their offence might be pardonable; and if combination among employers was the only means of limiting the distortions in the labour market arising from union action, it might even be justifiable. Having admitted that his association was as guilty as the unions of interfering with 'the action of those natural laws of supply and demand', one witness before the 1867 Royal Commission went on to say he was 'for having them all abolished, I should be glad if this were the result of this commission'.[1]

A history of British employers' associations would be needed to determine the validity of this hypothesis, and there is no such history. Its absence is not primarily due to lack of information. Much of the material used for writing trade union history is also relevant to employers' associations. Many associations have preserved their records and some have made them available to students. Histories of several individual associations have been published. Royal Commis-

[1] 1867 Commission, *Minutes of Evidence*, Qs 3489–90.

sions and other public inquiries have taken volumes of evidence from the spokesmen of employers' associations. In the absence of anything better, therefore, reference to some of these sources allows a rough sketch of the main outlines of the development of organization among employers to be presented here. It indicates that the hypothesis that employers' associations developed as a reaction to the unions is partly, but only partly, correct.

For one thing, dealing with labour problems is not the only motive for combination among employers. They also come together to concert action on commercial issues—for example to fix prices—and that cannot be excused as a response to trade union action. An association concerned with commercial issues only is now called a trade association, and is outside the scope of this book; but many associations handle both types of issue and are therefore employers' associations, whatever else they may be as well. There have been associations of this kind from the start.

Whatever the motives for combination, employers' associations can be traced back about as far as the unions. Associations of master printers existed in the eighteenth century.[2] Cotton employers were not far behind in combining in Glasgow and in several Lancashire towns.[3] As with trade unions, early organization was often informal and ephemeral, or spasmodic. 'There was no real West Riding Masters' Association' in coalmining, 'but they met when there was any special action taken on the part of the men, or when it was thought necessary to have a reduction or any advance in the price of coals'.[4] The Preston Master Spinners' Association 'took cognisance of disputes having reference to wages up to the year 1846, after which it was said to have been inactive up to 1853'.[5]

Most associations were limited to a single town or region until late in the nineteenth century, although there was intermittent action on a wider scale. In 1833–4 the 'document'—an undertaking binding workers to have nothing to do with trade unions—was imposed by employers in London, throughout the Midlands and in Yorkshire and Lancashire. In December 1864 the ironmasters 'of North and South Staffordshire, Sheffield, Derbyshire and the North of England met together and decided to give simultaneous notice of a reduction

---

[2] Ellic Howe, *The London Compositor, 1785–1900*, p. 10.
[3] National Association for the Promotion of Social Science, *Trade Societies and Strikes*, pp. 393, 396, 433.
[4] 1867 Commission, *Minutes of Evidence*, Q. 12521.
[5] *Trade Societies and Strikes*, p. 209.

of wages, equal to 10 per cent'.[6] About the same time some of the local building employers' associations were brought together in a General Builders' Association which was active for several years. The Mining Association of Great Britain, founded in 1854, regarded industrial relations as the exclusive concern of its constituent coalfield associations. Even so, 'it is impossible to overlook the opportunities which it must afford the coal-owners, by simply bringing them together from all parts of the kingdom, for preparing and concerting their measures towards the men'.[7]

One of the aims of many of these associations was to destroy the unions. The document was used again in the engineering lockout of 1852 and in the London building lockout seven years later, although many engineers continued to support their union after signing the document, and the withdrawal of the document was one of the conditions on which the building lockout was terminated. But many of them had other objectives as well. The setting of both prices and wages by the coalowners in each county was the general practice in coalmining long before stable unions were formed. The South Staffordshire Ironmasters' Association, so the 1867 Royal Commission were informed, had for many years held quarterly meetings at which 'the selling prices of iron for the district have been fixed, and wages were invariably regulated by these prices until recently'.[8] Before 1879, when they signed an agreement with the union, the Cleveland ironmasters 'met together and agreed as to whether they could ask for a reduction of wages or not, and then each works negotiated with its own men separately'.[9]

Moreover, the associations were always ready to deal with the unions when it suited them. At the end of the eighteenth century the working day of the London bookbinders was reduced from eleven hours to ten 'by mutual agreement after considerable negotiation. . . . It would appear that it was arranged with a combination of employers'.[10] The pay of the London printing trade was regulated by 'decisions on a scale made in 1810 with additions, definitions and explanations arranged at a Conference of Master Printers and Compositors in 1847'.[11] Even the anti-union General Builders' Associa-

---

[6] 1867 Commission, *Fifth Report*, p. 20.
[7] *Trade Societies and Strikes*, p. 20.
[8] 1867 Commission, *Fifth Report*, p. 57.
[9] Industrial Council, Inquiry into Industrial Agreements, *Minutes of Evidence*, Q. 9035.
[10] *Trade Societies and Strikes*, pp. 95–8.   [11] *Ibid.*, p. 86

tion which justified its objections to trade unionism before the 1867 Royal Commission on several grounds, including that 'they exercise coercion over both masters and men and tend to separate masters and men',[12] nevertheless arranged with the Birmingham building unions for 'a public meeting of masters and operatives connected with the building trades for the purpose of appointing delegates on both sides to draw up trade rules'.[13]

Some employers' associations took the lead in establishing collective bargaining. Led by Sir David Dale, a Quaker, the North of England Ironmasters approached the Ironworkers' Association to set up a conciliation board in 1869, which agreed to regulate wages by means of a selling-price sliding scale. He was following the example of A. J. Mundella who took the lead in forming a conciliation board for the Nottingham hosiery trade in 1860. A Hosiery Association was then set up to supply the employers' representatives on the board. The industry was highly competitive and both sides had an interest in preventing cut-throat wage reductions.

In the closing years of the nineteenth century local employers' associations in a number of major industries came together in national federations. In most instances federation was unquestionably a response to increasing trade union power. The upsurge of trade unionism on the waterfront which was the central feature of the 'new unionism' of 1889 prompted the foundation of the Shipping Federation in 1890. Within three years its vigorous and extensive strike-breaking activities had reduced the new unions of seamen and dockers to feeble remnants.[14] Other federations, faced with established unions of skilled workers, might defeat them, but they could not destroy them. Instead they tried to limit and control union action by imposing industry procedure agreements upon them. Under these agreements, union branches or districts were forbidden to strike over a local issue or claim until a national joint meeting of the federation and the union had considered it and tried to resolve it. Union leaders might be expected to take a wider and more cautious view of the matter than local hotheads; and union leaders also appreciated that these new procedures reinforced their authority over their branches.

[12] 1867 Commission, *Minutes of Evidence*, Q. 297.   [13] *Ibid.*, Q. 3074.

[14] The federation maintained three vessels to house and transport strike-breakers, as well as launches on the Mersey and the Tyne. Large sums were spent on paying, guarding and feeding these men, as well as providing them with 'beer tokens'. (L. H. Powell, *The Shipping Federation*, pp. 8. 144.)

The most outstanding example of this development was the foundation of the Engineering Employers' Federation in 1896, followed by the 1897 lockout and the 1898 settlement;[15] but it was not the first. In 1891 the Federation of Master Cotton Spinners' Associations had been formed to counter the growing strength of the rich and powerful Spinners' Amalgamation. After massive lockouts during the next two years the two bodies established a central procedure known as the Brooklands Agreement. Faced with outbreaks of local disputes, several employers' associations in footwear federated together in 1890. Their lockout, which lasted for seven weeks, came in 1895, and at the end of it the union was forced to accept a central procedure which included the novel feature of financial penalties for breaches of the agreement by either side. The National Federation of Building Trade Employers goes back to 1878, but they did not begin to play a prominent part in industrial relations until the nineties. In 1899 they locked out the plasterers with the result that a central procedure was agreed for the plastering trade and followed in 1904 by another which covered the whole building industry. The Shipbuilding Federation was set up in 1891 to counter the power of the Boilermakers. They eventually locked out the Boilermakers and the other shipbuilding unions in 1908, and the stoppage was ended by an agreement which included a central procedure for handling disputes.

The trend towards federation among employers was a consequence of trade union growth and activity, but, once established, the federations wrested the initiative from the unions. They forced the unions into industry-wide conflicts in place of the favourite union strategy of picking off one group of employers at a time, and they used their victories to redesign the system of industrial relations to a pattern of their own choice—the central procedure agreement.

The next step towards a system of industry bargaining was to regulate terms of employment directly by central agreements on pay and hours of work. By 1914 three industries had centralized the general adjustment of wages upwards or downwards—cotton weaving, cotton spinning and shipbuilding—and the footwear industry was moving in the same direction. In each of them the employers deserve a large share of credit for the innovation. Central pay settlements had been among the objectives of the cotton weaving and shipbuilding employers' federations from their foundation. But

[15] See pp. 20–1.

with the war initiative passed to the government. Piecemeal district negotiations over pay were poor instruments to cope with rapid wartime inflation, especially when one claim after another was referred to the wartime compulsory arbitration tribunals set up by the government. Most major industries therefore came out of the war with industry agreements on pay and hours of work, many of them originating in tribunal decisions or adopted under government control or pressure. Other industries followed shortly after the war. Encouraged by the Whitley reports, government intervention also helped to introduce industry bargaining into industries which had no central procedures before the war, and in some instances little bargaining of any kind. New employers' organizations were called into being for the purpose, including the Chemical and Allied Employers' Association, the Federation of Gas Employers, and the National Association of Port Employees.

By 1921, when the postwar slump precipitated government retrenchment and a return to non-interventionist policies in industrial relations, Britain was covered by a patchwork of industry agreements, far from perfect, with many gaps and some further holes to be torn during the next few years, but nevertheless providing regulative protection of at least minimum conditions for the majority of manual workers in most major industries. Industry bargaining was now the norm in British industrial relations.

With nearly twenty years of unprecedentedly high unemployment to come, employers' associations were in a powerful bargaining position and had ample opportunity to modify and develop this system of bargaining to suit themselves. What use did they make of it? To begin with, they did not get rid of the system. Coalmining and wool manufacture, it is true, reverted to district bargaining, but the coalowners were untypical in their passionate opposition to their national wage agreement which had been imposed on them by the coal controller during the war. More representative of the general opinion among organized employers were the cotton weaving employers. When serious undercutting of their agreed industry wage rates threatened to destroy the central regulation of pay in the early thirties, they joined with the unions in seeking and securing statutory support for their agreements.

To the extent that employers' associations sought to modify the system, most of the changes which they advocated were in the direction of greater centralization. This was particularly true of pay agreements. Most industries still had regional or district pay differentials. In some instances the industry agreement specified, and from time to time adjusted, two or more rates which applied in defined areas. In others the agreement determined a single national rate which was paid as a supplement to district rates inherited from the past. Generally the associations wanted to reduce the number and spread of rates in the first kind of agreement. Since this was almost invariably accomplished by levelling-up, the unions usually took the initiative and wanted to go further than the employers would agree. In the second type of agreement the associations tried to limit or eliminate the authority of district negotiators to adjust district rates. Where they succeeded, district rates were frozen and pay adjustments could come only through industry negotiations. This form of centralization commonly met with trade union opposition, for the branches and districts were reluctant to lose their right to make local pay claims.

The engineering pay agreement was of the second type. During the twenties the unions pursued a number of claims for increases in district rates, and, when these were rejected, they turned to national claims for increases in particular branches of engineering such as car manufacture and electrical engineering. Although the industry was generally depressed, these branches were expanding and the unions believed that they could afford to pay more; alternatively, they claimed district advances in those parts of the country where these sections of the industry were concentrated. But the federation was adamantly opposed to both these approaches and the unions lacked the strength to force the issue.

In the long run the employers' attitude may have helped to undermine the system of industry bargaining over pay which they intended to strengthen. Pressure for pay increases in the plant in the inflationary years after 1939 might have been contained to a greater extent if there had been scope for district or sectional adjustments to absorb some of the pressure where it was most acute. But that was not foreseen at the time.

There were many major strikes and lockouts during the interwar years, most of them concentrated in the years 1919–26. The slump in prices in 1921–3 brought a series of disputes over wage reductions, and there were several more in 1929–33 although on this occasion, despite unprecedented unemployment, the price level fell slowly and some industries suffered only modest pay cuts while in other industries cuts were avoided altogether. The great majority of these disputes arose out of claims for reductions or advances in pay, and were not concerned with the structure of collective bargaining. An exception was the engineering lockout of 1922 when the Engineering Employers' Federation returned to the issue of managerial prerogative. The unions had terminated the 1898 settlement shortly before the war, and with the shortage of skilled engineers during the war the bargaining strength of union district committees and shop stewards grew to unprecedented levels. In the eyes of the employers, they had been responsible for

a policy of interference, urged on by the unions and encouraged by war conditions . . . with a view to shifting the frontier into management's territory. . . . Complaints of obstacles placed in the way of executing orders poured into the Employers' Federation from all quarters.[16]

During the lockout the House of Commons was told by an engineering employer of

the intolerable conditions imposed upon us in our daily work. Lines of demarcation, disputes as to how many men shall be put on a machine, overtime conditions, . . . are being brought up to us from day to day and we . . . are being met by every particle of opposition which it is possible to put against us . . . because of the wild men who are assuming control of the trade unions.[17]

Given the violence of the employers' emotions, and the weakness of the unions, the terms of settlement were surprisingly moderate. Having acknowledged that matters regulated by agreement could not be altered except by agreement or after procedure had been exhausted, the agreement went on to say that a management proposal for an alteration in working conditions which were not governed by an agreement must nevertheless be notified to the workers if it would 'result in one class of workpeople being replaced by another in the establishment', in order that the workers could challenge it through procedure if they wished. If the issue had not been settled within ten days the management could make a temporary decision pending the completion of the remaining stages of pro-

[16] A. Shadwell, *The Engineering Industry and the Crisis of 1922*, p. 63.
[17] *Hansard*, 20 March 1922, cols 89, 95.

cedure. A proposal for change which did not replace one class of worker by another might be implemented without delay, but the workers were still entitled to seek its reversal through procedure. These provisions were far removed from those of the 1898 settlement. They acknowledged the right of workers to participate in decisions on the organization of work and manning even if managers were given a considerable advantage by their licence to put their proposals into practice pending a final decision.

By 1939, therefore, it must be assumed that organized employers in Britain had secured a system of collective bargaining which suited them. They had taken the initiative in its construction before 1914. They had accepted most of the extensions introduced by the government under wartime controls and immediately after the war, and they had chosen to sustain and reinforce the system during the interwar years when they had the power to make radical changes if they had wished to do so. Among its advantages for them were that it helped to avoid or resolve industrial conflict; limited competitive wage–cutting; and at least appeared to support managerial authority in the plant.

THEIR CURRENT FUNCTIONS

(a) *Pay Bargaining*

Already by 1943 one of the limitations of the system had become apparent, notably in engineering: it provided no means of controlling earnings in the plant. During the interwar years when it was in the interest of employers to keep a tight rein on piecework and to be sparing in their use of merit rates and other supplements, it had been reasonable to assume that pay in federated firms was regulated by the agreements between the federation and the unions. But, under conditions of labour shortage and cost-plus wartime contracts, engineering employers exercised less restraint. Earnings rose faster than rates, and the increases were spread unevenly between workers and plants. In 1943 an arbitration award tried to reverse this trend by increasing rates in such a way as to exclude high–earning pieceworkers. The award was unpopular, led to a number of strikes and had no noticeable effect on the growth of earnings.

In 1950 the federation put forward its own proposals for restoring the regulative power of its agreements with the unions by what was called a *pro tanto* clause. An increase was granted to the low earners in each grade; the amount of the increase was graduated down for those who earned more; and the highest earners received nothing. On this occasion there was no differentiation between pieceworkers and timeworkers. The unions agreed, partly because this was a period of government pay restraint. They thought a fairly substantial increase could be justified more easily if the benefits went primarily to the low paid. But this agreement proved as unpopular as the 1943 award. Once again a rash of strikes frustrated its intentions by securing plant increases for the higher paid to preserve their earnings differentials.

Thereafter the federation resigned itself for more than a decade to a continuing decline in the regulatory force of its pay agreements. But in 1964 a further period of government incomes policy brought a new approach to the problem. This time minimum earnings levels for each grade were increased in stages over a period of three years; and another package deal for a further period was signed in 1968. The repetition of the agreement showed that it was less unpopular than its predecessors in 1943 and 1950. This was not because high-paid workers had become reconciled to a decline in their relative earnings. The evidence is that the package deals had scarcely any effect in that respect.[18] It was rather because the growth of plant bargaining had reduced the impact of industry settlements of any kind on pay packets in high-earning plants, and this trend was accelerated by another aspect of the incomes policy—the government's enthusiastic encouragement of productivity agreements which were exempted from the limits on pay increases imposed by the policy.

Up to this time many federated employers in engineering and other manufacturing industries, although by no means all of them, had felt free to increase earnings by payment by results, lieu rates, merit rates (even 'merit rates commonly applied') and other supplements, but they had not thought it right to negotiate their own basic rates. One consequence was to encourage fragmented bargaining in the plant, raising an extremely complex structure of supplements and allowances on top of the industry rates. Another was that the whole structure was raised by the amount of the increase in national

[18] The increase in minimum earnings levels for skilled engineering workers between January 1965 and January 1968 was 21.7 per cent. Excluding overtime, average earnings rose by 21.1 per cent for skilled timeworkers and 20.7 per cent for skilled workers paid by results. (National Board for Prices and Incomes, *Pay and Conditions of Service of Engineering Workers*, p. 12.)

rates each time these were adjusted. It was to avoid this consequence that the engineering package deals switched to the adjustment of minimum earnings levels. But it was a central tenet of productivity bargaining that most forms of payments by results, and reliance on regular overtime, encouraged inefficient practices in order to increase earnings, and they should be replaced by high basic rates to remove the temptation. The acceptance of productivity bargaining therefore led to the licensing of federated firms to negotiate their own structures of basic rates. Where they took advantage of their new freedom, the link between the industry rates and plant rates was broken. Industry rates no longer had any direct effect on plant rates so long as plant rates were ahead of them. They became 'safety-nets'.[19]

The change did not come about without heart-searching and stress. The original Fawley productivity agreement was viewed with little enthusiasm by employers' associations. In 1964 Esso, followed by other oil companies, withdrew from the Employers' Panel of the Oil Companies' Conciliation Committee in order to introduce a productivity agreement in its distribution operations. The panel operated as an employers' association for this branch of the oil industry's activities, and its rules insisted on a strict application of its pay agreements.[20] Even where withdrawal from an association was not obligatory under its rules, 'the proposals of a particular company may demand an agreement so different from those prevailing in the rest of the industry as to render continued membership of the association a serious embarrassment. It was on such grounds that Alcan decided to withdraw from the South Wales and Monmouth-shire Iron and Steel Manufacturers' Association, and for similar reasons the Milford Haven refinery left the Welsh Engineers and Founders Association whose agreement had previously applied to their maintenance craftsmen.'[21] In the autumn of 1965 Shell was in discussion with the National Union of Seamen on manpower economies by means of the introduction of 'general-purpose crews' on its oil tankers in return for a pay increase beyond the rates agreed by the National Maritime Board. Negotiations were halted when the Shipping Federation told Shell that their proposal would 'prejudice

---

[19] See p. 18.
[20] In 1968 the defunct panel was replaced by the Petroleum Industry Employers' Committee on Employee Relations which confined itself to exchange of information.
[21] National Board for Prices and Incomes, *Productivity Agreements*, p. 36.

arrangements for the introduction of general purpose crews on other types of ship'.[22]

By that time, however, employer opinion was changing. In the same year the Confederation of British Industry told the Donovan Commission that it recognized 'the benefits created by many plant productivity bargains but considers it essential that they should be closely related to the national collective bargains in the industry'.[23] Given the nature and purpose of productivity agreements this was a silly observation, but not unfriendly. In July 1967 the rubber industry replaced its existing pay agreements by a new 'minimum basic wage'. There were to be no 'consequential increases for workers whose present earnings are above the minimum weekly wage. . . . Earnings for skill, responsibility and incentives will be determined at local level by local negotiation.' Later that year the Chemical Industries Association[24] negotiated a new agreement with both the process and the craft unions which had previously negotiated separately. The parties accepted that 'the wage rates in national agreements are minima'. Productivity bargaining was to be encouraged, but 'it cannot be done by a national negotiating committee. . . . While in certain cases relating to a company framework, it must . . . take place for the most part at works level.' A joint committee and advisory service were set up to encourage and guide productivity negotiations and to authorize departures from the national agreements other than wage agreements (where no authorization was required). In the same year the final report of the Pearson Court of Inquiry into the Shipping Industry recommended that experiments should be permitted in 'the way that seamen might be deployed and rewarded for more flexible working',[25] and shortly afterwards agreements on general-purpose crews were signed by several oil companies. In 1968 the Engineering Employers' Federation issued a paper on *Productivity Bargaining and the Engineering Industry* by its research director, E. J. Robertson, which recommended productivity agreements to its members so long as they were properly negotiated and carefully operated.

Although the rules of the Employers' Panel in oil distribution

[22] *Donovan Report*, p. 197.

[23] Donovan Commission, *Selected Written Evidence*, p. 269.

[24] This had been formed by a recent merger of the Chemical and Allied Employers' Association with several other associations which dealt mainly with commercial matters.

[25] *Final Report*, p. 34.

forbade any departure from their agreed rates, formal provisions of this kind were exceptional. In a 1966 survey of twenty-four associations which negotiated industry pay agreements, twenty settled 'basic rates only, allowing management at local level to agree to higher or supplementary rates'. Four said they settled 'effective rates, with very little freedom to negotiate other rates at local level'. These four organizations were asked how they prevented members who wished to pay more than the agreed rates from doing so. The spokesman of one of them said that there was no attempt at control, the respondent for another retracted his statement and admitted that in fact minimum rates only were negotiated. The two remaining associations relied on 'diplomatic letters' or 'purely persuasion'.[26] The change to encouraging individual members to negotiate their own pay structures was therefore a modification of attitudes, not rules. In the shipping industry the Pearson Report found that 'centralisation seems to have been accepted as the natural order of things. The major oil tanker companies have told us that they now take the view that the National Maritime Board has not paid enough attention to their special problems. We think there is substance in this complaint and welcome the decision of the Shipping Federation to establish a tanker section. But the neglect of special tanker interests is nothing new, and the Federation responded as soon as the companies demanded attention. It would seem that for many years the needs of the tanker companies went unrecognised because it did not occur to them that the prevailing centralisation could be challenged.'[27]

Even today there are wide variations in the extent to which associations and their members expect their pay agreements to be observed. Freedom for individual plants and companies to negotiate their own pay structures is the general, but not universal, rule in manufacturing. It is the norm in engineering, metal manufacture, and the chemicals and food manufacturing groups of industries (except for baking) which together account for about two-thirds of manufacturing employment. Most smaller industries have adopted a similar approach, but in footwear pay is determined either by an industry agreement on minimum rates and piecework, or by a detailed industry incentive agreement, and parts of the cotton industry still work to their standard piecework lists.

There is and always has been freedom for employers to exceed the

[26] Munns and McCarthy, *Employers' Associations*, pp. 92–3.
[27] *Final Report*, pp. 2–3.

statutory minimum rates in the private services which are covered by wages councils, whether by adding supplements to the minimum rates or by designing their own pay structures. The associations represented on the employers' side of the councils might try, if they chose, to hold their members to the statutory rates, but it does not appear that they have ever done so. Indeed it is doubtful how far these bodies should be counted as employers' associations. The Commission on Industrial Relations described the 45 employers' associations which then nominated members to the nine retail distribution councils as 'still predominantly trade associations'[28] which had been persuaded to provide nominees but otherwise confined themselves mainly or entirely to commercial matters. In road haulage the union side has been strongly organized for many years, but until 1977 every attempt to replace the council by voluntary collective bargaining failed because the Road Haulage Association was unable to undertake the normal functions of an employers' association. Its rules allow it 'to advise and assist its members in their industrial relations', but it 'does not negotiate with trade unions, and has no power to commit its members to any agreement or policy it advocates'.[29]

Industry agreements on pay have a very different status among employers in several of the private services which have developed effective collective bargaining. The largest of them is the building industry. In 1968 the National Board for Prices and Incomes conducted a survey of building earnings, and compared the composition of earnings in large firms with that in small firms.[30] The results, set out in Table 3, show that the large firms appeared to observe the industry agreement very closely. The correspondence was even more impressive than the table indicates since the agreed rates in London and Liverpool were 25p higher than elsewhere and this must account for part of the margin between the agreed rates and basic rates paid in large firms. It does not follow that the firms had no flexibility in paying their employees. Overtime can be manipulated to yield higher earnings, and payment by results arrangements in building are of very variable quality. On some sites earnings are closely related to output by careful measurement of work; in others there are no effective standards of measurement; and in many

[28] Commission on Industrial Relations, *Retail Distribution*, p. 35.
[29] Advisory, Conciliation & Arbitration Service, *Road Haulage Wages Council*, p. 24.
[30] *Pay and Conditions in the Building Industry*, p. 26.

instances the 'bonus' is in practice a flat supplement to the basic rate
of every worker on the site, or of every worker in a particular grade.
But the figures at least show that large building firms conformed
closely to the letter of the agreement.

Table 3

*Composition of Weekly Earnings in Building
in July 1968 by Size of Firm*

	Large firms (1000 or more operatives)		Small firms (10–24 operatives)	
	Craftsmen	Labourers	Craftsmen	Labourers
Agreed Industry Rate	£15.42	£13.17	£15.42	£13.17
Basic Rate	£15.69	£13.38	£17.51	£15.15
Overtime Pay	£4.33	£5.00	£2.11	£2.26
PBR Bonus	£6.56	£3.65	£0.58	£0.56
Other Pay & Allowances	£1.46	£1.17	£0.36	£0.21
Total Weekly Earnings	£28.05	£23.20	£20.66	£18.18

On the other hand, many small firms paid over the rate. It is
significant that whereas almost all large firms in building are federated, the majority of small firms are not. If non-federated firms feel a
need to pay more than the industry rates there is no reason why they
should disguise the payment as overtime (except in periods of government incomes policy) or go to the trouble of inventing a spurious
incentive payment system. Total earnings in small firms, however,
are a good deal closer to the industry rates than they are in large
firms.

Earnings in electrical contracting are even more closely regulated
by the industry agreement than in building because until 1972 the
union and the employers' association—the Electrical Contractors'
Association—refused to countenance payment by results. In 1967
they set up a National Joint Industrial Board to test and grade the

industry's workforce, and to promote technical education, provide welfare benefits and operate an employment service. The board also took over the negotiation and administration of agreements and the handling of disputes. Because of the wish of both sides of the industry to maintain central control over earnings, the board has striven to maintain its rates at a level substantially higher than industry rates elsewhere in construction. But this has proved a difficult task in periods of government incomes policy, and 'on some large construction sites electricians' earnings have fallen behind those of other trades. This has caused discontent and there are instances where the standard rate has been increased by unofficial bonuses and earnings boosted by fictitious overtime payments.'[31] Consequently, in 1971 the board was empowered to grant temporary dispensation to exceed the rate in special circumstances, and soon afterwards company incentive schemes were permitted. The reluctance with which this was done showed the strong support among the employers for the standard rate.

Despite the sanction given to company agreements on 'general-purpose crews' in 1967, the rates negotiated by the National Maritime Board continue to apply to the great majority of ratings in the industry.[32] Moreover, even those companies which negotiate their own agreements 'meet under the aegis of the Federation in order to co-ordinate payment systems and earnings levels and prevent leap-frogging'.[33] However, earnings are boosted by very substantial overtime. In 1966 the Pearson Report noted that 'ratings on foreign-going ships average a 66-hour week and those in the home trade average about 74 hours. In many cases these average figures are substantially exceeded.'[34]

Since the Devlin reforms the main burden of regulating pay in the docks has been assumed by port agreements, and in most ports these agreements are closely followed by individual employers. In road haulage there are now no industry rates at all, either statutory or voluntary. Pay is regulated by area agreements. There is nothing to prevent individual hauliers exceeding the rates in these agreements, but in practice they seem to conform to them fairly closely. In 1975 the basic earnings in the industry—earnings excluding bonus, over-

---

[31] Commission on Industrial Relations, *Employers' Organisations and Industrial Relations*, p. 24.
[32] In 1972 the proportion was given as 95 per cent (*ibid.*, p. 25).
[33] *Ibid.*, p. 25.　　　　　　　　　　[34] *Final Report*, p. 27.

time and shift payments—were just over £40. The area agreements uniformly prescribed a top rate of £40 for drivers of the largest vehicles with £35 as the lowest rate. Road haulage, however, is another industry with very substantial overtime working, and gross weekly earnings were then nearly £60 a week.[35]

Why do employers in these industries show such an unusual concern to maintain standard rates of pay? Special features are of relevance in shipping and electrical contracting. Given the firm opposition of the Shipping Federation and the officers' associations to any effective representation of ratings on board ship, there has been no opportunity for anything approaching plant bargaining to develop there; and the Electrical Contractors' Association deals with a single powerful union, the Electricians, who have given firm support to the observance of standard rates and been willing to exert considerable pressure on their members to keep them in line. But there are also at least two relevant characteristics common to most of these five services.

One of them is casual employment, which is common among manual workers in building, electrical contracting and shipping. Standard rates are a great convenience where workers move frequently from one employer to another. Thus the National Maritime Board negotiates standard rates of pay for ratings, whereas for officers, who constitute about half the total labour force and are permanent employees of the companies for which they work, the board settles minimum salaries only, and most large shipping companies have their own supplementary salary scales. In 1967 the National Board for Prices and Incomes found that the starting salaries provided by these scales averaged between ten and twenty per cent above the board's rates.[36]

Dock labour was also casual until 1967, and the dock labour scheme has continued to operate since then. Redundant dockers revert to the 'pool' until they are taken on by another port employer. The rapid introduction of container ships since the Devlin reforms has brought many redundancies. It is therefore not surprising that attitudes engendered by casual employment continue to have influence in the docks.

---

[35] Advisory, Conciliation and Arbitration Service, *Road Haulage Wages Council*, pp. 33–5.

[36] National Board for Prices and Incomes, *Pay and Conditions of Merchant Navy Officers*, pp. 9–10.

The second common feature is the small size of the employing unit. In 1972 the Commission on Industrial Relations reported that there were 11,500 federated building companies with 325,000 manual employees, giving an average of 28 employees to a company. Average employment in the 3,000-odd federated electrical contracting companies at that time was thirteen manual workers. By contrast, average manual employment in federated chemical companies was over 250 and in federated engineering *plants* (not companies) it was also over 250.[37] There is a good deal of doubt about the number of establishments in the private sector of the road haulage industry, but whatever figure is accepted, the average number of drivers per establishment is certainly less than ten.[38] Although there are a number of small employers in both shipping and the docks, there are a number of large port employers, and the British Council of Shipping, which has replaced the Shipping Federation, is dominated by large companies. Small units of employment cannot therefore be the sole explanation for support for standard rates of pay, but nevertheless it is easy to appreciate why standard rates should be attractive to small employers. They cannot provide themselves with sophisticated information services to assess the movement of pay in comparable firms. They lack the skills to design pay structures. Most of them are more vulnerable to competition than large firms, and anxious not to be undercut, or to lose their few key workers because they are not paying them enough. For all these reasons, standard rates have an appeal for them. By contrast in manufacturing, where the average size of firm and plant is much larger than in building, or electrical contracting, or road haulage—and the special features of shipping and the docks are not present—there is much less support for standard rates.

However, even if the average employing unit in manufacturing is much larger than in most private services, there are nevertheless many small manufacturers, even many small federated manufacturers; and they would have the same reasons as small employers elsewhere for desiring the protection of a standard rate. Their needs can supply one answer to the question; why continue to negotiate industry rates of pay in manufacturing? There have been no surveys

[37] Commission on Industrial Relations, *Employers' Organisations and Industrial Relations*, pp. 66–70.
[38] Advisory, Conciliation and Arbitration Service, *Road Haulage Wages Council*, pp. 14–18.

to explore the validity of this explanation, but it can be observed that many small engineering employers appear to rely on the increases in the industry rates to adjust their own wages, and association officers confirm that the negotiation of industry rates continues to be an important service for small employers in other industries as well. Indeed, it may even be true that employers' associations in manufacturing settle industry rates largely for the benefit of non-federated firms. The great majority of non-federated firms are small; they have the same need as small federated firms for the protection of an industry agreement; and since such agreements are not and cannot be kept secret, they can benefit from them without paying the cost of joining their associations.

This argument offers a supplementary explanation for the growth of plant and company pay structures in post-war Britain. Not only the state of the labour market, and the attitudes and organization of unions and employers, but also the growth in the size of plants must be included among the factors favouring this development. Managers in large undertakings felt a need for their own pay structures and they could acquire the information services and expertise required to negotiate and maintain them. Employers associations quickly revised their original hostile opinions towards productivity bargaining because many of their most influential members believed productivity bargaining was suited to their own needs. The combination of plant or company pay structures with industry agreements on minimum rates of pay has enabled employers' associations to satisfy both large and small employers. Similarly the authorization of payment by results in the building industry provided an outlet for larger building firms within an agreement originally suited to smaller firms.

The footwear industry is exceptional in operating two industry agreements on pay. The first is part of the National Conference Agreement which includes all the industry-level procedural and substantive rules except those contained in the second, the Agreement on Incentives based upon Time Study, which 'attempts to regulate such incentive schemes in detail at industry level' and applies to about forty large firms. 'The larger companies play a prominent and active role in' the British Footwear Manufacturers Federation. They are able to retain the protection of the procedure agreement and the agreements on working hours, holidays, short-time working, and so on, '*and* tailor the' agreement on incentives 'to their needs, without antagonising the small (generally piecework) companies'.[39]

An indication of the relative importance of industry and plant agreements in engineering is provided by a dispute over pay in 1971–2. In August 1971 the Confederation of Shipbuilding and Engineering Unions submitted a claim for a substantial increase in pay all round when the current three-year package deal ran out at the end of the year, together with: a £6 a week increase in minimum earnings levels for craftsmen and £5 for labourers; the immediate introduction of full equal pay for women; a 35-hour week; and four weeks' holiday with pay in place of three. During the autumn the employers offered a mere £1.50 a week on minimum pay, which was rejected. In January 1972 the unions decided to press their claims at plant level. The Sheffield and Manchester districts submitted district claims for an increase of £4 a week and the 35-hour week along with other concessions for all federated plants within their jurisdictions. In retrospect they were almost certainly misguided, for it might have been possible to make some progress by picking off one plant at a time. The local employers' associations offered a pay increase in line with the national offer, and in March the unions instituted an overtime ban in Manchester. A number of factories were occupied by their employees. In May a Manchester shop stewards' meeting decided to drop the claim for a reduction in the working week, and a round of plant pay settlements commenced there and throughout the country, many of them substantially above the national offer. Talks with the employers' federation opened again in August when national minimum pay was raised by £3 for craftsmen and £2.50 for labourers, with similar increases to follow a year later. There was also to be an additional day's holiday in 1972 with another in 1973. Thus an industry-wide pay claim was sufficient to trigger off an important dispute, but the decisive settlements were at plant level with the industry agreement providing a safety net. The dispute was complicated by the submission of district claims and especially by the attempt to secure a reduction in the working week by local or plant settlements.

(b) *The Working Week, Overtime, Holidays and Shiftworking*

Even today, flexible industry pay agreements seem to give most

[39] Goodman *et al.*, *Rule-Making and Industrial Peace*, pp. 90–1, 98.

employers all the room for manoeuvre that they need, and there is no variation between employers' associations or within them in attitudes to the observance of agreements on the length of the standard working week, the number of days of holiday each year, and premium rates for overtime and shiftworking. Candidates for membership of local engineering associations are required to give an undertaking to observe the federation's agreements on these matters.

Changes in agreements on them are far more infrequent than changes in pay agreements. Before 1914 there was a wide variation in the length of the recognized working week. Where it was governed by agreements—mainly district agreements—the range was from 48 to 60 hours, or even wider; and there does not seem to have been a marked coincidence in changes negotiated in different industries. However, the widespread introduction of industry bargaining over pay during the war was followed by a series of industry agreements on hours of work in 1918–20 when most major industries introduced a standard working week for manual workers of either 47 or 48 hours.

For twenty-five years thereafter there was no further general reduction, but two or three industries moved ahead on their own. Printing, for example, negotiated a 45-hour working week in 1937. The aftermath of the Second World War brought another demand for general improvement, and during 1945–7 the norm became 44 hours with 45 hours common in the textile industries. More than a decade of stability followed. From 1948 to 1959 the official average of normal weekly hours fell by only eighteen minutes from 44.7 to 44.4 hours. Then nearly thirteen million workers secured a reduction within two years and by 1962 the norm was 42 hours and the average was 42.4. But the 42-hour week was not a stable position. It had much less hold on trade union imaginations than the target of 40 hours. By 1964 new agreements were being struck, many of them providing for the introduction of the forty-hour week in two steps of an hour each. By 1967 the norm was 40 hours and the average was 40.5; and there has not been much change since then.

Annual holidays were exceptional for manual workers in private industry before 1938. A committee under the chairmanship of Lord Amulree estimated that out of 18.5 million manual and lower-paid white collar workers in Britain at that time less than eight million were entitled to them. The committee recommended that annual holidays with pay should be extended to all employees and their proposal that statutory wage-fixing bodies should be empowered to introduce them within their jurisdiction led to the Holidays with Pay Act 1938. By the end of the war there were few workers who were not entitled to at least one week's holiday in addition to bank holidays. In the early fifties there was a general shift to two weeks, and towards the end of the sixties came a further move to three weeks. Since then many industries have granted additional days (often taken at Christmas) and in 1975 four weeks was agreed in engineering, but imitation has been delayed by Government incomes policy.

Outside the public sector there is relatively little industry bargaining for white collar employees, and their working hours and holidays are settled in the company or the plant, whether by bargaining or by the employer. The standards are therefore more diverse, and less well recorded, than those for manual workers. Nevertheless it is probable that the majority of white collar employees have a working week somewhere between 35 and 38 hours and four to five weeks' holiday appears to be the norm.

The timing of general adjustments in the working week and holidays at intervals of ten years or more indicates the importance of concerted action by employers, and also between employers' associations, for one or two settlements in major firms or by employers' associations might set off a new wave. During the sixties the Draughtsmen's Association (as it then was) drew attention to the danger by a vigorous campaign, backed by strikes, to persuade individual engineering companies to grant their members an extra week's holiday. As a result the Engineering Employers' Federation tried, without success, to persuade the white collar unions in their industry to enter into an industry agreement to set standards on this and other aspects of employment. Besides that, an alteration in the time spent at work is a much more permanent addition to costs than a pay increase. An injudiciously large addition to pay one year may be recouped by an unusually modest settlement the next, but a reduction in the working week or a longer holiday is virtually irreversible. The relative disadvantage disappears only when other employers move into line. For this reason employers value the protection of a standard agreement. Finally, changes in these aspects of employment are far more visible than most alterations in pay. Many pay agreements are complex and earnings may rise substantially in a plant without attracting much attention outside, but a shorter working week or an extra week's holiday is clear-cut and forced on the attention of others. For all these reasons employers, both large and small—in manufacturing, private services or the public sector—are predisposed to support standard agreements on these issues; and the agreements serve as guides to non-federated firms also.

To some extent the same arguments apply to premiums for overtime and weekend work, to premiums for the many different patterns of shiftworking, and to the guaranteed week and lay-off provisions which provide some protection to the great majority of manual workers who are still 'hourly-paid' although they may be statutorily entitled to several weeks' notice. In this last respect white collar workers paid by the week or the month enjoy an advantage, but their overtime provisions are generally well below the norms agreed for manual workers. Most manual workers receive a premium of 50 per cent during the week (with perhaps 25 per cent for the first two hours) and 100 per cent for Sunday working—generally referred to as time-and-a-half, time-and-a-quarter, and double time. Many white collar workers are expected to work a margin of overtime without payment. When payment is given it may be at the normal hourly rate. When there is a premium it may be less than the premium for manual workers. Since one common explanation for overtime premiums is that they discourage employers from using overtime by raising its cost, it is worth observing that manual workers, with higher premiums, almost universally average more overtime than white collar workers.

(c) Disputes Procedures

A third service which employers' associations provide for their members is assistance in the resolution of disputes through the procedures which they have agreed with the unions. The disputes which their procedures may be asked to handle fall roughly into two groups; disputes about the application of industry or regional agreements to a particular plant or company; and disputes about plant issues which may be covered by plant or company agreements or customs, but are not normally regulated by industry agreements. The first group are called interpretation disputes, and the second domestic disputes.

There is no direct evidence on the relative incidence of disputes in these two categories in British industrial relations as a whole; but the annual figures of strikes and of conciliation cases handled by the Advisory Conciliation and Arbitration Service can provide an indirect indication. Analyses of strikes and conciliation cases by the reason given for the dispute are published annually.[40] There are fluctuations from year to year, but roughly half the strikes in Britain each year are due to disputes over pay. All but a tiny fraction of the remainder fall under one of five other headings. In descending order of importance in the 1977 analysis, they are: manning and work allocation; working conditions and supervision; dismissal and other disciplinary measures; trade union matters (including recognition disputes); and redundancy. The analysis of conciliation cases is under slightly different headings. Pay and terms and conditions of employment account for half or more of them. Even excluding statutory recognition cases under Section 11 of the Employment Protection Act,[41] recognition disputes constitute almost half of the remainder. Then come: dismissals, redundancy and 'other trade union matters'.

Disputes which lead to strikes or to conciliation by the Service are certainly not a random sample of disputes in British industry as a whole, and probably not a representative sample, but they lead so clearly to one conclusion about the distribution of interpretation and domestic disputes that it can reasonably be accepted as valid for disputes as a whole. The great majority of recognition disputes occur in areas where no union has so far achieved recognition. They cannot be interpretation disputes because there are no agreements to interpret where no union is recognized to negotiate. Manning and work allocation, working conditions and supervision, and discipline and redundancy, are not normally regulated by substantive agreements at industry level in private employment. This leaves pay and 'terms and conditions of employment'. Whether or not disputes on these issues are interpretation disputes is also determined by the extent to which they are governed by industry agreements. In private industry, so far as pay is concerned, for the most part they are not. Therefore it seems reasonable to conclude that interpretation disputes do not predominate in the private sector.

Where industry agreements claim to regulate substantive conditions of employment, it is essential for them to provide a means of

---

[40] An annual review of stoppages of work due to industrial disputes is published in the *Employment Gazette*, normally in June. Figures of conciliation cases are given in the annual report of the Advisory Conciliation and Arbitration Service.

[41] See pp. 408–9.

resolving interpretation disputes; but the need for an industry disputes procedure to deal with domestic disputes is rather more problematic. If the objective is to find the proposal most likely to be acceptable to the two sides in the plant or company, then an industry disputes procedure has the same purpose as the public conciliation service or as those private conciliators or mediators who are sometimes asked to assist with industrial disputes. It is true that an industry procedure has advantages. It is manned by people with intimate knowledge and experience of the industry; and, being drawn from the unions and the employers' association, its members may be able to exercise some pressure on the disputants to accept a recommended solution. Nevertheless their objective is the same as that of other conciliators and mediators. On the other hand, the industry disputes procedures set up before 1914 in engineering and other industries had another objective as well. The employers hoped that they could use it to prevent the unions from picking off one local association at a time. It follows that in any particular dispute the employers might reject the proposal most likely to achieve an amicable settlement because of its possible repercussions on other districts; and no doubt in other instances the unions might do the same because of its implications for them.

The conflict between these two objectives can be even more acute under plant bargaining. With hundreds or thousands of federated employers each making their own pay settlements, the likelihood of awkward repercussions from the acceptable solution to any dispute are multiplied; and this is especially true when a dispute reaches the national stage of dispute settlement, where there are representatives from all over the country, each considering the implications of a proposed settlement for his plant and locality.

This conflict of objectives may help to explain some of the criticisms of the engineering procedure as it existed before 1971 which were widely expressed during the sixties, not least by the Donovan Commission. They reported that 'the procedure functions slowly'; and that of the 519 cases which reached central conference in 1966, thirteen were withdrawn; 55 were settled; 85 were 'referred back'; 127 were 'retained'; and 'failure to agree' was recorded in the remaining 239 cases.

Reference back normally implies that some compromise arrangement has been found which will keep the peace in the factory but cannot be recorded as a settlement for fear of the implications for other factories elsewhere; and this is also the ultimate conclusion of many of the cases which are retained.[42]

Moreover, the prospect of central conference had an effect on the previous stage of procedure. One witness gave evidence to the Commission on his experience as chairman of local conferences.

> You sit with all the shop stewards and district officers, and here you have the panel of the employers and here you have the official representative of the association who does the talking; and although you, as chairman, are in charge theoretically, you dare not open your mouth, because what everybody is concerned with is not the issue but what goes into the verbatim notes, because the next stage is York,[43] so that anything once on the notes becomes a precedent; so that the official who is conscious of all the traps that lie in agreements and procedure does all the talking and you can see him manoeuvring that he gets the right things on the notes, never mind the issue; and then pressure is brought to bear on the individual company to settle somehow and not let it go any further.[44]

The Donovan Commission tried to make an assessment of disputes procedures by asking full-time trade union officers for their opinions of the procedures which they operated. Four major sets of procedures were mentioned by more than twenty officers. The Commission summarized their views by deducting the percentage of officers who said that a particular procedure was inadequate from the percentage who said it worked well. The scores were: Gas, Water and Electricity Joint Industrial Councils, +34; Chemicals Joint Industrial Councils, +17; Building and Civil Engineering Procedures, −3; and Engineering, −40.[45] It is therefore not surprising that both sides of the engineering industry were ready to accept some of the Donovan Commission's criticisms and to set about negotiating a new procedure. They were able to agree on a number of proposals, but the wording of the proposed *status quo* clause could not be settled.[46] The unions therefore gave notice to terminate the procedure which ran out in 1971. The consequence was that the industry

---

[42] *Report*, pp. 17, 106.
[43] Central conference was held monthly at York.
[44] *Minutes of Evidence* Q. 4198.
[45] *Workplace Industrial Relations 1966*, p. 63. [46] See p. 29.

had no formal disputes procedure for manual workers, but it did not follow that there was no means of dealing with those disputes which could not be settled in the plant. Under the old procedure such a dispute went first to a formal works conference with officials of the union or unions and of the local employers' association in attendance, and then to a local conference between representatives of the association and the union with a member of the association's team in the chair. Even after 1971 it was still possible for the disputants in the plant to ask their officials to come to a works conference; and if that did not settle the issue, to ask the local association to arrange an 'informal' conference with the union or unions to make a further attempt to resolve it. The difference was that the only alternative to finding a solution at a local conference was final disagreement; reference to central conference was no longer available. The emphasis was therefore more on finding a solution for the dispute and less on 'what goes into the verbatim notes'.

A new procedure agreement was signed in 1976. It was a very different document from its predecessor. Besides a generous *status quo* clause, it offered enlightened guidance on the selection and credentials of shop stewards and the provision of facilities for them, and gave official recognition for the first time to the post of 'chief shop steward'. One external stage of procedure—a local conference—was to be available where a dispute could not be settled domestically, except that 'matters which concern the interpretation or application of this or any other National Agreement shall be referred for discussion at national level'. A year later the Coventry association commented that the new procedure was 'already proving to be an effective mechanism for dealing with problems unresolved in domestic procedure. It is of course true to say that in Coventry the Association has noticed no great change in the way the disputes procedure operates, since the principle of a single "external" conference involving full time officials from both sides was effectively operating during the years following the termination' of the old procedure.[47]

Complaints against the defects of the engineering procedure have no longer been widespread since 1971, either when there was no official procedure, or since the new procedure has come into operation. Until recently the federation had separate but similar agree-

[47] Coventry and District Engineering Employers' Association, *Annual Report*, 1976.

ments with each of the five white collar unions which they recognize. These were never so fiercely criticized as the manual workers' agreement, which is common to all the manual unions. For one thing they did not contain a managerial prerogative clause, like the former manual agreement. But the general satisfaction with the end of central conference for manual workers has led to a renegotiation of the white collar agreements to make local conference the final stage of procedure for domestic disputes, and three of the unions have signed a common agreement. One important feature of the new arrangements for both manual and white collar workers is that disputes are not so liable to delay as in the past.

No other procedure in Britain has come in for anything like the volume of criticism which was directed at the former engineering procedure. No other procedure in private industry covers anything like so many employees as engineering, and no other procedure covers such a diverse range of technologies and product markets. Even allowing for the number of employees covered, no other major procedure handles anything like the volume of business that passed through the old engineering procedure. The National Federation of Building Trade Employers comes next to the Engineering Employers' Federation in terms of coverage of employees. Before 1970 the building industry had two procedures, one being an emergency procedure for handling disputes which threatened to cause a stoppage of work. In that year the emergency procedure was terminated, and since then all disputes have been processed through the standard procedure. From 1960 to 1967 the average number of cases reaching the National Conciliation Panel or a National Emergency Disputes Commission was 29;[48] from 1972 to 1975 the National Conciliation Panel averaged 26 cases a year.[49] Between 1960 and 1974 the number of cases reaching a national disputes committee in the chemical industry varied between three and sixteen, with an average of six.[50]

In its own way each of these procedures has an advantage over the old engineering procedure. Most of the disputes which come through the building procedure are interpretation disputes. The need to interpret a new agreement on incentive payments in 1970 raised

[48] Marsh and McCarthy, *Disputes Procedures in Britain* (2), p. 58.
[49] D. J. Keohane, *An Account and Assessment of two Employers' Associations in Building and Civil Engineering*.
[50] Marsh and McCarthy, *op. cit.*, p. 45 and B. Robinson, *The Nature and Extent of Employer Organisation: The British Chemical Industry and its Multi-Nationals*.

the annual average number of disputes reaching the national level to 70 in 1970–1.[51] The building procedure is therefore largely free of the heavy load of domestic disputes which burden the engineering procedures. In the chemical industry's procedure the stage before a national disputes committee is not a local or regional conference, but a 'headquarters conference'. Despite its name, it is held at the plant in which the dispute arose. National officials from the Chemical Industries Association and the union or unions concerned attend a joint meeting as conciliators. This procedure has a considerably higher rate of success in settling disputes than local conferences under the old engineering procedure, and is probably a more satisfactory method of finding a solution for a domestic dispute than they were.

Some types of dispute are rarely referred to industry disputes procedure in the private sector because none of these procedures can handle them effectively. Disciplinary dismissal, for example, is a perishable issue. Once the employee has left the plant his main concern is usually to find another job. If he finds it, he may begin to lose interest in an appeal. In the plant his job is filled and his former colleagues may begin to forget his case. Moreover, the form of the appeal may not inspire confidence in him or them. Unless there is provision for arbitration—and that is rare—the appeal can only succeed with the consent of the employers' side. The right of the manager to get rid of an employee whom he considers unsatisfactory is central to notions of managerial prerogative. It is one thing for employers to suggest to one of their colleagues that he might have offered a slightly larger pay increase, and quite another to override his decision to dismiss.

The 1976 engineering procedure tried to surmount one of these obstacles to the use of procedure in disciplinary cases by providing that where the reason for his dismissal is not 'gross industrial misconduct which necessitates instant dismissal' an employee who appeals to the procedure 'will remain an employee of the company until such time as either agreement is reached, or the procedure is exhausted'.

In any event, since the Donovan Report and the termination of the old engineering procedure, attention in industrial relations has shifted from alleged defects of industry procedures to the design and negotiation of domestic procedures—plant and company procedures to handle disputes up to the point at which the shop stewards

[51] D. J. Keohane, *op. cit.*

and managers admit they cannot settle them, and hand them on to the industry procedures. It is now generally agreed in manufacturing that industry negotiators cannot any longer lay down a standard domestic procedure and expect it to be followed. Consequently, in dealing with these procedures, employers' associations no longer act as negotiators or rule makers, but as advisers and consultants.

(d) *Advisory and Other Services*

The major area of expansion in the work of employers' associations over the last ten or fifteen years has been their advisory services. Advice on the design of domestic disputes procedures forms part of their general industrial relations advisory services which the Commission on Industrial Relations in 1972 found were provided by 80 per cent of the employers' associations which they surveyed, and had been expanded by 'just over threequarters' of them since 1967.[52] Another important aspect of industrial relations handled by these services is advice on pay, including work study, job evaluation and productivity agreements. The associations of employers in the cotton and wool industries established work study departments in the early post-war years as part of their campaign to extend the use of this technique. The work study centre set up by the Wool (and Allied) Textile Employers' Council in 1954 has been expanded into a management services centre which offers its services also to non-federated firms and firms in related industries. The introduction of incentive payments in the building industry in 1947 led the National Federation of Building Trade Employers to provide a comparable service to its members which now forms part of its comprehensive Building Advisory Service. The 1968 agreement sanctioning productivity bargaining in the chemical industry led the Chemical Industries Association to develop a new advisory service which now deals with questions of long-term strategy in industrial relations. The Engineering Employers' Federation set up their Advisory Service Department in 1969 to undertake reviews of industrial relations in member firms and, if necessary, to recommend the use of professional consultants; and the British Printing Industries Federation and the Newspaper Publishers' Association both offer similar services. Several local engineering associations had a range of advisory ser-

[52] Commission on Industrial Relations, *Employers' Organisations and Industrial Relations*, p. 35.

vices some years before the federation set up its central department, the associations in the West of England and Coventry having been among the pioneers. All these developments are part of a general trend in employers' associations away from direct regulatory functions towards the provision of services.

The majority of associations which do not negotiate with white collar unions can proceed only by advice on the question of white collar recognition. The Chemical Industries Association has been advising its members on white collar recognition since 1967. It has devised a model recognition agreement, and offers to be included as an external stage in procedure when the internal stages have been exhausted.

The extraordinary growth in the volume of labour legislation over the last ten or fifteen years has further encouraged the growth of advisory services. Busy managers want to be told the meaning of each significant piece of legislation and its relevance for them. They want to be informed of the more important court cases and tribunal decisions. They need advice on handling recognition disputes, designing disciplinary codes and procedures, and negotiating 'union membership agreements',[53] in such a way as to avoid potential legal difficulties. Many of them want their association officials to represent them before industrial tribunals. In 1972 the Commission on Industrial Relations reported that 55 per cent of the associations covered by their survey offered this last service.[54] A number of associations offer an advisory service on safety and accident prevention and the Health and Safety at Work Act 1974 has added to the scope of their work.

The rapidly expanding volume of labour legislation, which many managers consider to be far too large, needlessly restrictive, and requiring them to undertake many largely profitless tasks, has led to a growing demand from the members of employers' associations for their views to be represented to departments, to ministers, to parliament and to public inquiries. Association officers spend much of their time preparing and presenting briefs and evidence, either individually or through the Confederation of British Industry.

In addition to advising individual members, the major associations distribute a good deal of information to all their members not only on these matters but also on current negotiations and problems;

---

[53] This is legal jargon for the closed shop.
[54] *Employers' Organisations and Industrial Relations*, p. 35.

on settlements; and on wages and earnings. A number of them also provide training, not only to personnel managers and to other managers and supervisors, but also to shop stewards and other workplace representatives. Although the Commission on Industrial Relations estimated that employers' associations between them provided only four per cent of the industrial relations training in Britain in 1970,[55] several associations attach considerable importance to their training services. The Chemical Industries Association was a pioneer in developing joint courses for managers and shop stewards in industrial relations skills; and several of the larger local engineering associations have their own training colleges or training centres.

One further service of a very different kind is a financial indemnity to members involved in stoppages, provided they have followed their association's guidance. But this practice seems to be a relic of earlier, more combative days, and is almost unknown in associations formed since 1914. It is not considered to be an important incentive to firms to join their associations or to maintain their membership. Today the moral support of their fellow employers in a dispute is probably more important to them. Indeed the opportunity to discuss trends and problems with colleagues from other firms, to exchange experiences, and to enjoy a community of interest and attitude, with the prospect of sympathetic support in an emergency, may be one of the most valued benefits of membership of an association, and emphasizes the similarity between an employers' association and a club. The typical method of admission to an association 'is normally similar to that of a club'.[56] The Engineering Employers' Federation informed the Donovan Commission that the advantages of membership 'are such as would accrue from the membership of any "club"'.[57] Writing of local engineering associations, Arthur Marsh commented that 'some aspects of the "club" tradition still colour all associations, whether large or small'.[58] For those employers who do not have a high regard for this benefit, the financial advantage of the advisory services compared with employing their own staff or consultants may be a major consideration. According to the Donovan Commission, 'the readiness of employers to federate does not . . . arise from a desire for strong organisation'.[59] Their survey of mana-

---

[55] Commission on Industrial Relations, *Industrial Relations Training*, p. 16.
[56] Munns and McCarthy, *op. cit.*, p. 25.
[57] *Selected Written Evidence*, p. 403.
[58] *Industrial Relations in Engineering*, p. 65.   [59] *Report*, p. 22.

gers found that only eleven per cent of the respondents thought that their associations had a lot of power; 54 per cent thought they had a fair amount of power; and a quarter thought they had no power at all. Moreover, when the 80 per cent who thought their associations had no power or only a fair amount were asked whether they thought their associations should have more power, only about a quarter thought they should.[60]

THEIR MEMBERSHIP AND STRUCTURE

Statistics of organization among employers are less precise than trade union returns. The Department of Employment maintains a list of employers' organizations, but most of them are local associations.[61] Many of them are affiliated to other organizations on the list, such as the engineering and building federations, and are therefore more akin to the regions or districts of trade unions than to trade unions themselves. Others are 'left-overs from the nineteenth century, provide no service at all, and are being rapidly merged into larger organizations.[62] They hardly count.

There is also a problem of definition. The current legal definition of an employers' association is: an organization consisting 'wholly or mainly of employers or individual proprietors . . . whose principal purposes include the regulation of relations between employers . . . and workers or trade unions'.[63] This covers those which, like the engineering federation, deal exclusively with industrial relations and related matters, and those, such as the building federation and the Chemical Industries Association, which deal *both* with industrial relations *and* with commercial matters; and are therefore employers' associations and also trade associations. (This is now the more common type. Following the formation of the Confederation of British Industry in 1965, bringing together the formerly separate confederations dealing with industrial relations and commercial matters, there

---

[60] *Workplace Industrial Relations 1966*, pp. 95–6.

[61] In 1971 nine hundred out of 1,200 associations on the list were local bodies (Commission on Industrial Relations, *Employers' Organisations and Industrial Relations*, p. 13).   [62] *Ibid*.

[63] Trade Union and Labour Relations Act 1974. Before the 1974 Act most employers' associations probably came within the definition of a trade union under the 1871 and subsequent Trade Union Acts. Now they can choose between being companies or unincorporated associations.

were parallel mergers of employers' organizations in a number of individual industries, including chemicals, rubber, shipbuilding and shipping.) There is doubt, however, over the application of the definition to the considerable number of trade associations, mainly in the private service sector, which have been pressed into undertaking one or two industrial relations responsibilities, such as nominating members to serve as employers' representatives on wages councils. Whether or not the legal definition covers them, they are certainly not the counterparts of trade unions.

Consequently there is no real comparison between the thousand or so employers' organizations on the Department's list, and the roughly five hundred organizations on their list of trade unions. In fact, there are few occasions for a student of industrial relations to pay attention to many employers' associations beyond the fifty-three which were affiliated to the British Employers' Confederation before it merged into the Confederation of British Industry.[64]

Assessing the size of individual associations presents other problems. Trade unions count their individual members. But in engineering the individual members of employers' associations are plants whereas in building they are companies. Moreover, membership fees in the great majority of associations are related to numbers employed, and it seems reasonable to assess their strength in the same way. Thus the five thousand federated engineering plants employing over two million workers outweigh the ten thousand federated building companies with only about three hundred thousand employees.

For some purposes a more useful assessment of the strength of an association is given by comparing total membership with potential membership. A few associations, such as the Federation of Civil Engineering Contractors, include nearly all the eligible firms. But this is exceptional and the explanation is that there are few small firms in civil engineering. At the time of the Donovan Commission the building federation reported that 'its membership covers nearly all large contractors employing more than 250 men, 60 per cent of medium sized firms employing between 100 and 250, and a diminishing percentage with each smaller size group'. At that time there were over eighty thousand building firms and about sixteen thousand of them were federated. The federation estimated that its members employed about 60 per cent of the private building labour

---

[64] Grant and Marsh, *The Confederation of British Industry*, p. 32.

force.[65] It follows that the great majority of firms were non-federated and that these firms were predominantly small. In engineering there are over twenty thousand plants employing more than ten workers and five thousand federated plants. Since the Engineering Employers' Federation also claims to cover about 60 per cent of the relevant labour force, non-federated engineering plants must also be predominantly small. The engineering and building federations are probably more representative than the civil engineering federation. In fact, the engineering federation, covering over two million employees (1,360,000 manual employees and 690,000 staff) in a potential coverage of about 3.5 million, is several times larger than any other employers' association or federation, and its potential coverage is not very far short of half of total employment in manufacturing. Its returns therefore have very heavy weight in any overall statistics of employers' associations. It is therefore probable that the majority of private undertakings are not federated; and, since a coverage by associations of 60 per cent of the relevant labour force appears to be not untypical,[66] that the majority of them are relatively small compared with federated undertakings.

Employers are fond of contrasting the simple and rational structure of their organizations with the contorted complexity of British multi-unionism. It is true that most employers' associations or federations are confined to a single industry or part of it—provided that engineering is classed as a single industry—and that there is nothing like the general unions on the employers' side of industry, but the contrast with the unions is nevertheless not quite so sharp as employers claim. Within each industry there may be complexities in employer organization as well as among the unions. There is a multiplicity of associations in both printing and clothing; and the position in engineering is less simple than engineering employers generally allow. They contrast their federation with the twenty-two members of the Confederation of Shipbuilding and Engineering Unions, many of whom also recruit members in many other industries as well. But the same unions negotiate with the shipbuilding employers, several other small employers' associations in engineering, with the British Railways Board in respect of their engineering

[65] Munns and McCarthy, *op. cit.*, p. 22.

[66] The Confederation of British Industry informed the Donovan Commission that 'in many major industries federated companies employ 80 per cent or more of the industry's labour force, and in few industries in the proportion below 50 per cent' (*Selected Written Evidence*, p. 259).

workshops, with the government departments concerned with ord-nance factories and Admiralty shipyards, and with hundreds, or even thousands, of non-federated engineering undertakings. If the unions could determine the bargaining unit according to the structure of their organization, the union confederation would confront a multi-plicity of employers, public bodies and employers' associations. As it is, the employers settle the bargaining unit according to the structure of their organization, and thereby confer on their organization a degree of simplicity and rationality which is to some extent an optical illusion.

Employers' associations have less difficulty than trade unions in communicating with their members. For one thing, they have far fewer members. The building federation, with ten thousand mem-bers, has a larger membership than any other association which can seriously claim to be an employers' association. For another, the members are themselves organizations and not individuals. In most of them one person, or a section or department, will be responsible for dealing with the association so that its communications are not likely to be tossed away unread.

As for communication *from* the members, in small associations they can all be represented at a general meeting. The Newspaper Publishers Association, for example, has eight members. Larger associations can collect opinions from meetings called by each of their local associations, or regional organizations or specialist divi-sions. Generally associations aim 'to obtain a consensus of opinion rather than to take a vote'. But voting is sometimes used. A vote was taken among federated electrical contractors

> before the crucial decision . . . to adopt a policy of uniform wage rates. . . . In the [local] engineering associations voting by the membership is resorted to on national wage claims. Members' votes are weighted in relation to their wage roll. . . . The result of the voting is reported to the Federation Management Board which takes the decision in the light of the support or opposition to the action proposed.[67]

The federation also consults its local associations by means of ques-tionnaires, leaving to each one whether to consider the answers at a meeting or to circulate it for members to answer individually.

[67] Munns and McCarthy, *op. cit.*, p. 66.

The governing body of a major employers' association is generally a committee or council of elected local or sectional representatives together with office-holders—presidents, past presidents, vice-presidents and so on. In most instances this body is too large to meet more than once a quarter so that its main functions are to appoint committees to conduct the business of the association and to review and ratify their work. There is normally an executive or management committee or board; perhaps with a separate committee on finance; a negotiating committee; a disputes committee; a training committee; a safety committee; further specialist committees; and where the association also handles commercial matters a set of committees to deal with them. The General Council of the Engineering Employers Federation consists of representatives of the local associations and federation office-holders, about 120 members in all. They normally meet once a year, and the conduct of business is in the hands of a Management Board drawn from three sources: members elected on a regional basis; federation office-holders; and members co-opted by the board itself. The board meets monthly, and it is the board, not the council, which appoints the standing committees of the federation.

The management board's power to co-opt is intended to bring on to it 'persons who, from their wide industrial experience, can make a valuable contribution to the deliberations and discussions of the Management Board'.[68] In fact it is used mainly to bring on to the board the chief executives and personnel directors of major national engineering companies who would be unlikely to find their way to the board by regional elections. This practice illustrates a continuing problem of most major associations—to meet the requirements of large and small employers within a single organization. The building federation has a similar problem. Almost all the national building contractors have London head offices, and therefore affiliate to the federation through the London association which has formed a special group of them, about eighty strong. The federation itself has also set up a consultative committee of the twenty-odd largest contractors.

The problem arises not only from the difficulty of giving due weight to large companies in the government of the associations, but also because of the dissatisfaction of some of those companies with the restrictions imposed even now by policies and agreements suited

[68] Donovan Commission, *Selected Written Evidence*, p. 399.

to the requirements of small association members. That the problem continues is demonstrated by defections such as that of Chrysler from the engineering federation in 1971, the Mirror Newspaper Group from the Newspaper Publishers' Association in 1974, and Montague Burton from the Clothing Manufacturers' Federation in 1975. The Chemical Industries Association has gone further than others to meet the special needs of companies of this kind by instituting a category of non-conforming members, who are entitled to enjoy the services of the association and participate in its discussions, but take no part in its negotiations with the unions. They are not bound by the association's agreements, and negotiate separately with the unions. There are about fifty non-conforming members, including ICI, and their total employment exceeds that of the conforming members.

It is not always easy to man association committees. 'Not all members are ready to accept the duties of office, and those who show themselves ready to do so are frequently re-elected. Difficulties are experienced in persuading both small employers and the chief executives of large firms to spare the time for association work, and some associations have found it necessary to stipulate that the representatives of firms should be actively concerned in the management of the business.'[69] The work of committee chairmen and other senior office-holders unquestionably makes very heavy demands on their time, and the president of a major association sees very little of his company during his term of office. However, the task of finding committee members has been eased in recent years by the rapid growth in the number of personnel managers, including senior personnel executives and personnel directors. In many instances their companies appreciate that there is an advantage to the business from allowing them to spend some of their time on their associations.

There has also been a growth in the number and professionalization of association staff with the change in association functions and the extension of advisory services. There was, for example, an increase in the headquarters staff of the Engineering Employers' Federation from 29 officers in 1967 to 41 five years later.[70] Associations now rely less on lawyers and accountants and more on officers

[69] Munns and McCarthy, *op. cit.*, p. 65.
[70] Commission on Industrial Relations, *Employers' Organisations and Industrial Relations*, p. 67.

with industrial relations skills. Nevertheless, it does not follow that there is now an enlightened rule of senior personnel executives and professional association staff among organized employers.

Personnel managers and directors, and association officers, have to live with the unions, work with them and make the best deals they can with them. But majority opinion among British managers has been critical of trade unions for a decade or more. Line managers believe that their work is hampered by agreements and practices imposed on them by the unions, their time eaten by endless and often unprofitable discussions and consultations with shop stewards, against a background of volumes of legislation rushed through parliament to appease the unions. To many of them their colleagues in personnel posts may appear, at least sometimes, as the people who sell them up the river with ever more compromises with unions and shop stewards, thus putting further obstacles in the way of line managers achieving the results they should. Chief executives must be responsive to widely held opinions of this kind, and the directors of employers' associations certainly pay attention to the opinions held by the chief executives of major companies within their associations. For an association director is not in the same position as the general secretary (or full-time president) of a trade union. The general secretary holds the most important post in his union. He may be a national figure, reported in the press and interviewed on television. It is rare for an association director to have an equivalent public stature, and his status is probably no higher than that of the chief executives of the major companies in the industry.

During the middle years of the sixties, productivity bargaining enjoyed fairly widespread popularity among British managers. It was widely welcomed by personnel managers because it extended their function into the central task of the business—the improvement of profitability. Many line managers were persuaded to give it their support because it promised to relieve them of some of the restrictions which hampered their control over production and the deployment of manpower. Chief executives gave it their support and the initial opposition of the associations soon melted away. Many doubters and critics remained, but the tide of popularity turned only after the flood of 'phoney' productivity agreements encouraged by the policies of the Labour government from 1968 to 1970.

The report of the Donovan Commission received a more mixed

response. Many personnel managers welcomed it, along with the research paper entitled *Industrial Sociology and Industrial Relations* written for the Commission by Alan Fox, as expressing a philosophy of industrial relations in tune with the realities of modern British industry as they saw them. But majority opinion among line managers found the report too 'soft' on the unions. They wanted greater legislative controls over the unions and particularly over the use of the strike. Their opinions carried the day with many chief executives. Employers' associations came forward with one proposal after another for legal restrictions on the unions. In 1970 and 1971 it appeared that most managers and employers' associations were generally behind many of the Conservative proposals embodied in the Industrial Relations Act, at least until the Act began to operate. Policy-making in employers' associations is still affected by these different currents of opinion.

NON-FEDERATED EMPLOYERS

The majority of private employers are non-federated. They can be classified into four groups. Probably the largest in terms of numbers, though perhaps not in terms of the numbers they employ, are small employers who rely on personal dealings with their few employees. Aside from the relevant legislation, they have little use for the formal regulation of industrial relations, although they may rely on agreements negotiated in their industries to guide them on the length of the working week, holidays, overtime and pay increases. Their employees are not likely to include many trade unionists.

The second group includes many employers with a labour force of up to a hundred or even more. They recognize trade unions, at least among their manual employees. They probably have no written procedures, but there may be one or two shop stewards in the plant who are entitled by custom to discuss shopfloor problems with managers, and there may be occasional visits from a full-time trade union officer when more serious difficulties arise. In many instances there is an understanding that the employer will normally apply the provisions of the relevant industry agreements, along with one or two agreements (written or oral) peculiar to the plant, for example its own piecework or bonus system. Most of these employers do not have a principled objection to federation, and are fairly ready recruits to their associations when trouble arises beyond their capacity to handle—a strike, a redundancy, an adverse tribunal decision over a dismissal, or the unionization of their foremen. The majority of new recruits to associations come from this class.

The third group are companies which do not recognize trade unions, and set out to devise alternative means of regulating industrial relations domestically, often in conjunction with a staff association or elected staff committee—a 'company union' in trade union terminology. Some of them—Mars, IBM and until recently Kodak—are major companies with a large and sophisticated group of personnel staff. Most of them profess neutrality towards trade unions. They would be willing to recognize a trade union which recruited a majority of their employees. But their existing arrangements inhibit trade union growth, and their professions of neutrality ignore the impact on unorganized employees of a marked lack of enthusiasm for trade unionism on the part of their employer and managers. Many of them offer rates of pay and conditions of employment as good as, or even better than, unionized firms in the same industries; and this may also be interpreted as a device to keep the unions out. The notorious non-union firm of Grunwick paid relatively low wages until it came under union pressure.[71]

The fourth group consists of companies, including some of the largest in the country, which recognize trade unions, negotiate with them over a wide range of issues, provide sophisticated procedures and consultative arrangements, but prefer to handle their industrial relations for themselves without whatever limitations might be imposed on them by full membership of an association. Some of them, including ICI, Ford and Vauxhall, have highly centralized systems of industrial relations with company-wide agreements regulating pay and other conditions of employment in some detail. Others, such as Chrysler, have close central control of plant negotiations with company-wide agreements as an ultimate aim. In the first group of companies there must be a company disputes procedure to regulate the application and interpretation of agreements, and there is also an inevitable tendency in the others towards central intervention in disputes which cannot be resolved in the plant, for there is no external procedure for the plants to turn to. Generally these non-federated companies employ a larger personnel staff than their feder-

[71] *Scarman Report*, pp. 15–16.

ated colleagues since they have to provide the whole range of services for themselves.

Centralized negotiations and control over plant industrial relations has permitted some of these companies to make advances which would hardly have been possible for federated firms at the time. One example is the company-wide productivity agreements of ICI.[72] Apart from their ineligibility under the rules of the Chemical Industries Association which allowed members 'to pay wages at rates higher than those nationally agreed, but not to consolidate such payments into a salary as ICI proposes to do',[73] no major multi-plant federated company had the negotiating machinery or the managerial control to carry through such agreements. Another example is the 1966 productivity agreement covering the 55 plants and depots of the Gases Division of British Oxygen which was also non-federated.

However, the differences between these non-federated firms and federated companies of similar size has diminished since that time. The growth of personnel staffs; the negotiation of plant-wide agreements, and of company-wide agreements for white collar employees (and also for manual employees in some instances); and the development of company personnel policies have all brought the conduct of industrial relations in major federated companies much closer to that of this group of non-federated companies. The contrast between the structures of industrial relations in British Leyland and Ford, so marked ten years ago, is now much less sharp. One of the main differences has disappeared now that British Leyland has persuaded the unions to accept company-wide pay negotiation. Similarly there may not be very much difference in the structure of industrial relations between a federated chemical company which negotiates its own supplementary agreement and one of the non-conforming members of the Chemical Industries Association.

This instance points to another development which has obscured the contrast between federated and non-federated companies. The non-conforming chemical companies are non-federated only in the sense that they negotiate entirely on their own. Chemicals is not the only industry in which this can happen. The Mirror Group Newspapers continue to contribute to the Newspaper Publishers' Association and to enjoy their services; Montague Burton continues to have

---

[72] See pp. 150–1.
[73] National Board for Prices and Incomes, *Productivity Agreements*, p. 36.

close contact with the Clothing Manufacturers' Federation; and local engineering associations permit associate membership.

<h2 style="text-align:center">PUBLIC EMPLOYERS</h2>

Following the decision in 1919 to permit fully-fledged collective bargaining in the civil service, a National Whitley Council was instituted to deal with common issues, including the pay of general classes of civil servants employed in a number of departments—clerical grades, executive grades, administrative grades and scientific grades for example. The 'official' side now consists of senior civil servants appointed by the Civil Service Department. Departmental Whitley Councils deal with departmental issues, including a whole range of matters concerned with the organization and running of the department, and with the pay of 'departmental' classes such as tax officers—without reference to the National Council, but certainly not without reference to the Civil Service Department. Each council draws its members from senior officials of the department and from the unions recognized as representing its staff.

Once the councils were established there remained the question of what would happen if the two sides did not agree. Although strikes in the civil service are not unknown, neither side could contemplate strikes as a regular means of settling disputes; and 'it is clear that striking, even if not illegal, is a disciplinary offence on the part of a civil servant'.[74] A wartime arbitration board, set up in 1917 to deal with the impact of inflation on civil service pay, was abolished in 1922, leaving no appeal against the final decision of the Treasury. This was unacceptable, and in 1925 the right to arbitration was restored, at first by reference to the Industrial Court, and from 1936 by access to a separate Civil Service Arbitration Tribunal. Certain subjects, such as salaries above a specified level, superannuation, and the granting and withholding of established status, were excluded from arbitration, and there were two further conditions: that 'the Government will give effect to the awards of the court . . . subject to the overriding authority of Parliament'; and that the government 'must also reserve to itself the right to refuse arbitration on "grounds of policy"'.[75] The first proviso has never been directly invoked,

---

[74] H.M. Treasury, *Staff Relations in the Civil Service*, p. 20.
[75] *Ibid.*, p. 24.

although it has been clear under all formal incomes policies since 1966 that governments would not accept an award which overstepped their limts. The second was used once, to exclude the issue of equal pay for men and women, which has since been settled.

These arrangements applied to non-industrial civil servants. For industrial civil servants three Trade Joint Councils were set up—for shipbuilding; engineering; and miscellaneous trades—to deal with common conditions of service; along with departmental councils to handle domestic matters. Where the two sides could not agree, they were free to submit the dispute to arbitration by the Industrial Court, now replaced by the Central Arbitration Committee.

Although over the years many devices have been developed to provide flexibility and marginal adjustments—without which the business of the civil service would grind to a halt—it remains a formidably centralized bureaucratic system. But this is not because the civil service has a single employer. The same regulations apply with equal force to the nominally independent employing bodies which are staffed by civil servants. It is not common employment but membership of a single and largely self-governing civil service which is the source of this centralization. Under the rather remote supervision of parliament and government, senior civil servants negotiate a vast code of rules with the representatives of every grade of civil servant including their own trade union officers.

The irrelevance of common employment to the centralization of the civil service is demonstrated by the existence of several other almost equally centralized public services in which there is no common employer. The largest of them is the National Health Service. The management side of its joint councils consists of representatives of the various regional and area authorities established to run the hospitals and practitioner services. In addition, there are officials from the Department of Health and Social Security and the Scottish and Welsh Offices, although none of these bodies has any claim to be a health service employer. The reason is evident. All but a fraction of the money spent by the employing authorities comes from the Exchequer. Departmental representatives are therefore not only present, but also have the last word on major issues of pay, although they are in a minority on the management side. More precisely, it is the officials of the Treasury who have the last word, since they must be consulted before the departmental officials can agree to substantial increases in expenditure, and in most recent years there has also been the need to determine whether any proposed concession conforms with current government incomes policy. Even so, soon after the health service was set up, the Minister of Health, who was then the responsible minister, was given powers to confirm the decisions of the joint councils by embodying them in regulations.[76] In 1958 the Minister refused to confirm an agreement reached in the functional council for administrative and clerical staffs, and it remained inoperative. There is no obligation on either side to accept arbitration, but normally the management sides have been willing to allow disagreements to be referred to the Industrial Court.[77] In contrast to the civil service, the health service is centralized but not—at least apart from the medical profession—self-governing. The pressure for centralization comes from outside, from government departments. The rules negotiated by the joint councils are supplemented by a great many regulations laid down by the department on its own authority, and on the councils themselves the unions effectively negotiate, not with their employers, but with representatives of the government.

Until 1965 the Burnham Committees, established in 1920 to settle teachers pay, consisted of representatives of the teachers' unions and of the local education authorities and their education committees. In 1963 the difficulties of this arrangement were demonstrated when the Minister of Education (as he then was) decided that an agreement on schoolteachers' pay was unacceptable, but could not persuade the relevant committee to amend their decision to his liking. Deadlock ensued, for the department's legal advisers had ruled that it would be *ultra vires* for the committee to have recourse to arbitration.[78] In the end the Minister imposed his own salary scales. This drastic action seems to have been taken as much to force a reorganization of the system as to overrule the agreement made by the committee, undesirable though it was in his eyes. In 1965 the Remuneration of Teachers' Act introduced department representatives into the employers' sides of the Burnham Committees, and also established an arbitral body to resolve disputes. Henceforth the Minister's views

[76] S.1 1373 of 1951, made under Section 66 of the 1946 Act.

[77] At one time it was suggested that frequent recourse to arbitration in times of financial stringency showed that the government preferred to shift the responsibility even for justified pay increases to a tribunal. (Clegg and Chester, *Wage Policy and the Health Service*, p. 94.)

[78] Although the committee had previously introduced a form of arbitration by referring disputed issues to 'independent advisers'.

would carry due weight during negotiations, and there was a device for clearing deadlocks.

This reconstruction was the completion rather than the cause of the centralization of the regulation of employment in the education service. Previously the wide powers of the department to issue regulations, the heavy dependence of the employing authorities on government finance, and the desire of the teachers' unions for standardization, had already achieved a high degree of uniformity.

Negotiations in the police and probation services are on much the same footing as in the health service and education. The National Joint Council for Fire Brigades does not include departmental representatives, but its decisions require confirmation. By contrast the local authority service is in a rather different position from all the services mentioned so far. Before 1914 the local authorities regarded themselves as sovereign employers. This did not mean that they necessarily refused to deal with the unions, but they would not accept that an association could negotiate on their behalf. Each authority retained its own sovereignty. The doctrine continued to have an influence even when joint councils were set up nationally and in each region after the war. The authorities would not accept that an employers' side consisting of representatives of their associations, such as the Association of Municipal Corporations (as it then was) could negotiate agreements on their behalf. They insisted that the employers' sides of the regional councils should be directly representative of the authorities in the regions, and that representatives elected by the regional employers' sides should sit alongside association representatives on the national council.

Soon after the Second World War the Local Authorities' Conditions of Service Advisory Board was set up to co-ordinate the work of the employers' sides in the various councils dealing with local authority manual workers, white collar staffs, land drainage workers, building craftsmen and so on. Meanwhile the growing dependence of local government on central government grants, and the increasing volume of central government regulations and controls, had brought pressures for standardization, supported by the desire for a single career structure in local government. The once-prized autonomy of the individual employing authorities is now almost forgotten; the local authority service is almost as unified as the health service; the Advisory Board plays a large part in the decisions of the various councils; and the employers' sides have to have close regard for government views on acceptable settlements. Nevertheless central government still has no official part in their work, nor—incomes policy apart—do their decisions require ratification. Whatever discussions there may be with departments have no official standing.

Although there were a few experiments in nationalization before 1945, such as the setting up of the London Passenger Transport Board in 1934, the nationalized industries are very largely a postwar creation. The Acts which established them laid a duty on their boards to make provision for collective bargaining. Section 46 of the Coal Industry Nationalization Act of 1946 obliged the Coal Board to draw up with the unions machinery for 'the settlement by negotiation of terms and conditions of employment, with provision for reference to arbitration in default of such settlement . . .'. Similar phrases were inserted in the other nationalization Acts. In most instances the obligation to bargain over the terms of employment of manual workers was met by taking over existing machinery, although some new features were added, notably in coalmining. For white collar employees, however, most of the nationalized industries, other than the railways, had to set about devising industry negotiating procedures for the first time, and there were substantial increases in the membership of the relevant unions.

Whether publicly- or privately-owned, the former individual railway, gas and electricity undertakings, were already operated as public services, and each industry had at least some of the characteristics of a common service. The Post Office grew up within the civil service as a government department and its translation to a public corporation has not affected its character as a national service. But there have been much greater problems with coal and steel. Both of them were pieceworking industries. District autonomy was a major feature of collective bargaining in coalmining, and branch autonomy was equally embedded in steel industrial relations. Progress towards centralization has been slow, and has still a long way to go in the steel industry. These differences, however, have little to do with the structure of the employing authorities. The Coal Board, the Railways Board, the Post Office and the Steel Corporation are all single centralized employers. In gas and electricity, by contrast, most of the workers are employees of the regional boards. But this makes little difference to industrial relations.

The formal authority of the government over the nationalized industries rests on the power of the responsible ministers to give 'directions of a general character as to the exercise and performance by the Board of their functions in relation to matters appearing to the Minister to affect the national interest',[79] but this power is very rarely used. Indirectly, however, the minister has great influence over the boards whose members he appoints and may decide not to reappoint at the end of their terms of office. One instance was the humiliation of Mr Steven Hardie, chairman of the short-lived Iron and Steel Corporation, who was forced to resign in 1952.[80] Pay settlements in nationalized industries normally require the blessing of the cabinet, if not its formal approval. For many years the government tried to maintain the fiction that labour matters were within the managerial discretion of the boards, and board chairmen were required to support this pretence. However, since 1958 the secret has been less well kept. In that year, and again in 1962 and 1965, successive Prime Ministers themselves conducted the final stages of negotiations on railway pay, and in 1972 and 1974 another Prime Minister had to negotiate with the Mineworkers.

The principle of fair comparisons has figured prominently in postwar pay negotiations in the public sector. Comparisons with other workers are commonly quoted in pay negotiations in private employment, but several parts of the public sector have constructed formulas intended to ensure that public sector pay keeps in step with pay in private employment. The civil service has led the field. Governments need to show that they are not squandering the nation's resources on overpaid civil servants, and also that they are not grossly exploiting their own employees while exhorting others to be good employers. The best defence is to show that each grade of civil servant is being paid what employees elsewhere receive for similar work. In 1931 the Tomlin Commission on the Civil Service enunciated the principle that 'broad general comparison between classes in the Service and outside occupations are possible and should be made'.[81] There is, however, wide scope for debate over the application of broad general comparisons, and in 1955 another Royal Commission on the Civil Service (the Priestley Commission) not only reiterated the view that the pay of civil servants should be settled by 'fair comparison with current remuneration of outside staffs employed on broadly comparable work, taking account of

[79] This is the wording of the Coal Industry Nationalization Act.
[80] W. A. Robson, *Nationalized Industry and Public Ownership*, pp. 238–40.
[81] *Report*, p. 85.

differences in other conditions of service', but also recommended that a specialized unit should be set up to identify staff employed on comparable work and to investigate their pay and conditions of service.[82] The Civil Service Pay Research Unit was set up to do this job and to pass the information on to the negotiators for them to evaluate. The unit's techniques can only be applied to those classes of civil servants for whom 'outside analogues' can be found, and there are many, such as tax officers, whose jobs have no counterparts outside. For them the Priestley Commission recommended the use of 'internal relativities' whereby their pay could be related to that of another class of civil servants which had been settled by outside comparison.

In order to cope with accelerating inflation, the interval between 'pay reviews' was gradually reduced to two years, with general upwards adjustments each year for the grades whose review had taken place the year before. Between 1938 and 1955 civil servants generally had lost ground in pay relationships despite the 'Tomlin formula'.[83] For a number of years thereafter many grades received larger increases than were common in private employment and the pay review system proved popular. Civil service unions protested when pay reviews were postponed or set aside under successive incomes policies.

The settlement of the pay of industrial civil servants by 'fair comparison' has an even longer history. Since 1891 there has been a 'fair wages resolution' of the House of Commons setting out the terms of employment which must be applied by government contractors. The current version obliges them to observe terms not less favourable than those agreed between unions and employers' associations for that trade and district. In 1910 the government undertook to apply these terms to its own employees. From 1940 to 1967 this was done by setting two craft rates, one for London and one for the provinces, by averaging minimum timework rates for 22 outside industries (21 for London), and two 'M' rates for labourers by averaging rates paid in 34 outside industries (32 for London). In practice this worked differently from the pay reviews of the non-industrial civil servants. The Pay Research Unit investigates remuneration, not minimum rates alone. Few, if any, craftsmen in manufacturing receive the minimum time rates for their industry, and not

[82] *Report*, pp. 25, 27.
[83] Guy Routh, *Occupation and Pay in Great Britain 1906–60*, pp. 124–5.

many labourers either. Equally most industrial civil servants earned more than their minimum rates. Craftsmen were paid supplementary rates according to skill and experience; semi-skilled workers were paid 'lead rates' added to their 'M' rates; in addition there was overtime; and in 1966 about 15 per cent of the total labour force were paid by results.[84] No one, however, checked whether the additional earnings of industrial civil servants matched extra earnings elsewhere until the National Board for Prices and Incomes found that they did not—'although the present system is designed to give industrial civil servants pay comparable with that of their counterparts in private industry, it often fails to do so'.[85] The board's reports led to a separation of industrial civil servants into industrial groups with pay settled by comparison with the earnings (excluding overtime) in the private sector of the same industry, and additional pay where appropriate productivity agreements could be reached. The outcome was a considerable increase in pay for most grades of industrial civil servants.

Formal collective bargaining does not extend to the highest grades of the civil service. Following the Priestley Report, an independent Standing Advisory Committee was set up to review their pay. To guide its decisions, the committee collected 'information about how salaries in other public services and in broadly comparable employment outside the public services [has] moved since its last review'.[86] There is no doubt that the new system worked to the advantage of higher civil servants.

It is not surprising that other employees in the public sector began to show an interest in fair comparison. In 1960 the Royal (Pilkington) Commission on Doctors' and Dentists' Remuneration compared their pay with that of other selected professions. They found that average remuneration among doctors and dentists was higher than in any other profession, although doctors came slightly below actuaries if allowance was made for differences in age distributions. They held, however, that the disadvantages inherent in the working lives of doctors and dentists warranted an even higher differential, and recommended substantial increases. Subsequently a review body, similar to that for higher civil servants, was established to examine their pay from time to time, and to propose further adjustments.

[84] National Board for Prices and Incomes, *Pay of Industrial Civil Servants*, p. 4.
[88] *Ibid.*, p. 9.
[86] National Board for Prices and Incomes, *Pay of Higher Civil Servants*, p. 2.

In the same year the Royal (Willink) Commission on police expressly rejected 'fair comparisons' but went on to recommend a substantial pay increase for the police based on a formula which started with an average of the rates of selected skilled manual occupations, adding 45 per cent for their supplementary earnings and a further 25 per cent for the dangers and drawbacks of the policeman's job. The Guillebaud Committee on Railway Pay which had been commissioned 'to conduct an investigation into the relativity of pay' of railway workers compared with other workers and to 'establish the degree of job comparability between them', tried to find outside analogues where they could, and to use internal relativities where they could not, in the manner of the Civil Service Pay Research Unit; but in the absence of reliable earnings figures,[87] the pay comparisons were on the basis of minimum rates only, neglecting substantial supplementary earnings on both sides of the comparison. In 1964 the report of the Phelps Brown Committee recommended that the pay of London busmen should be linked to the earnings of men in the engineering industry in the London area, for which figures were available.

The National Board for Prices and Incomes roundly condemned the use of the Guillebaud formula in one of their early reports.[88] Next year they turned their onslaught on to the Phelps Brown formula.[89] Both formulas were abandoned. The board were able to point to technical deficiencies in some of the devices to secure fair comparisons, but more important was the conflict in principle between fair comparison and the kind of incomes policy which the board were required to administer. The policy provided for exceptional increases in certain circumstances, such as approved productivity agreements, and fair comparison would have fed these increases through to the public employees concerned. In addition there is some degree of 'slippage' in every incomes policy, and it is unevenly distributed. This would have been fed through as well. Consequently the pay of the public employees would have risen faster than the pay of employees to whom the policy was strictly applied. However, the board were not entirely consistent, for they recommended fair comparison to settle the pay of industrial civil servants, at least initially. The government did not refer the system of fair

---

[87] Adequately detailed figures of earnings for most British industries became available only with the publication of the first of the *New Earnings Surveys* in 1968.
[88] *Pay of British Railways Staff.*   [89] *Pay of Busmen.*

comparison for non-industrial civil servants to the board for examination. Such a reference might have presented a problem to a body staffed by non-industrial civil servants.

Review bodies for senior public servants (now extended to other groups in the public sector besides civil servants), for dentists and doctors, and for the armed forces have continued in being. The National Board for Prices and Incomes believed that such bodies were likely to develop a special concern for their clients at the expense of the national interest; and that all such reviews should be conducted by a single body, namely the board. The government's only response was to make the board responsible for reviews of the pay of university teachers, whose bitter hostility was aroused by the board's first report on the subject.[90]

The operation of the surviving systems of fair comparison was suspended during the periods of statutory incomes policy from 1966 to 1969 and from 1972 to 1974, but restored when they terminated. In 1975 the 'social contract' brought another suspension.

There is no great difference between public sector agreements and industry agreements in the private sector in their regulation of hours of work, overtime, shifts, and holidays, but whereas most employers' associations leave the regulations of pensions, sick pay, redundancy, and discipline to their members, these issues are centrally regulated in most public industries and services. The public sector has also been able to go further in controlling work organization by agreement than has any employers' associations, even a tightly-knit association such as the Electrical Contractors Association or the Shipping Federation. The powerloading agreement in coalmining is one example; and no employers' association has accomplished anything like the electricity supply 'status' agreements in 1965–6—so-called because they were intended to bring the status of manual workers nearer to that of white collar workers. In return for increases in basic pay and other concessions, average hours worked fell from 51 to 39 a week in generation and from 49 to 43 in distribution with 'an overall saving to the industry'.[91] Individual companies may perhaps have achieved results equal to these in productivity or measured daywork agreements, but the next accomplishment of

[90] *Standing Reference on the Pay of University Teachers in Great Britain*. Not only did the board recommend smaller pay increases than university teachers believed they deserved, but also proposed methods of relating pay to performance which they considered undesirable and unworkable, and which were not adopted.

[91] National Board for Prices and Incomes, *Productivity Agreements*, p. 20.

electricity supply has not so far been equalled by any multi-plant company. So successfully had the status agreements been applied that, despite the increases in pay, the cutback in overtime had held the growth of average earnings behind that of other industries. Something had to be done to improve earnings. In 1968 the industry negotiated an incentive payment scheme to apply to almost all its manual workers. Payment started at 3 per cent above the agreed rate for a performance of 65 per cent of standard, with stepped increases up to 33⅓ per cent for the standard performance or better. The unique feature of the scheme was that a central 'data bank' of performance standards was built up to provide uniformity throughout the industry. According to the agreement the standards were to 'be determined solely by work study', and management was entitled to use any of the accepted work study techniques. The scheme took some years to put into operation, and in 1971 a court of inquiry into a dispute over a general pay claim in electricity supply tried to compensate for this by providing 'lead-in' payments where it was not yet in operation but where the workers accepted 'such work study and work measurement as management find necessary', and 'the need to run down staff numbers'.[92] Eventually the scheme was in operation throughout the industry, and standard performances were being generally achieved. In fact there had to be local negotiations over the proposed rundown in numbers which may have modified the universality of the standards to some extent, but figures for overall manual employment in the industry indicate that the scheme has been remarkably successful. Certainly there is nothing to compare with it elsewhere in Britain, nor, it seems, abroad either.

The contrast in procedures is that whereas those in the private sector—certainly in manufacturing—deal mainly with domestic disputes, disputes of interpretation predominate in the public sector with its centralized agreements prescribing standard practices. Some of the pressures at work in the public sector can be illustrated by the experience of coalmining. The original procedure agreement between the Coal Board and the Mineworkers prescribed arbitration at three stages, at colliery and district level as well as at industry level. The assumption was that the issues in dispute could be divided into pit, district and national issues. District agreements have declined in importance and with them the district arbitrators, but the prevalence of piecework continued to provide work for pit arbitrators, known

[92] *Wilberforce Report* (electricity supply), p. 44.

as 'umpires', up to the time of the national powerloading agreement. They provided a speedy resolution of disputes, but the assumption that pit disputes could be settled as 'domestic' matters without repercussions elsewhere proved to be mistaken. A liberal award on piecerates or allowances at one pit led to demands for similar concessions in neighbouring pits. Each district had its own umpires, some nominated by the union and others by the board, and the normal arrangement was that they handled cases in rotation. Decisions therefore tended to be erratic. Another consequence, reported to the Donovan Commission by the Coal Board's spokesman, was 'a disposition to buy off because if you go to the umpire you may have something worse'.[93] Under the powerloading agreement the main decisions to be taken in the pit were the task to be performed by each powerloading team and the size of the team. Both the board and the union were determined not to leave these issues to the umpires. Instead a committee of two a side, whose members must be knowledgeable about 'powerloading systems in other parts of the District', visit the face and report their findings to a 'meeting of the parties at District level for decision'.

MODELS OF COLLECTIVE BARGAINING

Between them, this chapter and the last chapter have introduced some of the dimensions of collective bargaining structure: *levels* of bargaining (industry, regional, company, plant, and departmental or sectional) and the *scope* of bargaining (the range of issues negotiated at any level). The extent to which union representatives and managers are involved in the interpretation and application of rules and practices has been discussed, and this constitutes a third dimension, the *depth* of bargaining. Another aspect of the structure of bargaining is the relationship between levels of bargaining within an industry, company or plant.

There is no relationship to discuss where all bargaining takes place at one level; but that must be a rare situation. Even in a non-federated, single-plant company the agreements have to be administered, and it is hardly credible that departmental and sectional dealings between managers, foremen, shop stewards and workers do not lead to understandings and practices which amplify and modify the

[93] *Minutes of Evidence*, Q. 780.

plant agreements. However, where these understandings and practices do not go far beyond the minimum necessary to make the plant agreements work, the dealings from which they emerge could be called *administrative bargaining*. Where informal bargaining within the plant deals with issues not covered by formal collective agreements at higher levels, or goes beyond the administration of those agreements, it is called *fragmented bargaining*. There are also instances where higher agreements specifically provide for bargaining at lower levels over certain issues. Examples are the local authority agreement on incentive payments for manual workers which empowers individual authorities to negotiate schemes with local union representatives; and the productivity agreement in chemicals which empowers individual companies to negotiate their own productivity deals with local union representatives. These are instances of *controlled bargaining* since the agreements in both local authorities and chemicals have to be vetted by joint committees to see that they conform with the industry agreements. Where there are no controls of this kind, and the lower level negotiators are unsupervised so long as they do not stray beyond the subjects with which they are authorized to deal, bargaining may be described as *federal*. Plant pay bargaining in engineering and some other manufacturing industries can reasonably be classified under this heading since the only limitation imposed by the industry agreements is that the rates which are settled in the plant shall exceed the industry minima, a requirement which has no practical significance in most major plants.

Two simple models can help to show how collective bargaining structures work. The first starts with a substantive agreement on all matters currently subject to joint regulation. This agreement governs relations between the parties until it reaches the end of its term when a new agreement is negotiated. In the meantime it is the job of the procedure laid down in the agreement to settle disputes about its interpretation. Disputes about matters outside the agreement cannot be settled by the procedure but must await the termination of the agreement when they may be resolved by amendments or extensions to the agreement if the parties are willing. Industrial action is permitted only at the end of the agreement as a means of reaching a new agreement. Managers are therefore free to take their own decisions on matters outside the agreement for the unions cannot appeal to the procedure on such issues with any hope of success, and they are debarred from taking industrial action. This can be called the *statute law model*.

The second model is the *common law model*.[94] It starts with an agreed disputes procedure to resolve differences between the parties. Any dispute may be referred to the procedure, which resolves it by reference to any relevant substantive rule there may be between the parties, or to a custom which appears to be generally accepted by the parties, or by finding a compromise which is acceptable to the parties. For the model recognizes no sharp distinction between *disputes of right* under existing agreements and *disputes of interest* concerning the terms of a new agreement. Industrial action is allowed whenever the procedure has failed to resolve a dispute, or whenever one party has given notice to terminate an existing substantive agreement and the notice has expired. In this model, agreements have no fixed term, and there is no need for a single comprehensive agreement. Substantive matters can be regulated by as many agreements as the parties choose to make. The procedure may experience considerable difficulty in resolving disputes over managerial rights unless the matter is specifically regulated by agreement. Once procedure has failed to resolve the issue, however, the union is free to take industrial action against a managerial decision.

Although collective bargaining in several overseas countries, notably Sweden[95] and the United States, fits the statute law model fairly well, no part of the British system of collective bargaining gives so good a fit. Nevertheless the patterns of bargaining in the public sector come much nearer to this model than manufacturing industry does. Admittedly the substantive agreements in a public industry or service do not constitute a single body of rules which is periodically revised, and, apart from specific instances of fixed term agreements in the past, notably in the early sixties, notice can be given at any time to revise or add to any substantive agreement. However, at any one time these agreements constitute the agreed rules governing employment in the industry or service. Since a new substantive agreement may, subject to notice, be negotiated at any time, a dispute about a matter which is not covered by an existing agreement may admittedly be resolved without undue delay by negotiating an addi-

[94] These two models have a good deal in common with the static and dynamic types of collective bargaining identified by Kahn-Freund ('Intergroup Conflicts and their Settlement').

[95] Swedish collective bargaining may shift away from the statute law model as the Industrial Democracy Act 1976 takes effect.

tional agreement. However, the procedure is limited to the interpretation of disputes which arise under the existing agreements, and its task is to determine such disputes. Admittedly industrial action is allowed whenever negotiations on a proposal for the revision of a substantive agreement or for a new agreement have been concluded without reaching a settlement. However, industrial action is not allowed on any matter which is covered by the existing agreements. Finally, the formal assumption of public sector bargaining, as of the statute law model, is that managers are free to take their own decisions on matters which are not subject to collective agreements.

On the other hand, collective bargaining in manufacturing, and notably in engineering, comes nearer to the common law model than to the statute law model. The first agreements in engineering and several other major industries were procedure agreements which dealt with disputes as they arose. Apart from occasions where it was called on to deal with disputes about the rights of the parties under the procedure agreements, most of the disputes which came before procedure were claims for amendments or extensions to district agreements and were therefore disputes of interest. Subsequently industry agreements were negotiated on substantive matters, and the procedure could be called on to interpret them. More recently the staple business of procedure has become the settlement of domestic disputes. At least since 1922 the engineering agreements have recognized certain types of custom as having a status similar to substantive agreements, and the 1976 procedure agreement extended it to every custom. There is no difference in methods of dealing with disputes of interest and disputes of right concerning plant agreements. Both are handled by the procedure which now terminates with a local conference. Whereas both the 1898 and the 1922 agreements spelled out areas of managerial prerogative, the 1976 agreement has virtually put an end to the notion of managerial prerogative in engineering procedure, except where a plant agreement or custom specifies matters which managers are entitled to decide. Otherwise any innovation by a manager could be challenged as a breach of an existing practice.

The advantage of collective bargaining systems which approximate to the statute law model is their certainty. The existing agreements run for a fixed period; they can be amended or extended only when the period runs out; that is the only occasion on which industrial action is permitted; the procedure can deal only with disputes of interpretation and it has authority to determine them. So long as such a system of bargaining works effectively, industrial relations within its ambit are likely to be orderly. However, it has two disadvantages. The first is its rigidity. It offers no means of dealing with the new industrial relations issue which quickly blows up into a major problem. In this respect British public sector bargaining systems do not reflect the defects of the model for they can negotiate on such an issue without waiting for a fixed period to run its term. Nevertheless the initiation of new negotiations is not so flexible and speedy as handling the issue through a disputes procedure. The second defect is that the statute law model is not well adapted to multi-level bargaining. Ideally the model requires all agreements to be made at the same level and to provide uniform rules which apply throughout the system. In practice a certain amount of administrative bargaining at lower levels is inevitable, and some controlled bargaining at these levels can be permitted; but, given the unity of the system, controlled concessions within one part of the system may lead to strong pressure for their extension elsewhere. There is also the danger that the rigidity of the system will promote covert fragmented bargaining as a means of flexibility.

The main advantage of bargaining systems which approximate to the common law model is their flexibility. They can handle any kind of dispute; and because of that, multi-level bargaining presents them with no special problems. The defects of this kind of system are that the substantive rules are likely to be more complex and varied than in the statute law model; the central negotiators have less control over the system; and substantial differences in conditions of employment are likely to develop, and may give rise to pressures that the system cannot easily contain.

There are, however, substantial areas of British collective bargaining to which neither of these models applies. One of them is bargaining over discipline, at least outside the public sector. Unions rarely agree disciplinary codes, and most disciplinary procedures lack their consent. Much of the concern of shop stewards in disciplinary cases is to modify the employer's rules by establishing an acceptable set of precedents. They do not necessarily accept that an offence has been committed when one of their members faces a disciplinary charge, and, where they have not agreed to the procedure, they are in no way bound to agree with the final verdict. In many respects this method of dealing between managers and trade unions resembles the more primitive forms of industrial relations which preceded formal collective bargaining. At that time managers were in principle free to make their own rules on discipline or any other aspect of employment as they thought fit. For its part the union tried to impose rules of its own choosing on the employer and held itself free to challenge management decisions, and to refuse to operate them. In those circumstances there was no ban on industrial action until procedure had been exhausted, for there was no agreed procedure; and it is reasonable to question the relevance of a ban on industrial action in disciplinary cases in most private undertakings today.

In the statute law model the justification for the ban is that the only question before procedure is how the agreed rules apply to the particular issue. Since the union has negotiated and agreed the rules and the procedure, it is only reasonable that they should accept the proceedings and the verdict. If they believe that the rules should be amended, their opportunity will come when the agreement has run its term, and they will be free to employ industrial action at that stage if they choose. There is no similar obligation in disciplinary matters as they are generally handled in private employment in Britain today. In most instances, neither rules nor procedure have been agreed, and the union has no guarantee of the impartiality of the final decision. In the common law model the ban on industrial action has a different justification. It applies only until the procedure has been exhausted, and the procedure is not limited to the interpretation of agreements. All that the parties commit themselves to observe is a ban on industrial action until they have tried to resolve their dispute by negotiation through the prescribed stages. In general this appears to be a reasonable undertaking, although the perishability of dismissal cases may make industrial action impossible if it is not taken at once. But the industry procedure now normally operates after there have already been one or more stages of appeal under a plant procedure which has probably not been agreed by the union, and in which managers alone interpret a disciplinary code for which they alone bear responsibility. The question is not so much whether the union is obliged to refrain from industrial action if it refers the matter to the industry procedure, but whether the obligation applies while plant procedures to which they are not party are in operation.

Another instance is redundancy. Agreed redundancy procedures are the norm in the public sector. They set out the arrangements for consultation with the union over redundancy proposals, over how many employees are to go, and over their method of selection; and some of them fix levels of compensation for redundant employees above the statutory minimum. They do not bind the undertaking to secure union consent before declaring workers redundant, nor do they bind the unions to accept redundancy. After consultation the unions are therefore entitled to take industrial action if they wish. Some private companies have similar standing agreements, but most of them try to reach an *ad hoc* settlement with the unions when an occasion arises. Some trade unions in private employment are not keen to negotiate redundancy arrangements. Many shop stewards prefer work-sharing to redundancy, and for many years the official policy of the Engineers has been to refuse to accept redundancy, although full-time officers and shop stewards of the union have entered into redundancy agreements in a number of instances. The justification for refusing to negotiate is that the union should not share responsibility for putting their members out of a job, and that refusal to co-operate may help to postpone a decision until a change of circumstances has removed the need for a reduction in manpower, or natural wastage has accomplished it.

Redundancy, like dismissal, is a perishable issue. If industrial action is to be taken with any chance of success it must be done before workers have been declared redundant and accepted their redundancy pay, or in the case of a closure before the dismantling of plant has made closure inevitable. Reference to an external industry procedure is extremely unlikely to halt a proposed redundancy, for a panel of employers would be even less prepared to overturn the decision of one of their fellows on a redundancy than on disciplinary dismissal. Where there is no redundancy agreement in the company, therefore, the obligation not to undertake industrial action until the disputes procedure has been exhausted does not carry much moral force.

A further area of collective bargaining to which the two models have only limited application is the organization of work. Except where work organization is covered by specific agreements, the statute law model relies on the managerial prerogative that managers have the right to settle all issues not covered by an agreement. Few British agreements have tried to affirm managerial prerogative as a general principle, and whether or not employers assume that their agreements imply such a right, trade unionists do not accept that there is any such implication. A great many agreements, especially in recent years, specify rules governing particular aspects of work, and the obligations of employees to accept managerial decisions on specific matters. In practice these rules are sometimes repudiated by trade unionists even though they have been signed by their unions. But much more commonly the rules are circumvented. Where the agreement obliges them to accept work study, trade unionists will allow the work study engineers to carry out their investigations but query the results. If the agreement binds them to accept the findings of work study, they will not challenge the results themselves, but assert their right to negotiate over the new manning scales which management proposes to introduce on the basis of the findings. Should the agreement bind them to accept manning scales proposed by management, they may accept them, but the managers may find to their disappointment that the output is less than they had expected, and that manning will have to be increased again if orders are to be met.

The common law model appears to have greater relevance to British practice on bargaining over work organization, especially where the authority of custom is acknowledged by *status quo*. The procedure can accept any dispute about work organization and try to find an acceptable solution before either side resorts to industrial action; but there is a problem. Where managers fail to persuade their employees to accept a change in working practices, there is very little chance that the procedure can help them; for by admitting the existence of a custom they have admitted the right of their employees to take industrial action after procedure has been used, and there is little likelihood that union officers at the higher stages of procedure will enter into a settlement binding their members to accept a change in working practices which their managers have failed to persuade them to adopt. On the other hand, if managers introduce a new working arrangement forthwith, on the grounds that it involves no breach of custom, and their employees take the view that a custom has been overriden, the employees are likely to stop work at once. Disputes over working arrangements become perishable issues once the new arrangement has been introduced. With every day of its operation the chances of restoring the *status quo* become less. But in addition to that, the employees have right on their side, for in their view it is the managers who have already broken the agreement by acting without reference to procedure, and they themselves are therefore free to take industrial action. The obligation to refrain from industrial action therefore has little relevance in disputes over work organization. Even where *status quo* is not formally recognized, employees may assert a moral right to protect established customs by taking action at the moment most opportune to prevent their destruction.

It is evident that neither the statute law nor the common law model give much help to understanding collective bargaining over discipline, redundancy, and the organization of work in manufacturing. There is a need for a third model which might be called the *primitive bargaining model*. It starts with the proposition set out in the beginning of the engineering agreement of 1922: 'The Employers have the right to manage their establishments and the Trade Unions have the right to exercise their functions.' Their respective rights entitle both employers and unions to make rules, and to take industrial action to impose them on the other side. But in order to avoid anarchy, they try to make agreed rules where they can, and elsewhere they do their best to avoid conflict by meeting to settle disputes as they arise.

This model has no claim to be more applicable to British industrial relations than the other two models. But it does account for bargaining practices on some subjects in manufacturing better than the other two models do.

Chapter 4

MANAGERS AND MANAGERIAL TECHNIQUES

Little was heard about the individual firm in industrial relations before 1914. The Royal Commission on Labour which was appointed in 1891 and reported in 1894 conducted by far the most exhaustive inquiry into British industrial relations prior to the Donovan Commission. They sat in three committees to hear 583 witnesses in 151 sittings; they circulated questionnaires to trade unions, employers' associations, trades councils and public employers; they appointed a staff of assistant commissioners to conduct special inquiries; and they issued their evidence and reports in 65 blue books. For all that the Commissioners paid almost no attention to management in the 113 foolscap pages in which they summarized the evidence and set out their recommendations.[1] These dealt with relations between trade unions and employers' associations, and with the advisability of further legislation to control wages, hours of work, 'sanitary conditions' and the closed shop. The numerous observations and memoranda appended by members of the Commission and the minority report of the four trade unionists recorded different or supplementary views on the same issues.

The exception was a paragraph entitled: 'Trade unions and single establishments'. It concluded that 'there seems to be no sufficient reason why the conversion of separate establishments into independent industrial polities consolidated on a footing of partnership, should not exist side by side with trade unionism as a means of solving the problems which the relations of capital and labour present'.[2] But the only means to this end to be mentioned was profit-sharing, and the paragraph was clearly a concession to a member of

[1] Royal Commission on Labour, *Fifth and Final Report*.   [2] *Ibid.*, p. 38.

the Commission, Sir George Livesey, a life-long champion of profit-sharing who added a memorandum on the subject as an appendix to the report.

At the time there was nothing surprising in this neglect of the firm, for industrial relations was generally regarded as an external matter. The direction and deployment of workers within the undertaking was limited by the customs of the trade or industry which applied throughout a district if not more widely; they were in many instances restricted by agreements between employers' associations and trade unions as well, also generally covering a district; in addition, they might be bounded by the rules of a trade union, but these also came from outside the firm. In order to change, interpret or challenge rules of these types, employers had to work collectively through their associations; within the rules, each of them could set about managing his own business.

Employing and managing may therefore be seen as distinct functions, although both may be carried out by the same person. At that time most employers were individual proprietors who ran their own businesses, whereas today in most companies of any size the employer is a corporate body normally represented by a manager.

By the end of the nineteenth century, the growth in the size of businesses—both through the increasing number of large plants and through the development of multi-plant undertakings—had led to specialization in management. At some point in the growth of his business even the most versatile proprietor must devolve responsibilities, and this is often done by handing over specific functions—finance, sales and purchasing for example—to subordinates who thereby become specialists; but specialist managers had not yet emerged in the field of industrial relations.

The main reason for this was that the direction and deployment of workers appeared to be an essential element in the organization of production. It could not be split off as a separate function in the same way as keeping the accounts or selling the products. Consequently, the responsibility for handling labour matters was not devolved to specialists, but to subordinate 'line' managers and foremen, or to sub-contractors. Sub-contracting was common through much of the nineteenth century in the iron and steel industry, in coalmining and in construction. The sub-contractor undertook a specific task for a given price. He might be supplied with materials and equipment, but the responsibility for engaging, directing and paying his workers was entirely his. By means of sub-contracting, a large undertaking was able to operate as a cluster of small units, and shed most of its responsibilities for labour management. The situation was not radically different under the typical nineteenth-century foreman. He also selected his workers, disciplined them, and was empowered to dismiss them; and he might have considerable freedom in settling pay, for example by deciding piecework prices or allotting merit money.[3]

By the end of the century the practice of sub-contracting was on the decline, and specialists in incentive payment, financial control and elementary forms of work study were beginning to restrict the foreman's authority. It was, however, from welfare work that the profession of personnel management emerged in Britain. The Institute of Personnel Management started life in 1913 as the Welfare Workers' Association. Its first secretary had been employed as a welfare worker in Rowntree since 1896, and many of the other members came from Quaker firms.[4] The number and functions of welfare workers expanded rapidly during the war with encouragement from the Ministry of Munitions which set up a welfare section in 1915 with Seebohm Rowntree as director. By 1921 the association had a full-time secretary and a journal; and a two-year training course at university level had been approved.[5] Large firms began to employ specialist labour managers soon after the war. Rowntree was again a pioneer, and ICI took over a labour manager from one of its constituent companies, Brunner Mond. In 1931 the association changed its name to the Institute of Labour Management in order to attract such people into membership, and in 1936 it declared that labour management was an integral part of management, and that every firm should have a labour policy approved by the board to govern the work of the labour manager.

The Second World War was another period of rapid expansion, and by 1960 the Institute of Personnel Management, as it was now called, had three thousand practising members. Whereas in 1939 most personnel managers had been women,[6] men now constituted nearly 70 per cent of the institute's members, and almost half the

---

[3] The argument of this paragraph is set out more fully in an unpublished essay by Howard Gospel—'The Development of Managerial Organisation in Industrial Relations—A Historical Perspective'.

[4] M. M. Niven, *Personnel Management, 1913–63*, pp. 21, 37.

[5] *Ibid.*, pp. 59–65.

[6] G. R. Moxon, *The Growth of Personnel Management in Great Britain during the War 1939–1944*, p. 28.

members had had a university education.[7] Salaries had risen with the change in sex distribution and status. However, most personnel managers were not members of the institute. Personnel work could 'be done by two groups of people, the one specialising in human relations aspects of management all their lives and getting their experience by moving from one personnel management specialist post to another; and the other kind staying with one company and learning to take responsibility in many aspects of management, personnel management being only one in a series of these experiences. The Institute would seem to cater for the first type of personnel officer.' In 1960 there were 'various estimates from 10,000 upwards' of the total number of personnel managers.[8]

Since 1960 growing concern with the reform of industrial relations has further emphasized the importance of personnel management. In striking contrast to the neglect of the firm by the Royal Commission on Labour, the Donovan Commission's recommendations were directed primarily to companies and their personnel policies, and to the handling of industrial relations issues within companies and plants. New tasks have also been added to the work of the personnel department, such as 'manpower planning', which involves estimating future needs for employees of various skills and qualifications, and making plans to meet those needs; 'management development', which is the design of careers for managers to develop the potential of each of them through appropriate stages of training, experience and increasing responsibility; and 'organizational development' which involves reviewing the structure and working of the organization, and planning change where it seems to be needed. Even more important has been the impact of new legislation on the personnel manager's job. New statutory duties and liabilities for managers concerning redundancy, unfair dismissal, recognition of trade unions, disclosure of information, avoidance of discrimination, health and safety, and other aspects of employment have greatly extended the areas in which the personnel manager is expected to give expert advice and take on new executive responsibilities.

There are no serious estimates of the number of personnel specialists today. Several years ago Turner and his colleagues conducted a survey of 45 manufacturing plants and found that 'the ratio of such specialists to the establishment's total payroll strength in fact varied

[7] Ann Crichton, 'The IPM in 1950 and 1960'.   [8] *Ibid.*

widely—from nil up to nearly 12 per 1,000 employees'. The median was between two and three per thousand.[9] It may not be too far off the mark to treat this relationship as representative of other sectors of the economy, for recent years have brought a rapid expansion in the number of personnel appointments in the public and private service sectors, notably in local government and the health service. On that assumption, the total number of personnel specialists in Britain today may be as high as fifty thousand.

The status of personnel managers can be gauged by their salaries which now rank well up among the main specialist groups in British management, and by the practice, which is now fairly general among large companies, of appointing main board directors with special responsibility for personnel work within the firm. Some of them, such as Pat Lowry of British Leyland and the late Sir Jack Scamp of GEC, are among the small group of British managers whose names have become widely known, not only in industry, but also to the general public.

Through all this development there has remained a fundamental ambiguity about the job of the personnel manager. The management of labour is an integral part of the production manager's task. How can it be shared with a personnel specialist? The customary answer is a reference to the principle of 'line and staff'. As part of the 'staff', the personnel manager may have direct responsibility only for members of his own staff and such central services as the maintenance of personnel records. Selection, promotion, dismissal, negotiation and handling grievances may remain the responsibility of 'line' supervisors and managers in a direct chain of command up to the board, although they are asked to have regard to the expert advice of the personnel department. In practice, however, many line managers are eager to shift responsibility for these matters to the personnel specialists. 'In major areas of labour relations policy—such as employment, negotiations, communications and training—line management may shed all the details of administration, while retaining ultimate authority and an illusion of responsibility.'[10]

Many advocates of industrial relations reform supposed that this ambiguity could be resolved, or at least minimized, if companies adopted clear and positive personnel policies as recommended by the Donovan Commission; but this has not happened. The Department

[9] Turner *et al.*, *Management Characteristics and Labour Conflict*, pp. 40–1.
[10] Flanders, *The Fawley Productivity Agreements*, p. 254.

of Employment found that where companies have tried to put their industrial relations in order through negotiating wide-ranging company or plant agreements over both substantive and procedural issues, the personnel department has been enlarged and the status and influence of personnel managers has been increased because of 'the need for co-ordination of management action in industrial relations if agreements are to operate as intended'. Without co-ordination by the personnel department there may be discrepancies between senior and junior line managers, between departments, and between present and past decisions. 'Trade union representatives will be likely to make full use of such discrepancies in extracting concessions'. Accordingly 'top backing for the personnel function' needs to be 'beyond question'.[11] Such a situation places the personnel manager in a more authoritative situation than the normal line and staff relationship.

The truth of the matter is that there are always strains and conflicts of priorities in any business. If line managers are left to handle industrial relations issues for themselves, the pressures of production are likely to lead to *ad hoc* and contradictory decisions. If there is a personnel department, they may well hand on their industrial relations problems to be settled by the department on a 'fire-fighting' basis. If a personnel policy is introduced to promote consistent decisions on industrial relations issues, its effectiveness may depend on granting authority to the personnel department to override the natural priorities of line managers.

The remaining sections of this chapter deal with some of the industrial relations issues faced by managers—whether line or specialist—and the techniques which they have developed to cope with them. All of them are intended, one way or another, to influence the behaviour of their workers.

WORK STUDY

In the nineteenth century employers' associations and trade unions regulated piecework by drawing up 'lists' of piecework prices to apply throughout the area of their jurisdiction. There were town or district lists in clothing, hosiery, lace, iron and steel, printing and shipbuilding. From 1892 cotton weaving had a single 'uniform' list

[11] *The Reform of Collective Bargaining at Plant and Company Level*, pp. 82–4.

for the main class of its products, and two district lists for Bolton and Oldham determined the pay of mule spinners throughout Lancashire. In coalmining a price might be settled for a seam of coal throughout the district in which it was worked, although varying geological conditions might bring a good deal of bargaining over special allowances pit by pit.

Geological conditions, however, are not the only feature of the situation which can vary. The assumption of a standard piece-price list is that products, machinery and production methods are also standardized. The success of the Lancashire cotton industry's lists was due to the gradual perfection of the 'mule' as a spinning machine and of the 'powerloom' as a weaving machine during the course of the nineteenth century, and to the reluctance of British firms to experiment with newer methods of production, such as ring-spinning and automatic looms even when they were proving successful abroad. Ring-spinning acquired its own uniform list in due course, but as automatic looms were gradually introduced, the pay for the weavers who operated them was settled mill by mill.

The widespread introduction of piecework into the engineering industry at the end of the century therefore did not lead to regulation by piece-price lists, for the new mass-production machinery was not standardized and methods of production changed frequently. Consequently piece-prices, or the 'time allowed' to complete a job,[12] were fixed for each job in each plant, and, following the 1898 agreement, trade union regulation was left to the shop stewards. Subsequent agreements laid down minimum conditions such as a provision that the price or time should allow a worker 'of average ability' to earn a certain minimum level of pay; but actual earnings were still determined by prices and times set for each plant. The increase in the proportion of pieceworkers from about 5 per cent of the male labour force in 1886 to about 50 per cent in 1927[13] entailed a substantial transfer of control over pay from collective agreements outside the plant to dealings within it.

The growth of payment by results in other industries cannot be

[12] 'Time allowed' relates piecework payment to a time rate by allowing the production of a stipulated output in a given time to qualify for the time rate and paying the pieceworker who exceeds that output a bonus related to 'time saved'.

[13] The figure for 1886 is taken from *Report of an Enquiry by the Board of Trade into Earnings and Hours*, 1906, Vol. VI, and the figure for 1927 is from a survey by the Engineering Employers' Federation quoted in M. L. Yates, *Wages and Labour Conditions in British Engineering*, p. 118.

traced with the same precision as in engineering, but the general trends are fairly clear. 'The spread of mass production methods to other industries including chemicals, rubber, food manufacture and light metals led to systems of payment by results akin to those of engineering.'[14] Many of these systems involved the payment of a variable 'bonus', related to output, in addition to a timerate, and were called 'incentive schemes' rather than piecework. Since the First World War the same arrangement has applied in the engineering industry, but there the term 'piecework' was firmly-rooted and continues in use. Meanwhile new methods of production in long-established industries were gradually undermining the traditional piece-price lists inherited from the nineteenth century. Some of them have continued to apply to diminishing sections of their industries, as plant after plant shifted to its own incentive system; others dropped quietly into oblivion.

It is often supposed that a pieceworker is paid for his output. But this impression is shown to be incorrect by the almost universal provision in agreements on payment by results that prices or times are to be revised whenever new methods, machinery or materials are introduced. Such changes make it easier or more difficult for the pieceworker to produce a given output. They increase or diminish the effort required to earn a given level of pay. It is generally held to be unfair to penalize a worker because a tougher material takes longer to cut or to machine, and therefore requires a greater effort to reach the given level of pay. In other words, pay is related to effort and not to output.

Individual ability also varies, and a price or time fixed for an outstandingly able worker would require unusual effort from the general run of pieceworkers to reach an acceptable level of pay. So the agreements require the standard to be set for the worker of 'average ability' or the 'qualified' worker. It is also important that the method used when a job is being timed or priced should be the method used in production. If not, the earnings of the worker of average ability may diverge from the intended level. Traditionally the setting of the time or price was the responsibility of the foreman or of a specialist 'ratefixer' who relied only on 'his own knowledge and past experience'. The National Board for Prices and Incomes found that 'this method of work measurement is usually unsatisfactory'.[15] It is subjective and erratic, yielding 'tight' or 'loose' times or

---

[14] *Donovan Report*, p. 23.   [15] *Payment by Results Systems*, p. 49.

prices, with some workers toiling hard for meagre rewards and others earning generous rewards for modest efforts. The remedy recommended for these inequities is 'work study'.

Work study is defined by the British Standards Institution as consisting of a number of techniques but particularly method study and work measurement. Work measurement is 'the application of techniques designed to establish the time for a *qualified worker* to carry out a specified *job* at a defined level of performance'. Method study is 'the systematic recording and critical examination of existing and proposed ways of doing work, as a means of developing and applying easier and more effective methods and reducing costs'.[16] Method study can ensure that the method chosen for timing is an effective method which has been carefully specified.

These techniques had their origin in the work of an American, F. W. Taylor, 'the father of scientific management'. The strength and weakness of his methods were evident in his famous experiment in the handling of pig-iron in which he claimed to have discovered 'the law governing the tiring effect of heavy labour on a first-class man'.[17] By analysing the job and training workers in new methods suggested by the analysis, the average tonnage shifted per man went up by 250 per cent.

The simplification which made Taylor's work possible was that workers could be *studied* as if they were machines, and that their work could be controlled as if they were machines. Since Taylor claimed that 'every single act of every workman can be reduced to a science',[18] and since it was his intention to remove from the worker all control over his work in order to subject him entirely to the control of the manager,[19] his theories seemed to be based on the gross error that workers can and should be *treated* as if they were machines.

The error was widely recognized in Taylor's own day[20] and many subsequent exponents of work study not only developed Taylor's techniques of empirical research but also became more modest in the claims which they made for their findings. In Britain the new Ministry of Munitions established the Health of Munitions Workers Committee in 1915 to advise on 'industrial fatigue, hours of labour, and other matters affecting the personal and physical efficiency' of

[16] *Glossary of Terms in Work Study*, p. 6.
[17] F. W. Taylor, *The Principles of Scientific Management*, p. 57.
[18] *Ibid.*, p. 64.
[19] Harry Braverman, *Labor and Monopoly Capital*, chapter 4.
[20] Georges Friedmann, *Industrial Society*, chapter 1.

munitions workers.[21] Studies were conducted into the effect on output of hours worked and shift work, into factors affecting 'lost time', as absenteeism was then called, and into the relationship between output and factory conditions, especially lighting, heating and ventilation.[22] By the end of the war industrial psychology was an established discipline. The National Institute of Industrial Psychology was established in 1921. When its principal, C. S. Myers, brought out his *Industrial Psychology in Great Britain* in 1926 he forcefully dissociated himself and his subject from Taylor's error. The 'intuitive opposition of British workers to such ideas had', he said, 'a sound psychological basis'. By contrast the Institute's research had 'gained the confidence of the worker' by aiming 'to ease the difficulties which may confront him'.[23]

However, work study was still used mainly to design and improve systems of payment by results. The firm of Bedaux (now Associated Industrial Consultants) brought its techniques of work-studied incentive payment across the Atlantic about 1930. Their application led to a number of strikes investigated by the Trades Union Congress, but business expanded rapidly. A year or so later the consultancy firm of Urwick Orr was set up. Others followed and the production needs of the Second World War greatly expanded the demand for their services which continued to grow after the war. Although industrial consultants advise on many other aspects of management besides pay systems, and other aspects of pay besides payment by results, nevertheless, at least until recently, the staple business of the major firms continued to be the installation of systems of payment by results on the basis of work study.[24]

Throughout this time the status of work study has continued to be an issue of debate. Critics point out that it can never achieve complete precision. There are bound to be small margins of error with any timing device, including a stop watch, and allowances for rest pauses are bound to be somewhat arbitrary. Of greater importance is the need for 'effort-rating'—judging whether the individual under study is working at an acceptable piecework pace, and making appropriate adjustments upwards and downwards for any deviation

---

[21] *Official History of the Ministry of Munitions*, Vol. V, Part 111, p. 1.

[22] H. M. Vernon, *Industrial Fatigue and Efficiency*.

[23] pp. 28–9.

[24] In 1968 the National Board for Prices and Incomes found that 'about threequarters of the payment systems' which consultancy firms 'had installed involved conventional PBR'. (*Payment by Results Systems*, p. 20.)

from this standard. Tests with groups of work study engineers show that there can be wide variations in ratings of the same worker doing the same job. There are also

> certain jobs which are anathema to work study engineers. . . . A polisher, for instance, presses the part he is working on against a revolving buff and the speed with which he achieves the required finish depends upon the pressure he applies. During the work study it is easy for the man being timed to appear to press harder than he does in fact and, once a job value has been awarded, he can exploit the slack job value.[25]

Then there is the 'learning curve'. There is evidence to show that workers employed on repetitive jobs improve their performance not only from the first month to the second, although at a diminishing rate, but also from the first year to the second year and beyond.[26] In these circumstances the notion of a qualified worker loses precision; and the common provision or custom that the level of piecework earnings will not fall when modifications or new models come into production yields an automatic shift upwards to a new level of earnings through the learning process.

The work study engineer has answers to most of these charges. It is possible to achieve and maintain a fair degree of consistency in effort-rating where work study engineers are trained in the same methods and their work is checked fairly frequently. Even greater consistency can be achieved by using 'synthetic' times, which are

> records of times for tasks or job-elements which have been established and accepted by workers in the past. A work study department which has built up a library of such times is . . . often able to construct acceptable standards for new jobs from elements that have already been studied.[27]

In any case

> work study need not achieve universally applicable standards to justify itself; it need only apply consistent standards within individual establishments or other areas of common reference.[28]

[25] William Brown, *Piecework Bargaining*, p. 70.
[26] National Board for Prices and Incomes, *Payment by Results Systems* (Supplement), Paper 3.   [27] *Payment by Results Systems*, pp. 50–1.
[28] William Brown, *Piecework Bargaining*, p. 6.

He can also point out that work study has other uses, besides providing work values for payment by results. It is the most accurate method of estimating labour costs for accounting and pricing, and for planning new developments and new products. Finally, if there is to be payment by results, and if payment is to be reasonably fair as between one worker and another, and between one job and another, work study, for all its defects, is the fairest method of settling job values which is currently available.

In practice the 'degeneration' or 'demoralization' of payment by results systems which has been a common feature of post-war British industrial relations

> is not usually the consequence of a poor work study or ratefixing department. . . . It usually arises because too low a priority is given to the integrity of an establishment's payment system by top management itself.

In some instances managers 'deliberately allow PBR standards to slip for some workers so as to yield attractive earnings to a scarce grade of labour'.[29] When frequent minor changes in specification occur, there is a temptation to neglect the revision of work values by the work study department on the ground that the effect of any one change is marginal and there will almost certainly be difficulties in gaining acceptance for the new values. But a series of changes is likely to have a cumulative effect so that 'earnings will tend to rise unequally and without any increase in workers' effort'.[30] Bargaining pressures can have the same effect, with high earnings going to the most experienced bargainers, or the workers most strategically placed to put pressure on their managers and supervisors, and not to the most efficient workers. In these circumstances workers no longer accept the official 'conversion factor'—the factor by which the standard time for a job should be multiplied to give an appropriate level of pay—for their target is now the level of earnings paid on the more remunerative jobs. As a consequence work study engineers, ratefixers and supervisors are forced to diverge further and further from the official conversion factor in order to win acceptance for new job values; and the clamour grows louder for old jobs to be retimed to yield earnings closer to the current 'going rate'.

In its survey of payment by results systems the National Board for

---

[29] *Payment by Results Systems*, p. 54.   [30] *Ibid.*, p. 55.

Prices and Incomes found instances of payment by results under close control providing an undoubted incentive to effort and based on a careful use of work study.[31] They also found many instances which fell short of this standard. At one firm 'average wage earnings must have risen by 75 per cent between 1963 and 1967, much faster than the most optimistic estimate of a real increase in output, an increase which was in any case brought about by increased capital investment'.[32] In some plants there were 'wide discrepancies in pay . . . between individuals doing much the same kind of work: at one factory the spread of skilled pieceworkers' earnings was from £14.15.0d a week to £50 a week, with the highest and lowest earners in the same section . . . Once a PBR system gets out of effective management control, it takes on a life of its own as individuals and groups seize on any chance of raising their earnings to the level that they think is "fair"'.[33]

In a subsequent inquiry into pay in the building industry the Board investigated incentive payment on twenty-six sites. They classified six of them as 'good'—

> distinguished by relatively high efficiency and a payment system at least fairly well under control. The 9 'bad' sites, conversely, were all notable for a payment system out of control and relative inefficiency. On the 'indifferent' remainder, bonus earnings were not particularly high and neither was efficiency.[34]

It is not surprising that by the time the Board were preparing and publishing these reports new trends in pay systems were evident in Britain, seeking to make use of work study without relying on traditional methods of piecework and incentive payment. But before these trends are discussed it is necessary to give some account of a technique which has been developed to regulate the pay of the majority of manual workers and the great majority of white collar workers who are paid by time, namely job evaluation.

JOB EVALUATION

Traditionally craft industries paid one rate to the craftsman and a

[31] *Payment by Results Systems* (Supplement), Paper 6.
[32] *Payment by Results Systems*, p. 34.   [33] *Ibid.*, pp. 28–9.
[34] *Pay and Conditions in the Building Industry*, p. 32.

considerably lower rate to the labourer. When semi-skilled workers began to appear they were allotted an intermediate rate according to some estimate of the degree of skill involved in their jobs. In industries in which skill was acquired by experience and promotion by seniority, payment could not be explained in terms of either skill or experience, for a man might have accumulated all the skill and all the experience required for the most senior and highest paid job, but he still had to wait his turn. What clearly differed from one job to another was the level of responsibility. The senior man in the team was responsible for the team's work and output, and the second member of the team took charge when the senior man was absent. But other factors besides skill and responsibility are also relevant. If pieceworkers are paid for their effort it is reasonable that a timeworker should receive additional payment for a job requiring unusual effort or exertion, for example in handling heavy equipment or materials; and unusually dirty, disagreeable, hot or dangerous conditions are also widely held to warrant a higher rate of pay. Dangerous and unpleasant conditions and unusual exertion may be relatively rare among white collar workers, but skill and responsibility are widely argued as criteria for settling their pay differentials. Technicians and professional staff argue the value of skill—and qualifications—whereas supervisors and line managers emphasize the need to reward those who carry heavy responsibility.

Conflicts result from pressing the claims of different criteria for pay differentials. One that has attracted a good deal of attention is the dispute between production workers and craftsmen in the steel industry. Traditionally the production workers were paid according to their position in the team, and promoted by seniority. The top men were responsible for the output of their teams, as the first hand melter was for the output of the furnaces, and they expected to be well paid for it. As time has passed the industry has become more dependent on the craftsmen who maintain its increasingly complex equipment, and demand payment for their skill. Each of the two groups believe that they have a claim to be the highest paid manual workers in the industry, and several important postwar strikes have arisen out of their disagreement. In addition to major disputes of this order, quarrels over differentials between individuals and groups are a source of frequent friction in many plants as technological and social change alter the content of jobs and the regard in which they are held.

The techniques which have been designed to help in resolving differences of opinion over pay differentials are known as 'job evaluation'. The simplest technique is 'ranking' whereby a number of jobs are placed in a rank order of what appears to be their 'value' after the evaluators have examined what is involved in each of them. The most widely used is 'points rating'. This technique begins by specifying the factors, such as skill, responsibility and physical exertion which are held to warrant more than a minimum level of pay. Each job under examination is then awarded points on a numerical scale for the degree of each factor which it is judged to require. If it is considered that the factors are not of equal importance in determining pay their relative importance is allowed for by weighting the scales. Where, for example, skill is held to be more important than physical exertion, the former might be given a scale from 0 to 10, and the latter a scale from 0 to 5. The points for each job are added up, and the jobs are grouped into grades so that, for example, jobs with 46–50 points might be assigned to grade A, those with 41–45 to grade B, and so on. Finally a rate of pay is settled for each grade. Most of the more sophisticated devices have been developed from points rating.

The advantage of points rating and similar devices is that they provide a means of rationalizing conflicts over pay differentials. If the parties to the dispute fail to agree about the factors which warrant pay differentials, they must argue this difference out before proceeding further. Once that is settled, they must agree on the weight for each factor. So long as these two issues can be resolved, any difference of opinion over a differential can be reduced to an argument over the degree of skill or responsibility, or of another factor, required by the jobs under debate.

Job evaluation is not 'objective'. The only objective test of the value of a job would be the price put upon it by the labour market if that could be determined—but most labour markets are capable of putting very different prices upon what appear to be identical jobs. The test of the market must therefore be set aside in favour of an administrative or negotiated decision, which is necessarily subjective. The techniques of job evaluation help the parties to pinpoint differences in their subjective judgements and therefore to compromise over them. For this reason the techniques often form the basis for a negotiated pay structure, with joint committees of managers and union representatives—who may have received training in job evaluation to enable them to participate effectively—working out their own factors and weights, and rating individual jobs. Thereafter the committee may remain in existence to hear appeals and regrade jobs whose content has changed.

Nevertheless job evaluation is by no means trouble-free. Despite the efforts of the British Steel Corporation, it has not yet been accepted by the steel unions as the means to resolve the problems of the industry's pay structure. With one or two minor exceptions, such as tobacco and jute, it has not been used in private industry to design industry-wide pay structures, so that it does little or nothing to reduce discrepancies in pay between plants and companies. Within a company or plant an evaluated structure of basic rates may be distorted by incentive payments which provide variable earnings above the basic rates, or pressures for sectional increases, or by shortages of staff in particular grades. 'There are often pressures from managers and supervisors too, since a job-evaluated pay structure reduces their freedom of discretion.'[35] Periodic regradings on a large scale may come close to a general pay increase and could be used to circumvent a government pay policy.

In 1967 the National Board for Prices and Incomes conducted a national survey which found that the coverage of job evaluation was highest among white collar employees, with 30 per cent of managerial jobs evaluated and 27 per cent of 'staff' jobs. Non-craft manual workers came close behind with 26 per cent, but only 11 per cent of craftsmen were covered.[36] Although it was not conducted on a strictly comparable basis, a survey published by the Institute of Personnel Management in 1976 indicated that there had been a considerable extension of job evaluation schemes. Out of 213 companies, 168 had schemes in operation and another ten were about to introduce schemes. White collar employees were still well ahead of manual workers, ranging from clerical staff who were covered by schemes in 150 companies to technicians who were covered in 113 firms. Semi-skilled and unskilled manual workers were covered in 87 companies and skilled manual workers in 75.[37] Perhaps the higher coverage among white collar workers may be explained by the lower level of trade union membership among them in private industry, for some unions are reluctant to accept job evaluation. Certainly the insistence of many craft groups that all craftsmen are

[35] National Board for Prices and Incomes, *Job Evaluation*, p. 24.
[36] *Ibid.*, p. 10.
[37] Institute of Personnel Management, *Job Evaluation in Practice*, pp. 9, 16.

entitled to a standard craft rate, whatever their jobs, is one of the reasons for the relatively low coverage of job evaluation among skilled manual workers.

PRODUCTIVITY BARGAINING

At the beginning of 1960 the management of the Esso refinery at Fawley presented a detailed set of proposals to the unions representing their manual employees. The proposals arose out of extensive discussions in the refinery in which

> shop stewards took a major part. The basic idea . . . was that overtime should be drastically cut . . . and that basic wages should be increased (by a total of 40 per cent . . .) to compensate for this.

In order to achieve the cut in overtime without taking on more workers

> a number of changes were proposed. . . . Where craft skills 'over-lapped', demarcation lines were to be flexibly interpreted and process workers were to be permitted to perform some basic craft jobs. Craftsmen were to work without mates who were to be trained as craftsmen or given other jobs at the refinery. . . . Tea breaks and other unproductive time allowances were to be eliminated. . . . The Company promised that no man could be made redundant as a result of any agreement on the proposals.

Negotiations led to agreements which embodied most of the proposals, although the craft unions accepted 'only about half the proposed inter-craft flexibility items' and most of them refused to countenance the training of mates for craft jobs. As a result, the company was able 'to reduce its employment of contractors and to carry out a far-reaching reorganisation of its manpower'.[38]
Although no precise calculations of the gains for the company was possible, and the overtime targets were only partially achieved, there is no doubt that the agreement was very much to the company's

---

[38] National Board for Prices and Incomes, *Productivity Agreements*, pp. 50–1.

advantage, and at the same time the employees were placed, at least for the time being, 'among the highest paid in the country'.[39] The agreement therefore attracted a good deal of attention, and by the time that Allan Flanders published his book on *The Fawley Productivity Agreements* in 1964—which greatly augmented public interest—several other companies were already planning or even negotiating similar agreements. By 1966 the National Board for Prices and Incomes calculated that productivity agreements covered about half a million workers, by far the largest single contribution being made by the 'status' agreements in the electricity supply industry. Thereafter the rate of growth accelerated as productivity bargaining became the only approved means to pay increases over and above the 'norms' and 'ceilings' of the current incomes policy which was generally available.[40]

The popularity of productivity bargaining despite the prolonged and difficult negotiations involved was due to the contribution which it seemed to offer to resolving some major problems of British industrial relations which were becoming widely recognized at that time. The first was the use of overtime to provide acceptable levels of pay rather than to get work done.

In his study of the Fawley agreements, Flanders explored the process of overtime growth up to high and sustained levels. Shortages of equipment, of experienced managers capable of accurate planning, and of craftsmen in some trades were all met by overtime working. But when the shortages were alleviated and overtime might have been expected to diminish,

> the familar ratchet forces come into play. . . . There is no need to assume that overtime is 'manufactured' deliberately, though this may happen in some places. What makes overtime systematic is the almost automatic adjustment of work habits and behaviour that its regular working induces among workers and supervisors alike.

When special efforts and inducements brought a twelve per cent increase in the number of craftsmen at Fawley the reduction in average hours worked was 'little more than three per cent'.[41] In any event managers were not always eager to take advantage of oppor-

[39] Flanders, *The Fawley Productivity Agreements*, pp. 196–7.   [40] See pp. 352–5.
[41] Flanders, *The Fawley Productivity Agreements*, pp. 57–61.

tunities to reduce high levels of overtime. In one company 'the Chief Engineer's objections to the overtime cuts were not that the work could not be done without overtime, but that he would lose his staff'.[42]

Systematic overtime, however, was only one aspect of the under-utilization of manpower which was widely diagnosed as a major feature of the British economy during the sixties. The Devlin Committee drew attention to the practice of 'welting' in Liverpool docks 'whereby only half a gang is working at any given time; for each half it is one hour on and one hour off. During his hour off the man does what he likes; he is resting or smoking or having a cup of tea'.[43] The practice helped to sustain a high level of overtime which was encouraged by the unusually high overtime rates—double-time after 5 p.m. on weekdays and quadruple time at weekends. But the function of the 'blow' on Fleet Street—which is equivalent to welting—is not to provide overtime, but to maintain a large number of highly-paid jobs. Multiplicity of crafts or grades with rigid demarcation lines between them entails delay as one worker waits for another to do a job that he is perfectly capable of doing himself but is debarred from doing by the demarcation rules. The consequence may be systematic overtime or higher staffing than would otherwise be necessary, or both. Prolonged tea breaks and other pauses slow down the pace of work. The employment of craftsmen's mates at Fawley promoted idleness. The company calculated that mates were actually working 'about $3\frac{1}{2}$ hours a day on average'.[44]

The objective of productivity bargaining was to remove or curtail practices of these kinds by agreement with the unions. The detailed contents of the agreements varied widely. Most of them related to manual workers only, but some of them covered white collar workers as well, and a few affected white collar workers alone. Many were plant agreements or sectional agreements within a plant, but there were also company agreements and one or two industry agreements. Changes in working practices could be specified in detail or left to generalizations such as 'maximum flexibility'. New tasks and manning levels were based on careful work study in some instances, and on rough assessements in others. Job evaluation was often used in

[42] Whybrew, *Overtime Working in Britain*, p. 89.

[43] *Final Report*, pp. 16–18. In some instances it was a turn off and a turn on, or even a day off and a day on.

[44] Flanders, *The Fawley Productivity Agreements*, p. 170.

devising new pay structures, but by no means always. Many of the agreements introduced or revised shift systems. Pledges of no redundancy were common. Rates of pay were raised substantially in many agreements, although not usually by as much as Fawley's 40 per cent and, as at Fawley, many of the increases derived largely from a consolidation of overtime earnings or other additional payments. Consolidation, however, meant that a much larger part of the total pay packet was now used for the calculation of holiday pay, sick pay and pensions. Where overtime was cut, leisure was increased. A number of agreements raised the conditions and fringe benefits of manual workers nearer to those of workers with 'staff status'.

In order to assess the economic results of productivity bargaining it is useful to distinguish the agreements reached up to 1966 from those introduced under the pressure of incomes policy from 1967 to 1969. There is little doubt that the first group as a whole achieved substantial reductions in unit labour costs.[45] Of the second group the National Board of Prices and Incomes reported that 'in three-quarters of the companies we examined we were able to conclude that the net effect of the agreement was the achievement of lower costs per unit of output'.[46] However, other authors have concluded that this verdict is too optimistic.[47] In any event, the long-run economic gains have not been large. It is not at all easy to discern any impact of productivity bargaining on the overall performance of the economy; and many of the companies which had negotiated apparently successful productivity deals in the sixties were again faced with problems of low performance and substantial overmanning during the seventies.

In the long term probably the most important consequence of the popularity of productivity bargaining was the impetus which it gave to reform of the structure of collective bargaining. Its contribution to the recognition of the authority of shop stewards and to the formalization of plant bargaining have been noted in Chapter 2. The main concern of this chapter is its effect on management. According to McKersie and Hunter, 'by far the most important impact of productivity bargaining on managerial style has been the emergence of

[45] Donovan Commission, *Productivity Bargaining*, p. 38; National Board for Prices and Incomes, *Productivity Agreements*, pp. 21–2.

[46] *Productivity Agreements* (2), p. 28.

[47] McKersie & Hunter, *Pay, Productivity and Collective Bargaining*, pp. 249–55; H. A. Clegg, *How to Run an Incomes Policy*, p. 38.

planning as a key function. . . . Probably the most important result of productivity bargaining for British management has been the elevation of the industrial relations function. In many companies it now stands on a par with the other key functions of finance, production and marketing.' Furthermore, there has been an extension 'in the range of subjects and issues for which industrial relations personnel have assumed responsibility'.[48]

MEASURED DAYWORK

Several of the early productivity agreements included the termination of an outworn incentive scheme and the consolidation of incentive earnings as one item in the package, but generally the problems of pieceworking firms with degenerated systems of payment by results seemed far removed from those of Fawley or the electricity supply industry. The major worries of such pieceworking firms were strikes and wage drift.

The National Board of Prices and Incomes emphasized the 'stress and friction involved in constant bargaining', and reported that in one Midlands factory 'relationships between the ratefixers and the shop floor were described in terms of "battle" and "war" and a good shop steward was defined as one who spends "at least fifty per cent of his time in the ratefixing office, arguing"'.[49] Strikes and the use of other sanctions may be endemic in circumstances such as these, and during the sixties, managers, politicians and the public became more and more worried about unofficial strikes. In some of the most strike-prone industries, especially vehicle manufacture, the heavy incidence of strikes was widely attributed to piecework.[50]

Another consequence of this kind of piecework bargaining was that it 'produced a situation in which earnings are determined as much by bargaining skill and strength as effort'[51] so that the relationship between earnings and output was weakened. Bargaining over allowances for time lost due to machine breakdowns, shortage of materials, or other causes, can also lead to increased costs for a given output; and the nearer the allowances approach the level of average

---

[48] *Op. cit.*, pp. 322–6.
[49] *Payment by Results Systems*, pp. 19, 40.
[50] See pp. 274–5.
[51] *Payment by Results Systems* (Supplement), pp. 59–60.

earnings, the less the incentive to hasten back to work. The common practice of 'cross-booking' allows time actually spent on one job to be recorded against another, thus obscuring particularly high earnings on one job which might, if discovered, lead to a revaluation. Where a worker is paid partly on measured work and partly on unmeasured work, cross-booking can record less time on piecework jobs than they have actually taken. If the time spent on unmeasured work is paid by the hour the pay packet is thereby inflated. If the rate of pay for unmeasured work is the average hourly piecework earnings, the size of the pay packet is swollen further, for the smaller number of hours recorded against piecework yields higher average hourly piecework earnings. The practice of storing tickets for completed work 'at the back of the book', to be handed in when the worker chooses, serves to cushion him against fluctuations in earnings and to confuse the accounting system. All these practices and many more weaken managerial control over costs and lead to an upward 'piecework drift' in earnings.

There were many practices associated with piecework of which managers were anxious to be rid, but there did not seem much to be gained by trying to bargain over them in a typical productivity deal. The obvious way to get rid of them was to terminate piecework. Once every hour yields the same pay, there is no bargaining over allowances for lost time; and there is no use cross-booking jobs when the practice has no effect on earnings. What concerned managers in these firms was how to maintain output if piecework was abolished, and on this question productivity bargaining had something to offer. The new level of hourly rates introduced by the first Fawley agreement was accepted by the management in the belief that the refinery would be able to maintain or improve its performance with a given labour force and a set overtime target. If pieceworking firms were able to go further than that and switch to daywork with an explicit understanding that the new rates were to be paid only where stipulated performance targets were achieved, their problem might be resolved. Measured daywork appeared to be the means to achieve this aim, for it is defined as a situation in which

the pay of the employee is fixed on the understanding that he will maintain a specified level of performance, but the pay does not fluctuate in the short term with his actual performance. This arrangement relies on some form of work measurement or assessment, as a means of both defining the required level of performance and of monitoring the actual level.[52]

Even if such an arrangement fails to hold the performance of individual workers precisely to the former piecework levels there should be compensating advantages in cutting out the costs of administering piecework and of piecework disputes. In addition the firm should gain increased flexibility in deploying their labour force because workers need no longer fear loss of earnings which could easily be the consequence under piecework; and the introduction of new methods and equipment should not meet with the same resistance as under piecework once it is clear that earnings will not suffer as a consequence.

The first major agreement based squarely on the replacement of piecework by measured daywork was the national powerloading agreement in coalmining in 1966. Chrysler followed in 1969, and in 1970 British Leyland began the massive transfer of their scattered labour force to measured daywork. When the Office of Manpower Economics published the results of their survey of measured daywork in 1973, the system was found to be spread widely across manufacturing and other industries, but within manufacturing the vehicles industry came far ahead of the others, accounting for 30 per cent of the workers affected. However, the survey covered firms switching to measured daywork from both piecework and timework (for the system offered companies which operated unmeasured timework the opportunity to increase their labour productivity). In fact the numbers of measured daywork employees who had previously been on timework outnumbered those who had switched from piecework. Car workers accounted for more than 40 per cent of the manufacturing employees switched from piecework to measured daywork.[53]

The industrial relations consequences of measured daywork agreements have a great deal in common with those of productivity bargaining. Both involve a radical overhaul of methods of wage payment and the organization of work. Almost invariably they entail instituting and maintaining a system of formal negotiation with shop stewards where it does not already exist. The agreement becomes one of the chief means of achieving corporate objectives. If

[52] Office of Manpower Economics, *Measured Daywork*, p. 8.
[53] *Ibid*., Appendix B.

it is to work, its effective implementation has to take priority over most other objectives for line managers. The status of the personnel manager is almost inevitably raised, but even so, success is not likely to be achieved unless the plant manager, by taking a major part in negotiating and administering the agreement, ties his reputation to making it work.

In their report on *Measured Daywork*, published in 1973, the Office of Manpower Economics found 'an overall improvement in the industrial relations climate. Indeed in some cases the number of strikes and disputes fell dramatically'; and said that among those of the respondents to their survey 'who declared their aim in introducing MDW as being improved effort, 93 per cent said it was now better'.[54] Further experience suggests a less favourable verdict. It is true that the powerloading agreement was followed by several years of sharp decline in the annual total of stoppages in coalmining, but the figures for strikes in the docks and car manufacture show no clear reduction following the introduction of measured daywork in London and other ports, and in British Leyland and Chrysler. All three industries experienced a marked fall in productivity during the early seventies, leading to the reintroduction of payment by results in the London docks and on the coalface; and by 1977 it was the firm intention of British Leyland to follow suit as soon as they could arrange to do so. Disappointing results in the car industry may have been the consequence of inadequate planning. The government's 'think-tank' reported in 1975 that:

> in many plants the changes took place *before* soundly based manning levels and output standards were available. As a result many of the plants where MDW has been introduced are substantially overmanned and the grounds for dispute have switched from piecework rates . . . to manning levels. . . . Workers are said to lack any positive incentive to keep the lines moving.[55]

In both the car industry and coalmining it is now suggested that the replacement of piecework by daywork was an essential preliminary to the introduction of soundly-based and controlled systems of incentive payment which will yield high performance without provoking industrial unrest. Time will tell.

[54] pp. 34, 42.
[55] Central Policy Review Staff, *The Future of the British Car Industry*, p. 102.

WORK DESIGN

The assumption behind the technique known as 'work design'—and also as 'work organization', 'work structuring', and 'improving the quality of working life'—is that many workers are employed in jobs which fall short of their capacities in at least two ways. They are monotonous—making demands on only a few of the workers' capabilities; and they offer very little discretion so that workers have little or no choice in what they do during the course of the working day. The novelty is to suggest that work should be re-designed to remedy these defects. Many employers have paid attention in the past to alterations in the organization of work to make it safer, healthier, less onerous and less uncomfortable; and some employers may have altered jobs to make them more interesting or satisfying to those who perform them; but to advocate redesign of work to make it more interesting and satisfying as a central item in industrial relations policy is a new departure.

Monotony is relieved by 'job enlargement', adding new tasks to the job, in order to yield greater variety during the course of the working day. This process can be pushed further by 'job rotation', whereby several workers in a group are allowed or encouraged to swap jobs, either in a fixed cycle or as the spirit moves them. Lack of discretion is remedied by 'job enrichment'—limiting supervision or dropping rules so that workers can take more decisions for themselves. Rotation of jobs within a group at will is one example of discretion; another is allowing workers to order their own supplies; a third is making workers responsible for checking and inspecting their own products. Where a group of workers is allowed considerable discretion in organizing their own work activities the arrangement is described as an 'autonomous work group'.

The first example to attract widespread attention was the 'composite work team' in the British coalmining industry. The traditional method of coalgetting in Durham was extraction from a number of small 'places' at each coalface in each pit. Teams varying in size from two (one man on each of two shifts) to six (two men on each of three shifts) prepared the face, cut the coal, loaded it for transport, supported the roof and cut away stone in order to get at the face. The teams were self-selecting. A man who did not fit in, or work at the pace of the team, was dropped. The cycle of operations was continuous. Each man took over where the last man left off, and every man had an interest in leaving the place ready for the next man, for all shared equally in the piecework earnings of the place. When coalcutting machinery was introduced the pits changed to 'conventional' longwall operation. Coal was cut for the length of the face by machines operated by 'cutters'; 'Fillers' loaded coal, each in his own section of the face; 'Stonemen' cut the stone; and 'pullers' moved the conveyor forward and pulled out the roof supports where they were no longer needed. Different tasks were performed on separate shifts; and each task had its own price. There was little incentive to leave things ready for the next shift, and the oncoming shift might have to complete the previous element in the cycle of work before getting on with their own. Tensions grew. The faceworkers depended 'entirely on external control in order to carry out the indivisible primary task of completing the cycle'. Yet close supervision is impossible at the coalface. 'Such a situation inevitably breeds disorganisation unless the cycle group, through the pattern of its own internal organisation, is capable of exercising a high degree of self-regulation.'[56]

The requisite pattern was provided by composite longwall working, introduced in special circumstances in Durham and elsewhere. A single price was set for the whole team on the face, covering all three shifts and including every task to be performed, together with a performance bonus for completion of the cycle. Tasks and shifts were interchangeable at the discretion of the group. 'Composite workmen are multi-skilled miners qualified at least in filling and stonework, and often also in pulling, drilling and cutting.' The composite team was self-selecting and self-regulating, and shared a common interest in the completion of the cycle. Since this was management's objective also, 'the improved quality of relations with officials was in striking contrast to the atmosphere prevailing in conventional settings', and the officials could concentrate on giving 'technical leadership' rather than attempting to control operations at the coalface.[57]

Although composite organization was found to possess characteristics more conducive than the conventional to productive effectiveness, low cost, work satisfaction, good relations and social health,[58] the introduction of powerloading machinery and measured daywork rendered composite longwall working obsolete. Subse-

[56] Trist *et al.*, *Organisational Choice*, p. 66.   [57] *Ibid.*, pp. 78, 86.
[58] *Ibid.*, p. 291.

quent developments in work design have occurred overseas—in Scandinavia, Holland and the United States—more than in Britain. But one further British experiment—the Weekly Staff Agreement of ICI—deserves attention if only because it was an attempt to make use of work design techniques on a large scale.

In 1965 ICI signed a productivity agreement with the union representing its manual workers. It had much in common with the Fawley agreement. The company hoped to achieve flexibility between craft trades and flexibility between craftsmen and process workers to enable them to deploy their labour force more effectively. In return they offered higher rates of pay which were to absorb existing incentive schemes and compensate for reductions in overtime. But the agreement did not spell out the flexibilities which the companies sought. That would not have been possible in an agreement intended ultimately to cover the whole company with its ten divisions and eighty-odd plants. Instead 'jobs were to be examined, analysed and re-designed' by means of 'local discussions and agreements on each works or site', with retraining where necessary.[59] The redesigned jobs were then to be assessed and placed in one of the eight grades of the new pay scale which replaced the former structure. The outcome of the agreement in increased flexibility and improvement in manpower utilization was therefore to be determined by plant negotiations. The intention had been to test the agreement at some trial sites and then gradually extend it through the company. Some considerable successes were achieved, but the agreement ran into more opposition than had been expected, especially from craft shop stewards, and progress was slow. In 1969, therefore, a new Weekly Staff Agreement replaced the old Manpower Utilization and Payment Structure with a further increase in pay and rewording on flexibility designed to sooth the susceptibilities of the craftsmen. The revised agreement was rapidly adopted throughout all but a few of the company's plants. Meanwhile the company's central personnel department had absorbed the theories of work design and had 'tirelessly preached them throughout the company . . . to groups of managers, supervisors and shop stewards'.[60] The implementation of the agreement was therefore guided by these ideas. For a time there was 'intense experimentation and learning' leading to 'the development of specialised expertise', but 'as the "one-off" aspects of WSA were absorbed into a more on-going routine programme, . . . man-

[59] Joe Roeber, *Social Change at Work*, pp. 65–9.   [60] *Ibid.*, p. 153.

agers having satisfied the requirements of their superiors in introducing the programme turned their interest back to the day-to-day problems of management; unions turned their energies to issues where further concrete benefits could be obtained'.[61] By 1973 the central personnel department was beginning to look in new directions for further incentives to improve performance.

As yet work design is too untested a technique in Britain for any serious assessment to be made of the part which it might ultimately play in industrial relations.

JOINT CONSULTATION AND PARTICIPATION

The term 'employee participation in management', which has come into common usage in recent years, is one of the more opaque expressions in the industrial relations vocabulary. Taken literally, it might be held to include the whole of collective bargaining because, without collective bargaining, many of the issues with which bargaining deals would be decided by management, and collective bargaining therefore gives employee representatives a share in managerial decisions. Usually, however, it is taken to apply to managerial decisions which have not traditionally been subject to collective bargaining. Thus productivity bargaining has been said to recognize 'that workers have a right . . . to participate in the design of any new work system'.[62] The term is therefore used of *extensions* of the frontiers of bargaining, although this gives little indication of the issues which it includes, since the frontiers between collective bargaining and managerial prerogative vary widely over time, and between industries and plants. However, collective bargaining, narrowly defined, is not the only channel for employee participation in managerial decisions. Another technique has been in use for more than half a century—joint consultation.

Joint consultation was the business of the works committees whose establishment had been recommended by the Whitley Committee towards the end of the First World War in order to set up and 'maintain a system of co-operation in . . . workshop matters'.[63] Although many of the committees which had been brought into being in private industry were swept away in the depression of the

---

[61] *Ibid.*, p. 210. [62] McKersie and Hunter, *op. cit.*, p. 334.
[63] See pp. 31–2

early twenties, the inter-war years nevertheless brought important developments. A number of major firms which led the field in personnel management set up and maintained works committees on the Whitley model. Among them were Rowntree and Cadbury and in 1927 they were joined by the new industrial giant, ICI, which proposed to set up committees throughout its plants without reference to the unions. Under union pressure the firm agreed to complete its consultative structure with a Central Advisory Labour Council where managers met senior trade union officers, but shop stewards were not recognized and works committee representatives were elected by and from the whole body of workers regardless of union membership.

This was the model generally adopted when the Second World War brought a new upsurge in workshop democracy. On this occasion the mood on the shop floor was less rebellious than in 1914–18. There was general support for the war effort and for expanding output. The first Joint Production Committees appear to have originated in individual plants late in 1940. By the following summer the engineering unions were demanding their introduction throughout engineering, and the Trades Union Congress had given its blessing to the movement. In February 1942 the Director General of Ordnance Factories made an agreement with the unions for Joint Production Consultative Committees to be set up in all factories operated by the Ministry of Supply, and in the following month the engineering employers and unions made general provision for Joint Production Consultative and Advisory Committees in federated firms. The Ministry of Supply reported that by July 1943 there were 4,169 'joint production committees or similar bodies' operating in private firms in engineering and allied industries, covering two and a half million workers.[64] In addition there were pit production committees in coalmining, site committees in building and similar developments in many other industries.

By the end of the war joint consultation had received ideological support from two very different quarters. The first was the 'human relations school' developed in the United States by Elton Mayo and his colleagues on the basis of their findings from the 'Hawthorne experiment'.[65] They contrasted restriction of output in the 'bank wiring room' with rising output in the 'relay assembly test room'

[64] International Labour Office, *British Joint Production Machinery*, p. 88.
[65] See p. 54.

which they explained by the involvement of the girls in the experiment and the good relations among themselves and with their supervisor.[66] Mayo argued that 'a small society lives in an ordered manner such that the interests of its members are subordinated to the interests of the group'. But industrialization had destroyed this condition, and 'planlessness . . . is becoming characteristic both of individual lives and of communities'.[67] The danger was that informal groups in industry would try to create their own defences against planlessness and in doing so work against the aims of management. The challenge to society was therefore to recreate in industry a situation in which work groups could serve as a means of effective, purposeful and satisfying collaboration. Joint consultation seemed to be an ideal instrument for the purpose, and Mayo's teachings became accepted doctrine among British personnel managers for many years.

The second source of support was the Trades Union Congress. During and after the First World War many British unions adopted the objectives of workers' control or joint control which held that industry in a socialist society should be run by the unions or by joint boards half of whose members should be from the unions and half chosen by the government. Only if workers ran industry through their own organizations, held the proponents of these schemes, could 'wage-slavery' be ended. Their proposals came under attack in the debate over Herbert Morrison's London Passenger Transport Bill under the Labour government of 1929–31. Morrison proposed that members of a board to run a nationalized industry should be selected on their merits, and not as representatives.[68] However, it was not until 1944 that the unions made firm alternative proposals for the achievement of industrial democracy. In that year the General Council of the Trades Union Congress brought out their *Interim Report on Post-War Reconstruction* which accepted Morrison's position, although suggesting that 'experience gained in the collective organisation of Labour is a strong qualification' for board membership. Trade union officers appointed to the boards of nationalized industries should, however, 'surrender any position held in, or formal responsibility to the Trade Union'. But this arrangement by

---

[66] Subsequent re-examination of the Hawthorne experiment suggests that its evidence does not support these conclusions (Alex Carey, 'The Hawthorne Studies: a Radical Criticism').

[67] Elton Mayo, *The Human Problems of an Industrial Civilisation*, pp. 124–5.

[68] Herbert Morrison, *Socialisation and Transport*, 1933.

itself could hardly fulfil the objective of extending 'the influence of workpeople over the policies and purposes of industry' which rested 'primarily on the simple democratic right of workpeople to have a voice in the determination of their industrial destinies'. How was this right to be established now that workers' control and joint control had been rejected? The Council's answer was joint consultation. They pointed to the wartime joint production committees whose value had 'been recognised on all sides'. Consultation should be 'retained as a permanent feature of our industrial organisation' by setting up works councils. This could most easily be done in the public sector for 'in socialised industries there would, of course, be no difficulty in ensuring that such Works' Councils were set up and consulted'.[69]

But the same objectives could also be, and had been, achieved in private firms. There was therefore no automatic link between public ownership and industrial democracy.

In 1946 the Coal Industry Nationalization Act of the post-war Labour government placed an obligation on the National Coal Board to agree with the unions upon joint machinery for consultation on questions of safety, health and welfare, on the organization and conduct of the industry and on other matters of mutual interest.[70] Subsequent nationalization Acts contained similar provisions, and systems of consultative committees were established at workplace, regional and national levels. Meanwhile the government had run into economic difficulties which led to the first postwar incomes policy and the first postwar devaluation. It seemed to them that increased production was as urgent as during the war. In 1947 the National Joint Advisory Council to the Minister of Labour recommended that joint consultative machinery should be set up wherever it did not exist 'for the regular exchange of views between employers and workers on production matters'.[71] In 1948 a survey of 54 industry bargaining bodies conducted by the Ministry showed that twenty-six had agreed to recommend the establishment of joint committees to their members, eight had decided that existing machinery was enough, seventeen wished to leave the matter to local action and three had failed to reach a decision.[72]

---

[69] pp. 7, 21–3.   [70] Section 46.
[71] *Industrial Relations Handbook*, 1944 ed., Supplement No. 3, p. 4.
[72] Ministry of Labour and National Service, *Annual Report*, 1949, p. 110.

After the fall of the government in 1951, or perhaps even before that, joint consultative committees began to decline in numbers and importance. Marsh and Coker estimated that the number of joint production committees in federated engineering establishments fell by a third between 1955 and 1961, when fewer than one in ten federated establishments still had a functioning committee.[73] This decline coincided with a growth in the number and influence of shop stewards. 'Few consequences of workplace bargaining', reported McCarthy,

> have been so well investigated as its effect on joint consultative committees. . . . Either they must change their character and become essentially negotiating committees carrying out functions which are indistinguishable from . . . shop-floor bargaining, or they are boycotted by shop stewards and, as the influence of the latter grows, fall into disuse.[74]

These changes led to revisions in the theory of joint consultation. Previously it had been generally held that consultation and bargaining required separate forms of representation even where both functions were carried on within the plant. The duty of shop stewards was to press for the best possible deal for their members, whereas consultative committee representatives were partners in a continuous process of exchanging information and attitudes so that the decisions taken within the plant could reflect the view of everyone from labourers to senior managers. Bargaining was often sectional, whereas consultation required a single committee representing all grades of employee. Support now began to gather for the view that consultation and negotiation are both parts of a single process of involvement of workers and their representatives in decisions affecting their working lives. Both the practice and the theory of joint consultation seemed to be in disarray.

Interest revived during the seventies. The misfortunes of the British economy cut profits and brought redundancies and closures. Managers had good reason to seek the co-operation of their employees in increasing profits, and unions had an urgent interest in company manpower plans and in proposals for investment which can destroy and create jobs. Although discussion of these issues had long been part of the business of regional and national consultative

---

[73] 'Shop Steward Organisation in the Engineering Industry'.
[74] *The Role of Shop Stewards in British Industrial Relations*, p. 33.

committees in the nationalized industries, they were not subjects of regular dealings between managers and unions in most private companies few of which had company-wide consultative machinery suitable to handle them.

One of the first company councils designed for this purpose was established in GEC by Sir Jack Scamp to handle the series of redundancies and closures which followed the mergers with AEI and English Electric. The union representatives were full-time officers. Perhaps because discussions over these kind of issues at this level seemed to go beyond traditional joint consultation, the word 'participation' came into vogue. When Chrysler and British Leyland set up company consultative arrangements with shop stewards after their government rescue operations, they were therefore called 'participation agreements'. Their prime purpose was to discuss the means of keeping the companies in business; and survival has become an urgent reason for consultation in other companies. In 1977 the Confederation of British Industry reported on the findings of a survey of a sample of their members which showed that 'an enormous amount of consultation and communication takes place in companies of all sizes. . . . The majority of companies have arrangements which give employees and their representatives the *right* to regular information and consultation; and 16% of companies with more than 1,000 employees say they have formal participation agreements.' In addition to traditional topics, discussions covered lay-offs and redundancies, and 'significant minorities of companies also say they consult on recruitment, and in larger companies, on investment, research and development.'[75]

SUPERVISION

One way of evaluating the consequences of the managerial developments which have been reviewed in this chapter is to examine their effect on foremen (or supervisors) for, although line and personnel managers shape industrial relations policies, negotiate agreements and devise procedures, most of their dealings with their employees are conducted through supervisors.

It is generally agreed that there have been considerable changes in the job and status of the foreman since the war, and that most of them

[75] *In Place of Bullock.*

have been to his disadvantage. Growth in the size of plants and companies have diminished his position in the hierarchy. In an undertaking with only one foreman, or with two or three, the foreman reports directly to the boss and is likely to have considerable scope in running his section. In a large concern he comes near the bottom of the managerial hierarchy, and is subjected to a complex body of rules and directives handed down from above.

Rising educational standards of management have diminished the foreman's chances of promotion. A study by the Acton Society Trust analysed seventeen characteristics in the educational and industrial experience of managers, and found that service as a foreman seemed to be the least advantageous to prospects of promotion.[76]

With the growth of specialization, more and more decisions which used to be taken by the foreman now fall within the province of the specialist. The personnel department takes over much of the responsibility for selection, discipline and dismissal. The work study department decides the time in which a job should be done and works out standards of manning. Job evaluation schemes and measured daywork take away the foreman's ability to influence the pay of workers in his section. He remains responsible for the section's performance, but without the freedom he once enjoyed to choose his workers to suit himself, to organize their work as he sees fit, and to offer them incentives and rewards.

Plant bargaining and participation schemes both open up direct lines of communication between shop stewards and higher management. This change has two important consequences. Firstly, decisions taken by the foreman in matters affecting his section may be overriden by higher management on appeal. Secondly, more general decisions affecting industrial relations in the plant may become known to the shop steward and through him to the men in his section before the foreman has been informed.

Besides all these blows to his prestige, the foreman's pay differential has been reduced because 'increasing wages have benefited hourly-paid workers relatively more than their supervisors'.[77] The popular image of the foreman has come to be the 'forgotten man of industry'.

Most of the recent changes in collective bargaining have acceler-

[76] Acton Society Trust, *Management Succession*, pp. 28–9.
[77] National Institute of Industrial Psychology, *The Foreman*, p. 78.

ated the trend. In anticipation of the first productivity deal at Fawley, the chargehands were given staff status. 'They had welcomed this improvement in their position and prospects and it should have predisposed them to look with favour on the reorganisation as a whole.' But in fact there was a

> lack of pronounced enthusiasm for the new order, and quite a widespread and sustained nostalgia for the old. . . . Many of their problems, especially those concerned with the ambiguities in their role and the consequent weakening of their authority, remained unresolved. . . . Their difficulties [were] multiplied by the struggle in which—without their consent—they had become engaged.[78]

During their survey of measured daywork, the Office of Manpower Economics frequently . . . found there was no recognition by management that the supervisor's job would change, or that he should be involved in planning the new payment system. . . . Again few firms deliberately revised the supervisors' job descriptions; in most cases responsibilities evolved in reaction to changing work pressures. . . . In several firms there was considerable discontent over delay in adjustments [to] the pay of supervisors following increases given to the operatives. . . . The case studies showed that in only a few cases did management systematically tackle the problems of supervision arising from MDW.[79]

Work design has brought similar consequences for foremen.

> They have rarely been sufficiently—if at all—involved in exercises like WSA. First, management attention was drawn to shop stewards as the workers' representatives. . . . Secondly, given the opportunity, the shop stewards did all they could to freeze the supervisors out of discussions, fruits of an ancient enmity. . . . Lastly, the supervisors have traditionally been among the most loyal of ICI's employees and their compliance could be taken for granted.

But work design is an even greater threat to the foreman than are productivity bargaining and measured daywork.

---

[78] Flanders, *The Fawley Productivity Agreements*, pp. 211–12.
[79] *Measured Daywork*, p. 38.

Self-supervision, autonomous working . . . have to reduce the role of supervisor. And to loss of authority was added the insecurity of severe redundancies; between 1965 and 1973, the numbers of supervisors dropped by 28% while that of weekly staff dropped by 14%.[80]

The most recent *Workplace Industrial Relations* survey provides a check on this dismal account of the position of the supervisor. 'By-passing' the foreman is unquestionably common in British industry. About two-thirds of the foremen surveyed said that stewards were supposed to raise an issue with them before taking it higher, and almost as many said that the stewards were supposed to ask permission before approaching higher management. About two-thirds of the latter group said that there were ways in which the stewards could gain access to higher managers direct. The most common way was to go to see the manager or phone him, but he could be stopped on the shop floor, or the matter could be raised at a meeting or taken up through the convener. In addition three-quarters of the senior managers said that individual workers could gain access to managers by similar methods without going through the foreman.[81]

Only 42 per cent of the foremen said that their industrial relations decisions were always backed by higher managers; 36 per cent said that their decisions were usually backed; and 17 per cent said 'sometimes'. On the other hand, 64 per cent of foremen thought that managers kept them 'well enough informed if and when they decided issues with stewards', and 52 per cent thought that higher managers fully appreciated their problems in dealing with stewards. Twenty-eight per cent of foremen (40 per cent in plants with five hundred or more employees) said that they had to refer some issues raised by stewards to higher managers although they felt they should have been free to settle them themselves. The topics most frequently mentioned were pay and discipline. But only 7 per cent said that they were dissatisfied with their authority to deal with issues raised by stewards; 45 per cent were fairly satisfied; and 42 per cent were satisfied.[82]

The latest *Workplace Industrial Relations* survey asked no questions about the promotion prospects and pay of foremen. The 1966 survey

[80] Roeber, *Social Change at Work*, pp. 281–2.
[81] *Workplace Industrial Relations 1973*, pp. 46, 51.   [82] *Ibid.*, pp. 22–3.

found that 69 per cent of its sample of foremen were interested in promotion, and about half of these thought there was a reasonable hope of it. The average *net* income of the sample exceeded that of the sample of trade union members by 24 per cent and that of non-members by 37 per cent, but that does not prove that some super-visors were not earning less than some of the workers under their control.[83]

These findings demonstrate that the foreman's lot is far from trouble-free, but the picture they paint is not entirely black. They indicate considerable variety. It may be that the supervisor's job is not generally more vexatious or anxious than many other jobs in many industries and services, but that his problems are particularly aggravated where industrial relations tensions are most acute—in strike-prone firms, where shop-floor pressure is high and where industrial relations and collective bargaining are experiencing rapid change.

Nearly thirty years ago a study of foremen concluded that: 'It has been said again and again that the supervisor holds a key position in industry. At the moment, he is holding that position against consid-erable odds.'[84] The importance of the supervisor has continued to be reiterated over the years since then, but in many companies the odds have been stacked against him more than ever. This might be evi-dence of the stupidity and incompetence of those who run British industry. But it could also be that the traditional job of the foreman is no longer tenable where 'the interface between management and the shopfloor'[85] is subject to acute pressure, and that responsibility for performance must be placed on someone else, whether higher man-agement or the workers themselves.

STYLES OF MANAGEMENT

So far this chapter has dealt with changes in managerial approaches to industrial relations over time. Earlier chapters have drawn atten-tion to important differences in industrial relations behaviour from one undertaking to another, and to some of the causes of divergence. Managers in large plants handle industrial relations in a different way

---

[83] *Workplace Industrial Relations 1966*, pp. 98–9.
[84] National Institute of Industrial Psychology, *The Foreman*, p. 104.
[85] Roeber, *op. cit.*, p. 281.

from their colleagues in small plants; the conduct of industrial relations in multi-plant companies which centralize personnel matters differs from that of decentralized companies; and many characteristics of industrial relations in the public sector contrast with those of the private sector. These variations might be described as different styles of managing industrial relations.

At one time Joan Woodward took the view that technology was a major determinant of managerial style. She classified production systems into three types: unit and small-batch production to customers' orders, including the making of prototypes; large-batch and mass production, classified together and including assembly lines; and process production which covers continuous flow production of liquids, gases and crystalline substances and the batch production of chemicals. Using evidence from a survey of a hundred firms she argued that the organization of a firm is shaped by its system of production. The main contrast is between small batch and process production on the one hand and large batch or mass production on the other. The last two systems tend towards more rigid organization and clear-cut definition of duties, along with elaborate production control procedures, whereas in small batch and process systems organization is flexible and the exercise of control is a relatively easy matter. This has its consequences for industrial relations, since 'the intractable problems of human relations were concentrated in the technical area where production control procedures were most complex, and sometimes more rigorously applied'.[86]

Several years later, however, further research led her to argue that it was better to classify production systems according to the control process than by technology. The categories which she suggested were: unitary and personal controls, where one man effectively runs the plant, using 'his personal authority both to direct and check' the work of others; personal and fragmented controls, where several managers exercise personal control in different departments; mechanical and fragmented controls, where there are mechanisms 'for ensuring that what ought to be done has been done, for detecting deviations, and for taking any corrective action that may be necessary . . . as opposed to random orders or *ad hoc* prescriptions', but these mechanisms are still applied department by department; and, finally, mechanical and unitary controls, where the control mechanisms are unified into a single control system for the undertaking as a whole.

[86] Joan Woodward, *Industrial Organisation: Theory and Practice*, pp. 180–1.

This classification had the advantage that it could distinguish the system of management in one large batch or mass production undertaking from that of another; whereas classification by technology could not do so, although 'there was much more variation in the kind of managerial control applied' than in small batch or process production. When the findings of the original survey were reclassified into the new categories they showed a high concentration of unit and small batch production in the personal and unitary category with a minority under the personal and fragmented heading; there was a very high concentration of process production under the mechanical and unitary heading; and large batch and mass production undertakings were spread across all four control systems, although more were located in the two fragmented types than in the unitary types. Consequently there appeared 'to be more freedom of choice for the management of batch production firms than for other categories, in deciding what kind of control processes to use'.[87] This version of her theory comes much closer to the analysis which has been adopted in this book. Although industrial relations are influenced by production systems, the latter are not determined by technology alone, but also by the choice of control process. This process is an integral feature of managerial organization, which in turn is influenced by such factors as size of plant, centralization and decentralization in the company, and the pressures of public ownership.

The most renowned account of differences of style in the management of industrial relations, however, is Alan Fox's distinction between 'unitary' and 'pluralistic' frames of reference. The first is a structure with 'one source of authority and one focus of loyalty', like a team whose members 'strive jointly towards a common objective, each pulling his weight to the best of his ability'. Managers who accept this frame of reference, he says, 'can be found deploring any reference to "the two sides of industry" in the belief that such talk encourages the wrong attitudes'.[88] The pluralistic frame of reference recognizes both 'the legitimacy and justification of trade unions in our society' and 'the reality of work-group interests which conflict quite legitimately' with those of management and provide a rational basis for

restrictive practices and resistance to change. . . . This leads on

---

[87] Joan Woodward (ed.), *Industrial Organisation: Behaviour and Control*, pp. 39, 48–9, 52–5.   [88] *Industrial Sociology and Industrial Relations*, pp. 3, 12.

directly to the necessity of the pluralistic frame of reference for the development of more sophisticated bargaining techniques designed to reconcile management and work-group interests at a higher level of mutual advantage. Such techniques are now emerging under the name of 'productivity bargaining'.[89]

In practice neither frame of reference is commonly found in its pure form. 'Most employers and managers have been obliged to accept trade unionism'—'as a necessary protection for the worker in the economic aspect of his employment'. But recognition of the role of trade unions in regulating *market* relations in this way often went along with a rejection of their role 'within the workplace itself in regulating *managerial* relations, i.e. the exercise of management authority in deploying, organizing and disciplining the labour force after it has been hired'.[90] This distinction roughly coincides with the frontier between what were once recognized as the areas appropriate to collective bargaining and those which came within the scope of joint consultation. When Fox was writing in 1966 this frontier had for many years been pressed back on the shop floor as workplace organizations extended their control over manning, work organization and methods, and the rules governing overtime and piecework; and economic pressures and government incomes policies were already pushing managers into recognizing the right of unions within the plant to negotiate over many aspects of managerial relations through productivity and measured daywork agreements.

Fox's frames of reference are therefore not of much use in drawing distinctions among the majority of sizable British firms which accept that trade unions have a substantial role to play in the regulation of both market and managerial relations—although they still indicate some of the differences between these firms and the firms which refuse to recognize unions or grant them a very limited degree of recognition. Today the main value of his analysis is in examining variations in managerial attitudes within firms. Recognition of the right of unions to share in the regulation of some aspects of managerial relations does not imply that managers have fully accepted the pluralist frame of reference with all its implications. Some managers, for example, were actively warding off trade unionism among their white collar employees at the same time as they negotiated productivity agreements with the unions representing their manual work-

<hr>

[89] *Ibid.*, pp. 7, 10.   [90] *Ibid.*, pp. 7, 10.

ers. Most managers shift from one frame of reference to another according to the issue before them; and the appropriate frame for each type of issue changes as the frontiers of job regulation move under the pressure of events—with a time-lag. The managers who appeared to be sharing power effectively yesterday may be today's autocrats unless they modify their attitudes again. The storm of anger and resentment with which British managers greeted the proposals of the Bullock Committee for equal representation of shareholders and trade unions on the boards of companies with more than two thousand employees demonstrated that there were still some issues which the great majority of them interpret through a unitary frame of reference.

Size, centralization of control and public ownership therefore remain the main explanatory variables available to account for differences in styles of industrial relations management between one undertaking and another; but that is not to say that they offer adequate explanations or provide satisfactory tools of analysis. The truth of the matter is that the study of management in industrial relations is in a primitive state.

Chapter 5

TRADE UNIONS

STRUCTURE

In relation to trade unions the word 'structure' usually carries a narrower meaning than is customary in the study of organizations. It is confined to their morphology or external structure—the coverage by each union of industries and occupations. Their internal structure—the relationship between their parts—is commonly called trade union government.

Categories are available for the analysis of trade union structure. Traditionally there were three: craft, industrial and general. If the first of them is restricted to unions of apprenticed craftsmen, then it becomes one type within a larger category of occupational unions. H. A. Turner has suggested that the concepts of 'open' and 'closed' unions might be more useful analytical tools for many purposes. Open unions are those which recruit over a fairly broad front and closed unions restrict membership to one or two grades of worker.[1] John Hughes proposes supplementary categories of 'sectoral' and 'sectoral-general' unions as well.[2] A sectoral union recruits workers in several industries within a given sector of the economy; and a sectoral-general union is open to all workers within such a sector. But all these categories are of very limited value in describing the unparalleled complexity of British union structure. There is no acceptable alternative to examining individual unions in turn.

Since, according to the official returns, there are 462 British trade unions,[3] it is impossible to examine them all in a single chapter. But

[1] H. A. Turner, *Trade Union Growth, Structure and Policy*.

[2] John Hughes, *Trade Union Structure and Government* (1), pp. 8–9.

[3] This is the 1976 figure. Unless otherwise stated all membership statistics used in this chapter are derived from the figures of unions and union membership collected by the Department of Employment for 1976. The returns for 1977 were not all available when the manuscript went to the printer.

most of them are very small: more than half have less than a thousand members. Almost 88 per cent of total union membership is in the 39 unions with over fifty thousand members.[4] A brief survey of the structures of unions with over fifty thousand members can therefore serve as a fair introduction to British union structure in general. They can be separated into three groups for the purpose, although it should be emphasized that these groups are certainly not analytical categories. The public sector unions constitute the first group, and the membership of the eighteen public sector unions with more than fifty thousand members is set out in Table 4.

The National and Local Government Officers Association started out as a professional association for senior local government officers, and the National Union of Public Employees as a breakaway union for manual employees of local authorities. The Public Employees now recruit manual workers employed in the health service, by water authorities and by universities as well as by local and education authorities. The National and Local Government Officers recruit all grades of white collar employees in local authorities and water authorities; most grades of white collar employees in the National Health Service; administrative, clerical and supervisory staff in gas and electricity supply and in road passenger transport; and clerical and supervisory staff in universities. They also have groups of members in one or two other public services. Both unions recruit nurses, but the major unions for nurses are the Confederation of Health Service Employees, which also recruits manual hospital employees and is particularly strong in psychiatric hospitals; and the Royal College of Nursing, which is not affiliated to the Trades Union Congress and still regards itself as a professional association as much as, or more than, a trade union.[5]

The National Union of Teachers is the main union for schoolteachers, with particular strength in primary schools. The National Association of Schoolmasters and Union of Women Teachers is a

[4] The official returns treat the technical administrative and supervisory section of the Amalgamated Union of Engineering Workers as a separate union (although the foundry section, also with over 50,000 members, is not so treated). All three are regarded as one union here, so that the total would be 38, except that the official returns exclude the Police Federation on the grounds that it is not a union, whereas it is included here, so that the total becomes 39 again.

[5] Before 1974 professional associations either had Royal Charters or registered as companies. Either way they could not legally be trade unions. However, the Trade Union and Labour Relations Act 1974 permitted them to be, and to seek certification as, trade unions.

Table 4

Public Sector Unions with over Fifty Thousand Members

	Membership 000s
National and Local Government Officers Association	683
National Union of Public Employees	651
National Union of Teachers	289
National Union of Mineworkers	260
Civil and Public Services Association	231
Union of Post Office Workers	201
Confederation of Health Service Employees	200
National Union of Railwaymen	180
Post Office Engineering Union	125
Police Federation	109
Society of Civil and Public Servants	105
Iron and Steel Trades Confederation	104
Institution of Professional Civil Servants	100
National Association of Schoolmasters and Union of Women Teachers	86
Royal College of Nursing	81
Transport Salaried Staffs Association	74
Inland Revenue Staff Federation	64
National Association of Teachers in Further and Higher Education	60
Total	3603

recent amalgamation of two unions which recruit mainly in secondary schools. The National Association of Teachers in Further and Higher Education covers teachers in further education colleges, technical colleges, and polytechnics, but does not include university teachers. They have their own union.

Apart from managers and some supervisory and clerical staff, the National Union of Mineworkers is the sole trade union in coalmining. Their unchallenged position among the manual employees of the Coal Board was achieved by a special arrangement with the Engineers, the Electricians, the Transport and General Workers, and the General and Municipal Workers, each of which had some thousands of members in the industry before nationalization, whereby the Mineworkers represent them in all industrial matters, leaving administrative and friendly benefits to their original unions.

Most civil servants are members of unions which cater for a group of civil service grades across all government departments. The largest is the Civil and Public Services Association which covers mainly clerical grades; the Society of Civil and Public Servants recruits mainly executive grades; by contrast the Institution of Professional Civil Servants is the union for professional, scientific and technical staff in all grades from the highest to the lowest. There are also one or two civil service unions which cater for particular classes in a single department, such as the Inland Revenue Staff Federation for tax officers. The inclusion of 'public services' in the title of the clerical and executive unions dates back to the time when the Post Office was hived off, for both unions have members there who ceased to be civil servants. The two main Post Office unions are the Union of Post Office Workers, which recruits postmen, sorters, telephonists and counter clerks, and the Post Office Engineering Union which includes engineering and related staff from labourers to technicians.

The National Union of Railwaymen and the Transport Salaried Staffs are the two main unions for railway employees, although the Associated Society of Locomotive Engineers and Firemen also commands a good deal of attention. Both of them have a number of interests elsewhere in public transport due to the wide ramifications of the old railway companies into London Transport, road transport (both passenger and freight), docks, inland waterways, shipping, travel agents and elsewhere. The unions followed the companies and have retained their positions. The Police Federation's official status as a trade union is debatable because the Police Act 1919 which constituted it debars members of a police force from membership 'of any trade union, or of any association having for its objects, or one of its objects, to control or influence the pay, pensions or conditions of service of any police force',[6] but it unquestionably acts the part of a trade union and was for some years included in the official trade union returns. Finally, although a dozen other unions are recognized by the Steel Corporation, the Iron and Steel Trades Confederation is the major union for both manual and white collar employees in the industry. It has for some time been discussing a merger with the Steel Industry Management Association. The Confederation also has a

[6] These words were repeated in the Police Act 1964.

relatively small group of members in related branches of the engineering industry.

One of these unions—the Mineworkers—has a reasonable claim to be considered an industrial union. The Railwaymen and the Iron and Steel Confederation make the same claim, but, because other unions recruit large numbers of railwaymen and steelworkers, it is an aspiration rather than an accomplished fact. Several of them can be classified as occupational unions since they cover professions rather than industries. They include the teachers' unions, the Police Federation, the Royal College of Nursing, and the Inland Revenue Staff Federation. The other civil service unions, however, must be considered 'grade unions', for they cover a wide range of occupations whose common feature is that they are included in a band of grades, or a group of associated bands, by the civil service grading system. The Post Office Engineers might fall into the same class, but the range of grades and occupations in the Union of Post Office Workers is more heterogeneous than in any of the civil service unions in the list. The National and Local Government Officers is a sectoral' union since its field of operation is the public services; and the Public Employees might even be classed as 'sectoral-general'. However, there is one characteristic which they all share. Despite difficulties of classification, the main principle on which each one is constructed is fairly readily comprehended; and that is more than can be said of many other large British unions.

Nevertheless there are some unions in private industry with relatively simple structures. Eleven of them with more than fifty thousand members are listed in Table 5. Three are from the printing and paper group of trades. The Graphical Association has brought together most of the former craft unions in print, and is the main union for skilled (and for the most part apprenticed) printing workers. The Society of Operative Printers is predominantly a union for white collar and less-skilled manual newspaper workers, although it has skilled members as well, and recruits outside the newspapers. The Graphical and Allied Trades also include skilled workers—for example bookbinders and papermakers—but their membership is mainly among the less-skilled in newspapers, magazines, general printing, and paper and board making. Among these eleven unions they have perhaps the least claim to be classed among unions with a simple structure.

Four unions are in the clothing and textiles group of industries.

The Tailors and Garment Workers approximate to an industrial union for the clothing industry other than hosiery, and the Hosiery and Knitwear Workers to an industrial union for hosiery. The Footwear Leather and Allied Trades come near to constituting an industrial union for footwear, although they have interests outside. The Dyers Bleachers and Textile Workers cover both the manufacture of woollen or partly woollen cloth, and the finishing stages of the textile trades in general—cotton, wool and manmade fibres.

Originally a craft union, the Bakers became an industrial union for that section of food manufacture in England and Wales which is now expanding into other branches of food manufacture. There is a separate Scottish union. The Agricultural and Allied Workers are the main union for farmworkers, including factory farms, although the Transport and General Workers also have a sizable agricultural section. The major section of the Furniture and Allied Trades was an industrial union for the furniture industry until amalgamation with the Woodcutting Machinists gave them wider interests. Banking is a

Table 5

Private Industry Unions with relatively
Simple Structures and over Fifty
Thousand Members

	Membership 000s
Society of Graphical and Allied Trades	194
National Union of Tailors and Garment Workers	113
National Union of Bank Employees	112
National Graphical Association	108
Furniture Timber and Allied Trades Union	87
National Union of Agricultural and Allied Workers	85
National Union of Hosiery and Knitwear Workers	72
National Union of Footwear Leather and Allied Trades	67
National Union of Dyers Bleachers and Textile Workers	59
Bakers Food and Allied Workers' Union	56
National Society of Operative Printers Graphical and Media Personnel	53
Total	1006

white collar industry, so that the Bank Employees claim to be both a white collar union and an industrial union for banking; but the separate staff associations of the various banks also account for a large number of bank employees.

The membership of these eleven unions is only a relatively small part of total union membership in manufacturing and the private services. Another relatively small part is to be found in unions with less than fifty thousand members. But the majority of trade unionists in these two sectors, and a large minority of public sector trade unionists as well, are members of ten 'conglomerate' unions with over fifty thousand members. The details are set out in Table 6.

The four largest of these unions have members in almost every major industry in the country. With the Engineers[7] and Electricians

Table 6

*Conglomerate Unions with over Fifty
Thousand Members*

	Membership 000s
Transport and General Workers Union	1930
Amalgamated Union of Engineering Workers	1412
General and Municipal Workers Union	916
Electrical Electronic Telecommunication and Plumbing Union	420
Union of Shop Distributive and Allied Workers	413
Association of Scientific Technical and Managerial Staffs	396
Union of Construction Allied Trades and Technicians	294
Association of Professional Executive Clerical and Computer Staff	142
Amalgamated Society of Boilermakers Shipwrights Blacksmiths and Structural Workers	128
National Union of Sheet Metal Workers Coppersmiths Heating and Domestic Engineers	75
Total	6136

[7] Henceforth only the Amalgamated Union of Engineering Workers is referred to as the 'Engineers'. The dominant engineering section of the union (formerly the Amalgamated Engineering Union) is called 'Engineers (engineering section)'.

the main reason for this is that almost every industry employs skilled maintenance fitters and electricians, relatively few of whom are non-unionists or members of other unions. In addition, in a good many instances both unions insist that their members must be supervised by members of the union, so that they include foremen in many industries; the Engineers are the union for draughtsmen, and many industries employ draughtsmen; and it is the normal practice of the Electricians to recruit electricians' mates in any industry. Both unions also have their strongholds. Not far off a million members of the Engineers come from the engineering group of industries where the union caters for a range of skilled manual operations, draughtsmen and allied grades, some supervisors, and—in competition with other unions—large numbers of less-skilled workers, both men and women. The Electricians have three strongholds. Theirs is the only union in electrical contracting, and the main union in electricity supply, but their largest single group of members is in engineering. In some electrical engineering plants they recruit less-skilled workers of both sexes.

In manufacturing the two general unions cater predominantly for production and ancillary manual workers other than craftsmen, especially in the engineering, food manufacturing, chemicals, and building materials groups of industries, but they have groups of members elsewhere, for example in the textile groups of industries. The Transport and General Workers are the dominant union in road passenger transport, road haulage, and the docks. The General and Municipal Workers is the recognized union for much of the catering group of industries, but it has so far had only modest success in recruitment. Both unions have an interest in construction; in local government; in the health service; in gas, electricity and water supply; and in goverment industrial establishments.

Both unions have substantial white collar sections, each with its own title: the Association of Clerical Technical and Supervisory Staffs in the Transport and General Workers; and the Managerial Administrative Technical and Supervisory Association in the General and Municipal Workers Union. Both unions also include sizable groups of craftsmen. The largest group in the General and Municipal Workers is the gasfitters; and in the Transport and General Workers the plasterers.

There are two white collar conglomerates: the Scientific Technical and Managerial Staffs and the Professional Executive Clerical and

Computer Staff. Both of them recruit every grade of white collar employee (as also do the white collar sections of the two general unions) but the first caters mainly for supervisors, technicians, and managers, except in insurance and banking where it is primarily a clerical union; and the second is predominantly clerical. Both of them have their largest group of members in engineering, but the remainder are scattered over a wide range of industries including some in the public sector. The Scientific Technical and Managerial Staffs has, for example, considerable groups of members in civil air transport, the health service, and universities; and the Professional Executive Clerical and Computer Staff in coalmining and other nationalized industries.

The Shop Distributive and Allied Workers are primarily a shop assistants' and shop managers' union but they also represent manual workers in a number of manufacturing industries, mainly in the food manufacturing and chemical groups. One of their constituents was a union for co-operative employees which recruited workers in co-operative-owned factories as well as co-operative shops, and amalgamated with a localized general union with members in many manufacturing plants.

The Construction Allied Trades and Technicians have brought together most but not all of the one-time independent building crafts including carpenters, bricklayers, painters, and stonemasons. They also compete with the general unions—mainly the Transport and General Workers—for non-craft building employees. In addition, their members are employed in most major industries as building maintenance workers; carpenters are employed as production workers in, for example, the finishing of ships and the construction of car bodies; and bricklayers are employed in the lining and relining of steel furnaces.

Similarly the Boilermakers are an amalgamation of a number of originally shipbuilding crafts. With changing technology, welding has emerged as the main skill, and with the decline of shipbuilding there is more demand for welders in engineering than in shipbuilding. In addition the union's members are employed on maintenance in a large number of industries. The Sheet Metal Workers cover an even more diverse group of skills, straddling engineering and construction; and they also have widely scattered groups of members employed in maintenance.

A further contrast may be drawn between the public sector unions and the rest. Twelve of the eighteen public sector unions in Table 4 are white collar unions; and, given that several other unions in the table have substantial white collar membership, white collar members account for about two-thirds of the total membership of those eighteen unions. By contrast, of the twenty-one unions in Tables 5 and 6, only four are white collar or predominantly white collar, three of them conglomerates. Even when allowance is made for the white collar sections of the remaining unions, white collar workers cannot account for more than a fifth of the total membership of the twenty-one unions. One reason for the contrast is that the conglomerates between them include large numbers of manual employees in the public sector, and relatively few white collar workers there.

ITS CAUSES

How did this bizarre and complex structure come about? The first reason is that the British trade union movement is the oldest in the world and its present structure is an inheritance from the nineteenth century. At that time unions were mainly organizations of skilled workers, either apprenticed craftsmen or the top men in promotion lines. Union structure for both groups was dictated by the way they went about their business. Craftsmen strove to reserve the skilled jobs for themselves and place all other workers at a distance. They wanted all craftsmen in the union, and everyone else excluded. Top men, by contrast, could easily be replaced by the next men in the line. Their position depended on the strict enforcement of the promotion rules. They wanted all other workers in the line to be in the union and subject to union discipline, preferably in a subordinate capacity.

Mighty unions were constructed on these principles. They provided substantial protection for skilled workers. But they did nothing for less-skilled workers in the craft trades and they had no lesson to offer industries in which there was not a sufficiently large and powerful group of skilled workers to build a union to one of these two models. Hence labourers' unions came into existence. With no principle of organization to restrict them they strung together groups of labourers in craft industries with groups of recruits from previously unorganized industries and services. After the outburst of 'new unionism' in 1889 they shrank back into small and fragile organizations for the next twenty years, although the craft unions still confined their recruitment to skilled workers. In 1911 there began a decade of union growth from 2.5 million members to over 8 million by 1920. Naturally the increase in membership was greatest in areas where the unions had previously been weakest, and the labourers' unions—now renamed general unions—grew from barely a hundred thousand members to over 1.5 million during the decade.

Nevertheless the strength of the craft unions enabled them to recruit skilled maintenance workers almost everywhere they could be found; and, as increasing mechanization augmented the need for maintenance, they became a power in many industries besides those in which they had originated. But mechanization also decreased the demand for skilled production workers, especially in engineering; and in 1926 the Engineers finally resolved to open their ranks to all classes of male engineering workers. Within a few years they were recruiting energetically among less-skilled workers in the car industry and other sections of engineering, and in the Second World War they opened membership to women as well. The Electricians and other craft unions followed their lead. Having opened their ranks too late to prevent the development of the general unions, the craft unions did so when the result was bound to be a further complication of union structure.

With the growth of white collar employment, trade unionism among white collar workers was already an important issue by the end of the First World War. In the public sector, with its clearly demarcated civil and local government services, and the separation of civil servants into distinct grades each with its separate entry requirements, the pattern of trade union organization followed the structure of the services. But there were no such guidelines to follow in private industry. At first white collar unions in private employment were guided by occupational boundaries. One organized clerical workers, another draughtsmen, a third foremen and a fourth laboratory technicians, without regard for industrial boundaries. But all of them except the draughtsmen remained weak until long after the Second World War. They consisted of scattered groups of members in plants and companies all over the country. Where one of them had organized a group of members there was every reason to recruit workers in related white collar occupations in the same plant, if they could, for the unions badly needed members and the workers would otherwise probably have remained unorganized. Thus they became conglomerates with little regard for either occupational or industrial boundaries. The one exception, the draughtsmen, later merged with a conglomerate, the Engineers. But, because white collar workers were already well-organized in most of the public sector, these unions made relatively little impact there.

Thus British trade union structure had taken on something recognizably like its current shape as long as fifty years ago; and was even more like it by the end of the Second World War. But there were two important causes of further change: amalgamation; and growth and decline.

Amalgamation is likely to meet with opposition in any organization. Whatever its advantages, a good many individuals and groups may lose by it. A trade union amalgamation can lead to a merging of branches with consequent loss of status and income for some branch secretaries; and mergers of districts entailing the abolition of district posts and the disbanding of district committees. Rights of representation at conference, elections to the executive, and opportunities to compete for full-time posts may all be affected. Since the disadvantages are immediate and evident, whereas the gains are mostly long-term and hypothetical, organizational interests at the lower levels of the unions usually favour the *status quo*. However, things may be different at the top. Full-time officers in a declining union may want a merger to protect their jobs and pensions. Trade union leaders are respected for the votes at their command, and the quickest route to more members is amalgamation. Leaders may try to convince their members that a merger will bring more bargaining strength, more adequate services, and more secure financial benefits; they may promise that rationalization will not be set in hand for several years after the merger; and they may be able to promise important posts in the new union to key individuals. One or two amalgamations can start a competitive race as individual unions strive not to be left behind. Consequently the structural history of British trade unionism records long periods of stagnation interspersed with bursts of amalgamation. The first came after the First World War, aided by an amendment to the law in 1917 to ease the legal requirements for union amalgamation. Its most notable products were the Transport and General Workers in 1921 and the General and Municipal Workers in 1924. The second was set off by a further change in the law in 1964. It has had relatively little impact in the public sector, although the Schoolmasters have joined forces with the Women Teachers and several small civil service unions have been absorbed by their larger associates; or in the unions listed in Table 5, despite one or two absorptions there also. Its main impact has been on the conglomerates. The Construction Allied Trades and Technicians and the Scientific Technical and Managerial Staffs have been created by it; the structure of the Boilermakers and Sheet Metal Workers has been substantially changed; the formation of the Amalgamated Union of Engineering Workers gave the former Amalgamated Engineering Union a substantial white collar section; the Transport and General Workers have taken over the Vehicle Builders, the Plasterers and the Chemical Workers; and the Electricians have absorbed the Plumbers. Accordingly, although the total number of British unions fell from 1,323 in 1900 to 664 in 1960 and 462 in 1976, the consequence has not been a rationalization of trade union structure but increasing complexity due to the further diversification of the conglomerates.[8]

Total trade union density reached a peak in 1948 with 45 per cent of the labour force (9.4 million members). Membership increased slowly over the next twenty years but not so fast as the labour force, so that by 1968 trade union density was 43 per cent. Then began a new period of growth to 12.4 million and a density of over 50 per cent by 1976. The increase in 1969 and 1970 was attributed to the 'wages explosion' which followed the decay of the Labour government's incomes policy; and subsequent investigation confirms this explanation. Bain and Elsheikh have constructed an economic model of union growth which indicates that the rates of change of pay and prices have been highly significant determinants of growth during the whole period since figures became available in 1892. Their model also accounts for the failure of union growth, although continuing, to maintain its pace after 1970. The rate of inflation continued to rise, but the model shows that the impact of rising prices on union growth begins to lose its force after they pass 4 per cent a year; and

---

[8] According to the records of the Department of Employment, 27 unions with more than five thousand members were absorbed into larger unions as a result of amalgamations during the years 1965–74. Membership at the time of the mergers totalled approximately 550,000. Sixteen of them, with about 400,000 members in all, joined conglomerates. If the merger which formed the Amalgamated Union of Engineering Workers had been included, the conglomerates would have accounted for eighteen unions and about 550,000 members out of 29 unions with 700,000 members.

unemployment, which has a significant negative effect on union growth, began to rise.[9]

The twenty years of stagnation in total union membership between 1948 and 1968 were not a period of stability in the composition of the total, and subsequent growth has also been unequally distributed. Manual trade union membership has remained almost stable, but manual density has increased with the decline in manual employment, from 51 per cent in 1948 to 58 per cent in 1974. Meanwhile white collar membership has more than doubled, but a large part of the increase is due to the expansion in white collar employment, and the rise in density was only a little faster than for manual unions, from 30 per cent to 39 per cent. The number of women in trade unions nearly doubled between 1948 and 1974, and density rose from 26 per cent to 37 per cent, a good deal faster than the increase in density for men. This change was not due only to the disproportionate number of women in white collar employment, for women also provided a rising share of manual employees and trade unionists over the period, while the number of male manual trade unionists fell, although not so fast as the decline in the male manual labour force.

These overall changes were accompanied by considerably larger changes in individual industries and industry groups. The main changes in the size of the labour force in major industries or groups of industries are given in Table 7, and the most striking changes in union densities are set out in Table 8. Most of the major industries not included in these tables recorded a modest growth in employment and a modest growth in union density over the period, although there were some modest falls as well. The figures help to account for some of the changes in the membership of major unions set out in Table 9 which records the growth between 1948 and 1974 of the fifteen unions with the highest membership at the end of the period.

Many of the unions in Table 9 experienced one or more amalgamations between 1948 and 1974. Most of these, however, were absorptions by a major union of comparatively small unions, and in those instances the membership of the major union in 1948 is compared with the membership of the amalgamated union in 1974. Examples are the Engineers, the Electricians, and the Transport and General Workers. In two cases, however, amalgamation has created

[9] Bain and Elsheikh, *Union Growth and the Business Cycle*, Chapter 4.

Table 7

*Main Changes in Employment in
Major Industries 1948–74*

	Percentage Change
Health	+123
Education and Local Government	+115
Insurance, Banking and Finance	+60
Post Office and Telecommunications	+44
Distribution	+30
Textiles	−36
Agriculture	−47
Coalmining	−61
Railways	−68

a new union: the Scientific Technical and Managerial Staffs, and the Construction Allied Trades and Technicians. The 1948 membership figure for the first adds together the members of the Association of Scientists Supervisors Executives and Technicians and of the Scien-

Table 8

*Main Changes in Union Density in Major
Industries 1948–74*

	Density 1948	Density 1974
Road Transport[10]	60	95
Gas, Electricity and Water	68	92
National Government	66	91
Education and Local Government	62	86
Metals and Engineering	50	69
Health	39	61
Clothing	34	60
Insurance, Banking and Finance	32	45
Chemicals	30	51
Construction	45	27

[10] These and other figures for union density quoted in this chapter are drawn from Price and Bain, 'Trade Union Growth Revisited'. They note that union density for road transport is overstated because they could not separate road haulage members of the Transport and General Workers employed by hauliers from those employed by manufacturing concerns. Haulage workers employed in manufacturing are included in the employment figures for the relevant manufacturing industry.

tific Workers, the two unions which combined twenty years later to form the present union. For the second the 1948 figure is the combined membership of the Woodworkers, the Painters, and the Building Trade Workers. Apart from these two unions, the table records without distinction growth due to mergers and growth from recruitment.

The decline of the Mineworkers and the Railwaymen is accounted for by the fall in the labour force in coalmining and the railways. Both rising employment and increasing union density in local government and the health service explain the exceptional growth record of the Public Employees and the National and Local Government Officers. Much more modest growth in the Civil and Public Services Association is due to an increase in union density more than offsetting a relatively small decline in national govern-

Table 9

Change in Membership 1948–74 of the Fifteen Largest Unions (in 1974)

	Percentage Change
Association of Scientific Technical and Managerial Staffs	+1055
National Union of Public Employees	+239
National and Local Goverment Officers Association	+209
Electrical Electronic Telecommunication and Plumbing Union	+128
Amalgamated Union of Engineering Workers	+92
Society of Graphical and Allied Trades	+70
Transport and General Workers Union	+46
Civil and Public Services Association	+41
National Union of Teachers	+41
Union of Post Office Workers	+29
General and Municipal Workers	+8
Union of Shop Distributive and Allied Workers	+3
Union of Construction Allied Trades and Technicians	−29
National Union of Mineworkers	−58
National Union of Railwaymen	−62
Total Trade Union Membership	+26

ment employment. Intermediate growth records for the Engineers and the Graphical and Allied Trades can be largely explained by a combination of increasing union densities and a moderate growth in employment in engineering and in the printing and paper group.

In several instances the trends in union growth appear to run counter to the change in employment and density. Despite rising density, the Post Office Workers increased in numbers at a slower rate than their industry group. The reason is that the expansion was on the telecommunication side of the Post Office. The Union of Shop Distributive and Allied Workers barely grew at all in an expanding industry.[11] But their stronghold was the co-operatives which were declining while total employment in distribution increased. The Teachers' growth was modest in a fast-growing industry, but the most rapid growth was of ancillary workers, not teaching staff, and the Teachers' stronghold was in primary education which expanded less rapidly than secondary or higher education. The Construction Allied Trades and Technicians lost members in an expanding industry because of the growth of self-employment.

Figures for changes in union density by industry conceal an exceptionally rapid increase in union density among white collar employees in manufacturing between 1968 and 1974, from 11 per cent to 32 per cent. This, together with the continued switch from manual to white collar employment, helps to explain the almost astronomic growth rate of the Scientific Technical and Managerial Staffs. A continuing growth in the demand for electricians in almost every industry helps to explain the growth of their union.

The wide spread of general union membership over most major industries makes it almost impossible to account for the growth of the two general unions by changes in employment and union density in individual industries, but it is perhaps significant that their combined growth rate is close to the growth rate of total trade union membership. Among the reasons for the widening lead of the Transport and General Workers over their rival general union are: the far greater success of the Transport and General Workers in attracting smaller unions into amalgamation; the loss by the General and Municipal Workers of their pre-war lead over the Public Employees in local government; and a geographical difference. The

---

[11] This was the position in 1976. In 1977 membership increased by 10 per cent, mainly due to growth in large private retailing companies. In 1978 Woolworth signed a company agreement with the union.

General and Municipal Workers have traditionally had greater strength in Scotland and the north where employment has declined, whereas the Transport and General Workers predominated in the midlands and the south where employment has grown.

All but one of the unions in Table 9 are either public sector unions or conglomerates, of which there are seven apiece. Five of the public sector unions and four of the conglomerates have grown faster than the overall rate, but the conglomerates provide three of the five fastest. This suggests that the major public sector unions, despite having achieved a higher rate of density than other unions and operating exclusively in the fastest growing sector of employment, nevertheless have not succeeded in out-distancing the conglomerates. In fact the fifteen unions in Table 9 accounted for 62 per cent of total trade union membership in 1948 and 67 per cent in 1974. Because of the decline of the Mineworkers and Railwaymen, the share of the public sector unions actually fell, from 20 per cent to 18 per cent, whereas the share of the seven conglomerates rose from 40 per cent to 47 per cent.

The foregoing pages have provided an outline account of how some of the main features of current British union structure have developed; but there remains a puzzle. If the structure of nineteenth-century unions was determined by the way they strove to achieve their objectives, should not the same be true of twentieth-century unions? Sidney and Beatrice Webb defined a trade union as 'a continuous association of wage-earners for the purpose of maintaining or improving the conditions of their working lives'.[12] Trade unions cannot do much about maintaining or improving conditions unless they can exercise some control over them. Because of the structures they had adopted, nineteenth-century craft and promotion-line unions had considerable control over key sections of the labour force which enabled them, at least in good times, to require employers to meet certain conditions if they wanted to employ union members. How, then, does the structure of unions today relate to their methods of achieving their objectives?

Trade union methods have changed since the nineteenth century. Unilateral trade union regulation of employment no longer tops the list. It has been replaced by collective bargaining which has developed and flourished to this day despite the complexity of British union structure. It has proved possible for a number of unions

[12] *History of Trade Unionism*, p. 1.

in one industry, in some instances a dozen or more, some of them having members in many other industries besides, to co-operate in the conduct of collective bargaining; and even in organizing industry-wide strikes. It has also turned out that collective bargaining actually confirmed and strengthened existing union structures. By entering into agreements with the unions, an employers' association recognized them as the appropriate unions to represent the workers—or at least the manual workers—in their industry.

The structure of craft and promotion-line unions was determined by the need for strong trade union discipline at a time when unions sought to exercise unilateral control over the conditions under which their members worked. To make such action effective the unions strove to recruit every craftsman, or every man in the production line, and to exclude everyone else. But what happens to union discipline under multi-union collective bargaining? The answer is that the enforcement of discipline is then unquestionably more difficult, but the need for discipline has been considerably reduced. The maintenance of acceptable terms of employment no longer depends on trade union discipline alone. Once a rule has been embodied in a collective agreement, the employers' association and its members are committed to its enforcement.

If the argument set out on the last few pages is correct, it follows that employers share responsibility with the unions for the current structure of British trade unionism. An account of the growth of white collar unionism in steel can help to substantiate the point. Although trade union density among manual steelworkers has been high since the end of the nineteenth century, white collar unionism remained weak until the second nationalization of the industry in 1968, for most steel companies had little sympathy with it. Nevertheless the Iron and Steel Trades Employers' Association took a step towards white collar recognition in 1943 when they decided that if there was to be recognition, it must be confined to the unions already recognized to represent their manual employees. They therefore made an agreement with the Iron and Steel Trades Confederation on procedural arrangements for clerical staff, laboratory staff, and foremen which were to apply where a company chose to recognize the union to represent these grades. The agreements 'provided a shield behind which an employer could take refuge if approached for recognition for staff grades by an "outside" union',[13] without being

[13] G. S. Bain, *Trade Union Growth and Recognition*, p. 54.

forced to grant recognition to an 'inside' union. Over the next twenty years the Steel Confederation did not appear to overexert themselves on behalf of white collar employees in the industry, and two 'outside' unions managed to establish sizable pockets of membership, and local recognition by employers, in several areas. They were the unions now known as the Professional Executive Clerical and Computer Staff and the Scientific Technical and Managerial Staffs. By 1968, however, the decline in the steel labour force had convinced the Steel Confederation that they faced a future of dwindling membership unless they recruited more successfully among white collar staff, and they and the other nationally recognized steel unions[14] persuaded the British Steel Corporation to reaffirm the 1943 arrangement. Since the nationalization statute obliged the Corporation to bargain with trade unions, a large influx of white collar employees into the unions was expected, and the two outside unions protested vigorously. During the summer of 1968 they called a strike at a car plant which was one of the Corporation's major customers in order to demonstrate the intensity of their feelings. A court of inquiry was set up and found that there were strong grounds for recognizing the two outside unions.[15] Rather reluctantly, the Corporation began to take steps in this direction, but they were held up when the Steel Confederation, supported by the other recognized unions, ordered their members to disregard instructions from supervisors who were members of the outside unions. The General Council of the Trades Union Congress then intervened and decided that the two outside unions should not be recognized. Early in 1969 the Corporation announced that they would not give national recognition to the two unions, but continue existing arrangements for local recognition and grant further local recognition where one of the two unions could prove majority membership, and where no nationally recognized union was already the accredited representative of the group concerned. This arrangement is still in force. Under it the Steel Confederation has recruited and represents the vast majority of white collar employees in the industry, although the two outside unions retain pockets of membership and local recognition rights. Union structure is far more tidy among white collar

---

[14] Most of these other unions had a few white collar members, mainly supervisors who had maintained their membership after promotion.

[15] *Report of a Court of Inquiry under Lord Pearson into the Disputes between the British Steel Corporation and Certain of their Employees.*

employees in steel than among manual workers, and although the Steel Confederation may claim a major share of responsibility for it, another considerable share belongs to the former employers' association and the Corporation.

The Trades Union Congress also has some authority over union structure. Since 1921 its disputes committee has heard complaints from one union against another, most of them arising out of the 'poaching' of members or the pursuit of negotiating rights in another union's territory. Over the years its decisions have established a body of case-law, codified in the 'Bridlington' principles of 1939. They recommend that no union should enrol a member of another union without inquiry; and that no union should begin organizing activities in an establishment in which another union has a majority of workers and negotiates for them, except by agreement. This limitation also applies where a union is trying to organize 'in the face of exceptional difficulties' and has not yet recruited a majority of the workers, or even where it once had a majority but has lost it.[16]

The preamble to the Bridlington principles also recommends unions to agree on spheres of influence, on recognition of each others' membership cards, and on conditions of transfer. Working arrangements of this kind constitute 'a large and important hinterland of multilateral and bilateral union agreements', which is 'largely unmapped territory'.[17] The most important of them is an agreement between the two general unions providing for transfer without loss of accumulated rights. Along with informal understandings between local full-time officers, these agreements have helped to avoid or minimize conflict between unions.

The Bridlington principles and inter-union arrangements for the most part sustain and legitimate existing rights. They do not prevent competition among unions which have already achieved recognition, as is shown by the dramatic growth of the Public Employees largely at the expense of the General and Municipal Workers, and the success of the Engineers, once they had decided to open their ranks, in recruiting less-skilled workers. Their aim is only to 'set agreed limits to inter-union competition'. Equally, 'they do not stretch to any positive powers to pursue rationalisation'.[18]

[16] The evolution of the Bridlington principles is described in Shirley Lerner, *Breakaway Unions and the Small Trade Union*, Chapter 2.
[17] John Hughes, *Trade Union Structure and Government* (1), p. 30.
[18] *Ibid.*, p. 29.

Congress has from time to time debated the rationalization of union structure, and its General Council have prepared reports on the subject, all of them cautious documents. Reviewing past reports in 1963, the Council noted that 'at the end' they had 'always contented themselves with giving general approval to all efforts to achieve greater unity and with offering the General Council's help to reach amalgamation or arrangements for closer unity in particular cases'. The 1963 report then went on to 'consider how best to stimulate and to guide the process of piecemeal and ad hoc developments by which changes in the structure of unions have come about in the past'.[19]

More recently, with the approval of Congress, a statutory method of intervention in some aspects of trade union structure has been introduced by the Employment Protection Act 1975, through the procedure whereby the Advisory Conciliation and Arbitration Service handles recognition disputes under section 11 of the Act.[20]

THE INDUSTRIAL CONSEQUENCES OF UNION STRUCTURE

The compatibility of British trade union structure with collective bargaining does not prevent problems arising in collective bargaining as a result of union structure. Competition between unions for members may lead to industrial disputes, as it has done in steel and elsewhere. In addition, multi-unionism complicates the conduct of collective bargaining because many plant managers, companies, public boards, and employers' associations have to deal with a number of unions. By now, however, there are well established patterns of union co-operation in most industry negotiations. Joint industrial councils and other negotiating bodies have their 'workers' sides' which meet separately before the full sessions to decide their line of action. They have their own officers and procedures. Over the years precedents have been established to distinguish the kinds of issues which they can settle for themselves and those that have to be referred to the executives of the several unions. Similar procedures are followed in regional joint councils, whose workers' side secretaries maintain contact with the national workers' sides. Each government department has its own Whitley council, but there is also a National Whitley Council to deal with issues common to the

[19] Trades Union Congress, *Annual Report*, 1963, pp. 123–4.   [20] See pp. 408–21.

whole civil service. Its 'staff side' has a full-time secretary with his own office and staff, and over the years it has developed into a channel for joint action by civil service unions. The Post Office unions withdrew from it when the Post Office became a separate public corporation and established their own federation, the Council of Post Office Unions.

Outside the public sector, trade union federations have been on the wane in recent years. Amalgamation among printing and building unions has led to the demise of the Printing and Kindred Trades Federation and the National Federation of Building Trade Operatives. The General Federation of Trade Unions, originally established to provide a centralized strike fund for British unions, now survives to provide common services for a group of relatively minor unions. By far the most important remaining federation (other than the Trades Union Congress itself) is the Confederation of Shipbuilding and Engineering Unions which conducts negotiations affecting manual workers in engineering, shipbuilding, and one or two other industries. It is distinguished from most workers' sides by its annual conference of delegations from affiliated unions; by formal rules deciding the relationship between the federal bodies and the constituent unions, including rules on industrial action; and by having its own headquarters, full-time officers, and staff. But all this gives the Confederation no clear-cut advantage over a workers' side. There may be some value in having formal provisions for calling strikes, but workers' sides have conducted strikes—for example the strike of local authority manual workers in 1970—and when the Confederation called national engineering and shipbuilding strikes in 1957, they found they could only do so by breaking their rules.[21] The Confederation's district committees are not noticeably more powerful than the regional workers' sides of some joint industrial councils. However, no workers' side has so many constituent unions as the Confederation with its twenty-two affiliates.[22]

[21] There are two rules on stoppages. One prescribes 'a ballot vote of affiliated membership' and the other refers to 'a decision . . . taken in accordance with the rules governing the societies affiliated to the Confederation'. Neither procedure was used, partly to avoid delay, and partly to prevent an adverse vote by a minority of unions. Each union called its own members out, in many instances in breach of its own rules. (Clegg and Adams, *The Employers' Challenge*, pp. 98–102.)

[22] Over forty unions and professional associations are represented on the staff sides of the various Whitley councils in the health service; but the largest number on any one functional council is thirteen; and the staff side of the General Council consists of elected representatives from the staff sides of the functional councils.

An alternative to federation is provided by the industry committees of the Trades Union Congress. Nine of these bodies have been
set up over the last ten years or so.[23] They consist of representatives
of the General Council and of the unions in the relevant industry or
industrial group, and their main business is to co-ordinate union
responses to proposals for legislation or regulations, and to actions
by government or other public bodies. Since Congress is the recognized spokesman of British trade unions, there is a clear advantage to
affiliated unions in dealing with this kind of issue under its aegis. But
some of the committees undertake other activities. Perhaps the most
important of them is the Steel Industry Trade Union Joint Consultative Committee, which is exceptional in having no General Council
representatives although it is serviced by Congress staff. It has
become the negotiating body for the steel unions over common
conditions of service for both white collar and manual employees.
The Printing Industry Committee has set up a disputes liaison procedure through which unions are required to keep each other
informed about problems which may lead to industrial disputes. In
1976 it joined with the employers to set up a Joint Standing Committee for National Newspapers which agreed on a policy for dealing
with the consequences of new printing technology by a series of
measures including redundancy, pensions, and decasualization,
which was later rejected by the members.

However, there are still problem areas of union structure. White
collar negotiations are generally separated from manual negotiations, and this may cause problems as moves towards 'staff status'
take effect, so that some terms of employment are common to both
groups and settlements for one of them may affect negotiations for
the other. To date, however, few problems of this kind have arisen.
Separate negotiations for process workers in 'general' or 'industrial'
unions and for maintenance workers in 'craft' unions are the practice
in most industries, but in some instances where this division has
caused specific difficulties the two groups of unions have entered
into joint negotiations as they did over the general agreement on
productivity bargaining in chemicals in 1967.[24] The railway procedure entitles the three railway unions to negotiate separately or
together. Rival claims from the Railwaymen and the Locomotive

---

[23] They cover construction, fuel and power, health, hotels and catering, local
government, printing, steel, textiles, and transport.
[24] See p. 73.

Engineers and Firemen (who compete for membership among footplate staff) have been a frequent feature of post-war pay negotiations, and were a major cause of the national railway strike of 1955.

The steel industry also provides examples of important strikes in which union structure has been a major influence. There was a national stoppage of maintenance workers in the summer of 1956, and a prolonged strike of maintenance craftsmen at Port Talbot from December 1963 to February 1964 cost more working days than any other British strike between 1962 and 1966. The central grievance in both disputes was the higher levels of pay enjoyed by senior process workers in the Steel Confederation, aggravated by the growing numbers and responsibilities of the maintenance craftsmen, due to the rapid increase in sophisticated machinery.

In addition to separate negotiations for maintenance workers, the steel industry has traditionally dealt separately with each union representing production workers, of which there are now four: the Steel Confederation, the Blastfurnacemen and the two general unions. Since nationalization the steel committe of the Trades Union Congress has taken over responsibility for settling common conditions of employment, but pay remains a matter for discussion between each individual production union and the Corporation. The Blastfurnacemen have long held the view that the Steel Confederation has been favoured by steel managers, under both private ownership and nationalization. The construction of a new blastfurnace at Llanwern, the biggest yet in Britain, gave them the opportunity to try to remedy their grievance. They held out for higher pay for the men who were to operate the new furnace than the Corporation was willing to offer. The dispute was brought to a head in September 1975 by the Corporation's decision to commission the new furnace and the refusal of the men to start work. The threat of a national stoppage led to a court of inquiry which recommended a compromise but went on to say that 'the aim should be to move towards a parity of basic wages of [blastfurnace] keepers and steelmakers in due course as a cornerstone of a reformed wages structure'.[25]

Rivalry of this kind can of course occur between sections or groups within a single union, but, where it does, there is a greater likelihood that it will be settled within the union and without involving the employer in a dispute. Overall, therefore, it is undeniable that

[25] *Court of Inquiry into a dispute between the National Union of Blastfurnacemen and the British Steel Corporation*, p. 42.

multi-unionism complicates the conduct of industry collective bargaining; but, on the other hand, it is remarkable that the great
majority of these complications are handled as smoothly as they
are.

Multi-unionism also has an effect upon industrial relations in the
plant. A considerable share of responsibility for the strength of
workplace organization in Britain is commonly attributed to it.
Where a plant manager faces an issue which affects employees
belonging to two or more recognized unions, it is unlikely to be
settled by a discussion with the full-time officer from one of them.
To arrange a meeting with one full-time officer usually takes time,
with two of them it takes longer, and with three, four or more it can
be a task of some magnitude. It is much easier to call together the
shop stewards in the plant, and if the matter can be settled with them,
there will probably be no need to bother about the full-time officers.
In this way multi-unionism induces employers to recognize and
augment the authority of shop stewards.

The survey conducted by William Brown and his colleagues
confirms the relationship between multi-unionism and the strength
of workplace organization. They found that, 'in multi-union manufacturing workplaces, the probability of there being a full-time
steward, an executive committee, and regular steward meetings is, in
each case, at least half as great again as in single-union workplaces. . . . In smaller plants it makes a significant difference to the
likelihood of there being senior stewards.' Even where the unions in
the plant show little sign of co-operating with each other, workplace
organization is more developed than in single-union plants, but it is
still further developed where there is evidence of substantial co-
operation. The authors conclude that 'multi-unionism stimulates the
development of steward organisations, and steward organisations,
as they develop, become more able (and probably find greater necessity) to cope with multi-unionism'. In other words, multi-unionism
at plant level tends to create its own remedy. If multi-unionism
makes it more difficult for managers to deal with unions outside, it
also tends to create an organization in the plant which overcomes
some of the defects of multi-unionism. Brown and his colleagues go
on to say that 'the extent to which stewards can develop their
organisations, and in particular the extent to which they can cope
with the problems of multi-unionism, appears to depend to a
considerable extent upon management'—for example, on whether

managers are prepared to set up joint committees with the stewards.[26]

The association between one of the most criticized features of post-war plant bargaining—fragmented bargaining—and multi-unionism is not so close as is commonly supposed. Fragmented bargaining can flourish where there is only one union. The best examples are the railways and the steel industry. Plant bargaining in the railways is conducted by local departmental committees. One set of these committees is dominated by the Locomotive Engineers and Firemen, and another by the Transport Salaried Staffs, but the other three are the Railwaymen's preserves. There are departmental committees, and therefore fragmented bargaining within one union, because railway employers have chosen to organize their business on a departmental basis. In steel, despite the large number of unions in the industry, the great majority of production workers in most plants are members of the Steel Confederation. Each department has its own union branch which negotiates separately for that department. This unusual branch autonomy is authorized by the union's rules, but the rules in turn reflect a system of organization chosen by managers which dates back to the days when the work of each department was sub-contracted with a separate agreement between the firm and the sub-contractor.

Collective bargaining on behalf of white collar workers in manufacturing is conducted at company level more than plant level, but either way it is in many instances fragmented, especially in engineering and chemicals. It is common in large engineering plants for the Scientific Technical and Managerial Staffs to represent supervisors, middle managers, and some groups of technicians; for the Engineers (technical administrative and supervisory section) to represent draughtsmen and associated grades; and for either the Professional Executive Clerical and Computer Staff or the white collar section of the Transport and General Workers, or both, to represent clerical workers. Furthermore, each of the several grades represented by the Scientific Technical and Managerial Staffs may have its own branch which negotiates separately from the others. This fragmentation contrasts with the plant-wide agreements for manual workers which are now widespread in large engineering plants, and reflects the situation at industry level where, in contrast to the manual unions which have a common procedure agreement, two of the five white

[26] Brown *et al.*, *op. cit.*

collar unions still have their own separate procedures; and the Scientific Technical and Managerial Staffs have two procedures, one for technicians and the other for supervisors. Over the years in which the original agreements were signed, the Engineering Employers Federation made no great effort to persuade the white collar unions into a common procedure which might have encouraged them to co-operate in plants and companies.

Multi-unionism also has important industrial consequences through demarcation, or the boundaries between occupations. Where several craft trades are employed in the same workplace, as in engineering, shipbuilding, or building, or more generally in the maintenance of machinery and buildings, there must be some means of dividing up work between the crafts. To some extent the training of the individual crafts dictates the division of labour, but there are large areas of common ground where two or more craftsmen are competent to carry out a particular item of work. Nevertheless 'custom' allocates it to one craft or another, and disputes over the drawing of the boundaries may lead to stoppages in which the employer is penalized, as he sees it, in a quarrel which is none of his making. Demarcation disputes, however, are a relatively minor cause of strikes in Britain. In 1964–6 they accounted for 2.6 per cent of all strikes.[27] Shipbuilding is the industry most prone to disputes of this kind, with 12 per cent of their stoppages due to demarcation over those years. The industry has had a special procedure agreement for handling demarcation since 1912. Decisions taken under it have led to district 'books of apportionment' drawn up between the unions and accepted by the employers. Neither the Boilermakers nor the Shipwrights were party to these agreements, however, and they continued to rely on the direct enforcement of the custom of their trades.[28] The amalgamation of the Boilermakers, the Shipwrights, and the Blacksmiths in 1963 therefore had a considerable effect on demarcation in ship construction, and a new demarcation agreement was signed by all the unions in 1969.

Strikes are not the most important consequence of demarcation rules. Their effect on the utilization of manpower is more crucial.

[27] *Donovan Report*, pp. 100–1. These are figures for the proportion of *unofficial* strikes due to demarcation, but as there were few official strikes the difference is probably insignificant.

[28] Shipbuilding demarcation practices are discussed in J. E. T. Eldridge, *Industrial Disputes*, Chapter 3, and in G. Roberts, *Demarcation Rules in Shipbuilding and Shiprepairing*.

Strict interpretation of demarcation rules may require three or four men to carry out a task which one of them—perhaps any one of them—could have completed on his own. It is now widely recognized that output per employee in most British industries is generally lower than in France, Japan, the United States, West Germany and most other developed countries even when allowance has been made for differences in equipment and in the length of production runs.[29] But the difference is not spread evenly over the whole production process; the maintenance of machinery and plant is an area in which the contrast is particularly sharp.[30] Managers commonly explain this contrast by demarcation rules between craft unions, and it is a plausible explanation. However, it is not the whole story.

Demarcation rules continue to operate inside craft unions as well as between them—in the new amalgamation of ship construction trades, in the Construction Allied Trades and Technicians, between different craft groups within the engineering section of the Engineers. It may be easier to resolve disputes and arrange for greater flexibility within unions than between them, but union boundaries, especially of conglomerates, are not the cause of demarcation rules. Nor are such rules confined to crafts, or to the boundaries between craft and non-craft employees. Most workers, both manual and white collar, have a notion of what they may reasonably be expected to do, and with the spread of job evaluation, many of them have written job descriptions. Their unions or workplace organizations quite commonly insist on observing the limits of these notions or descriptions, especially as a means of pressure on employers. 'Working to rule' is a traditional form of industrial action now being overhauled by its modern equivalent, 'working to job description'.

Furthermore, union restrictions of whatever kind are not the only cause of low utilization of manpower in Britain. An area in which the contrast with countries overseas may be even more unfavourable than in maintenance is white collar employment in manufacturing.[31]

[29] See, for example, C. F. Pratten, *Labour Productivity Differentials within International Companies.*

[30] In 1972 a team of managers and trade union officials sponsored by the Economic Development Committee for the Chemicals Industry found that the number of production operatives per unit of output was 10 per cent higher in Britain than in the chemicals industries of West Germany and the Netherlands, whereas the number of manual maintenance employees per unit of output was 50 per cent higher (Chemicals EDC, *Chemical Manpower in Europe*, p. 14).

[31] The Chemicals EDC team found that their industry 'appeared to have twice as

As the majority of white collar employees are still not unionized, and the majority of unionized employees are relatively recent recruits, the explanation for this contrast must be sought somewhere else than in the unions.

UNION CONSTITUTIONS

So far this chapter has tried to explain the development of British trade union structure, to show the various devices and practices which have emerged to mitigate or avoid the consequences of its extreme complexity, and to argue that some popular views about its effects are probably exaggerated. Even if that is accepted, however, there remains a disparity between the unions and the subjects of the three previous chapters: workplace organizations, managers, and employers. Industrial relations in the plant have altered substantially since the war. Workplace organizations have changed in step, or perhaps it would be more correct to say that changes in workplace organization have been an integral part of the alteration in plant industrial relations. Workplace organizations have grown in number, in strength, in function, and in formality. The number of personnel and industrial relations managers has increased several times over, and a series of new managerial techniques have developed to cope with postwar industrial relations issues. Employers' associations, for all their conservative tendencies, have radically revised their functions during the last ten or fifteen years. However union structure outside the workplace has, it seems, remained fundamentally unaltered—perhaps unalterable—and such changes as there have been, some amalgamations for example, seem to have arisen from considerations which have very little to do with developments on the shop floor.

At first sight the processes of decision-making in trade unions seem to be almost equally impervious to change. The formal constitution of the Transport and General Workers is much the same as the original rulebook designed for the new amalgamation in 1921. Many unions have been absorbed since then and the framework has been able to contain them with little adjustment, which shows how well the constitution was designed to facilitate further mergers. The

many administration employees' as the French and Dutch chemicals industries—i.e. white collar employees other than managers (*ibid.*, p. 15).

dominant engineering section of the Engineers still operates under a constitution whose main lines had been established before the end of the nineteenth century, and the amalgamation with the unions which are now the technical administrative and supervisory section, the foundry section, and the constructional engineering section has so far had almost no effect on the government of the engineering section. In many important respects forms of government in the General and Municipal Workers still follow the rules drawn up within the old Gasworkers' union before 1914. Many other union constitutions have experienced equally little change. Is this impression of immutability correct?

Just as it is impossible to discuss British trade union structure without some knowledge of the structures of at least some of the major unions, so it is pointless to try to answer this question without a preliminary account of some of the features of government in some of the larger unions. Happily, however, there is somewhat more regularity in patterns of government than in union structure. Since the Steel Confederation introduced a representative conference in 1977 all major unions have such conferences, which meet annually, or in some instances biennially. Their job is to review the work of the union, to discuss and determine policy, and in most cases also to decide upon amendments to union rules. Each major union has its executive committee or council, called 'the executive'. All unions have general secretaries who, except in the smallest unions, are full-time officers, although several large unions also have full-time presidents whose authority may match or even exceed that of their general secretaries. In all but the smallest unions the members are grouped into branches, and most large unions have regional or district organizations, or both, to serve as links between the branches and headquarters.

Many of the major variations on this basic pattern can be illustrated by reference to the three major unions. The conferences of the two general unions consist of representatives elected from the branches, although a considerable number of full-time officers attend the conference of the General and Municipal Workers with the right to speak but not to vote. They include the ten regional secretaries, who act as the leaders of the 'district delegations'. These delegations normally meet separately outside conference to consider how to cast their votes on important issues. In 1977 there were about 450 delegates at the annual conference of the General and Municipal

Workers and roughly 1,100 at the Transport and General Workers' biennial conference. The engineering section's conference, known as the 'national committee', has only fifty-two delegates, two elected by each of the twenty-six divisional committees which consist of representatives from the district committees. The district committees are partly elected from the branches and partly by district meetings of shop stewards.

The most significant difference in function is that the conferences of the two general unions exclude from the agenda all resolutions concerning negotiations or settlements in particular industries. In these two unions, and in others such as the Electricians, any issue affecting one particular industry is of direct concern only to a minority of the delegates. To permit conference to decide such an issue would make it possible for a majority with no direct knowledge of the issue, or personal stake in the outcome, to override the wishes of those directly affected. Most members of the engineering section, and most of the delegates to the national committee, work in the engineering industry, and resolutions on negotiations and settlements in both engineering and other industries are allowed on the committee's agenda.

To compensate for the incapacity of conference to decide questions which for many trade unionists, probably most of them, are the most important which their unions have to resolve, the Transport and General Workers' constitution has trade groups covering particular industries or groups of industries. Members working within each industry or group elect a trade group conference which meets annually to consider its affairs. There are also regional trade group committees and a national trade group committee which are charged with carrying out the decisions of the conference, subject only to the overriding authority of the union's executive. In 1969 the General and Municipal Workers made a modest move in the same direction when they provided for periodic industrial conferences in the regions and nationally to discuss industrial business and to give advice to the regional and national officers responsible for negotiations. The engineering section has no such machinery.

The 39 members of the Transport and General Workers' executive are 'lay' members—not full-time officers—28 of them directly elected by the members in the regions and eleven chosen to represent the national trade group committees. The General and Municipal Workers' executive consists of three representatives from each of the ten regions. Two are lay members chosen by the regional council, which is elected by the members, and the third is the full-time regional secretary. After the general secretary, the ten regional secretaries are the union's senior full-time officers. The executive of the engineering section consists of the president and seven executive councillors who are elected by the members in electoral divisions created for the purpose. The job of executive councillor is a full-time salaried post and, in addition to attending to executive business, the councillors act as the union's senior officers after the president and the general secretary, representing the union on outside bodies and taking responsibility for negotiations in particular industries.

The use of the term 'lay member' in trade unions requires explanation. A lay member is any member of the union who is not a full-time officer (and in most instances not a full-time staff employee) as defined by rule. But a lay executive member may be a full-time shop steward; many members of the Transport and General Workers' executive and some of the members of the General and Municipal Workers' executive hold offices of this kind. Even without such a post, so much time may be taken up with executive meetings, sub-committees, negotiating meetings, representing the union on other bodies, and perhaps also part-time commitments as shop steward or branch secretary, that a lay executive member may rarely or never work at the job which he nominally holds. He is paid a daily fee and expenses while on union business. Some unions also classify full-time branch secretaries as lay members. Originally this practice arose because individual branch secretaries built up their branch membership to a point where the commission on subscriptions provided sufficient income to live on, but it has persisted in some unions where full-time branch secretaries are salaried and pensionable employees of the union. At one time the majority of lay members on the General and Municipal Workers' executive were full-time branch secretaries of this kind. The rule has now been changed to classify these posts as full-time union offices, but there are still full-time branch secretaries appointed under the old rule who are eligible for membership of the executive.

The general secretaries of the two general unions are elected by their members for life whereas the president and general secretary of the engineering section, who automatically hold the same offices in the amalgamated union, are subject to periodic re-election. The president is responsible for union policy and industrial issues, and the general secretary for administration.

Each of the three unions has a considerable body of full-time officers and a sizable clerical and administrative staff. All full-time officers of the engineering section are elected, and subject to re-election after their first three years and thereafter at intervals of five years, except where the date for re-election would have fallen within five years of retirement. The full-time officers of the Transport and General Workers are appointed by the executive. The General and Municipal Workers' procedure is more complicated. Regional offic-ers are initially appointed by the regional committees for a period of two years. If they are considered satisfactory they then stand for election. Any qualified member of the union may run against them. In the hundreds of elections since the procedure was introduced in 1926 the official candidate has never lost, and now most elections are unopposed. An elected officer of the union may proceed to any senior post except that of the general secretary without a further election. In addition the union has district officers, full-time branch officers, and recruitment officers who are not elected officers. They must seek appointment as regional officers if they wish to rise in the union.

Methods of election vary. For many years the engineering section cast individual votes at branch meetings, but recently they have changed to the postal ballot. The Transport and General Workers allow either distribution of ballot papers at the plant or postal votes as alternatives to voting at the branch. The normal method in the General and Municipal Workers is to take a vote at a branch meeting. The votes of all the branch members in good standing are then cast according to the decision of the meeting.

The main link between the headquarters of the engineering section and its branches are its over two hundred district committees and district secretaries. The district committees have inherited wide powers from the period before 1914 when their predecessors in the Amalgamated Society of Engineers were responsible for determin-ing the customs of the trade and for negotiating district rates of pay and hours of work with local employers' associations. The rules empower them to 'regulate rates of wages, hours of labour, terms of overtime, piecework and general conditions affecting the interests of the trades in their respective districts'. This authority is of little direct value to district committees since district agreements in the engineering industry are almost extinct. Instead their powers serve as a constitutional shield for the autonomy of plant bargaining. In practice the importance of the district committees, apart from their administrative functions, rests on their ability to co-ordinate plant action because they include many important senior stewards in their districts. In 1970 the thirty-three members of one committee included eleven conveners and fifteen other stewards. Four of the remaining seven members had been stewards, and one of them had also been a convener.[32] In comparison with the district committees the divisional committees are of little importance and the main function of the divisional officers is to service the engineering disputes procedure.

The Transport and General Workers' headquarters has two links with the branches, one through the regional organization and the other through trade groups, the former dealing with administrative and the latter with industrial issues. In addition the executive has power to create districts within the regions, but until the late sixties this power was used sparingly.

The primacy of the General and Municipal Workers' regions is unchallenged. They are the sole formal channel of communication with the branch, and the regional secretaries and their committees have unusual administrative autonomy which is protected by the presence of regional secretaries on the executive and by the organization of conference into district delegations. The institution of industrial conferences has given national industrial officers closer contacts with the relevant officers and shop stewards within the regions, but so far this is no more than a marginal closing of the wide gap in authority between them and the regional secretaries. The 1973 conference authorized the appointment of district officers to take responsibility for large branches or groups of branches, but no district committees were established and the district is not yet a level of major importance in the union's administration.

This brief survey of the formal provisions of the constitutions of Britain's three largest unions has introduced some of the main variations in forms of union government, enough to allow an elementary analysis of some theories of union government which may help to make sense of the process of government in these three unions and others as well.

[32] Boraston *et al.*, *op. cit.*, p. 25.

OLIGARCHY AND DEMOCRACY

The most popular academic theory of union government is the 'iron law of oligarchy' expounded by Robert Michels in his book on *Political Parties* first published in Germany in 1911. The essence of his argument is that full-time officials secure a monopoly of power in large-scale voluntary organizations. They use it to keep themselves in office, and they are helped in this by the low level of participation among the members. Michels believed that his theory applied with equal force to trade unions and to political parties.

There is a good deal of evidence to suggest that it has some application among British trade unions. Branch attendance generally is below 10 per cent.[33] Some branches never meet, and in some instances the branch has been dispensed with. One of the case studies reported in *Workplace and Union* investigated a district of the Tailors and Garment Workers with nearly four thousand members in three branches. Only one of these held meetings and had a branch committee. The work of the other two branches was transacted by the full-time officer who acted as secretary for all three branches. There was no district committee. Another of the studies described a district of the Hosiery and Knitwear Workers with nearly seven thousand members. A few of them were in two small specialist branches. For the rest, formal union business was transacted by the district committee elected, when an election was necessary, by postal ballot; but usually the number of nominations did not exceed the vacancies.[34] Polls are low in many unions which vote at branch meetings. Before they changed to a postal ballot, the engineering section achieved 'a rate of 7 per cent in elections to major office'.[35] The General and Municipal Workers disguise the size of the branch vote by translating it into a block vote of the branch membership, but the figure of members actually voting is probably less than in the engineering section, since average attendance at branch meetings is lower in the General and Municipal Workers.[36]

There is, therefore, evidence of a low level of participation by union members in the official machinery for taking decisions; but by

[33] See p. 44.

[34] Boraston *et al.*, *op. cit.*, Chapter 7.

[35] John Hughes, *Trade Union Structure and Government* (2), p. 47. With the postal ballot, the proportion of eligible members who cast their vote in the presidential election of 1978 was 32 per cent.   [36] See p. 44

itself that does not constitute oligarchy. An oligarchy exists only if leaders are willing to exploit the opportunities created by apathy and have the power to do so. Many trade union chief officers enjoy considerable power. There are provisions for dismissal in all unions, but they are rarely used.[37] In the minority of unions which require their chief officers to submit to periodic re-election, there is an opportunity to challenge their leadership, but challenges almost invariably fail.[38] In those unions in which the executive appoints the general secretary, they might be expected to have some control over him. One such union is the Public Employees among whom Bryn Roberts, general secretary from 1934 to 1962, established an almost autocratic sway; and another is the Steel Confederation whose successive general secretaries have acquired a reputation for unusually strong leadership. In these instances the expectation was not realized. A dramatic example of the influence which the chief officer of a union can exert was the switch in the political and industrial policies of the Transport and General Workers towards the left in 1956 when Frank Cousins, after a brief interregnum, succeeded Arthur Deakin as general secretary. Another example is 'Carron's law'. Between the accession of the Labour government in 1964 and his retirement, Lord Carron used his position as president of the Engineers to cast his union's block vote at the Trades Union Congress and the Labour Party conference in accordance with what he regarded as an overriding obligation to support the government, rather than with a close regard to the decisions of his own union on specific issues or to the wishes of the union's delegation.

There are wide variations in the authority of trade union executive members. No lay member of an executive carries anything like the weight of a full-time executive councillor of the engineering section; but it does not follow that full-time executive members are inevitably more authoritative than lay members. In contrast to executive councillors in the engineering section, the full-time members of the executive of the Construction Allied Trades and Technicians have no specific representative and negotiating functions, and some of them perhaps cut less of a figure in the trade union world than some

[37] The Railwaymen requested J. H. Thomas, their political secretary, to resign in 1931, the Engineers dismissed their president in 1932, and the Foundry Workers dismissed their general secretary in 1937.

[38] The general secretary of the Engineers was defeated by his opponent in 1913, and in 1962 the courts decided that the general secretary of the Electricians had been fraudulently elected. The post was awarded to his opponent.

of the senior stewards in major plants who serve as lay members on the Transport and General Workers' executive. Other factors also affect the situation. The Railwaymen oblige their executive members to stand down at the end of three years. There are therefore no 'elder statesmen' with long continuous service to guide them, and members have to make their mark quickly. This factor, together with their number, which exceeds that of the total body of full-time officers, and their practice of arranging that their work lasts throughout the year, gives the Railwaymen's executive a capacity for wilful behaviour. Traditionally senior local government officers played a large part in the executive of the National and Local Government Officers. Their method of conducting executive business appeared to reflect the vexations which they suffered in their local authorities where senior professional officers are under the control of elected councils and committees. Until recently the general secretary was not the spokesman for the executive at conference, and in most instances central negotiations with employers were conducted by the lay chairman of a negotiating committee and not by the full-time officer responsible for that industry. Since affiliation to the Trades Union Congress, however, the union's practices have shifted nearer to those of other unions.

A weak executive can easily become an instrument of oligarchy. Overawed by the knowledge, experience and skills of their general secretary and other senior officers, and perhaps also subject to pressures, the members may become appendages to a ruling clique. A powerful executive may be an effective check on the chief officer, but they may prefer to work with him to dominate their union. Before 1975 the executive of the General and Municipal Workers consisted of five of the ten regional secretaries and a lay member from each of the five remaining regions. Given the high status of the regional secretaries within the union, and their grip on its administration through the practice of regional autonomy, this made the executive an unusually powerful body provided that they worked together with the general secretary, which they usually did. In 1959, much to the surprise of the leaders, the press, and the delegates, the union's conference voted by 150 to 126 in favour of a resolution supporting unilateral nuclear disarmament by Britain. The general secretary, Sir Thomas (later Lord) Williamson persuaded the executive to recall conference two months later for the sole purpose of reconsidering the decision, which was reversed by 194 votes to 139. The executive would not have been likely to take such a step if their political views had not been in tune with his on this issue.

Considerable influence is exerted by the 'platform' at most union conferences. With very few exceptions, the chief officer of the union is the central figure. In many unions he is supported by a phalanx of executive members and senior full-time officers. Even if the chairman of conference is a 'lay' member, he is usually a member of the leading group, and if his rulings veer from strict impartiality they will probably favour the platform. Since there are almost invariably too many resolutions from the branches or districts to consider separately, they are 'composited' by a standing orders committee so that there is only one, or perhaps two, resolutions on one topic. The wording of a composite resolution can influence its chance of success, and most standing orders committees work closely with the platform. In many unions the executive itself presents a number of resolutions on major issues.

Even in those unions whose membership is found to be entirely or largely in a single industry there are special problems in relation to conference control over negotiations. Any policy approved at conference must in practice leave the negotiators with room for manoeuvre, both in determining what concessions are acceptable, and in deciding whether to settle or to recommend a strike. There is little likelihood that conference will be in session for consultation when a particular negotiation reaches a critical stage. Special conferences may be called to consider proposed settlements, but they are expensive, and convening conference is by no means the general practice in these circumstances. Moreover, even where one union has most of its members in a single industry, it may have to take account of the views of other unions in the same industry. Its conference may decide that certain demands should be submitted to the employers, but what is actually put to them has to be settled at a meeting of a workers' side or a federation. This need to reach a compromise between several unions puts power in the hands of the full-time officers who lead union delegations at such meetings, and in many instances constitute the whole delegation.

If the General and Municipal Workers' method of confirming the appointment of full-time officers by a subsequent election is counted as appointment, then eight of the ten largest British unions, and fourteen of the twenty largest, appoint all their full-time officers apart from the general secretary. The Electricians appoint all their full-time officers except their general secretary and full-time executive members who are subject to periodic elections. Two of the remaining five—the Mineworkers and the Railwaymen—elect their officers for life. The Construction Allied Trades and Technicians and the Graphical and Allied Trades elect most officers but appoint others. The engineering section is the only union among the top twenty which provides for periodic re-election of all its full-time officers. These differences in methods of selection affect the job of full-time officers. All of them have two responsibilities within the union, one to the members with whom they deal and the other to the executive which has general oversight of the conduct of the union's business; but the relative weight of responsibility varies with the method of selection. Appointed officers owe primary responsibility to the executive, who appoint them, supervise their work, and may dismiss them. Where they are elected and subject to re-election, full-time officers owe a greater allegiance to their members who give them their jobs and have a regular opportunity to review their conduct and vote them out of office. Election for life balances the two responsibilities more finely. The officer must initially be the members' choice, and if he runs for a senior post he must again present himself to the members; but otherwise it is the executive who review the way in which he discharges his office, and take action if they consider it necessary. The full-time officers of most major British unions can therefore normally be relied on to support and apply the policies approved by the executive and by conference.

Most unions possess wide disciplinary powers. In addition to specific rules, the majority of them are armed with a general power to suspend, expel or otherwise penalize a member who acts detrimentally to the interests of the union as seen by the appropriate disciplinary body.[39] It is possible for a union to use a rule of this kind to silence or get rid of full-time officers or union members who challenge their leaders. Where there is a closed shop, expulsion from the union may cost a lay member his job, and a disciplinary case against an officer may lead to his dismissal. The Donovan Commission reported that 'some members of the Electrical Trades Union in the recent past, before its change of leadership, faced expulsion and

---

[39] In an unpublished study F. P. Graham found that 66 out of 80 unions with 94 per cent of the membership covered by the Trades Union Congress had such rules (McCarthy, *The Closed Shop in Britain*, p. 100).

possible loss of their jobs for protesting against union malpractices'.[40]

This brief survey indicates that there are several important features
in the government of many British unions which might lend themselves to oligarchy. But it does not follow that British unions are
oligarchies, for there are other influences at work. The two most
important are parties or factions, and the power of workplace organizations in union affairs. They are dealt with in the two following
sections.

PARTIES AND FACTIONS

In 1956 an American sociologist, Martin Lipset, and two colleagues
published a study of the social structure and government of the main
American printing union, the International Typographical Union.[41]
It is one of the few trade unions in the world in which office-holders
and candidates for office are organized into two rival groups which
compete for office openly, and in which the minority group at any
one time stands a fair chance of ousting the majority and becoming
the 'administration'. The authors used their findings to amend the
iron law of oligarchy. There is, they concluded, one chance of
avoiding the operation of the iron law in a trade union. It is to
establish a two-party system. So far as they were aware the International Typographical Union was the only union in the world which
had done so, and much of their sociological analysis was designed to
show that the development of its two-party system was due to the
unique social composition of the union.

There is no precise British counterpart to the International Typographical Union's form of government, and British unions have a
traditional prejudice against organized opposition.

> The organisation of a collective opposition has always been
> looked upon as an activity seriously endangering the sense of unity
> and brotherhood which is the bedrock of trade union organisa-
> tion. To this end many unions have rules which forbid canvassing,
> the circulation of correspondence between branches and commit-
> tees . . . and the attendance of members of one branch at meetings
> of another.[42]

[40] *Report*, pp. 166–7.   [41] Lipset *et al.*, *Union Democracy*.
[42] B. C. Roberts, *Trade Union Government and Administration in Great Britain*,
pp. 243–4.

Nevertheless, factions have a long history in British unions. During the twenty-five years before the First World War many British unions experienced a protracted contest between 'lib-labs' and socialists, with the socialists often claiming to be the champions of militant industrial policies.

The lib-labs were not finally defeated until the 1918 election, and long before that a motley group of syndicalists, industrial unionists and other advocates of revolutionary trade union action were attacking orthodox Labour supporters from the left. During the nineteen-twenties the communists established themselves as the leading opposition group, and it was at that time that opposition was equated with disloyalty. Some individual unions banned communists from holding office, and the General Council of the Trades Union Congress ruled against sending communists as delegates to trades councils or to Congress itself. The justification for these decisions did not lie in the methods used by the communists within their unions. They may have contravened union rules, but the over-riding reason for withholding the toleration normally accorded to opposition groups was the control clearly exercised by Moscow over the policies and conduct of British communists.

With the 'popular front' of the thirties, and then the entry of Russia as an ally into the Second World War, the communists were able to re-establish themselves in a number of unions, and shortly after the war they assumed effective control of the Electricians. A few years later the Bevanites emerged as an organized left-wing opposition inside the Labour Party, and they were succeeded by the Tribune group. After the Russian invasion of Hungary in 1956 the communists began to splinter in all directions, and whatever else might be said about the dissident groups, they owed no allegiance to Moscow. Finally came Euro-communism which loosened the Russian grip on the official Communist party. These developments helped to rehabilitate opposition within trade unions, and today there is a fairly open conflict in many unions between a 'moderate' group which supports the offical policies of the Labour party and a 'broad left' coalition of left-wing Labour and official Communist party members, with occasional electoral support from 'Trotskyite' groups.

This conflict is particularly manifest in the engineering section. There have been moderate and left candidates in every presidential election for the last twenty years, and for the general secretary's post, all executive council seats, and most national and many divisional and district offices. The moderates were led by the president, Lord Carron, until he retired in 1966. In the election for his successor, the candidate of the left, Hugh Scanlon, defeated the moderate candidate, John Boyd. Boyd, however, succeeded another moderate as general secretary in 1975. When Scanlon retired in 1978 the moderate Terry Duffy defeated Bob Wright of the broad left for the presidency. For most of the period the moderates have held a slender majority on the executive and at conference, although not always at the same time; and they are now well ahead. During the seventies the lines between the two groups have become more clear-cut, and the selection procedures and canvassing of both groups have become more open.

The conflict has held up the progress of the four sections of the Amalgamated Union of Engineering Workers towards an effective merger. At the moment each section operates under the constitution which it had as an independent union. Representatives of the four sections meet together from time to time as the conference or the executive of the amalgamated union and take common decisions in which each union casts a block vote. This procedure allows the engineering section to determine the policies and actions of the amalgamated union, since voting strength is roughly according to membership; and so far it has blocked schemes for a unified constitution. Under a unified constitution the left majorities in the three smaller sections could combine with the large left minority in the engineering section in a single faction which might constitute a majority within the unified union.

The periodic elections for every full-time post in the engineering section offer an almost continuous test of the strength of the rival factions. The allegiances of the majority of the full-time officers are known, and these officers provide leadership and strength to each of the factions. The Mineworkers have developed almost equally powerful and clear-cut factions, although their officers are elected for life. Since the war the presidency has been held by moderates, and elections for the general secretary's post have been won by left candidates, although the current secretary, Lawrence Daly, has veered towards the moderates since his election. Among the areas of the union, Scotland, South Wales, and more recently Yorkshire have provided the voting strength of the left, and Durham, Nottingham, and several smaller areas have usually managed to give the moderates a precarious lead at conference and on the executive. Since full-time officers are eligible for election to the executive (and in fact occupy almost all the seats), and to attend and speak at conference, the chief officers of the areas are well-placed to provide leadership for the two factions.

The authors of a wide-ranging study of union democracy in Britain and the United States, Edelstein and Warner, deny that the factions of the engineering section and the Mineworkers can be considered to be parties, or that either of the two unions can be said to have a two-party system.[43] Their general theme, however, is a revision of the pessimistic theory of Lipset and his colleagues. Firstly, they suggest that democracy is likely to exist in any union where there is serious competition for the top posts. It does not matter whether the opposition succeed in ousting the administration or not, so long as the administration believe that there is a risk that they might, and are therefore under pressure to revise unpopular policies. Secondly, they argue that the existence of effective opposition does not depend on the social composition of the union alone, as Lipset and his colleagues suggested. Unions cannot do very much to alter the social composition of their membership; but if, as Edelstein and Warner believe, the constitution of the union has an important influence on the effectiveness of opposition, then the union and its members can influence the degree of democracy that they enjoy. This is obviously true of the number of elective posts and the frequency of elections. Edelstein and Warner also argue that effective opposition can be encouraged by such constitutional provisions as the protection of individual rights within the union and the creation of second-rank elective national posts whose incumbents are well-placed to compete for the top posts. They set out to demonstrate the relationship between such constitutional features and the strength of democracy, which they measure by comparing the proportion of votes going to the winner and the runner-up in elections for the two top posts in a union.

This test of democracy is not very suitable for British unions. The size of the vote for the runner-up in an election for one of the two top posts may be an indication of the strength of the opposition in unions

---

[43] *Comparative Union Democracy*, pp. 252, 285–6. They even refer to 'the absence of open factions in British unions' (p. 204). The factions in the engineering section and the Mineworkers are denied the status of parties because of the restrictions on canvassing and electioneering, and the two unions do not have two-party systems because two or more left candidates sometimes compete, and there are also frequent independent candidacies.

which hold regular elections for those posts. Its relevance in unions which elect for life is less obvious, and still less in unions which elect only their general secretaries (and that for life); and it has no relevance at all in unions which appoint all their full-time officers, including the general secretaries. Nevertheless, it is possible for unions of all these types to experience lively factional competition within their executives and at their conferences, which should presumably be accepted as an indication of democracy.

If a wider and less precise test of the contribution of opposition to union democracy is adopted—say strong evidence that opposition groups are able to push union administrations into policies or actions which they would not otherwise have favoured—it would cover unions to which the Edelstein and Warner test is not applicable. It would also indicate a growth in democracy in British unions since the war. For, if British union government generally ever warranted classification as oligarchy, it was during the period from the thirties to the fifties. By the end of the thirties most British unions were led by men who had lived through the heady years of trade union militancy 1910–20, in most instances as militants themselves, and had reacted to the subsequent years of unemployment and trade union decline. They had taken part in the development of industry bargaining, and welcomed the centralization in industrial relations and union government which had been one of the consequences. Their experience of the General Strike and the Communist party had made them cautious in their industrial tactics and hostile to factions within their unions. Their hold on their unions and the similarity of their views enabled them to provide a fairly consistent lead for the movement through the General Council of the Trades Union Congress, backed up by votes at the meetings of Congress itself.

Admittedly communist influence in the unions grew rapidly during the war, but once Russia entered the war the communists gave support to the policies of their union leaders, reverting to opposition only in 1947. The leaders' first serious defeat was in 1950 when the Labour government's incomes policy was rejected by Congress. This was the outcome of shifts in opinion and adverse conference decisions in individual unions through the previous twelve months which showed that, even then, the machinery of union government could be used to defeat apparently entrenched leaders.

The leaders, by now a new generation cast in the mould of their predecessors, soon regained their ascendancy and kept it for a number of years thereafter; but they were under attack. Systems of factional government were taking shape among the Engineers and the Mineworkers. The Draughtsmen (now the technical administrative and supervisory section of the Engineers) permitted the preparation of 'slates' and open canvassing for votes at their conference.[44] The leaders of the Railwaymen, the Post Office Workers, the Civil and Public Services, the Building Trade Workers (as they then were), and some smaller unions had to face challenges and occasional defeats from opposition factions. Subsequently substantial opposition groups began to show their strength at conferences of the Teachers and the National and Local Government Officers.

Conference votes on German rearmament, nuclear disarmament, Vietnam, the Common Market, and other questions of foreign policy may give some indication of opposition strength, but the defeat of the platform on an issue like that does not usually provide an accurate measure of the balance of power in a union. It is more likely to be due to mismanagement or a lack of interest among the delegates. Decisions on bargaining strategy, incomes policy, or union structure and rules provide better guidance. Opposition among the Teachers and the National and Local Government Officers has shown its strength both in the conduct of salary negotiations and in carrying resolutions which favour the introduction of a shop steward system.

Although successful opposition may be a sign of democracy, too much success may undermine democracy. Shortly after the war the communists won control among the Electricians, and the opportunities for democratic opposition dwindled as their grip tightened. The communist administration put every obstacle that they dared in the way of the determined group of opponents—many of them ex-communists—who were in the end able to amass sufficient evidence of electoral fraud to overthrow the communists in 1961, and to replace them. Soon after the war an electoral organization known as the 'bloc' was established in the Post Office Engineering Union in order to keep the communists out, and for many years thereafter enabled the general secretary to rule the union with little more than token opposition to his policies.[45] These, however, are exceptions, and in neither union has opposition ever disappeared.

---

[44] Graham Wootton, 'Parties in Union Government, the Association of Shipbuilding and Engineering Draughtsmen'.

[45] It has been suggested that in this union for 'both leaders and activists . . . the

The record of opposition in the two general unions has not been mentioned so far. The powerful positions of the regional secretaries (the 'barons') of the General and Municipal Workers in their own regions, on the executive, and at conference has given their union as good a claim as any to the name of oligarchy; but the regional autonomy which is the foundation of their power has also served to give expression to opposition views. A delegate who wishes to challenge the platform at conference has only to persuade a majority of his own regional delegation to back him in order to have the support of a recognized group with an unquestioned right to disagree with the platform and to vote against it. The London, Midland, and Lancashire regions have all from time to time offered a congenial home to heterodox opinions which have thus been able to make a fair showing at conference, even if they have had little chance of defeating the platform.

The powerful position of full-time officers in the General and Municipal Workers offers a mechanism through which their policies can be changed. Elections for the general secretaryship have been fairly close-run since the war. In the past they provided an opportunity for members of the ruling group to compete with each other without risk to their system of government; but in 1973, when Lord Cooper retired, several regional secretaries contested the succession with one of the national officers, David Basnett, who had for several years been serving as Lord Cooper's unofficial deputy. Basnett was therefore unquestionably part of the ruling group, but it was known that he favoured changes which were radical in the context of the General and Municipal Workers. He wished to alter the structure of the union's executive and diminish regional autonomy. Many of the union's full-time officers shared his opinions, along with other national officers. They associated the static membership of the union, and its failure to exploit opportunities for expansion, with its form of government. The regional officers are the main link between the union and the branches, which cast the votes in the union's elections. When the votes were counted, Basnett topped the poll. There is little doubt that the majority of the officers gave him their support because they believed it was time for a change, and that their support was crucial.

benefits of open dissent have been outweighed by consideration for the stability and viability of the union'. (Frank Bealey, 'The Political System of the Post Office Engineering Union'.)

Full-time officers are also important in the Transport and General Workers' policies. When Frank Cousins became general secretary in 1956 it appeared that the union's political and industrial policies switched from right to left overnight. Full-time officers who represented the union to the outside world had to speak and vote for resolutions they had formerly opposed. But the extent to which the new policies were effective within the union depended on the day-to-day conduct of business by the officers, many of whom retained sympathy for the outlook and methods of Arthur Deakin. Radical change began twelve years later when Jack Jones succeeded Frank Cousins and, among other alterations, set in motion a thorough-going reorganization of the disposition and duties of the union's full-time officers.

The crucial questions about the government of the Transport and General Workers, however, are how the switch from right to left came about and why Cousins was succeeded by a considerably more radical reformer. Deakin had been the assistant general secretary before he succeeded Bevin and was in turn succeeded by his assistant general secretary, Tiffin; so when Cousins was appointed assistant general secretary under Tiffin it was generally assumed that he was to be the next general secretary; and in fact he won the election easily when Tiffin died a few months later. But Cousins had already established a reputation within the union as a critic of Deakin's policies, so his appointment as assistant general secretary must have been a recognition that there was a good deal of dissatisfaction with those policies. The centralization of the union's administration under Bevin and Deakin, their condemnation of unofficial strikes, their insistence that it was the job of full-time officers to negotiate and settle without frequent reference back to the members, were policies unsuited to the growing power of workplace organizations in post-war Britain, and this was one of the causes of dissatisfaction. However, although Cousins showed more understanding and sympathy with shop stewards and their problems than his predecessors had done, he did not carry through a programme of union reconstruction to meet the needs of workplace organization, and the problems remained; some got worse. The one leading figure in the union who proclaimed a programme of that kind was Jack Jones, the secretary of the West Midlands region. Two years before Cousins was due to retire he was appointed to the new post of executive officer at union headquarters. The assistant general secretary was of an age with Cousins, and could not succeed him. Jack Jones was elected, and set about implementing his programme. Since then workplace organization has occupied a central position in the policies of the Transport and General Workers; but it has been important in the government of other unions as well.

WORKPLACE ORGANIZATION IN UNION GOVERNMENT

The main outlines of the constitution of the engineering section have already been described. The executive government of the union is in the hands of the president and general secretary, elected by the members nationally, and an executive council of seven elected in seven divisions of the union. The legislature is the conference or 'national committee' of fifty-two members, two from each of the twenty-six divisional committees consisting in their turn of district committee representatives. The district committees have extraordinarily wide powers, but their importance in the union is not due so much to these powers, which have largely fallen into disuse, as to the conveners and other shop stewards who sit on them.

These constitutional arrangements have been compared with the structure of government in the United States which combines a separation of powers with federation. The federal government is divided between the legislature (Congress), the president in whom is vested executive power, and a Supreme Court which can declare legislation and presidential actions unconstitutional. By itself this arrangement would not necessarily prevent the concentration of political power, for the president might achieve control over the legislature through a party system as the cabinet does in Britain. However, the constitution drives a wedge between the president and Congress by choosing him through what amounts to a vote of the whole electorate, whereas members of Congress represent constituencies; the members of one house, the Senate, being chosen to represent the separate states within the union. The states have wide independent authority under the constitution to run their own affairs. Their interests as represented in Congress may be very different from those of the whole United States as represented by the president.

If president is compared with president, Congress with national committee, and state with district, there is a tolerable parallel between the two systems of government, enhanced by the existence of a Final Appeal Court in the engineering section with an authority to override executive decisions which it is not reluctant to use. This method of government may not necessarily provide overall decisions in accordance with the wishes of the majority of the electorate (members) to a greater extent than more centralized governments, or even to as great an extent; it has often been condemned, both in the United States and in the engineering section, as an obstacle to any effective government at all; but it has two advantages for democracy. By decentralizing decisions to states (districts) it takes them nearer to the people (members); and by giving the legislators an independent source of power in their states (districts) it provides a potent check on autocracy or oligarchy in the central government.

Decentralization in the engineering section is primarily the consequence of the growth of workplace bargaining and organization. It just so happens that the system of workplace bargaining in the engineering industry fits fairly neatly into the constitutional provisions of the rulebook. When it was drawn up in 1921, the constitution of the Transport and General Workers was designed to suit a quite different system of collective bargaining. Subject to conference and executive, it vested authority primarily in the national trade groups and their secretaries in order to match the arrangements for industry bargaining which had by then been established in most of the industries covered by the union. Regional organization took second place, and in any event the regional offices were relatively remote from the workplace. Friction therefore arose as workplace organizations grew in strength, showing itself in unofficial strikes and movements, which sometimes made the union headquarters appear to be impotent.

The most glaring example of friction was in the docks, where an unofficial system of workplace organization based on the gangers had grown up unrecognized by the union and the employers. For years before the Devlin Committee was appointed in 1964 the need for new policies and methods was advertised by large-scale unrest in the ports; by the power of the unofficial movements in London; and by the incursion of the rival 'blue' union into Liverpool and Hull despite the opposition of the Transport and General Workers, the employers, and the Trades Union Congress. In 1961 Frank Cousins joined with the employers in announcing a new approach to the decasualization of employment in the docks, but negotiations were left to the trade group and nothing was achieved. In 1965 the Devlin report contained one of the most outspoken criticisms of a major British union to be found in a public document, and demanded that the union should launch 'a great campaign' to 're-establish its power and authority in the three major ports',[46] in order to be able to play its part in carrying through the report's proposals for the termination of casual employment in the docks. Decasualization was agreed and put into effect in 1967, but protracted unofficial strikes in London and Liverpool demonstrated the continued weakness of the union, and the persistent disaffection of many dockers. It was during the following year that an official system of shop stewards, recommended by the Devlin report, was instituted in the docks, and shop stewards were brought into the port and national committees which run the trade group and negotiate agreements.

This reform did not put an end to industrial trouble in the docks. Over the next few years the closure of the docks and wharves, due to rapid containerization, brought acute problems of industrial relations, which were exacerbated when some employers tried to use the Industrial Relations Act to curb industrial action by dockers. But these problems were mainly handled and finally settled through the union's committees by representatives who were able—though not without temporary upsets—to retain the confidence of their members.

Reconstruction of the union in the docks, however, was only one item in a general reform of the union. Jack Jones availed himself of the provision in the union's rules which permits district committees to be set up. These committees may be empowered to handle union business within their territory, including industrial matters, thus cutting across the trade groups. The facility had been used sparingly up to this time, although Jack Jones himself had been district secretary in Coventry for a number of years. Now he set up districts throughout most of the union. In one large district 'one outcome was the release of a great deal of energy and enthusiasm, not only among the lay members of the committee, but also among full-time officers. Most of these were young men who had chafed under the old arrangements and were convinced supporters of the "grass roots" philosophy of the new general secretary. They now felt that they had been released to run their union as a trade union should be run.'[47] Most of the new district secretaries were appointed from this type of

---

[46] *Final Report*, pp. 43–6, 105.   [47] Boraston *et al.*, *op. cit.*, p. 45.

officer. They were under specific instructions to foster workplace organization and to encourage workplace autonomy by assisting shop stewards to settle workplace grievances and negotiations for themselves. When they and other officers in the union were conducting negotiations at any level they were to consult the members and shop stewards over proposals and settlements, so that as far as possible the decisions would be made by those who would have to work under the agreements. One consequence of these changes was that regional organization was emphasized at the expense of the trade groups, for the regions were the main links with the districts, although in emergencies even they could be by-passed.

These reforms brought the official union structure closer to the members and the shop stewards at the plant. Steps were also taken to bring the shop stewards into the official machinery of union government. The powers of the district committees are delegated by the executive and differ with circumstances, being invariably more restricted than those of the engineering section's district committees. Nevertheless the district committee is an official body in which shop stewards from different plants can exchange information and ideas, sometimes co-ordinate action, and also transmit their views to higher bodies within the union. In addition, the number of stewards serving on these higher bodies has been increased. Previously the workers' sides of national, regional, and company negotiating bodies had consisted entirely or almost entirely of full-time officers. Now their representation was cut to provide seats for shop stewards. For several years there have been very few members of the union's executive who were not senior shop stewards or holders of equivalent posts. Whereas the structure of the Engineers permitted workplace organization to take an increasing share in the government of the union without major reforms, the Transport and General Workers reconstructed their union to encompass workplace organization. The change has not led to open factional contests within the union, although by 1977 the disagreements between a substantial section of the executive and the general secretary over the Labour government's incomes policy, in which he had been closely involved, were not a well-kept secret.

Although the General and Municipal Workers have a reputation for conservatism, they have been pioneers in shop steward training, which they undertook on a large scale in the fifties. They now have two residential colleges consistently occupied by shop steward courses, and spend a considerably larger part of their budget on training than other major unions do. The introduction of regional and national industrial conferences in 1969 was a first modest step to give shop stewards some share in decisions relating to their industry and to make national industrial officers more accountable; and the conferences are unquestionably popular with the shop stewards who attend them. The new grade of district officer introduced four years later was intended, like the district secretaries and committees of the Transport and General Workers, to bring the union closer to the workplace. But there was no provision for district committees and although a considerable number of district officers have been appointed they have so far had relatively little impact on the conduct of the union's business. Finally, the reconstruction of the union's executive from five regional secretaries and five 'lay' members to ten regional secretaries and twenty lay members has led to a slow increase in the number of senior stewards who share in the central administration of the union.

Both the general unions have made belated changes to cope with problems that have long been with them. By contrast the Public Employees reorganized their union to take account of workplace organization before they experienced similar problems. Shop stewards were introduced into the union on a large scale only after the National Board for Prices and Incomes recommended incentive payments in 1967, and shop steward organizations in the local authorities and the hospitals were still being built up in 1973 when the union commissioned a university research team to examine

> possible changes in the structure of the Union which would take into account, not only the reorganisation of Local Government, Health and Water Services in April, 1974, but also the continued growth and expansion of the Union and the need to maintain democracy and efficiency.

Among other proposals, the team recommended that, where possible, branches should be merged into 'district branches' matching the new local government and health authority boundaries. The shop stewards within each district should constitute the district committee; or, where a district consisted of several branches, both stewards and branch secretaries were to sit on the district committee and the branch secretaries were to be the senior stewards. District committees were to elect representatives to area and divisional committees to give the workplace a direct link with the higher levels of the union.[48] These proposals were accepted and put into operation, although the merging of branches into district branches has been slow. Since the union's shop stewards are still finding their feet it is too early to judge the effect of the reform, but it is undoubtedly the most far-reaching attempt yet to reconstruct a union in order to integrate shop stewards into its official procedures.

After the expulsion of their communist leaders, the Electricians' rules revision conferences of 1962 and 1965 introduced wholesale constitutional reforms. There were electoral safeguards and guarantees of members' rights; the part-time executive was replaced by a full-time body; small branches were merged into larger branches served by full-time secretaries; area committees were abolished, with area and national industrial conferences put in their place; subsequently, appointment of full-time officers was substituted for periodic election, except for the two top posts and seats on the executive which continued to be subject to election every five years; and in 1977 it was agreed that representatives from the industrial conferences should be included along with branch representatives at the union's national conference. Like most of the other changes, the abolition of area committees was intended to weaken the communist influence in the union and prevent a communist resurgence, for the area committees were thought to be centres of communist activity; but it is also significant that their place was taken by area conferences of shop stewards in the three main industries covered by the union, which elect their own area industrial committees. Because of its industrial spread, the union's area committees had been less effective bodies for handling industrial business than the district committees of the engineering section, in which engineering almost invariably outweighs all other industries by a wide margin. The new arrangement was therefore a superior means of keeping in touch with workplace organizations and giving shop stewards access to decision-making at the higher levels of the union; although the union still has a special problem in these respects because of the wide dispersion of electricians in relatively small numbers which gives it an unusually large number of small workplace organizations.

Other unions have also adapted their structures to meet the needs of workplace organization. Collective bargaining for white collar

[48] Fryer *et al.*, *Organisation and Change in the National Union of Public Employees*.

workers in manufacturing industry is concentrated mainly at company or divisional level. The Scientific Technical and Managerial Staffs therefore group their branches, which where possible are plant branches, into company councils with company conferences to facilitate contact between the plants and allow representatives to take part in company negotiations. Industrial conferences are now held by a number of unions. Among others, the Shop Distributive and Allied Workers have adopted them.

Workplace organization can also play its part in unions with centralized bargaining arrangements. The Post Office Workers is a highly centralized union with no full-time officers outside the London headquarters. Its district committees have no authority over the branches and are 'talking shops for local activists'. Most of the branches, however, are workplace branches, and the branch official's

> everyday work . . . consists of dealing with the grievances of members. The sort of things which occur constantly at work—a quarrel between a member and his superior, a protest over a sacking or other disciplinary action, a query over the proper rate of pay for a job—are all dealt with by branch officers. . . . This casework gives the local official a rather special relationship with the ordinary member.[49]

Despite the centralization of the union and the Post Office bargaining procedures, the branch officials' role in the grievance procedure gives them a position of some power. They are also represented in the union's central machinery of government since 'Annual Conference . . . is composed wholly of lay activists'.[50] Even in this highly centralized union, therefore, it is possible to find partial equivalents for the two outstanding features of the constitution of the engineering section: an official status in the union for workplace organizations which also possess some independent authority of their own as bargaining agents; and the representation for these workplace organizations in the union's legislative body.

One question posed by this discussion of the part played by workplace organizations in union governments is this: since most union executives, and all union conferences, regional and district committees, trade groups and so on are composed mainly or entirely of lay members, who were the lay members before shop stewards

---

[49] Moran, *The Union of Post Office Workers*, pp. 93, 96.　　[50] *Ibid.*, p. 29.

began to take on the job? The answer is that in most unions in which the branch is not a workplace organization there were and are branch secretaries and other branch officers prepared to devote themselves to keeping branch records, handling contributions and benefits, conducting correspondence, arranging meetings, and assisting members. They may also be willing to stand for election to committees of various kinds, to conference and even to the executive. Very likely they regard membership of these bodies as some reward for many tedious hours of paperwork. In many instances they undertake little workplace business. It was officers of this type who manned up higher trade union committees and conferences in the past.[51]

Such branch officers render a great service to their unions, but their position and authority derive almost entirely from the unions. They have not the independent authority of senior stewards who negotiate with plant managers, are in a position to obtain important benefits for the members in their plants, and probably have considerable influence over decisions to strike or operate other sanctions in the plant; and who may derive part of their authority as officers of a multi-union joint shop stewards committee, right outside the control of the union. The lay activist who does not derive his power from the workplace is therefore not in the same position as the senior steward to bring pressure to bear upon his union, nor so free to take part in an opposition faction. In the past such men and women have usually helped to provide solid support for the existing leaders and policies of their unions.

Trade union workplace organizations have therefore promoted democracy within British trade unions by bringing important decisions closer to the members; by exercising a direct influence over their trade union leaders; and by assisting in the development of factions. In addition a number of important unions have adapted their constitutions to give workplace organizations a recognized place within the machinery of government. However, while it may be true that a growth of factional competition and of workplace organization have both helped to promote democracy in British trade unions since the war, they do not by themselves constitute democracy. Democracy also rests on elections and individual rights.

[51] When the Electricians decided to include industrial conference representatives in their biennial conference, *Personnel Management* (February 1978) commented that the decision would 'be a direct injection of shopfloor opinion into a body whose branch delegates tend to be rather more elderly with many drawn from the public sector rather than manufacturing industry'.

ELECTIONS AND INDIVIDUAL RIGHTS

The poor attendance of trade unionists at branch meetings is not necessarily an insurmountable handicap to democratic government in the unions. Most members find little to interest them in branch meetings; they can learn what is going on in their unions more easily and conveniently through their shop stewards; and important decisions on workplace issues are often put to a vote in the plant. Postal or workplace ballots allow the members of some unions to participate in union elections without going to branch meetings; but poor attendances may not be fatal to democracy even where voting is at branch meetings.

In most union elections most of those eligible to vote do not know the candidates. It is not just that they do not know the candidates well, and are not well qualified to judge their experience and abilities. They do not know their names. A considerable number of trade unionists do not know the name of their general secretary. They are a good deal less likely to know the names of candidates for the general secretary's post. Ignorance increases in inverse proportion to the position of the post in the union hierarchy.

In these circumstances much of the art of electioneering is to get the candidate's name known. Press comment can publicize the names of candidates and some partisans of the left are adept at getting their names in the newspapers; but press publicity does not always work to their advantage. In the autumn of 1976 Terry Duffy challenged and defeated the incumbent, Bob Wright, in an election for a seat on the executive of the engineering section; and in 1978 Wright, now assistant general secretary, was defeated by Duffy in the election for the presidency. Wright is known and respected as an able and likeable negotiator, but he is a left-winger whereas Duffy is a moderate. On both occasions a considerable press campaign in support of Duffy emphasized the political leanings of the candidates and the poll (almost one-third of the electorate in the presidential election) was unusually high. Many of Wright's supporters argued that Duffy's victories were due to the votes of members of the union who knew nothing of the merits of the two candidates as trade union officers.

If these are the facts of trade union elections, a defence can be made for branch voting. The small numbers of union members who attend branch meetings are likely to include a high proportion of those acquainted with potential candidates for union office. They also include a high proportion of shop stewards.[52] Branch voting might therefore be represented as to some extent a form of indirect election in which trade union members rely on their representatives to make a choice among the candidates for elective posts within the union. If so, such elections are far from perfectly democratic, and open to manipulation, but they are not necessarily to be condemned as wholly undemocratic.

Apart from the communist ballot-rigging case among the Electricians, there is no evidence of electoral malpractices being used to maintain control of the central machinery of government of a major British union. There are plenty of technical infringements of electoral rules, and sometimes there is suspicion of local chicanery, such as the casting of a branch vote by the branch secretary without calling a meeting, or the disappearance of some ballot papers, but serious malpractice is probably rare.[53] In recent years a number of unions have tried to protect themselves from corrupt electoral practices by transferring responsibility for counting votes to the Electoral Reform Society. They include the Electricians, the Mineworkers, and the Railwaymen.

Even where trade unions act within their constitutions, the use of disciplinary powers against members who challenge their leaders may indicate a risk to democracy. From time to time union leaders discipline the leaders of unofficial movements and unofficial strikes. The Transport and General Workers have taken action against the leaders of unofficial movements among busmen[54] and dockers.[55] The Engineers have disciplined members of district committees for their part in unofficial strikes.[56] The General and Municipal Workers have imposed penalties on the whole body of members engaged in an unofficial strike.[57]

The closed shop is widespread in Britain. There has been no general survey since McCarthy's nearly twenty years ago, but trade

[52] See footnote 72 on p. 45. In an unpublished survey of General and Municipal Workers' branches (mentioned on the same page) it was found that shop stewards constituted two-fifths of average branch attendance overall.

[53] In a survey of a sample of 494 trade union members carried out for the Donovan Commission, only four claimed knowledge of elections 'not fairly carried out' in their unions. All four cases were branch elections. (*Report*, p. 172.)

[54] Clegg, *Labour Relations in London Transport*, pp. 126–30.

[55] Allen, *Trade Union Leadership*, pp. 209–10.

[56] Turner *et al.*, *Labour Relations in the Motor Industry*, pp. 283–4.

[57] Clegg, *General Union*, pp. 124–32.

union density has increased considerably since then, and the proportion of union members in closed shops has probably risen above
his estimate of two-fifths.[58] The recent Warwick survey returned a
47 per cent coverage in manufacturing, and there has been a notable
spread of closed shop agreements in the public sector in recent years.
The closed shop gives a union control over its members' livelihoods,
so that disciplinary dismissal—or the threat of it—is a powerful
weapon which can be misused. Nevertheless trade unions usually
employ it sparingly. After a series of unofficial dock strikes, the
Transport and General Workers investigated the activities of
seventy-seven members, expelled three, and debarred from office or
cautioned several others.[59] Punishment short of expulsion can create
martyrs with enhanced support at subsequent union elections. Two
of the London busmen disciplined for unofficial activities following
the London bus strike in 1937, A. F. Papworth and J. W. Jones, were
subsequently elected to the executive of the Transport and General
Workers, and were two of the very few lay members ever to sit on
the General Council of the Trades Union Congress. The outcome
can be the same even where the penalty is loss of job, provided the
union subsequently relents. British seamen cannot sign on for a job
unless their names are on the employment register which is maintained jointly by the employers and the Seamen. During unofficial
shipping strikes in 1960 the union struck the names of a number of
the leaders of the National Seamen's Reform Movement off the
register, including Jim Slater's. A year later he was allowed back on
the register, and in 1973 he was elected general secretary.[60]

The gravest crime which union malcontents can commit is to
form a breakaway union. Breakaways are by no means uncommon
in Britain,[61] and the recognized unions have little hesitation in using
the closed shop to suppress them where they can. Even so they
usually allow the deserters to return to the fold, as the Transport and
General Workers did in 1946 in London Transport when they used
the closed shop to destroy the National Passenger Workers Union.[62]
However, when, at the end of the Pilkington strike in 1970, a
considerable body of strikers left the General and Municipal Workers to establish the Glass and General Workers Union and were

---

[58] See p. 25.   [59] Allen, *Trade Union Leadership*, p. 209.
[60] John Hemingway, *Conflict and Democracy*, pp. 57–71.
[61] Hemingway lists 41 'breakaway unions which are known or believed to have
been formed in Britain since the last war'. (*Ibid.*, pp. 172–5.)
[62] Clegg, *Labour Relations in London Transport*, pp. 129–30.

allowed back to work only when they had rejoined their former union, some of the leaders were refused readmission.[63]

There are also disciplinary powers vested in union districts and branches, and even 'kangaroo courts' at the place of work whose activities are occasionally headlined in the newspapers. Little evidence is available to assess the use of disciplinary powers at this level, but the Donovan Commission's surveys questioned nearly five hundred trade union members about union discipline. Forty-five of them gave details of recent cases. The most common offence was a lapsed subscription, but there were also cases of strike-breaking, of defying an overtime ban or a prescribed overtime limit, of 'misconduct', of theft, and five cases of 'disobeying union rules'. In four of the forty-five cases the respondent thought that the punishment was unfair, but none of these were expulsions, nor did the accounts suggest that the motive for the accusations had been to injure a political opponent. Most of the cases appeared to have been heard at branch meetings. There were seven appeals to higher levels in the unions, and in all but one of the six cases in which the respondent commented on the appeal, the hearing was said to have been fair. Three of the seven appeals altered the original decision.[64]

The Commission's conclusion was that 'it is unlikely that abuse of power by trade unions is widespread'.[65] Nevertheless they proposed that a review body of two trade unionists with an independent chairman should be established by law to hear appeals against disciplinary actions and also against election malpractices.[66] The Industrial Relations Act attempted different and more complicated safeguards which had little opportunity to prove themselves, but, since those and many other parts of the Act were repealed, the Trades Union Congress has set up its own Independent Review Committee, chaired by a lawyer, Lord Wedderburn, with one trade union member and a second independent. It is not empowered to hear appeals against all disciplinary actions, nor against election malpractices, but only against expulsions or refusals of admission in circumstances where the appellant's job or prospective job is at stake. So far unions have accepted its verdict where appeals have been upheld, but that does not appear to have persuaded the employers concerned to

[63] Lane and Roberts, *Strike at Pilkingtons*, Chapter 8.
[64] *Workplace Industrial Relations 1966*, pp. 123–5.
[65] *Report*, p. 168.
[66] *Ibid.*, pp. 176–8.

restore the appellant's job or to offer him a job.[67] However, its hearings yield no evidence of widespread abuse of disciplinary powers by trade unions.

CHANGE IN THE UNIONS

The main changes in the external structure of British trade unions since the war have been substantial alterations in the relative size of unions, and a large number of amalgamations which have reduced the total number of unions by about two-fifths since 1945. Some public sector unions, such as the National and Local Government Officers and the Public Employees, have sustained a rapid growth but others, such as the Miners and the Railwaymen, have suffered heavy losses. The group which has gained most are the conglomerates, ten of which now account for almost half of total British trade union membership; and the conglomerates have been the main beneficiaries from amalgamations. Both the main forms of change have therefore helped to confirm the unique pattern of British trade unionism which was already clearly visible before the war.

Enthusiasts for industrial unionism must regard these developments as disastrous. Critics of trade unionism emphasize the ways in which multi-unionism obstructs efficient union organization; and employers stress the difficulties which it creates for the management of industrial relations and for the efficient use of manpower. There is substance in these criticisms, but they can be taken as a final verdict on conglomerate organization only by someone who ignores the history of conglomerate unions in postwar Britain. For some years after the war they might have been represented as inflexible bodies, unresponsive to the wishes and needs of their members, and to changes in their social and economic environment, but over the last two decades such a characterization would be manifestly false. The conglomerates have shown themselves to be highly flexible, capable of substantial growth despite a decline in manual employment and a growth in white collar employment; capable of adapting their forms of government; and capable of responding to radical alterations in the structure of collective bargaining. At least from a trade union point of view the balance of advantages and disadvantages may be in favour of conglomerate organization.

[67] *Industrial Relations Review and Report*, No. 173, April 1978.

The outstanding development within the unions has been the adjustment of methods of union government to meet the growth of workplace bargaining. To a considerable extent this was a response, even a belated response, to a trend which had been noticeable since before the war, and had travelled fast and far by the time the unions recognized the need for change. Once they had responded to it, however, the unions, and especially the Transport and General Workers, began to encourage workplace bargaining in pockets of manufacturing industry which had so far been unaffected by the general trend. In the public sector, where workplace bargaining had made relatively little progress in the local government, education and health services, the unions took the lead in promoting shop steward organization and pressing employers into dealing with shop stewards; having begun with manual employees, they are now increasingly turning their attention to workplace bargaining and representation for white collar employees in these services.

The leaders in constitutional reform to bring the official machinery of union government closer to the workplace and to bring shop stewards into the official machinery of government have been the Transport and General Workers and the Public Employees, but most other major unions have also made considerable changes in the same direction. This development—the most important reform within the unions since the nineteen-twenties—has substantially strengthened union democracy. The opportunities for trade union members to have a say in the decisions which affect their working lives have been increased by the larger share which their workplace representatives now enjoy in the central and regional government of the unions; by the greater volume of issues affecting employment which are now settled by plant and company bargaining conducted by these representatives; and by the direct participation of trade union members in deciding these issues through either ballots or votes at mass meetings.

Before 1926 the ballot was the normal means of authorizing strikes and proposed collective agreements. In the years of unrest from 1919 to 1926 many strikes were called as a consequence of ballots which went against the advice of union leaders; and prolonged by further ballots which rejected proposed settlements. After almost seven months, the national coal stoppage of 1926 was terminated only when the leaders resolved to put the issue to a delegate meeting and not to a ballot. Thereafter the ballot fell into disuse, not because of formal revision of union rules, but because the leaders minimized the occasions for it and employed a broad interpretation of their own authority to take decisions. In recent years, however, the ballot has regained some of its former popularity as a means for sanctioning strikes and agreements at industry level; and, as a result of changed union attitudes, voting by the members is a normal way of settling the many major collective bargaining issues which are now decided in the plant.

Chapter 6

THE PROCESS OF BARGAINING

THE WORK OF THE BARGAINERS

The previous four chapters have introduced the parties to collective bargaining and outlined its structure, including the main structural contrasts between different sectors of employment. It is now appropriate to turn to the process of bargaining. In the manhours which it occupies this process matches a fair-sized industry. It employs about ten thousand trade union officers and staff members, and perhaps ten thousand full-time shop stewards; fifty thousand or more industrial relations and personnel managers, officers and staff; some thousands of officers and staff in employers' associations; and many hundreds of civil servants in government departments, the Advisory Conciliation and Arbitration Service and other agencies. Its part-timers include about three hundred thousand shop stewards and even more line managers, from managing directors to foremen. Some line managers complain that industrial relations occupies as much as three-quarters of their working time.

Endless heroic assumptions would be required to estimate the total manhours involved, but one simple calculation may give an impression of the order of magnitude. The total figure of full-timers can hardly be less than eighty thousand. If the average working time spent by shop stewards on industrial relations is taken as about five hours a week, they account for the equivalent of forty thousand full-time employees. Although the actual figure is probably much higher, for the purposes of the calculation it may be assumed that the part-timers on the management side account for an equivalent number of manhours. Rounding down the sum of these figures to avoid an impression of spurious accuracy leads to a total of about 150,000 full-time equivalents. This is more than total employment in the newspaper and periodicals industry or in rubber manufacture, and a little less than in instrument engineering. In addition the men and women involved are unusually talented and experienced, and many of them are highly qualified as well.

What do they do in this time? They attend meetings. Many industry negotiating bodies have regular sessions, generally each quarter, which require preliminary meetings of each side. In addition there are special meetings to handle annual pay claims and other important negotiations; and there may also be standing and ad hoc sub-committees. In many joint industrial council industries, the quarterly meetings and sub-committees are duplicated in each region although most of the regional bodies do not handle much business other than the administration and interpretation of industry agreements. In many parts of the public sector these arrangements are paralleled by consultative bodies which bring together similar groups to consider issues which are not formally the subjects of collective agreements. The management sides consist of association officers and committee members in the private sector and senior managers in the public sector, except in local authorities and the health service where members of local and health authorities take most of the places. On the union side there are full-time officers of the recognized unions, often accompanied in these days by a sprinkling of lay members. In many instances there are as many as twenty a side, but normally the talking, both at full meetings and separate meetings of each side, is left to the chairman and secretary of each side and perhaps to one or two other senior members of their teams. The rest are there to vote if either side requires to come to a decision—decisions of the joint body are by agreement of the two sides, not by voting—and to report back to their own organizations.

Other industries, such as engineering, have no regularly constituted negotiating bodies; but their customary procedures are nevertheless highly formalized and hallowed by time. Each side has a negotiating committee. In engineering the committees are appointed by the employers' federation and the Confederation of Shipbuilding and Engineering Unions. Joint meetings are arranged at the request of either side. Important negotiations require a series of meetings, and often a sub-committee as well. The behaviour of the two sides is very like that of their colleagues in negotiating bodies with formal constitutions.

Then there are disputes or grievance procedures[1] consisting of the

[1] Common usage is to treat 'disputes procedures' and 'grievance procedures' as

successive stages to which unsettled issues may be referred. These are either separate joint bodies or sub-committees of joint negotiating bodies, in most instances at both regional and industry level. The volume of business depends on the number of unresolved issues referred from the plants. The adjudicating—or conciliation—bodies[2] may meet regularly, or ad hoc, or both. The members are mostly senior managers (often acting in their capacity as association officials) and full-time trade union officers, although in the railways the union sides of the sectional councils which act as disputes committees are composed of elected lay members. In addition to the members of the disputes committee, meetings are attended by spokesmen to present the case on either side, and usually also by the individual whose case is under discussion, or representatives of the group in a collective dispute.

Negotiating arrangements and disputes procedures in those major multi-plant companies which negotiate at company level are very similar to the arrangements in the nationalized industries, except that full-time union officers play a less prominent part in some companies, and shop stewards a larger part. Like the nationalized industries, many of them also have consultative councils or even a group of councils and committees to discuss various aspects of the company's affairs which are held to be of interest to their employees.

The situation in the plant varies almost infinitely, size being probably the most important explanatory variable. In relatively small unionized plants, there may be nothing beyond occasional meetings between the manager and one or two stewards. At the other end of the scale, some large plants have negotiating bodies, disputes procedures, consultative committees, sub-committees, ad hoc committees, joint shop stewards' committees, and shop stewards' negotiating committees which rival the arrangements of some major companies in their number and in their calls on manpower. The difference is that senior stewards and shop stewards usually handle most or all of the business on the trade union side, and full-time officers have a minor role.

Committee meetings, moreover, are not the end of the story. Generally speaking formal meetings, and especially formal meetings

synonymous. It would be possible to confine the first to collective and the second to individual cases, but in fact practitioners also talk of individual disputes and collective grievances.

[2] Some of them are empowered to determine disputes; others merely recommend.

of, say, more than twenty people, are not suited to effective bargaining. They may have a significant ritual function in the bargaining process, but most of the important decisions which they record have been prepared in informal discussions elsewhere. At any level in the whole structure of collective bargaining an agreement, or the resolution of a dispute, at a formal meeting may have behind it dozens of other meetings within each side and between one or more individuals from either side.

Interchanges of this kind merge into still more informal contacts: line managers consulting the personnel department, chats between members of the personnel department, phone calls to the association and to company head office, consultation between stewards, a tour round the plant by the convener, calls to the full-time officer, chats in the pub at lunch-time or after work. It would be interesting to know what proportion of the national telephone bill relates to industrial relations calls.

In addition to personal contact there is paperwork. There are letters to write, and one grievance may accumulate a substantial file of letters before it is settled. There are cases to prepare. In some procedures written cases are exchanged before the meeting. Otherwise some full-time union officers and senior stewards may rely on oral presentations, but the management side normally has a brief. Many shop stewards rely on managers and their secretaries to provide most of the paperwork; but some shop steward committees have full records of their own meetings going back for many years. A survey of full-time trade union officers found that their three most time-consuming activities, out of a list of seventeen different kinds of activity, were, in order of the time they took: routine office work and correspondence; conducting negotiations with managers at the workplace; and preparing material for negotiation. The fourth was supervising and guiding the work of shop stewards or other workplace representatives, and communicating with them.[3] These were 'first-line' full-time officers: they excluded national and regional officers except where such officers were directly responsible for plant business. First-line officers are, it seems, primarily office-workers and plant bargainers.[4]

[3] Brown and Lawson, 'The Training of Trade Union Officers'.
[4] The importance of plant bargaining in the job of the first-line officer might be taken to indicate that he must play a larger part in plant bargaining than is suggested elsewhere in this book. However, given the modest number of full-time officers, this

Behind all these activities lie others less immediately linked to collective bargaining; such as the training of managers, full-time union officers and shop stewards in collective bargaining techniques; the work of research departments in trade unions and employers' associations; and much of the work of industrial consultants.

STYLES OF BARGAINING

To fill out this description of collective bargaining, distinctions must be made between different types or styles of collective bargaining behaviour. In Britain the best-known such distinction was drawn by the Donovan Commission in their assertion that Britain has 'two systems of industrial relations'.

> The one is the formal system embodied in the official institutions. The other is the informal system created by the actual behaviour of trade unions and employers' associations, of managers, shop stewards and workers.[5]

They went on to say that the

> formal system assumes industry-wide organizations capable of imposing their decisions on their members. The informal system rests on the wide autonomy of managers in individual companies and factories, and the power of industrial work groups.
> The formal system assumes that most if not all matters appropriate to collective bargaining can be covered in industry-wide agreements. In the informal system collective bargaining in the factory is of equal or greater importance.
> The formal system restricts collective bargaining to a narrow range of issues. The range in the informal system is far wider, including discipline, recruitment, redundancy and work practices.
> The formal system assumes that pay is determined by industry-wide agreements. In the informal system many important decisions governing pay are taken within the factory.[6]

They also asserted that the 'formal and informal systems are in conflict'.[7] To resolve the conflict, they proposed that 'industry-wide

survey finding is compatible with only a small share of plant bargaining being handled by full-time officers.

[5] *Report*, p. 12.   [6] *Ibid.*, p. 36.   [7] *Ibid.*, p. 36.

agreements should be limited to those matters which they can effectively regulate'[8] and companies should 'develop, together with trade
unions representative of their employees, comprehensive and
authoritative collective bargaining machinery to deal at company
and/or factory level with the terms and conditions of employment
which are settled at these levels', together with 'joint procedures for
the rapid and equitable settlement of grievances in a manner consistent with the relevant collective agreements'.[9]

There is room for argument, as they admitted,[10] about the extent
to which their description of industry and plant bargaining was
accurate at the time it was written; but that is not of immediate
importance now, since it certainly cannot be accepted as an accurate
description of collective bargaining today. The question is whether
the notions of formality and informality are helpful in understanding
contemporary collective bargaining.

What exactly is meant by the words 'formal' and 'informal' in
collective bargaining? According to the Donovan report,

> the formal system assumes that collective bargaining is a matter of
> reaching written agreements. The informal system consists
> largely in tacit agreements and understandings.[11]

Thus a substantive rule contained in a written agreement between a
trade union and an employer or an employers' association, and
signed by their authorized representatives, is a formal rule; and a
grievance procedure established by such an agreement is a formal
procedure. An example of informality might be an understanding
that, as far as possible, overtime in a given section will be distributed
in rotation; or tolerance of a practice that a shop steward can take a
grievance straight to the manager without notifying the foreman.

By itself, writing a rule down does not necessarily formalize it. It is
a common practice among shop stewards to make a note of an
informal concession in order to quote it as a precedent later on. Nor
are signatures wholly necessary to formality. Even today the procedures for promotion in the steel industry are not embodied in a
signed agreement, but no one doubts their authority; and the highly
formalized procedures for negotiating industry agreements in
engineering are not themselves the subject of a written agreement.
The crucial test of the formality of a rule is therefore its authority. If it

[8] *Ibid.*, p. 263.   [9] *Ibid.*, p. 45.   [10] *Ibid.*, pp. 36–7.   [11] *Ibid.*, p. 36.

has been either authorized by the relevant signatures or hallowed by time, then it is a formal rule.

There is, however, no clear division between formal and informal rules. Where it is generally understood that the spokesmen of the two sides of a formal negotiating body meet together from time to time to dispose of minor items which would otherwise take up the time of a full meeting, it may be called an informal arrangement but it would probably make no significant difference if the practice had been authorized by a minute of the joint body. An 'off the record discussion' during difficult negotiations might be rather less formal because the negotiators would not wish it to be publicized, but their colleagues would probably not challenge their right to explore possible solutions in this way. However, if they tried to commit their colleagues to an understanding reached between themselves at such a meeting, they might well be challenged. Formality and authorization are matters of degree.

The Donovan Commission held that informality was especially characteristic of plant bargaining; and even today, despite the increase in formal plant procedures and substantive agreements since then, informality continues to thrive in plant bargaining. In 1972 Thomson and Murray examined the working of procedures in thirty-five plants in carpet manufacture, chemicals, and food manufacture. Twenty-two of the plants had 'formal'—by which they meant written—procedures; the remainder relied on 'informal' arrangements. In practice, however, the difference between the two groups was less than might have been expected.

> What was surprising was the extent to which people did not relate to or even know about the formal procedure. Essentially, the actual process is much more complex in terms of the issues, the social organisation of the plant and its underlying normative values than the assumptions of the existing formal procedure can reflect, even in plants with a relatively simple structure. As a result, there was almost everywhere a willingness to permit informal methods of solution to embody the complexity of a given situation.[12]

One reason for this informality was the predominant view of grievance handling among managers 'as an extension of the adminis-

---

[12] Thomson and Murray, *Grievance Procedures*, p. 99.

trative process', but an extension in which they accepted the right of the workers to challenge, or seek clarification of, their decisions.

> In this administrative process, it mattered less that the grievance procedure was followed . . . than that the best answer was achieved in the shortest possible time. Moreover, the logical person to amplify or re-evaluate a decision need not necessarily be someone in the direct line of the procedure, and, given the problem solving approach, it might appear sensible to go straight to that manager.

The unions acquiesced.

> In particular, the senior stewards whom we interviewed greatly valued access to senior management. The possibility of a certain amount of 'forum shopping' on issues where there is no single clear authority is also an attractive aspect of the informal process.[13]

Informality, then, continues to thrive in plant bargaining which might in these instances still be described as a largely informal system. However, the Donovan Commission insisted that the informal system of plant bargaining at that time was 'in conflict' with the formal system. What did they mean by that? They could not have meant that informal procedures and understandings in the plant were literally in breach of industry agreements, for they had it on the authority of their research director that it was not so. Settlements in the plant, he wrote, 'concern matters that are either not generally regulated at national level at all . . . or else they are about issues which are normally only regulated nationally in the sense that certain minimum conditions or standards are laid down'. In a series of case studies he had found 'only two examples of domestic settlements which clearly violated national agreements'.[14]

What the Commission said was that 'the informal system undermines the regulative effect of industry-wide agreements. . . . Procedure agreements fail to cope adequately with disputes arising within factories.'[15] The consequence of dealing with so many issues informally in the plant was to diminish the importance of industry bargaining. Insofar as it was supposed that industry agreements

[13] *Ibid.*, pp. 117–20.
[14] McCarthy, *The Role of Shop Stewards in British Industrial Relations*, p. 26.
[15] *Report*, p. 36.

substantially regulated industrial relations at that time, there was a conflict between the informal system and the *pretences* of the formal system. The transformation since then of many industry pay agreements in manufacturing into 'safety nets', and the reform of the engineering disputes procedure, have considerably reduced the force of this argument.

The Commission went on to say that 'the assumptions of the formal system . . . prevent the informal system from developing into an effective and orderly method of regulation'.[16] One thing they meant by this was that the pretence that industry agreements were the main regulators of industrial relations prevented the negotiators at industry level from specifically authorizing plant negotiators to deal with the issues which many of them were handling in practice; and that this lack of authorization hindered development towards the 'effective and orderly' bargaining in the plant which the Commission wished to see.

There was, however, little pressure from workplace negotiators to be given formal authority of this kind. In discussing 'the almost universal reliance on informal arrangements and understandings in shop floor bargaining', their research director reported that it was primarily due to the reluctance of managers to convert '*de facto* practices' into '*de jure* rights', in other words to make them legitimate. His case studies had discovered four reasons for their reluctance to legitimize informal procedures: firstly, it would mean that the procedures could not be withdrawn; secondly, even if the present generation of stewards would not take advantage of legitimation, the next generation might; thirdly, if present procedures were legitimized, the stewards might seek a further set of even more advantageous informal concessions; and,

> finally, some *de facto* concessions could not be written down because management, particularly at board level, would not be prepared to admit publicly that they had been forced to accept such modifications in their managerial prerogatives and formal chains of command.

Shop stewards, by contrast, would have welcomed the formal recognition and status which an agreed procedure would have given them. In relation to substantive rules, however, managers and stew-

---

[16] *Ibid.*

ards were in agreement. Both parties saw advantages in maintaining the existing state of affairs. Shop stewards found that most managers were in practice willing to discuss with them issues which the managers held to be matters 'for management determination alone', and understandings often emerged. 'To insist on formalising such discussions in any way would merely have the effect of narrowing the effective scope of shop floor bargaining.' Managers held that formal agreements would more readily provide precedents for the future and for the unions to use in other plants; and admitted that 'formal bargaining on certain controversial subjects would be frowned on by some employers' associations and their members'.[17]

Accordingly legitimacy was at that time denied to much plant bargaining because managers and employers' associations were concerned to limit the erosion of managerial prerogatives and believed that open acknowledgement of their losses and defeats would increase the rate of decay. In some respects shop stewards were not anxious to challenge this managerial attitude, but in any event they could not insist on legitimation; and unions outside the plant did not do so, whether they could or not. The denial of legitimacy was facilitated by the existence of industry agreements, because the employers could assert that their associations were not prepared to concede further rights to unions or shop stewards beyond those in the agreements. However, industry agreements were not essential to the informality of plant bargaining. It was possible for managers in non-federated undertakings to show a similar preference for tacit understandings and covert arrangements beyond the limits of a company or plant agreement, as they did at Fawley before productivity bargaining was introduced, because they also did not want to acknowledge inroads into their prerogatives. For the same reason, informal bargaining with informal workplace representatives can be found even in plants where no unions are recognized and managers admit none but legal limitations on their rights.

The Donovan Commission's objection to the state of plant bargaining at that time, therefore, was its doubtful legitimacy and furtive character. They proposed formalization because they believed that open acknowledgement of the extent of joint regulation in the plant by all concerned would lead to a much-needed rationalization of the whole process of collective bargaining.

Paradoxically, the outcome of adopting their proposals was likely

[17] McCarthy, *The Role of Shop Stewards in British Industrial Relations*, pp. 27–9.

to be more rather than fewer conflicts between informal practices and agreed rules. Most plant practices on the distribution of over-time, manning, workloads, discipline, and so on were not in conflict with formal agreements at that time because those issues were rarely regulated by formal agreements. However, if plant agreements were negotiated to deal with them in accordance with the wishes of the Donovan Commission, there was the risk that old practices might continue to operate in breach of the agreements or that new practices would develop in conflict with them. Michael Terry has argued that the introduction of formal plant bargaining may promote a reaction towards informality wherever workers find the new rules disadvan-tageous and are in a position to put pressure on their foremen. In those circumstances a new crop of 'informal rules and understand-ings is likely to sprout up'.[18] An example of this process is to be found in many plants where measured daywork has replaced piecework. Because standard rates of pay are now negotiated, the practices whereby workers can manipulate piecework to secure higher earnings are no longer in use in these plants; but there is still a need to settle the tasks which are to be carried out in return for the standard rates, and the action to be taken where performance falls short of the prescribed targets. Measured daywork is subject to pressure at both these points, and, where performance falls short, the pressure is on the foreman. It readily leads to new practices which require additional manning or more overtime to achieve a given output. 'Effort drift' emerges to take the place of 'wage drift'.

Terry goes on to explain the behaviour of workers in situations such as these partly by their view of what confers legitimacy on a workplace rule. A formal rule, even if it is agreed by their shop stewards, does not necessarily take precedence over custom and practice 'because workers do not feel the same allegiance to the former as they did to the latter. They are not responsible for the formal rule as they were for the C. & P.' The Donovan Commission may therefore have had too simple-minded a view of legitimacy in industrial relations. What appears to be legitimate may depend upon where you are standing.

In the instances which Terry was discussing, the new customs were in the interests of the workers but not of the managers, but there are also instances in which both parties may find it to their advantage to disregard or circumvent agreed rules. On the basis of

[18] Michael Terry, 'The Inevitable Growth of Informality'.

their observations in a plant with a strong union organization and a long history of formalized procedures, Batstone and his colleagues argued that

> workers are concerned with protecting or promoting what they believe to be their interests. Managers are largely concerned with the maintenance of profitable production. Accordingly there are likely to be occasions when one or both parties believe their goals can be more easily achieved by breaking agreements. Such pressures apply equally to management and workers; and our observation suggests that these pressures apply as strongly to higher management as to lower management and foremen. When crises occur, and there is a choice between disrupting production when sales are vital and breaking an agreement, it would be a very 'ritualistic' manager who preferred to guard the agreement.[19]

It is now possible to offer a more sophisticated account of the relationship between formality and informality in industrial relations than the Donovan Commission did. If it is assumed that formal bargaining is necessarily legitimate, then informal bargaining may also be accepted as legitimate where it does no more than supplement and expedite formal procedures and rules; or it may be illegitimate because it conflicts with formal agreements; or it may be of doubtful legitimacy because it deals with issues outside the scope of formal agreements. The informal plant bargaining which concerned the Donovan Commission so much was mainly in this third category. The Commission may have been right in their view that a shift to formal procedures and agreements in the plant would, by granting legitimacy to plant bargaining, lead to a number of desirable consequences; but they did not foresee other consequences of such a shift, such as the likelihood of conflict between the new plant agreements and workplace practices; a danger that workers would see 'their' customs as more legitimate than the new agreements, even though the agreements were accepted by managers, unions and shop stewards; and a likelihood that managers or shop stewards, and sometimes both of them, would be driven to disregard the new rules by even more urgent considerations than their duty to respect agreements.

A revision of the Donovan Commission's analysis on these lines does not destroy their argument or render their recommendations

[19] Batstone *et al.*, *Shop Stewards in Action*, p. 264.

worthless. The contrast which they drew between the formal and informal systems remains a useful if crude approximation to the state of collective bargaining in manufacturing at that time; formalization roughly along the lines of their proposals has led to substantial changes in collective bargaining, especially in manufacturing; and the effect of these changes might be judged, at least from some points of view, to have been predominantly beneficial. What the revision does entail is that there is no simple choice between formal and informal systems of bargaining. All collective bargaining systems are a mixture of the two. A system which relies heavily on informality is apt to encourage the growth of procedures and arrangements of doubtful legitimacy—at least from the point of view of senior managers, employers' associations, and unions outside the plant. A system which emphasizes and extends formality risks conflict between the formal rules and practices. The overall mix in Britain has changed considerably since the Donovan report, but there is still a wide variety between industries, companies and plants.

So far discussion of bargaining styles has concentrated on formality and informality, for two reasons. Firstly, since the Donovan Report these aspects of bargaining style have been at the centre of debate in British industrial relations, and a crucial element in the reform of collective bargaining in manufacturing industry. Secondly, most British research into collective bargaining over the period has emphasized formality and informality. Nevertheless there are other important aspects of bargaining style.

One of them is the distinction between 'leaders' and 'populists' already mentioned, which was formulated by Batstone and his colleagues in their study of shop stewards, but may also be observed at other levels of bargaining. They showed that 'strong bargaining relationships' developed between managers and leader stewards. Such a relationship involves exchange of confidential information in off-the-record discussions, and giving support to the negotiator on the other side when he is or might be in difficulty; and it is 'a relationship of trust'. Its advantage is that it assists each of them to attain his objectives. The research team were able to show that leader stewards increased the earnings of their members faster than populists did. The managers with whom they dealt were 'less involved in trivial problems' than other managers, and their sections accounted for fewer strikes than other sections.

There is a connection between these styles of bargaining and the degree of formality. A strong bargaining relationship promotes informality between steward and manager because it 'goes beyond the minimum formal relationship which necessarily exists between them'.[20] On the other hand, populist stewards, whose main concern is to represent the wishes of their members, have less to offer managers and there is presumably little reason for either of them to go far beyond 'the minimum formal relationship'. Highly informal relationships with managers, however, are not confined to 'leader' stewards. In a plant belonging to a company to which they gave the pseudonym 'ChemCo', Nichols and Armstrong described a shop steward who had originally been 'selected by a foreman rather than the men', and trained by the company. As shop steward, and also stand-in foreman, he was able to avoid heavy work which he was not fit to do. This privilege affected his conduct as a steward, for, when standing up to managers 'might ultimately cost you your job as well as what remains of your health, any sane person would think twice'.[21] Here was a relationship with management which went beyond the necessary formal minimum required by the role of shop steward because of the weakness of the steward, not because he was a leader.

Another common aspect of bargaining style is described in an account of relationships between branch secretaries and managers in two collieries. Both branches 'were considered to be militant. . . and the union secretaries active in pursuit of their members' interests'. However, in the northern colliery, few disputes were

resolved at the expense of one party or the other. The management–union relationship was characterized by mutual respect and was described by both sides as very good indeed. The union secretary said he was well informed by management and consulted a great deal about matters of importance to himself and his membership. The manager said the points the union secretary raised were usually well founded and he tried to accommodate his suggestions and requests wherever possible. Out-and-out conflict occurred only when the manager or union secretary felt his prerogatives severely threatened, or where the manager was obliged to maintain area policy. The bargaining strategy of each side was one of conciliation rather than conflict. At the midland colliery, however, the management–union relationship was described by

[20] *Ibid.*, pp. 168–77.
[21] Nichols and Armstrong, *Workers Divided*, pp. 99–110.

both sides as strained and they saw their dealings together in terms of conflict rather than co-operation. . . . The N.U.M. secretary complained that the Lodge[22] was not sufficiently consulted or even informed about matters of importance to their membership while the manager felt the unions' demands were often unreasonable. Thus most negotiation took the form of confrontation and where the union got its own way it was through overt conflict rather than by influence or persuasion.[23]

Walton and McKersie argue that the degree of co-operation in a bargaining relationship is affected by the subject-matter under consideration. They distinguish *distributive bargaining*, in which one party's gain entails an equivalent loss to the other, from *integrative bargaining*, in which both parties can gain from one or more of the possible outcomes. They call the subject-matter of the first an 'issue', and that of the second a 'problem'.[24]

The most obvious examples of bargaining situations to which these two models apply are traditional pay negotiations and productivity bargaining. The traditional claim for an all-round increase of £x a week, or y per cent entails, if granted, an increase in costs to the employer (or employers) of an amount equal to the increase in the wage bill. Any reduction in the final settlement is a gain to the employer. If he makes a counter-offer lower than the claim, any advance on his figure is a gain to the employees. Managers often treat disputes over managerial prerogative as 'win-lose' situations as well. On the other hand a productivity agreement, in which working methods are changed to allow production to be maintained without need for systematic overtime, may grant an increase in pay sufficient to compensate for the loss of overtime earnings without adding to the employer's wage bill. Both sides have to acknowledge that work practices are subject to bargaining, but the employer gains from more efficient use of equipment, and the employees gain from a shorter working week and a stable pay packet.

In practice, bargaining situations are rarely as clear-cut as these examples. In negotiations over a straight pay claim, employers may introduce the possibility of union concessions which might offset part of the cost of the wage increase; and the size of the pay increase in productivity negotiations can be the subject of hard bargaining and

[22] 'Lodge' is another name for a miners' union branch.
[23] Christine Edwards, 'Measuring Union Power'.
[24] Walton and McKersie, *The Behavioral Theory of Labor Negotiations*, pp. 4–5.

strikes. Nevertheless many bargaining situations approximate to the one model or the other, and it seems that each of them has its own style of bargaining.

Walton and McKersie illustrated their theory with American examples, but it has been applied to Britain by Richard Hyman in a study of the operation in Coventry of the engineering procedure as it existed before 1971. He noted that

> the key function of procedure as a means of dispute resolution appears to lie in its creation of an artificial social situation. This artificiality is immediately apparent to the observer of a formal conference, and is emphasised by the contrast between the behaviour of the negotiators before its commencement and during adjournments, and their behaviour while the conference is in progress. In the former situation the opposing representatives employ first-name terms and engage in small talk and light-hearted banter; when procedural discussions commence the atmosphere alters perceptibly, and the exchanges become highly forma-lised. It is significant that in *both* situations the actors appear to be deliberately performing roles; if the formal courtesies of the conference seem artificial, the preceding bonhomie often appears equally contrived.

Both types of behaviour emphasize the artificiality of the formal negotiating situation in which the narrow definition of the issue to be settled and the conduct of business by professional negotiators assist the parties to reach a settlement.[25]

Hyman also noticed that about 30 per cent of 'works conferences' were held outside the agreed procedure. The subject-matter of these informal conferences differed sharply from the business of formal conferences. Almost three-quarters of the latter dealt with wages compared with only a third of the informal conferences. Moreover many of the pay questions discussed at informal conferences were not pay claims, but such topics as 'piecework problems in the machine shop'. The great majority of formal conferences arose from union references, whereas a considerable proportion of informal conferences had been requested by the employer. The terms of reference of informal conferences were not closely defined because an agreed definition of the problem was in many instances one of the objectives of the conference. The task of the professionals was to

[25] Richard Hyman, *Disputes Procedures in Action*, pp. 57–60.

assist the parties to explore the situation, and not to constrain them within the limits of an artificial procedure.

> Even if the references were specific enough to pursue formally, an ultimate failure to agree would merely give the company the right to act unilaterally—a right which in most cases it already in theory possesses as part of its 'managerial prerogatives'. Unions too may prefer to raise informally questions which affect 'managerial prerogatives'; a sympathetic response is perhaps more likely in this context than in formal procedure.[26]

VALUES IN BARGAINING

The previous section has dealt with some of the ways in which negotiators go about their business, and why their styles of bargaining differ. It has given little indication of what they actually discuss during the many thousand man-years which they spend each year talking and listening.

A considerable part of this time is spent in formal meetings which may appear to be largely ritualistic. In pay negotiations both sides may be aware that several comparable industries, or companies or plants, have settled for, say, 8 per cent. Nevertheless the union negotiators ask for, say, 12 per cent, although they know that they and their members are prepared to settle for 8 per cent, and they would be hard pressed to engineer a situation in which the members would strike for more than 8 per cent. Yet there may be a slight chance that by asking for 12 per cent they might bluff the other side into settling for 9 per cent. The employers offer 6 per cent, although they are quite content to settle for 8 per cent. They know that one of the few ways in which they could trigger off a strike would be to offer 8 per cent, for then the union negotiators might believe that there must be more to come if only sufficient pressure was applied. Consequently both sides make elaborate preparations for arguing a case which they do not believe is defensible. Proceedings of this sort can occupy a series of meetings spread over several months. At one time it was customary to describe them as 'the annual ritual dance'.

Claims for a reduction in the working week provide another example. The evidence shows that adjustments in the working week

[26] *Ibid.*, pp. 45–8.

are tightly bunched with intervals of up to two decades or more between them. But during the intervals hundreds, maybe thousands, of applications for a shorter working week are launched by trade unions. Perhaps a few of them stand a chance of starting the next round of reductions; but the majority are formalities. Nevertheless they take up the time of negotiators.

Many open-and-shut cases are submitted to disputes procedures. In some of them the union representative knows that his member, or members, are almost certain to lose, and even believes that they should lose, but prefers them to learn the weakness of their case from experience and not from him. However, if experience is to be their teacher, he must make an eloquent presentation on their behalf or they may think that their failure has been due to his incompetence. In other cases—not so many, but they exist—the employers' association official or the personnel manager knows perfectly well that he is wasting his time pursuing a reference, but cannot persuade the company, or his managing director, that the case should be conceded. So he must work up a presentation which may impress them, even if it has no influence on the union.

One of the means by which an experienced negotiator can assess the bargaining strength of the other side is to examine and probe the case which they present. From what they say he may be able to learn their sticking-points and the issues on which he may push them with very little risk. He may also be able to assess the degree of confidence or anxiety which they feel about the outcome of the negotiations. He may therefore be content to prolong proceedings for as long as they are willing to talk. He is probably not being persuaded by their arguments, but he is nevertheless learning from what they say.

In major negotiations it is usual for the union to put forward a package of claims: a general increase in pay, particular adjustments in differentials, an increase in shift-pay, a concession on travelling time, an extra day's holiday, and so on. The employers' side usually responds with a package of their own, refusing some points, going part of the way to meet others, showing a willingness to increase their offer given certain concessions on manning or flexibility. By listening to the presentation and asking questions, the experienced negotiator can discover not only the likely sticking-points on the other side, but also how to readjust his own tactics to extract further concessions from the other side over issues on which they do not seem likely to risk a breakdown.

The reasons given in the last few pages for talking and listening in collective bargaining have been analysed at length by Walton and McKersie under two headings: 'attitudinal structuring', which is concerned with 'influencing the relationships between parties', and 'intraorganizational bargaining', which is 'designed to achieve consensus within the union and within the company'—to bring their expectations 'into alignment with those of the chief negotiator'.[27] These two processes are not limited to 'playing to the gallery', or to professional conveying and receiving hints of the real intentions and expectations of the parties. They are also aimed to alter opinions; and the behaviour of negotiators leaves no doubt that this aim is sometimes achieved. 'That was a good point', says a member of one side or the other when they have retired for an adjournment, 'we shall have to make some concession there.' Alternatively, after a discussion during an adjournment, the comment may be: 'I feared he was selling us down the river, but now I see why we can't push any harder on this issue.'

What arguments are effective? Arguments used in pay negotiations have attracted most attention from academic researchers. In a book published in 1955 Barbara Wootton found that the arguments used to support pay claims were, in order of frequency: the cost of living, relativities, shortage of labour, productivity and profitability.[28] If frequency of use is an indication of effectiveness, then price increases were the most effective argument for pay increases at that time; and that is understandable, for if prices have risen since the last pay settlement employees are poorer as a consequence. It can hardly be denied that this is a reason for seeking, and granting, an increase. But if the index of retail prices has increased by 3 per cent it cannot justify a pay increase of more than 3 per cent unless the union negotiators can sustain an attack on the reliability of the index. This is attempted from time to time, but probably without much effect on the other side. To justify a larger increase the union has to look elsewhere; and increases already granted to other workers, or levels of pay achieved by similar workers elsewhere, provide the most readily available source of arguments.

There is a good deal of evidence that, over periods of some years, pay in different occupations moves fairly closely in step. Pay relationships, says Guy Routh,

---

[27] Walton and McKersie, *op. cit.*, p. 5.
[28] Barbara Wootton, *The Social Foundations of Wage Policy*, Chapter 5.

seem to have the capacity to regain previous shapes, sometimes after lapses of many years. . . . As between managers, foremen, skilled, semi-skilled and unskilled manual workers the structure was not much different in 1960 from what it had been in 1913. Coalminers and agricultural workers suffered from relative declines after the first world war, but regained their previous position after the second. The relative pay of railwaymen and Civil Servants was allowed to deteriorate during and after the second world war and was then restored by drastic upward revisions in the middle or late 1950's.[29]

Detailed studies of changes in industry pay agreements have been made by Knowles and Robinson[30] and by R. F. Elliott.[31] They were unable to descry a general annual wage round of increases of similar amounts given at similar intervals. The overall impression from one year to another is of variation rather than uniformity, although there are 'certain regular coalitions of groups' which keep fairly close to each other. But in the longer run their verdict does not conflict with Routh's.

The variability of the total increases secured by our groups over the full period was smaller (sometimes considerably smaller) than the variability of increases in shorter periods. In other words, there was more uniformity between the cumulated increases secured than there was between the increases in a 'round' or other short period.[32]

The absence of a regular wage round does not disprove the importance of comparison in pay settlements. There would be regular wage rounds only if comparison was the sole influence on pay settlements; and it is not. Barbara Wootton listed shortage of labour, productivity and profitability as further arguments for pay increases. Since changes in these items are unevenly distributed between industries and plants, they must, if they have any effect at all, push pay settlements apart. In recent years productivity agreements and measured daywork agreements have in most instances provided substantially higher increases in pay than the general run of settlements at the time.

[29] Guy Routh, *Occupation and Pay in Great Britain, 1906–60*, p. 148.
[30] 'Wage Rounds and Wage Policy'.
[31] 'The National Wage Round in the United Kingdom: A Sceptical View'.
[32] Knowles and Robinson, *op. cit.*

Another factor leading to dispersion in pay settlements is the uneven distribution of wage drift, which is generally more rapid where payment by results is in use. Earnings in timeworking industries and plants tend to fall behind. Sooner or later these industries and plants negotiate abnormally high increases in rates, so that earnings may catch up, and then their rates move out of line.

According to Routh, pay structure is

by its nature incapable of reaching a state of rest, because it is made up of a multitude of units (that is, units for the purpose of determining rates of pay) who have different ideas as to what their relationships to one another should be. Group A may claim parity with Group B, which may claim a differential of x per cent over Group A. Both groups cannot then be at rest at the same time.[33]

Many of the most radical adjustments in pay since the war have been the outcome of public inquiries. The 'drastic upward revision' of civil service and railway pay noted by Routh was the result of the Priestley Commission and the Guillebaud Committee. Among others, busmen, doctors, electricity supply workers, firemen, local authority workers, miners, nurses, policemen, and teachers have been the subjects of pay inquiries. The reports demonstrate the importance of comparisons in settling pay. In almost all of them the assessment of comparisons provided the central argument, and it was a moral argument. The justification for basing pay adjustment on comparison was not grounded in economic analysis or in assessments of bargaining strength, but in considerations of fairness.

What comparisons are fair? In a survey carried out in 1962, W. G. Runciman inferred from his evidence that, in assessing their own position, manual workers, particularly semi-skilled and unskilled, tend to make comparisons with other people at a similar social level to themselves. Because of this about a quarter of the whole population surveyed thought that no one else was faring any better than they were themselves, and the proportion was higher among manual workers.[34] His investigation was repeated by Political and Economic Planning in 1975. They found that the proportion who felt that others were not doing any better than themselves had risen almost to

[33] *Op. cit.*, p. 150.
[34] W. G. Runciman, *Relative Deprivation and Social Justice*, p. 193.

a third, and semi-skilled and unskilled manual workers were the least discontented.[35]

In assessing notions of fairness in collective bargaining, however, the opinion of trade unionists may count for more than that of non-unionists, and the opinions of negotiators may count most of all. Political and Economic Planning found that manual trade unionists were a little more contented than manual non-unionists (35 per cent of trade unionists felt that others were not doing better than themselves compared with 32 per cent of non-unionists); and, when trade union workplace negotiators were asked whether any other groups of workers were doing better than their members, no less than 51 per cent replied that none were. Among the minority who felt that there were groups doing better than their members, 55 per cent quoted another group of manual workers, and only 30 per cent referred to white collar, professional or managerial workers.[36]

In drawing comparisons, therefore, the horizons of trade unionists are limited, and those of their negotiators in the workplace are even more limited. As Hyman and Brough comment, 'the choice of pay comparisons is typically unambitious and powerfully shaped by custom: major inequalities which form an established part of the incomes hierarchy are rarely a focus of attention'.[37] This is conducive to the success of pay negotiations, for to be effective comparisons must be accepted by both parties, or in some instances by third parties; but it is nevertheless interesting to discover that trade unionists and their representatives not only *use* modest comparisons which have a reasonable chance of acceptance by others, but also *accept* them themselves. It is also of interest to find that pay comparisons, like so many other aspects of industrial relations, are shaped by custom. But how are the customs made and changed?

Anyone acquainted with the work of a number of negotiating bodies is aware that comparisons vary from one group to another, and from time to time. Fitters, drivers, labourers, clerical workers, and technicians all compare themselves with fitters, drivers, labourers, clerical workers, and technicians in other plants and industries. Miners and dockers cannot so easily find comparable groups of workers outside their industries. They therefore make comparisons with the general movement of rates and earnings elsewhere, and

---

[35] W. W. Daniel, *The Next Stage of Incomes Policy*, pp. 17–19.

[36] *Ibid.*, pp. 21–2.

[37] R. Hyman and I. Brough, *Social Values and Industrial Relations*, p. 61.

with general levels of pay. But comparisons are also drawn with
different groups in the same plant or industry. Fitters claim that their
differentials over other manual workers must be protected. Foremen
seek an increase in salary because the pay of the workers they
supervise has gone up. Unskilled workers complain that they have
little opportunity to increase their earnings over the basic rate and
they are therefore falling further behind the production workers.
Political and Economic Planning investigated the comparisons
which workplace negotiators took into account in pay negotiations.
Perhaps their most interesting finding was the close correspondence
between the replies of managers and shop stewards. Local comparisons with workers employed on similar jobs were referred to most
frequently by both of them, with managers (51 per cent) mentioning
them more often than shop stewards (41 per cent); other groups in
the same plant came second (22 per cent each); third were groups
elsewhere in the same industry (14 per cent and 16 per cent); and
groups employed by the same company in different plants came
fourth (6 per cent and 10 per cent).[38]

A detailed study of change in the use of comparisons in workplace
pay bargaining has been made by Brown and Sisson, using the long
run of detailed pay statistics available, grade by grade, for manual
workers employed in London newspaper production and Coventry
engineering. They were able to show that comparisons with workers in other London newspapers had a predominant effect on pay
movements in Fleet Street during 1961–4, but comparisons with
other grades in the same plant took over in 1964. External comparisons assumed increasing importance in Coventry engineering during 1964–71, but comparisons with other grades in the same plant
reasserted themselves after 1971. In both instances they were able to
link the change with an alteration in bargaining structure. From 1964
onwards there was a rapid development of productivity bargaining
in Fleet Street which for the first time settled 'comprehensive' rates
of pay for each grade in each newspaper, incorporating the myriad
components which had previously been separately negotiated items
in the pay packet. These 'comprehensive' agreements revealed
within each newspaper office 'the large differences in earnings that
had developed over the years when pay levels were obscure'. Consequently the individual chapels paid less attention to what their colleagues on other papers were earning, about which they were already

[38] W. W. Daniel, *The Next Stage of Incomes Policy*, p. 24.

fairly well informed, and took account of the overall levels of pay of other chapels in the same office. In 1971 the Coventry Engineering Employers Association terminated their local toolroom agreement 'which tied toolroom workers' earnings to a district rate', and was also used as a guide for the pay of other groups of skilled workers, thus freeing employers to negotiate settlements within their own plants, and to develop their own pay structures.[39]

There is very little evidence to indicate how typical these instances are of changes in the use of comparisons in workplace bargaining; and there are no recent studies of the use of comparisons in industry pay bargaining. But at least these studies of plant pay comparisons emphasize the importance of comparisons at that level, and give some notion of the ways in which they are used and changed.

There is even less evidence available on the arguments which are used in bargaining over other topics. The close bunching of changes in hours of work and holidays suggest that comparisons are decisive once a breakthrough has been made. The evidence of McCarthy and Coker indicates that the main concern of trade union representatives in disciplinary cases is to establish precedents which can serve to suggest what is fair in subsequent cases. More generally, and particularly with reference to bargaining over the organization of work, the widespread reliance of negotiators from both sides upon custom and practice again emphasizes the importance of fairness. The justification for following custom is that it is fair to maintain relationships which have been established in the past; and to seek the consent of those concerned before making a change.

POWER IN BARGAINING

Despite references to bargaining strength and strong bargaining relationships, this chapter has so far offered few hints of the extent to which power relationships permeate collective bargaining. In fact the mere existence of a collective bargaining relationship creates power resources for the negotiators. If there is a bargaining relationship, it persists because both sides believe that they have something to gain from it. Union negotiators and their members believe that they have obtained or might obtain some improvement in condi-

[39] Brown and Sisson, 'The Use of Comparisons in Workplace Wage Determination'.

tions of employment which would not be theirs without collective bargaining. The employer may merely believe it is better for his reputation that he should recognize the union, or he may attach some importance to his membership of an employers' association from which he would be bound to resign if he were to withdraw recognition. The value which each side finds in the relationship automatically gives power to the other side. The threat to withdraw from the relationship is two-edged, but it is a weapon. Without threatening to break the relationship, each side can show reluctance to make progress on concessions sought by the other side as a means of persuading the other side to pay more attention to its own claims.

The stages of a disputes procedure are another source of bargaining strength. Where one negotiator is reluctant to allow an issue to go on to the next stage, the other can put pressure on him. Managers are especially vulnerable to pressure of this kind in domestic procedures when the next stage of procedure involves their own superiors on whom their careers depend. A reference to the next level may entail informing the superior of past concessions or practices which the manager would prefer not to expose.

Power relationships in bargaining are not confined to those between the two sides. They exist also within each side. 'A strong bargaining relationship', according to Batstone and his colleagues,

> involves a large investment in terms of risk. In order to ensure returns upon that investment, each side has an interest in protecting and maintaining the power of the other. . . . Hence, much of the advice exchanged is aimed at preventing the other person getting into difficulties or being 'conned'. On several occasions we observed managers warning leader stewards and conveners that certain people were 'trying it on', and advising them not to get involved in the issue. Similarly, stewards sometimes cautioned managers with whom they had strong bargaining relationships about the activities of other managers.[40]

The advantage to each partner in a strong bargaining relationship depends on the other retaining the support of his own side.

The relative power of the parties can be influenced by the distribution of power on each side. In discussing the 'inevitable growth of informality', Michael Terry argues that managerial power derives

[40] Batstone *et al.*, *Shop Stewards in Action*, pp. 172–3.

from the top, but that is not true of trade unions, 'especially those with strong and autonomous shop floor bodies'.[41] Consequently, he suggests, the advantage is likely to lie with the union where the decision is within the authority of a foreman, and shifts further towards the other side the higher up the managerial hierarchy it is taken. Leftwing critics of the Donovan report and productivity bargaining argue that such a shift is the objective of the policy of formalizing plant bargaining. Tony Cliff described productivity agreements as 'part of a major offensive by the employing class of this country to shift the balance of forces permanently in their direction'.[42]

The case which Terry used to illustrate his argument was a measured daywork agreement which incorporated in writing the previous customs on mobility and flexibility between jobs. These customs had protected pieceworkers from loss of earnings when moved from one job to another. Managers and shop stewards supposed that the termination of piecework would have reduced the need for this protection, and were surprised by 'a positive spate of shopfloor complaints' which led to further restrictions on transfers. They 'reduced the speed with which transfers could be made' and 'ensured that men transferred were those who wanted to move'.[43] In this instance the response of the workers to formalization had been precisely as feared by the managers in McCarthy's survey. They sought and obtained a further set of even more advantageous informal concessions beyond those that had been formalized; and thereby prevented formalization from shifting decisions on work organization outside their control.

What has been the experience elsewhere? In the 'ChemCo' cement works studied by Nichols and Armstrong

the productivity deal . . . made the development of solidarity . . . a good deal more difficult. There seems to be very little the men can get their teeth into. Either they go on fiddling about with the grading system and wait for the national rises to 'come through' or they can escalate into a full blown challenge to the framework of the productivity deal itself—in which case they could well find their own union officials ranged against them as well as management. . . . By more or less eliminating the possibility of action at local level, the productivity deal makes it difficult for an emergent

[41] Michael Terry, *op. cit.*   [42] Tony Cliff, *The Employers' Offensive*, p. 3.
[43] Michael Terry, *op. cit.*

sense of solidarity to show results and so harden to the point where, national agreement or no national agreement, the men might take action on their own behalf.[44]

The ChemCo agreement was company-wide. In his study of industrial relations at two oil refineries, one in Kent and the other in Grangemouth, Duncan Gallie has assessed the longrun effects of a series of plant productivity agreements negotiated in each of them through the sixties. 'Productivity bargaining', he concluded,

> unquestionably shifted influence away from the full-time officials, and into the hands of the shop floor representatives. Equally, it strengthened the control that the workers could exercise over management decisions, by making existing powers more effective and by formally extending the scope of control to the whole sphere of work organisation.

Although 'grievance procedure was indeed formalised, . . . the shop stewards remained central to it'. Over questions of work organization there had been a 'shift from an informal tradition of cooperation to a formal recognition of a right of control. While not all formalization is necessarily advantageous to the work force or its representatives, formalisation of the right of control indisputably is.'[45]

There is no difficulty in finding explanations for the failure of the cement workers to increase their shop floor power through their productivity agreement. The agreement encouraged workers to share in redesigning their jobs, but rates of pay for the new jobs were determined according to a company-wide grading scheme under which disputed gradings were referred to a panel of managers. The scheme was designed to leave 'very little the men can get their teeth into'. Nevertheless a strong workplace organization might have been able to extract some advantage from it. (There is evidence that this happened elsewhere in ChemCo.) But the cement workers started with a weak shop floor organization and shop steward. They did not lose power as a result of the deal. They merely failed to increase their power.

Other variables might also be relevant to the impact of formalization on shop floor power, including, for example, the competence of

---

[44] Nichols and Armstrong, *op. cit.*, p. 112.
[45] Duncan Gallie, *In Search of the New Working Class*, pp. 172–6.

managers, technology, and the size of the undertaking. These and other factors would have to be investigated to provide an adequate explanation for the contrast in the experience of the oil refineries and Terry's plant compared with the cement workers, and compared with each other. Even without that, however, it is clear that there is no constant relationship between formalization of bargaining and the structure of power in industrial relations. Patterns of collective bargaining are too complex for that.

The one generalization which appears to hold good is that, other things being equal, a shift in the level of bargaining upwards or downwards leads to a redistribution of power in the same direction within each side. Thus the transfer of control over the pay of faceworking miners from colliery piecework negotiations to the national powerloading agreement transferred power from the branches to the Mineworkers' national conference and executive. However, it is a matter for debate whether this transfer left the union as a whole stronger or weaker. In their confrontations with the Coal Board and the government in 1972 and 1974 the Mineworkers did not appear to be weaker than they had been ten years before—although it must be admitted that the fuel crisis had buttressed their strength in the meantime. What the transfer of power within the union had unquestionably accomplished was to facilitate the achievement of some objectives at the expense of others. One of the chief aims of Will Paynter and the other miners' leaders who favoured the powerloading agreement was 'to reach and maintain a fair differential in wage rates between the different occupations'; to provide 'a wage-negotiating system where . . . all the workers in the industry advance together, not section by section'; to make 'possible the benefits of increased productivity being shared by all and not as a concession to a privileged grade'.[46] They wanted to harness the strength of the faceworkers to exert pressure on a wage structure which would include all miners, and thus raise the earnings of the daywagemen in relation to those of the pieceworkers; and their intentions were realized, for that was one of the outcomes of the agreement. However, the price of achieving their objective was the loss of the pieceworkers' power to bargain over their own earnings. The power of a union, or of a company or an employers' association can only be assessed when the objective to be attained is specified.

If that is true, then Terry's hypothesis about the effect of the level

[46] Will Paynter, *British Trade Unions and the Problem of Change*, pp. 116–17.

of bargaining on union power needs to be revised. Even with the strongest shop floor organization, the advantage can only be swung in the union's favour by allowing the decision to be taken on the shop floor so long as the issue *can* be decided on the shop floor. If the union's objective can only be achieved at a higher level—say a company-wide pay increase or a company pay structure or a standardization of working conditions across a company—it cannot be obtained by leaving the decision to the shop floor in each plant.

This line of argument calls into question the whole notion of a balance of power in collective bargaining. It cannot be assessed simply by counting victories and defeats on the basis of: 'you win some, you lose some', for results must be checked against objectives. Victories and defeats must be measured in relation to the importance to each side of their objectives—and that might be a matter of dispute, say between shop stewards and national leaders on the union side, or between different companies in an employers' association.

Another example of the inadequacy of a count of wins and losses in disputed issues as a measure of bargaining strength is provided by the comparison of two collieries quoted on p. 241. Analysis of the data showed that in the midland colliery, where the relationship was one of conflict, the branch secretary's bargaining power, when measured by the number of disputed issues won, was greater than that of his colleague in the northern colliery where relations were co-operative. When account was then taken of the issues settled without a dispute, however, the influence of the northern secretary as reckoned by both manager and union was well ahead of his midland colleague measured in the same way.[47]

Power in collective bargaining is also influenced by values. Batstone and his colleagues showed that the mobilization of support for collective attitudes increases the union's ability to achieve its objectives, whereas emphasis on individualistic values strengthens management. They went on to show that the parties had considerable scope in applying these general values to individual cases. Collective values may be mobilized to bring the whole plant out in support of a section in dispute, or to persuade a key section that they should use the procedure rather than strike and put their colleagues out of work.[48] Similarly notions of fairness can be used to select issues and support particular outcomes. Paynter and his colleagues emphasized the fairness of compressing differentials in support of the powerload-

[47] Christine Edwards, *op. cit.*   [48] See p. 60.

ing agreement. Eleven years later, when the introduction of incentive payments gave substantial advantages to the faceworkers, fairness was interpreted as requiring a high reward for those who were in a position to make direct contributions to raising productivity.

In this last instance, the Coal Board and the government lent their weight to support those miners' leaders who favoured incentives, showing that negotiators may employ values to influence the other side as well as their constituents. Similarly the leaders of the Coventry engineering employers were trying to influence the unions, as well as to mobilize the support of their own members, when they argued that the Coventry toolroom agreement should be terminated because the proper comparison for the pay of skilled timeworkers was the earnings of other skilled workers in their own plants rather than in the district as a whole. Since the civil service system of fair comparisons has developed an elaborate and fairly precise method of translating earnings figures for outside analogues into pay increases for civil servants, the main variable in civil service negotiations—except when the system is suspended—is the selection of analogues by argument over which comparisons are fair.

The process of bargaining cannot be understood without taking account of styles, values and power. However, with certain limited exceptions, current information about collective bargaining is far too meagre to permit patterns of styles, values and power to be discerned, plotted and explained. One exception is the shift towards formal plant bargaining in manufacturing, and a second is trade union density, which is one element in trade union power. Both these have already been discussed. A third exception is the most conspicuous aspect of power in collective bargaining—industrial action. It is the subject of the next chapter.

Chapter 7

STRIKES AND OTHER INDUSTRIAL ACTION

OTHER INDUSTRIAL ACTION

Since information about industrial action in Britain relates over-whelmingly to strikes, this chapter is largely about strikes; but it must be observed that strikes are not the only form of industrial action, and probably not the most common of them. Replies by both managers and shop stewards to questions in the Donovan Commission's surveys suggested that overtime bans were slightly more frequent than strikes, and that working to rule and 'go-slows' were relatively common.[1] Rather more precise questions were posed by subsequent *Workplace Industrial Relations* surveys. National (industry-wide) strikes were excluded, and managers and shop stewards were asked for their experience over the previous two years. In 1973 strikes were reported by 18 per cent of managers and 23 per cent of shop stewards; overtime bans by 25 per cent of managers and 36 per cent of stewards; threats to strike by 19 per cent of managers and 26 per cent of stewards; working to rule by 17 per cent of managers and 25 per cent of stewards; and 'go-slows' by 9 per cent of managers and 9 per cent of stewards.[2] There can be little doubt that the overtime ban is now the most common form of industrial action.

No official statistics are collected of the use of sanctions other than strikes, and few case studies have explored them in detail. Consequently we know little about them. From the point of view of the union and the employee they have the immense advantage of putting pressure on the employer at no cost to the union and at no cost to the employee except in lost overtime earnings. There is always the risk that the employer will send workers home when their action appears to involve a breach of contract, and the union may be forced to

[1] *Workplace Industrial Relations 1966*, pp. 32–4, 83–4.
[2] *Workplace Industrial Relations 1973*, pp. 79–80.

retreat or strike; but if the choice at this stage is for a strike the union has the advantage that the employer's stocks have already been reduced by the sanctions previously employed. In the famous contest between the miners and the Heath administration over the winter of 1973–4, the miners imposed a ban on overtime and on safety work in November, the first to run down stocks and the second to put pressure on colliery managers who had to carry out the work themselves. In January the shortage of fuel forced the country on to a three-day working week. At the end of the month the miners voted on the Coal Board's offer. Whatever might have happened if the question had been put the previous autumn, the majority in favour of a strike was four to one; and the miners were in a commanding position when they finally stopped work on 10 February.

In some industries the use of sanctions short of a strike may be even more effective than a strike. A railway strike causes a great deal of initial disruption, but within a day or two most individuals and organizations have made alternative emergency transport arrangements which may prove more durable than the strikers' capacity to hold out. An overtime ban or a work-to-rule causes considerable disruption and delay without turning most customers away. Even in industry-wide disputes, therefore, the railway unions have shown a preference since the war for these forms of sanction. A national strike in electricity supply is unthinkable. It would bring the nation to a halt, including hospitals and most other emergency services, and produce general chaos within a day or two. It is too powerful a weapon to use. During a dispute over pay in December 1970 the manual workers' unions in electricity supply applied a general work-to-rule and an overtime ban. The effect on production was greater than the unions had anticipated, and there were frequent and often prolonged 'blackouts' in all parts of the country. Within a few days the public reaction to electricity supply workers was so hostile that the union leaders were under strong pressure from their members to call the sanctions off. They did so on the promise of an independent inquiry into their claims. The inquiry, chaired by Lord Wilberforce, recommended substantial increases in pay early in 1971.[3] In October 1977 the application of similar sanctions unofficially in a minority of power stations was enough to cause widespread blackouts.

Perhaps the most telling evidence of the effectiveness of sanctions

[3] *Wilberforce Report* (electricity supply).

which curtail production but do not bring it to a halt comes from the newspaper industry. Lost production of a newspaper cannot be made good and customers lost to a competitor are not easily won back. Managers are therefore under great pressure to overcome any interruption at once, and frantic negotiations late at night are a common feature of Fleet Street industrial relations. In major disputes a newspaper may suffer daily, or frequently repeated, losses of production over periods of weeks. Newspaper workers rarely strike.

These instances of the use of sanctions short of strikes in a few industries cannot, however, give any more than the most sketchy clue to their general use in British industrial relations; but there is one more finding that can be extracted from the *Workplace Industrial Relations* surveys. The 1973 survey shows that where one sanction is used within a plant the others are likely to be employed as well. The figures are set out in Table 10, which reports the replies of senior managers. Plants with one strike were much more likely to experience all other forms of sanction than plants with no strikes, and plants with more than one strike were considerably more likely to experience all other forms of sanction than plants with only one strike.

Table 10

Experience of Industrial Action over the Two Years before 1973[4]

Other Sanctions	No Strikes per cent	One Strike per cent	More than One Strike per cent
Threats to Strike	13	38	60
Overtime Bans	19	51	63
Working to Rule	13	26	39
Go-slow	5	15	37
None of the Above	66	34	20

STRIKE PATTERNS

The Department of Employment attempts to record and classify all

[4] The figures in this table, drawn from information collected for *Workplace Industrial Relations 1973*, were supplied by its editor, S. R. Parker.

'stoppages of work due to industrial disputes' which involve ten or more workers and which last for at least one day, or which lose more than a hundred working days. No attempt is made to distinguish between 'strikes' and 'lockouts', since in many instances the matter is debatable, and the words 'strike' and 'stoppage of work' are therefore commonly treated as synonymous.

The minimum qualifications for inclusion in the official returns exclude a large number of strikes. In an account of the work of the Motor Industry Joint Labour Council, Sir Jack Scamp drew upon information supplied by eight major car producers to show that in 1967 '60 per cent of all stoppages lasted for less than four hours'.[5] Any of these which did not involve two hundred workers or more would not qualify.

Some strikes which qualify nevertheless go unrecorded. There is no obligation on employers to make returns. Except for the Coal Board and the Post Office which make their own returns direct to the Department, information is collected by its local offices. They have good local contacts; they study the local newspapers; and when a strike lasts any length of time there will be claims for supplementary benefit for strikers' families. Even so, the provisional results of the Warwick survey suggest that probably a half or less of the manufacturing strikes which meet the requirements are in fact recorded. The prominence of coalmining in postwar strike comparisons between industries is partly explained by the Coal Board's practice of central reporting.

Some stoppages are not returned because the managers concerned do not see them as strikes. Batstone and his colleagues report that this happens where managers see stoppages as 'legitimate', which 'is particularly common in relation to stoppages over such issues as safety and working conditions'.[6]

'Political' strikes are separately recorded by the Department and excluded from its annual returns and tables. In most recent years there have been one or two strikes which fall within the Department's definition of a political strike. The Department estimated that 1.25 million workers came out on 1 March and 18 March 1971 on one-day protest strikes against the Industrial Relations Bill then before parliament. At the end of July 1972 forty thousand dockers and 130,000 workers in other industries struck in protest against the

---

[5] *Report by Mr. A. J. Scamp on the Activities of the Council.*
[6] Batstone *et al.*, *The Social Organization of Strikes*, pp. 19–20.

imprisonment of five dockers for contempt of court in an action arising under the Industrial Relations Act. On 1 May 1973 about 1.6 million workers joined in a day of protest against the government's incomes policy sponsored by the Trades Union Congress.

Apart from political strikes, the stoppages excluded from the official statistics are mainly small strikes. The larger the number of workers on strike and the longer the strike lasts, the more certain it is to be reported. Consequently comparisons of the total number of workers involved in strikes and of the total number of working days lost in strikes between one industry and another or between one year and another are more reliable than comparisons of the total number of strikes, for small strikes make only a modest contribution to the totals of workers involved and working days lost. Even comparisons of total numbers of strikes may be fairly reliable so long as it may be assumed that standards of reporting remain fairly constant. The totals themselves are inaccurate, but the trends over time and contrasts between industries can probably be accepted without too much qualification.

Although the figures for workers involved and working days lost are more reliable than those for the numbers of strikes, they are nevertheless only estimates, and estimates vary.

If a stoppage affects only part of an establishment, the strikers may wish to exaggerate the extent of their support, while management may understate the impact of the dispute. Even if the factory is forced to close . . . there will be the problem of distinguishing those actively supporting the strike and those laid off in consequence. This distinction is impossible to apply accurately, short of interviewing every employee; and, even then, there is the difficulty that support is a question of degree rather than all or nothing. British statistics do however separate workers 'directly' and 'indirectly' involved at each establishment, even if the estimates must on occasion be little more than guesses. Perhaps wisely, the Department of Employment does not even attempt to guess the number of workers in other factories made idle by stoppages.[7]

The main trends in postwar British strikes are set out in Figures 1 and 2. Up to 1968 the main movements in the number of strikes were fluctuations up and down, although there was a fairly steady increase between 1950 and 1957. There was a slight tendency for the number

[7] Richard Hyman, *Strikes*, p. 18.

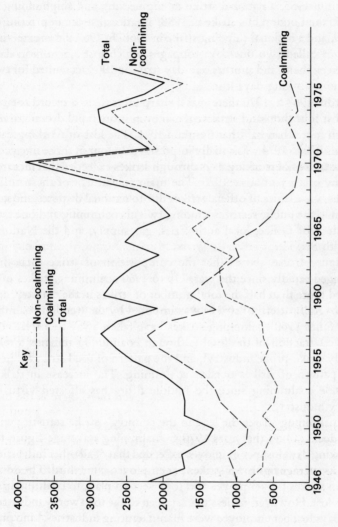

Figure 1. Number of Recorded Strikes 1946–77

of working days lost to increase over the same period, but it was heavily overlaid by wide fluctuations. Most of the peak years for losses were distinguished by one major strike: a national railway strike in 1955, a national strike in engineering and shipbuilding in 1957, the London bus strike in 1958, a national strike in printing in 1959, and a national shipping strike in 1966. In 1962 the engineering unions called two one-day stoppages which lost 3.5 million days between them, and another one-day strike in 1968 accounted for two million working days lost.

From 1968 to 1970 there was a sharp increase to a record total of almost four thousand strikes and an even more rapid decline to not much more than half that figure in 1971. The loss of working days from 1970 to 1974 was equally impressive. In four of those five years the total loss of working days through strikes exceeded that incurred in any other year since 1926. The main constituent of these heavy losses was a series of official strikes due to national disputes, most of them in the public sector, including two in coalmining and one each in the Post Office, local authorities, gas supply, and the National Health Service.

Figure 1 also shows that the composition of strike totals has changed rapidly since the war. Up to 1960 coalmining strikes provided more than half the total number of strikes in the country, and the overall pattern of strikes was imposed by the trend in coalmining. Since 1960 coalmining strikes have fallen away to a relatively modest fraction of the total (although coalmining remains a relatively strike-prone industry), and the pattern of total strikes is now the pattern of strikes outside coalmining. The increase in strikes outside coalmining since the middle fifties has affected virtually every industry.

Coalmining shares the lead in the country's strike statistics with the docks. Over the years 1970–5 coalmining's average figure for working days lost per employee exceeded that of all other industries, and its average figure for strikes per employee came third. The docks led in strikes per employee and took second place to coalmining in days lost. However, no less than sixteen of the top twenty industries for days lost per employee were manufacturing industries,[8] and only three of the top twenty industries for strikes per employee were not in manufacturing. Seventy-eight manufacturing industries exceeded

[8] These are industries classified as Minimum List Heading industries, of which there are 178 in all.

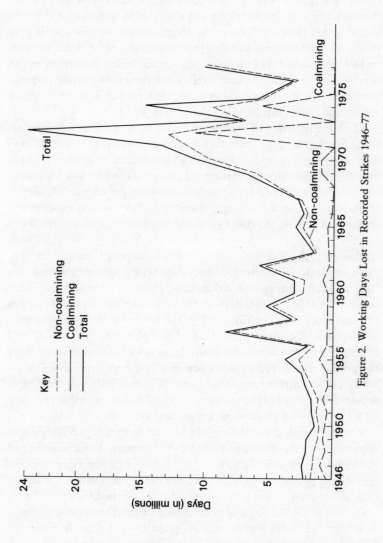

Figure 2. Working Days Lost in Recorded Strikes 1946–77

1.1 strikes a year per 10,000 employees; and 41 came below that figure. Three public sector industries came higher and eleven were below; and nine private services came higher, with 36 below. Taking the dividing line for working days lost at an average of 0.2 of a working day per employee a year, 72 manufacturing industries, five public sector industries and four private services came above the line, and 47 manufacturing industries, nine public sector industries and 41 private services came below. Strikes are therefore heavily concentrated in manufacturing industry, although the public sector makes a significant contribution to working days lost.[9]

The Department's figures indicate that there is a heavy concentration of strikes in large manufacturing plants. Over the years 1971–3 they give the average proportion of manufacturing plants which experienced no stoppage during the course of the year as no less than 98 per cent, and they accounted for 81 per cent of manufacturing employment. On the average, therefore, plants which experienced strikes had almost ten times as many employees as those which did not.[10]

However, the Warwick survey, which also covers manufacturing, gives grounds for treating these results with caution. It found that large plants had more strikes than small plants did, but when account was taken of the size of the labour force, small plants had more strikes and incidents of other forms of industrial action *per employee* than large plants did. Just under half of the plants in the survey had experienced some form of industrial action by manual workers over the previous two years, and 9 per cent had experienced action by white collar employees. Some form of industrial action had been reported by a third of the plants with 50–99 full-time employees, and by 87 per cent of those with a thousand or more employees.

Another result derived from the official figures is probably more dependable. Strikes tend to be highly concentrated in a minority of plants which experience strikes. According to these figures, 5 per cent of the plants which had strikes in 1971–3 accounted for 24 per cent of the strikes and 67 per cent of the days lost.[11]

One of the most famous conclusions of the Donovan Commission, derived from the figures supplied by the then Ministry of Labour, was 'that the overwhelming majority of stoppages—some

---

[9] Figures supplied by the Department of Employment.
[10] *Department of Employment Gazette*, November 1976.
[11] *Ibid*.

95 per cent—are due to unofficial strikes'.[12] Since then the Ministry, now the Department of Employment, has grown more cautious. It no longer records unofficial strikes but only strikes known to be official (which have continued to run at about 5 per cent of the total) and other strikes. The Donovan Commission's own surveys should have made them more careful in their use of words. They were aware that most union executives have the power to pay strike benefit in respect of strikes which have not received their authorization. Their secretariat examined the records of the fourteen largest unions in the country and found that benefit had been paid in two hundred such strikes in 1965, and probably in more than 150 in 1966. Moreover, most strikes are over before there is an opportunity for official authorization to be granted. In 1964–6 over half of all unauthorized strikes lasted less than two days, and four-fifths were over within the week. The Commission concluded 'that in the majority of unofficial strikes the unions do not officially declare an attitude; and that in a substantial proportion of the remainder they are prepared to pay dispute benefit after the event'.[13] That is not what the term unofficial strike is usually taken to mean.

A more fruitful way of expressing their findings would have been to emphasize the lack of central union control over the use of strikes. Whatever union rules may say, and whether union executives like it or not, the control of strikes is normally in the hands of workplace organizations. This conclusion applies even more forcibly to strikes which are too small to be recorded or fail to be recorded, for virtually all of them must be unauthorized. Moreover, it is probable that official authorization of the use of sanctions other than strikes is a good deal more rare than the authorization of strikes. Official authorization of overtime bans and working to rule is only relevant when there is need to co-ordinate action over a wide area. Within the plant it is irrelevant. No question of strike benefit arises. The use of sanctions in industrial disputes is therefore overwhelmingly a work-place matter except in major strikes.

A sharper distinction can be drawn between constitutional and unconstitutional disputes, for it turns on whether the issue in dispute has been through all the relevant stages of the agreed disputes procedure before the strike takes place. If not, the strike is described as unconstitutional whether a no-strike undertaking is explicit in the

[12] *Report*, p. 97.
[13] *Ibid.*, p. 109.

agreement, or merely implied or understood.[14] The constitutionality of other sanctions is perhaps more doubtful in some instances, but the 1976 engineering procedure tries to leave no room for uncertainty. It ordains that

> there shall be no stoppage of work, either of a partial or a general character, such as a strike, lock-out, go-slow, work-to-rule, overtime ban or any other restrictions, before the stages of procedure provided for in this Agreement have been exhausted.

There are no overall figures of constitutional and unconstitutional strikes, although the Engineering Employers Federation publishes figures for strikes affecting their members. In 1976 seventy-two (87.8 per cent) of the 82 white collar strikes were unconstitutional, as were 608 (95.1 per cent) of the 639 manual workers' strikes, giving an overall figure of 94.3 per cent unconstitutional strikes.[15] The Department's returns show that 3.4 per cent of recorded British strikes in 1976 were known to be official, compared with 5.7 per cent of engineering strikes in federated firms which were classified as constitutional. It seems plausible that the proportion of constitutional strikes should be much the same as the proportion of strikes known to be official. There are some instances of workers striking without authorization over an issue which has been through procedure, but probably the great majority of strikes which do not have official authorization by the union occur before procedure has been exhausted, many of them before it has been used at all. Similarly, unions occasionally call official strikes before procedure has been used, but not often.

A feature of the recent strike pattern which does not emerge from the official statistics is the use of the 'sit-in' strike, or the occupation of the plant by strikers, which became relatively common following the occupation of Upper Clyde Shipbuilders in 1971. In this instance the occupation was a 'work-in' which was therefore not recorded as a strike. Next year a number of Manchester engineering plants were occupied during a strike over claims for improved pay and conditions submitted to all federated firms in the district.[16] In many

---

[14] An analysis of industry procedures found that 41 per cent expressly prohibit both strikes and lockouts, and 24 per cent expressly prohibit strikes, until procedure has been exhausted. (Norman Singleton, *Industrial Relations Procedures*, p. 64.)

[15] Engineering Employers Federation, *Annual Review, 1976–7*.

[16] See p. 81.

instances occupations have been protests against threatened closures or redundancies. In some the aim was to secure better redundancy terms, whereas others were intended to elicit political intervention to prevent a closure. Several, like Upper Clyde, were successful, a few leading to the establishment of worker co-operatives. In others, like the engineering strikes in Manchester, the intention was to increase pressure on employers during disputes over more traditional issues. Hemingway and Keyser reported twelve redundancy sit-ins from January to June 1975, and fifteen over other issues.[17] The use of the sit-in may have been inspired by the example of France in 1968;[18] and its use in redundancies in Britain was due to rising unemployment and the manifest vulnerability of governments to this form of pressure.

EXPLANATIONS FOR THEM

An explanation of strike patterns presupposes a theory of why workers strike. Strikes have been described as 'both a reaction against frustrating situations and an instrument of positive action'.[19] It will be assumed in the following pages that the two main motives for striking are: to exert pressure on managers, employers' associations or the government in order to achieve a collective bargaining objective; and to express frustration over some aspect of the work situation. Both motives may be at work in a given strike. It is not uncommon, for example, for workers to strike over delays in handling grievances, thus giving vent to their impatience and putting pressure on the negotiators to deal with the issues.

In order to discover how these motives are related to patterns of strikes, information is needed on the actual issues about which workers strike. It is not easy to determine the principal cause of a strike since it may have several causes, and the overt issue may be less important than other grievances of the strikers. Nevertheless the Department of Employment classifies strikes by the reason given for them, and the figures they publish under this heading give the best indication available of the issues involved. Table 11 sets out their returns for the years 1974, 1976 and 1977. The first of them was the

[17] *Who's in Charge*, pp. 64–5.   [18] *Ibid.*, p. 5.
[19] S. Wellisz, 'Strikes in Coal-Mining'. This quotation is taken from Chapter 5 of Hyman, *Strikes*, which gives a fuller discussion of motives for striking.

Table 11

Reasons Given for Striking, 1974, 1976 and 1977

Reason	1974				1976				1977			
	Strikes Nos.	(%)	Days Lost 000s	(%)	Strikes Nos.	(%)	Days Lost 000s	(%)	Strikes Nos.	(%)	Days Lost 000s	(%)
Pay[20]	1,192	(66)	13,109	(88)	875	(43)	1,831	(52)	1,558	(58)	8,233	(79)
Duration and Pattern of Hours Worked	53	(2)	201	(1)	66	(3)	40	(1)	45	(2)	26	(−)
Redundancy Questions	85	(3)	99	(1)	86	(4)	199	(6)	77	(3)	166	(2)
Trade Union Matters	184	(6)	500	(3)	166	(8)	379	(11)	189	(7)	313	(3)
Working Conditions and Supervision	156	(5)	116	(1)	215	(11)	205	(6)	251	(9)	211	(2)
Manning and Work Allocation	263	(9)	409	(3)	398	(20)	399	(11)	354	(13)	905	(9)
Dismissal and other Disciplinary Measures	259	(9)	411	(3)	210	(10)	456	(13)	229	(8)	534	(5)
Total	2,922	(100)	14,845	(100)	2,016	(99)	3,509	(100)	2,703	(100)	10,378	(100)

[20] Strikes over pay are subdivided into strikes over wage rates and earnings levels, and strikes over extra wage and fringe benefits; but the latter are always a small fraction of the total.

last year which was, at least for most of the time, largely free from the restraints of strict incomes policy. The second was a year in which incomes policy was applied fairly successfully and with relatively little friction. By 1977 the policy was meeting a good deal of opposition. It seems to be generally true that the number and size of strikes over pay are affected by incomes policy, and such a relationship is clearly visible in these three years.

A different system of classification might have given different results. In examining twenty-four instances of strikes and 'near-strikes' in a single plant, Batstone and his colleagues listed all 'the reasons put forward by the workers for action'. (In most instances several reasons were given.) The most frequently mentioned were: 'management breaking agreements, "conning", adopting a hard line' (27 per cent); 'fairness, comparisons with other work groups' (16 per cent); 'mobility, manning, job description' (12 per cent); 'management ignore men's efforts, goodwill, and intentions' (12 per cent); and 'loss of money, security' (9 per cent).[21] Still another set of reasons might have been suggested by the managers, had they been asked. Given the categories adopted by the Department, however, pay emerges as far and away the most important overt reason for strikes, responsible for two-thirds of the strikes and 88 per cent of the working days lost in 1974. With a major miners' strike, 1974 was an exceptional year, but it illustrates the point that a heavy annual total of working days lost is almost always due to one or two major industry-wide strikes, and these strikes are almost always over pay. Even in 1976, which is an exceptional year because of its small number of strikes and low losses of working days, and because of the unusually small contribution of pay strikes to the totals, pay disputes accounted for 43 per cent of the strikes and 52 per cent of the days lost.

This predominance of pay disputes in the overall figures provides some explanation for the difference in strike patterns between the public sector, manufacturing and the private services. In the public sector, pay is settled in industry negotiations, and in manufacturing the plant is the most important level of pay settlement, with the company taking second place. Consequently strikes over pay might be expected to be relatively common in manufacturing and relatively rare in the public sector; but when strikes over pay occur in the public sector they might be expected to be large. In fact strikes in

[21] Batstone *et al.*, *The Social Organization of Strikes*, pp. 47–8.

general are far more common in manufacturing than in the public sector, and the contribution of the public sector to total working days lost is significantly larger than its contribution to total strikes. As a whole, the private services settle pay either in industry negotiations or by managerial discretion at the company or the plant, and trade unions are generally weak. In these circumstances it seems reasonable to suppose that there would be few strikes over pay and no reason to suppose that, when they occurred, strikes over pay would be relatively large. In fact the private services are relatively strike-free and make a particularly modest contribution to working days lost through strikes. The two major exceptions are port transport and road haulage. Negotiations over pay in the docks are mainly port by port, and in road haulage the main negotiations over pay are regional, supplemented by bargaining with individual employers. Both industries are highly unionized. In these respects therefore their industrial relations characteristics are more akin to those of manufacturing industry than to other private services. A third, and lesser, exception is construction, which supplements industry agreements on pay with a good deal of negotiation over 'incentive payments' on site, and has a higher level of unionization than most private services.[22]

So far the evidence lends support to a structural explanation of strikes over pay to the extent that they are 'instruments of positive action'. The structure of collective bargaining determines the points at which pressure for pay increases can be most effectively applied, and therefore exerts an influence over the pattern of strikes. This explanation helps to account for differences between the strike patterns of the three main sectors of the economy. Can it also account for the changing trends since the war?

Under the piecework system, collieries were the scene of a 'running battle between the manager and his pieceworkers over their wages and his costs'.[23] Piecework prices were settled face by face, and changes in the structure of the seam and conditions of work at the coal face could bring wide fluctuations in piecework earnings. There were therefore negotiations on allowances to compensate for

---

[22] The paucity of strikes in industries with a low union density is not primarily due to the absence of strike pay for non-unionists, since most strikes in unionized industries are not financed by the unions. It should rather be attributed to a low propensity to collective action where individualistic attitudes prevail, encouraged by managerial style and the small average size of plants.

[23] G. B. Baldwin, *Beyond Nationalisation, The Labor Problems of British Coal*, p. 176.

diminished piecework earnings. Men transferred from one face to another might suffer 'a drop in wages unless they could persuade the under-manager to increase the rate'; and if men did not complete as much work as he expected the under-manager 'would pay only for the amount of work actually completed' so that they would not get their allowances.[24] The pay of faceworkers was therefore settled in fragmented bargaining with small groups, and earnings fluctuated considerably despite the system of allowances. In examining strikes in four Lancashire pits, W. H. Scott and his colleagues sought to test the hypothesis 'that groups whose wages fluctuated from week to week would have a greater number of wage disputes than groups whose wages were more stable', and found that their evidence went some way to support it.[25] The faceworkers accounted for the great majority of the strikes, and among them the fillers and packers were the two most strike-prone groups. In matters of pay, 'for faceworkers, and particularly fillers, fluctuation in earnings was the problem', and 'under variable physical conditions and with advancing mechanisation, the main causes of variability of earnings lie increasingly outside the faceworker's control'.[26]

Pay settlement in coalmining was therefore extremely fragmented at that time. Although this fragmentation does not explain why the industry should be responsible for more than half the recorded strikes in Britain during the fifties, it is enough to account for its place at the top of the list of strike-prone industries. Within each colliery there were many points at which pressure might yield pay increases. The evidence also provides a link between the other main motive for striking—'a reaction to frustration'—and the pattern of coalmining strikes. There can be few more frustrating experiences for wage-earners than to suffer wide fluctuations in their earnings from week to week, especially when the causes of variability lie outside their control; and fluctuating earnings might be expected to make them less concerned with losses of earnings caused by striking.

From 1957 onwards the contribution of coalmining to the annual total of strikes began to fall. Part of the decline is due to the decrease in the labour force. It is now less than 40 per cent of the 1957 figure, but the average number of strikes for the five years 1970–4 was only 12 per cent of the average for 1953–7; so falling manpower is not the only influence at work. The other reason usually given for the downward trend in coalmining strikes is the powerloading agree-

[24] Scott et al., *Coal and Conflict*, p. 124.   [25] *Ibid.*, p. 130.   [26] *Ibid.*, p. 190.

ment of 1966 which has had the effect of transferring all but a handful of faceworkers from piecework to daywork. Thereafter their earnings fluctuated only with overtime and absenteeism. Rates of pay were settled in central negotiations between the Coal Board and their union. The main issue for negotiation at the pit was the work to be done in return for the fixed wage. There has not yet been time to assess the impact of the introduction of incentive payments at the end of 1977.

If the structure of bargaining accounts for strike patterns, the powerloading agreement can explain a sharp fall in the number of coalmining strikes. However, the bulk of the decline had already happened before 1966, so that, if the explanation is to be sustained, an earlier change in bargaining structure must be discovered. In fact the national powerloading agreement was the culmination of a long process of mechanization and consequent adjustments in the traditional methods of pay settlement. The proportion of coal output which was powerloaded rose from 4 per cent in 1950 to 70 per cent in 1965. During these years powerloading agreements were negotiated coalfield by coalfield. Except for the Scottish agreement which settled a time rate, these divisional agreements shared two features. They retained a margin of pay varying with output, but the major part of weekly pay was a fixed rate; and the main decisions on the pay of powerloading faceworkers were taken jointly by the divisional coal boards and area union officials, not at the pit. It is plausible to link these changes with the declining propensity to strike on the grounds that the opportunities to apply pressure for increases in pay were progressively reduced and that greater stability of pay reduced the faceworkers' frustrations.

Corroboration of the link between bargaining structure and strikes comes from the three other most strike-prone industries of the fifties and early sixties—car manufacture, docks and shipbuilding. Their systems of pay settlement had important similarities with that of coalmining. At that time most car plants, other than those owned by Ford and Vauxhall, operated piecework systems. Turner and his colleagues collected detailed evidence of wide fluctuations in one car plant in 1962–3, and reported that such fluctuations are characteristic

of earnings generally in the payment-by-results plants. . . . This is partly a consequence . . . of the general fluctuation in production to which it [the car industry] has become liable in recent years. It is also a consequence of such more minor disturbances to output as the effects of technical hold-ups, of breakdowns, sometimes of changes in models or equipment, and of strikes in other departments or plants. Occasionally, it results from methods of bonus calculation themselves.[27]

There was an opportunity for an increase of pay every time a new rate was set or an old time revised. Bargaining

tends to start from the assumption that the new task must be given at least the same earnings . . . as that with which the old task ended. . . . Moreover, workers' productivity tends to rise particularly fast in the first few weeks or months after a new task is undertaken. . . . Thus, the more frequently job-rates have to be changed, the faster earnings of production workers rise';[28]

and the more anxious were timeworkers in the same plant to catch up by means of lieu rates, or bonuses or plus-payments of one sort or another.

Frequent changes in piecerates were not a characteristic of the docks, for one of the industry's main problems was the failure to change them even with new methods and equipment.

Where mechanisation is introduced and piecework rates remain unadjusted, piecework earnings tend to 'run away' from the time rates. Attempts are then made to correct this tendency in a general way by granting wage increases which provide for a smaller percentage addition to piece-rates than to time rates. . . . A consequence of this is that for many piecework operations which have remained untouched by mechanisation or by the introduction of new methods, the rate is too low and no longer offers a reasonable incentive.[29]

A move from one type of cargo to another could therefore bring wide fluctuation in earnings. In Liverpool, however, the practice of 'welting' meant that piecework earnings contributed little if anything to the earnings of most dockers. The variable element was overtime and especially weekend working, paid at exceptionally

[27] Turner *et al.*, *Labour Relations in the Motor Industry*, p. 159.
[28] *Ibid.*, p. 157.
[29] Devlin Committee, *Final Report*, p. 23.

high rates, and pay fluctuated with the availability of weekend work. Prior to 1967 dockers were casual employees unless they were among the minority of 'perms', and when no work was available they were entitled only to 'attendance money' and a guaranteed weekly minimum far below the level of average earnings. This was another cause of fluctuations in pay. Because of opposition to the revision of piecework rates, bargaining concentrated on the allowances which could be paid for working cargoes which, due to poor stowing or some other unusual feature, did not yield normal earnings, or were unusually unpleasant to handle. Since every cargo differs from the last in some way, there was plenty of room for argument.

In the shipyards, piecework had long since ceased to be the normal method of paying the 'black squads' who build the main structure of a ship and were responsible for most of the industry's strikes. It had been replaced by lieu rates, which were separately negotiated yard by yard and ship by ship. According to G. C. Cameron, insecurity was 'a major cause of strikes in the shipbuilding industry'. It was caused not only by wide variations in the demand for ships, but also by methods of production.

> Shipbuilding is an assembly industry in which the skills of the many trades are used in turn, so when the work of any particular trade is finished on one vessel, there is the possibility that other vessels in the yard will not be at the stage of building which requires the skill of the particular trade which is seeking new work.

Moreover, 'the earnings opportunities for any trade' depend on 'the changing stages of vessel assembly. Thus even if a trade is not paid off at the conclusion of its work on one vessel, it may have its overtime opportunities reduced or completely removed, or be under-employed.'[30] Bargaining over pay occurred

> at a point where management greatly requires [a] particular skill. . . . A good example of this type of dispute is the pre-launching strike of the shipwrights. Amongst the duties of this craft is the preparation and control of the launching of each vessel, and this . . . provides a highly suitable occasion for a wage claim which can, if necessary, be backed by a short strike.[31]

[30] G. C. Cameron, 'Post-war Strikes in the North-East Shipbuilding and Ship-repairing Industry'.   [31] Ibid.

The characteristics of a strike-prone industry at that time can, therefore, be established with some confidence. They were: highly fragmented bargaining, and fluctuating earnings. These characteristics were in some instances associated with piecework, but they could also be found where bargaining concentrated on overtime and lieu rates, and where fluctuations in earnings were due to casual labour or to lay-offs. It is also relevant that dock strikes immediately interrupt the transit of goods, and that strikes of key workers in car manufacture, coalmining and shipbuilding rapidly bring the whole production process to a halt; although by no means all workers possessing equivalent economic power are strike-prone. For example, railwaymen, electricity supply workers and water supply workers are not.

However, these common characteristics of strike-prone industries do not explain why the number of strikes outside coalmining were rising while strikes in coalmining were falling. In fact the share of car manufacture, docks and shipbuilding in total strikes outside coalmining also fell during the sixties as strikes became more frequent in other manufacturing industries and services, and in the public sector as well. Without a detailed examination of the strike records of each one of them, or at least a number of them, it is impossible to give a convincing explanation for the general upward trend outside coalmining. It is, however, plausible to suggest that the rising trend in strikes might be associated with rising wage drift, which continued almost throughout the fifties and early sixties,[32] with the rising number of shop stewards, and with the growth in the volume of workplace bargaining which, it is generally agreed, went on over those years. The first provided increasing opportunities for fragmented bargaining and a growing risk of fluctuations in earnings, and the second and third characteristics indicated a greater capacity to exploit the opportunities for increasing earnings which fragmentation provided. But it must be observed that this explanation, which may be termed the 'Donovan' theory of postwar strikes, is not grounded in any detailed investigation of the evidence. It is little more than a plausible guess.

From 1968 onwards short-term shifts have dominated the British

[32] Measures of drift vary. According to the Department of Employment, between 1949 and 1953 average hourly earnings excluding overtime exceeded average hourly wage rates by 0.3 per cent a year. The difference rose to 1.5 per cent a year in 1961–5, and fell again to 0.8 per cent in 1965–9. (*Department of Employment Gazette*, August 1975.)

pattern of strikes. The upsurge in strikes to an all-time peak in 1970 might be due to unprecedented fragmentation of pay settlements, but there is no evidence that anything of the sort occurred, and if this explanation were to be entertained, it would add to the difficulties of accounting for the even more rapid slump in strikes in 1971. At the time this decline was attributed by some commentators to the impact of the Industrial Relations Act, but the sharp fall in strikes began in the autumn of 1970, more than a year before the Act's main provisions came into effect, and as soon as they were effective the number of strikes began to rise again. It seems more credible to attribute these fluctuations to four special short-run factors: incomes policy, unemployment, inflation, and union growth. The incomes policy instituted by the Wilson administration in 1965, and given statutory backing in 1966, began to totter in 1969 and collapsed in 1970. Just as relatively strict incomes policies are accompanied by a reduction in strikes, so the collapse of incomes policies leads to a wave of strikes, as in 1951 and 1974 as well as in 1969 and 1970. Secondly, rising unemployment is generally associated with a reduction in strikes, and unemployment rose sharply over the winter of 1970–1. Thirdly, 1969 and 1970 experienced the most rapid inflation of prices and wages—the wage explosion—for many years, and a rapid rate of increase in the rate of inflation is also generally associated with an increase in the number of strikes. Inflation was worldwide and almost every major 'western' country experienced a sharp increase in strikes about that time. Finally, there was also a rapid growth in trade union membership in 1969 and 1970, and union growth is also usually associated with an increase in strikes. A number of variables like this cannot be accommodated in a theory except by mathematical techniques. A model has been constructed by Robert Davies with highly encouraging scores in the relevant tests.[33]

Another explanation is required for the high levels of working days lost during the years 1970–4. The main contribution to the totals came from a wholly unprecedented series of major public sector strikes which arose from conflicts between the unions concerned and the Heath administration over the application of its successive incomes policies to them. More detailed examination of these conflicts must wait until Chapter 8; but the structure of collective bargaining can explain why, if there was to be a wave of pay

[33] R. J. Davies, *An Economic Analysis of Quarterly Strike Activity in the U.K., 1966–75.*

strikes in the public sector, it should consist of a small number of very large strikes.

Otherwise, the structure of bargaining appears to make only a modest contribution to accounting for post–Donovan strike trends. The major shift to plant-wide bargaining occurred over the years 1968–72, but there is no evidence that the incidence of strikes in manufacturing since 1972 is lower than before 1968.[34] The effect of the change in bargaining structures, had there been one, should have been concentrated in those industries in which the reform of bargaining structure had been most widespread. Two such industries were car manufacture and the docks. In 1968 piecework was still the dominant method of payment in the car industry, but Chrysler shifted to measured daywork in 1969 and British Leyland followed, plant by plant, over the next few years. For three years after the first stage of the Devlin reforms brought decasualization in 1967, the docks preserved their old systems of payment along with their new shop steward organization. Both the rate of increase in dockers' earnings and the number of dock strikes reached new heights.[35] But in 1970 came the second stage of reform which concentrated on pay structures, and introduced port-wide time rates in most ports including London. Nevertheless car manufacture and docks remain the two most strike-prone industries in Britain apart from coalmining.

It is possible to give reasons for this failure of car and dock strikes to wither away. The second stage of the Devlin reforms in the docks was followed by a major running battle over containerization which threatened to take most of the work of stowing and unloading cargo away from the docks into inland container depots. This caused many individual strikes and soured relationships generally; and for several years the risk that, if their employers went out of business, they would be 'returned to the register'—at a lower level of pay—kept many dockers in a state of insecurity. The new car plant pay structures were not immune from pressure. Most had job-evaluated systems so that individual grades could press for regrading, and back

[34] Turner *et al.*, *Management Characteristics and Labour Conflict*, report that their survey showed that 'so far from declining with the establishment and development of formal collective agreements, conciliation procedures and consultative arrangements, . . . the incidence of labour unrest appears, if anything, to increase' (p. 37). However, their measure of unrest is working days lost through strikes, and it is entirely consistent with the structural explanation of strikes that such strikes as occur after the formalization of plant bargaining should, as a result of centralization of bargaining within the plant, be comparatively large.

[35] Mellish, *The Docks After Devlin*, pp. 42–5.

their claims with strikes, as a number of groups have done. A special problem has arisen in some car plants over the relative pay of former pieceworkers and timeworkers. Skilled timeworkers, who once accepted that production workers on piecework could earn as much as themselves, resent production workers being on, or close to, their own rates now that they are all paid time rates. Many car workers continued to suffer insecurity through fluctuating earnings. For, although they are paid the new measured daywork rate for working a full week, they are still liable to be laid off, and lay-offs have been common in recent years, most of them caused by strikes in other plants within the same company, or by stoppages in the increasingly strike-prone suppliers of car components. Finally, striking can be something of a habit. If centralized bargaining is to put an end to fragmented strikes because they can no longer extract concessions, the effect will come only when the workers have learned the lesson that sectional strikes do not pay off; and, if concessions are made despite centralized bargaining, the lesson may never be learned.

There is, however, one series of figures which appears to show a clear effect of the growth of plant-wide bargaining on strikes. Stoppages which lasted for two days or less accounted for 63.0 per cent of all recorded strikes in 1964. Thereafter their contribution fell in every year but one up to 1974, when it was 30.2 per cent. The drop in the number of recorded strikes involving less than fifty workers was not as steep or as regular, but it was nevertheless substantial—from 41.5 per cent in 1964 to 29.7 per cent in 1974. For a few years after 1964 the two series must have been influenced by the decline in coalmining strikes, but by 1970 the downward curve of coalmining strikes had flattened out. Consequently these trends may be seen as evidence of the effect of a general decline in fragmented bargaining. Subsequently there have been modest fluctuations in both series, but in 1977 the proportion of stoppages lasting for two days or less stood at 30.3 per cent, and of stoppages involving less than fifty workers at 28.5 per cent.

The explanation of strike patterns so far has depended almost entirely on bargaining structures as they affect pay. Many strikes, however, are not about pay; and, although grievances over pay or frustrations due to irregular earnings may lead to strikes on issues other than pay, it is also possible that some strikes which are classified as pay disputes may be due to grievances or irritations about other issues. The main groups of other issues are classified by the

Department of Employment as: manning and work allocation, dismissal and other disciplinary matters, trade union matters, working conditions and supervision, and redundancy questions. There is no compelling reason why methods of pay bargaining should explain patterns in these strikes.

The heading 'trade union matters' includes recognition disputes. In some of these an outside union is challenging a recognized union, but most of them arise where a union is seeking recognition in a plant or company which has so far not entered into collective bargaining arrangements. Where this is so, the strike cannot be unconstitutional for the union has no agreement with the employer to break. The remaining issues—work organization, discipline, working conditions, and redundancy—are all matters which are very imperfectly covered by joint regulation in private industry. In most of the public sector they are covered by procedures, some of which have not been agreed with the unions, but which are generally accepted and operated by them. In private industry, however, they are not usually regulated by industry agreements, and coverage by agreements in most individual plants and companies, where they exist, is commonly partial and scrappy. Accordingly, where disputes arise over issues under these headings in private industry, they are much less likely to be contained by procedure than similar disputes in the public sector, and strikes might be expected to be more common than in the public sector over these issues as well as over pay issues; as is indeed the case when the public sector is compared with manufacturing. This reasoning also helps to explain why such a large proportion of British strikes are unconstitutional. The cause may lie more in the methods of bargaining than in the issues.

THE FINANCE OF STRIKES

A further reason can be given for the small proportion of British strikes which are known to be official. Union finance plays a small part even in most official strikes. In 1971 the majority of male trade unionists were in unions whose rules prescribed strike benefit for men varying between £4 and £6 a week.[36] In many instances the figures have not been revised since then. Today they are far below 10 per cent of average male earnings, and for many workers they are

[36] John Gennard, *Financing Strikers*, p. 65.

under 5 per cent. The explanation for this low level of benefits is to be found in the statutory arrangements for the payment of supplementary benefit to strikers' families. (The striker himself is not entitled to benefit except in instances of special hardship.) Up to 1971 any strike benefit over £4.85 was deducted from the supplementary benefit received by the striker's family. Since a considerable number of strikers do seek supplementary benefit, levels of strike benefit over £4.85 appeared to be subsidies from the unions to the state.

In 1971 the figure was reduced by the then Conservative government to £1. Their intention was to discourage strikes. Whether their action had this effect is debatable, but one of its consequences was to give unions cause to doubt whether the payment of any strike benefit at all was justifiable. No strike benefit was paid in either of the national coalmining strikes in 1972–4. It also meant that strikers who claimed supplementary benefit on behalf of their families had little financial interest in whether the strike was official or not. Indeed it is possible that their interest was best served by taking part in a strike which was called unofficially but subsequently, after it was over, given approval by the executive to the extent of authorizing the payment of benefit. For unless the amount over £1 a week was successfully reclaimed by the Department of Health and Social Security, those taking part in such a strike were better off than official strikers.

The importance of supplementary benefit to some strikers, and the payment of tax rebates to strikers by their employers under the 'pay as you earn' system, has given the 'state subsidy theory of strikes' a considerable following in Britain. The main tenet of this theory is that the number and length of strikes in Britain are substantially higher than they would be if supplementary benefit and tax rebates were not available to strikers or their families. It also holds that the proportion of official strikes is substantially lower than it would be if strikers were more dependent on their unions for financial support.

The theory gained support through ignorance of the ways in which strikes are in fact financed. Very few unions have the resources to finance a long strike by anything like their total membership. Most long strikes involving very large bodies of workers have therefore always been financed from other sources besides the funds of the unions concerned. The principle of providing public support for strikers' families, at that time from the resources of the

Poor Law Guardians, has been established since 1898; and major stoppages, such as the national miners' lockout of 1926 which lasted for seven months, have received substantial support from public funds. It may well be that the support is now more generous than it was then, even taking into account the intervening changes in price levels and average earnings; but there has been no marked overall increase in the relative value of supplementary benefit rates in terms of average earnings since 1956, and there is no clear relation between the 'take-up' rate of benefit by strikers and the fluctuations in the relative value of benefits.[37] In any event supplementary benefit normally becomes payable only after two weeks, because most British manual workers are paid a week in arrears and a pay packet is expected to last for a week, so that supplementary benefit is irrelevant in more than 80 per cent of strikes. Entitlement to supplementary benefit may help to prolong strikes which have already lasted more than two weeks, but if it is to be a major influence on decisions to strike, the workers concerned must have some idea of the prospective duration of the strike before it begins, and in many instances, unless it is specifically intended to be a brief demonstration stoppage, it is probable that they have not.

Tax rebates are a relatively new feature in strike finance. Very few manual workers qualified to pay income tax before the war; and the value of tax rebates, and the numbers entitled to them, have increased very considerably in recent years with the effect of 'fiscal drag'; but it does not follow that it is a major source of income for strikers.

Two recent pieces of research have provided the first reliable information on the sources of strikers' income. W. J. Cole interviewed a sample of strikers involved in the national building strike in 1972,[38] and Gennard and Lasko interviewed samples of strikers in the 1971 national postal strike and in a strike of electricians at the Chrysler plants in Coventry in 1973.[39] All three were prolonged strikes so that there was time for supplementary benefit to come into operation for a number of weeks. The figures are set out in Table 12.

The experience of the three strikes is not entirely comparable. Pay in hand was not included in the building survey. No income tax

[37] Durcan and McCarthy, 'The State Subsidy Theory of Strikes'; Gennard, *op. cit.*, p. 28.
[38] W. J. Cole, 'Research Note. The Financing of the Individual Striker: A Case Study in the Building Industry'.
[39] Gennard and Lasko, 'The Individual and the Strike'; Gennard, *op. cit.*, p. 132.

rebates were paid to the postal strikers during their stoppage because the clerical staff were also on strike. The Chrysler strike was the only one in which strike benefit was paid instead of hardship allowances in special cases; and the rate of benefit was substantially higher than the union's standard benefit of £4 a week. This accounts for the very low level of supplementary benefit in the Chrysler strike. For all three strikes, however, savings provided by far the largest source of income, with spouses' earnings exceeding supplementary benefit. In none of them did supplementary benefit and tax rebate together approach the contribution made by savings. However, the figures in the table are overall averages. Individual experience varied widely. Most strikers with large dependent families receive little in tax rebate, and probably have relatively small savings, but they have the highest entitlement to supplementary benefit. Supplementary benefit therefore makes a disproportionate contribution to the support of those who would otherwise be the first to feel the pressure to return to work; although that would also have been true of poor law assistance to strikers' families before the war. The state subsidy theory of strikes may be correct in suggesting that entitlements to supplementary benefit and to tax rebate have had an influence on the pattern of postwar strikes, particularly on the duration of long strikes; but the evidence suggests that their overall influence has not been great.

Table 12

Sources of Strikers' Income

Source	Postal Strike 1971 per cent	Building Strike 1972 per cent	Chrysler Strike 1973 per cent
Savings	32.3	45	28.6
Spouse's Earnings	15.6	17	11.8
Supplementary Benefit	14.5	16	1.4
Tax Rebate	–	10	13.7
Pay in Hand	18.1	–	9.8
Strike Pay or Hardship Allowance	1.6	2	21.9
Other[40]	18.5	10	12.8

[40] 'Other' includes casual work, family allowances, gifts, borrowing and deferred payments.

INDUSTRIAL ACTION AND COLLECTIVE BARGAINING

If methods of financing strikes have had relatively little influence on the pattern of postwar strikes, then the structure of collective bargaining remains the most successful explanatory variable. It offers a fairly satisfactory explanation for long-term changes in the overall pattern of strikes, and accounts for differences between the three main sectors of employment. Its deficiencies are its failure to explain some of the recent short-term changes in the overall pattern, and to account for continued strike-proneness in industries whose bargaining structure has changed in ways that might be expected to reduce the incidence of strikes.

The explanation relies on the assumption that strikes are used to exert pressure to achieve bargaining objectives. Bargaining structure determines where pressure is effective. If this assumption is accepted, there is no difficulty in extending the explanation to include the impact of incomes policy, unemployment, rising inflation, and rising union membership on the strike pattern, for all of them also affect the achievement of bargaining objectives. A strict incomes policy makes it unlikely that claims for pay increases over the limits of the policy will be successful, so that the number of strikes over pay may be expected to fall during the lifetime of such a policy; and unsatisfied claims to accumulate to cause an explosion when the policy slackens or comes to an end. Trade union pressure is more effective when economic activity is rising than when it is falling. Increasing unemployment therefore tends to reduce the overall number of strikes, although strikes may then be longer when they do occur, since employers will be less anxious to settle than when demand for their products is rising. An increasing rate of inflation makes unions anxious for quick settlements and for increases which take account of expected inflation as well as past inflation; so that they become more prone to strike. Increasing union membership adds to the pressure that unions can exert, and therefore adds to the likelihood of strikes.

It is not surprising that these four factors can obscure the relationship between the bargaining structure and the pattern of strikes for a period of years. During 1950–65 the long-term relationship between bargaining structure and strikes was unusually evident because incomes policies were few and feeble, variations in the level of unemployment were modest, the rate of inflation did not fluctuate wildly, and overall union membership was unusually stable.

However, exerting pressure to achieve bargaining objectives is only one of the motives which have been postulated for striking. The other is to express frustration over some aspect of the work situation. Why should the structure of collective bargaining affect the way workers express their frustration? There is no convincing reason why it should do so where frustration is the sole motive for the strike; but perhaps there are not many such strikes. The work of Batstone and his colleagues has demonstrated that even an unofficial sectional strike may involve a good deal of discussion and persuasion.[41] Where there has been discussion and argument before a strike, it seems reasonable to suppose that some of the strikers will have been persuaded that a strike can help in some way to remedy their grievances. If so, they will probably have given some consideration to the level at which those grievances can be settled; and bargaining structure will therefore have been one of the influences at work on the decision to strike.

The motive of expressing frustration nevertheless has an independent part to play in accounting for British strike patterns. There are marked differences between the strike records of industries with apparently similar bargaining structures. Printing and car manufacture, for example, are both highly unionized; both have exceptionally strong workplace organizations; although industry agreements count for a good deal more in printing than in car manufacture, both have highly-developed workplace bargaining; both are now predominantly timeworking industries; but car manufacture is one of the most strike-prone British industries whereas printing is relatively strike-free. One of the most striking contrasts between the two industries is in their technologies—between assembly-line manufacture of cars and craft methods of printing, even in the production of newspapers and periodicals. The frustrations of assembly-line production compared with the relatively high degree of job satisfaction in printing may help to account for the differences in strike records.

A similar comparison may be made between railways on the one hand, and coalmining on the other. Both are in the public sector; both have centralized systems of management and collective bargaining; both are highly unionized; until the introduction of incen-

---

[41] Batstone *et al.*, *The Social Organization of Strikes*, esp. Chapters 5 and 6.

tive payments into coalmining at the end of 1977, their payment system had been roughly similar for a decade. Nevertheless coalmining is strike-prone whereas railways are relatively strike-free. The technology of coalmining and in particular the dangerous and constantly changing working conditions of the pits might be expected to cause greater frustration than the technology and conditions of railway operation; and therefore help to account for differences in strike frequency.

Strikes, like quarrels, must have at least two parties. So far the discussion has been entirely in terms of the motives of workers and unions; but rare lockouts still occur, and it is not uncommon for an employer to take action which has the effect of precipitating a strike. Employers have their frustrations, too, which may influence what they do in industrial disputes, but where their aim is to achieve bargaining objectives, their motives provide the same kind of link between bargaining structure and strikes as do the motives of the workers and their unions.

Strikes are only one form of industrial action, and probably not the most common form in the plant, although strikes may be more common than other forms of industrial action in major industry-wide or company-wide disputes. All that we know about the pattern of other forms of industrial action is that their distribution appears to follow the distribution of strikes at plant level, and that their use in major disputes, like the incidence of strikes in major disputes, is relatively common in the public sector. It is therefore reasonable to suggest, in the absence of other evidence, that collective bargaining structure may have a similar relationship to the pattern of industrial action in general as it does to the pattern of strikes; although there may be another link between them as well. It has been suggested in earlier chapters that many British unions, and particularly their workplace organizations, exercise a high degree of control over production processes. This might be called a feature of collective bargaining structure, broadly defined; and it might help to explain the apparently high incidence of other forms of industrial action in Britain.

All forms of industrial action, however, constitute only one type of pressure in collective bargaining. There is also the whole range of administrative pressures which are available to all kinds of other organizations outside industrial relations, but are not neglected in industrial relations on that account. Unlike strikes and overtime bans, these pressures are used as readily by managers as by trade unions.

> Managers can suddenly become less co-operative, and unwilling to concede even the most insignificant claims. They can demand their rights under an agreement and seek to tighten up on facilities previously granted to the stewards. They can authorise more strict supervision, demand more output, clamp down on unauthorised breaks and declare war on all kinds of accumulated privileges.[42]

Because the use of administrative pressures in industrial relations has not been observed, counted, and analysed as strikes have been, there is not much to be said about them; but they should not be forgottten, for their use is almost certainly more general and more frequent than the incidence of all forms of industrial action. For industrial action is a relatively rare occurrence in the great majority of plants, although most of them, unless they are small, practise collective bargaining. Since collective bargaining does not proceed very far without pressure of some sort, it must rely on administrative sanctions where industrial action is not providing the pressure.

[42] McCarthy, *The Role of Shop Stewards in British Industrial Relations*, pp. 23–4.

Chapter 8

THE STATE IN INDUSTRIAL RELATIONS

In dealing with the organization and work of employers, managers, trade unions and shop stewards and with their relationship through collective bargaining, the preceding chapters have not given much attention to the role of the state in industrial relations. A good deal has been said about industrial relations in the public sector in general and in particular publicly-owned industries and services but it has been concerned with employment relations in public undertakings, not with intervention in industrial relations by the government, its departments and other state agencies, parliament, and the courts, whether in the public sector or elsewhere. There have been references to statutes and to government actions, but only incidentally.

There is justification for this approach. Everything cannot be said at once, so that the subject must be developed in stages, and the part played by the state in British industrial relations has always been considered as intervention from outside. The integral parts of the industrial relations system and their relationship must therefore be considered before intervention from outside can be described and analysed.

There is, however, a problem of exposition. Previous chapters have given attention to changes in industrial relations since the war, and especially over the last ten years or so. In most instances changes have been fairly continuous, as, for example, the developing character and structure of workplace bargaining and the more recent responses of trade unions and employers' associations to it. By contrast, changes in state intervention, which have been concentrated in the years since 1960, have not followed a steady trend. Instead there have been violent fluctuations as one government has succeeded another, or as a government has revised its approach halfway through its term of office. No one can be sure what will be promised at future general elections by way of new approaches or restoration of old practices.

This chapter therefore begins with the traditional doctrine of voluntarism and its application in various aspects of industrial relations. It then turns to the reasons for change and outlines the general directions of the changes. Finally, it deals with the Trades Union Congress and the Confederation of British Industry. These two bodies have developed primarily as agencies to represent their members in dealings with government, parliament, and government departments, so that they fit into the subject-matter of this chapter.

The analysis is taken further in the next two chapters which deal in greater detail with the two main areas of government intervention: incomes policy and labour law. The first analyses the experience of postwar incomes policies, mainly since 1964. The second examines current labour law and some proposals for legislation.

The doctrine of voluntarism in industrial relations rests on two principles: the abstention of the law, and the primacy of voluntary collective action. These are examined in turn.

THE ABSTENTION OF THE LAW

In 1954 Otto Kahn-Freund wrote:

> There is, perhaps, no major country in the world in which the law has played a less significant role in the shaping of [industrial] relations than in Great Britain and in which today the law and the legal profession have less to do with labour relations.[1]

The first part of this statement can be accepted without reserve; the second part remained true until 1971. However, the abstention of the law never implied the complete exclusion of the law from industrial relations. Rather it meant that, although legislation might be permitted on certain limited aspects of industrial relations, there were other areas from which the law was excluded.

The first area in which legislation has long been regarded as permissible, indeed essential, is safety and health. Where there is danger to life, limb or health at work, unions demand and employers accept, at least in principle, that the law should impose standards and

[1] Flanders and Clegg, *The System of Industrial Relations in Great Britain*, p. 44.

make provision for their enforcement. Traditionally this was done by successive Factories Acts which laid down minimum standards on such matters as ventilation and sanitation; on the guarding and proper maintenance of machinery and other equipment; on the provision of drinking water; on the notification of accidents and industrial diseases; and on penalties for failure to comply. Enforcements was in the hands of a professional factory inspectorate.

A second area of permissible legislation was the protection of groups considered to be unable to look after their own interests effectively. They included women and young persons under eighteen, whose hours of work were limited by the Factories Acts.

A third area is social security legislation, including unemployment and health insurance, and pensions. The alternatives are for trade unions to offer their own friendly benefits or for agreements to be negotiated with employers to institute schemes for their employees. But even the richest unions cannot offer satisfactory coverage for their members, and at the time that state schemes were first introduced in Britain, before the First World War, the notion that benefits of this kind could be a subject for collective bargaining had not yet been entertained by trade unionists or employers, at least outside the public sector.

Apart from these limited areas, the law was kept away from industrial relations. Collective agreements, for example, were not treated as legally binding contracts as they are in most countries overseas. One reason for this was section 4 of the Trade Union Act 1871 which debarred the courts from 'enforcing directly' any agreement between one trade union and another. Since most employers' associations, if not all of them, were trade unions in the eyes of the law until 1971, it followed that the agreements between unions and employers' associations could not be directly enforced. This provision did not affect agreements between unions and individual plants or companies, but all collective agreements, whether covered by section 4 or not, were generally regarded as 'gentlemen's agreements'. The parties 'do not intend to make a legally binding contract, and without both parties intending to be legally bound there can be no contract in the legal sense'.[2] There was some controversy among lawyers over the matter, but in March 1969 the decision in the *Ford case* confirmed the predominant opinion. The main consequence of this state of affairs was that unions and their officers and members

[2] *Donovan Report*, p. 126.

could not be sued for striking in breach of their collective agreements when they stopped work without giving due notice to terminate the agreement, or without making full use of the disputes procedure. That was the issue in the *Ford case*.

However, it did not follow that collective agreements had no legal effect. The relationship between employers and individual employees *is* contractual in a legal sense. The contract includes the pay and other conditions of employment of the worker, his obligations of service to the employer, and the notice required to terminate the contract. In the past the terms of the contract were frequently not written down nor even mentioned when the employee was taken on. They were assumed to be determined by custom, and where a collective agreement applied to the relevant trade in that part of the country, the courts held that its provisions became part of the individual contract between employer and employee unless there was evidence to the contrary.

In certain circumstances, however, the terms of a collective agreement were binding on employers even where they were clearly not party to it. The first 'fair wages resolution', dealing with the conditions of employment which must be observed by firms awarded government contracts, was passed by the House of Commons in 1891, and about the same time local authorities began to pass similar resolutions. With subsequent amendments the House of Commons resolution obliges the contractor to observe terms and conditions of employment not less favourable than those laid down in collective agreements for that trade or industry. Strictly speaking the resolution is not a law, but a direction to government departments to award contracts on those terms. However, the principle has been extended by legislation. The observation of 'fair wages' is a statutory condition of obtaining a licence to operate a road passenger transport service, and similar provisions apply in certain other industries.

In 1940, wartime regulations which provided for binding arbitration awards in industrial disputes also empowered the arbitration tribunal to compel an employer to observe terms of employment at least as favourable as those in the relevant agreement (if any), by awarding that the provisions of the agreement should be implied terms in the individual contracts between him and his employees. These arrangements continued in one form or another until 1959, when binding arbitration was terminated. Then the Terms and

Conditions of Employment Act 1959 empowered the Industrial Court to deal with complaints that the employer was not observing the relevant agreement and to compel him to do so.

The law was also kept as far as possible from the conduct of trade union business. The foundation of modern British trade union law was the Trade Union Act 1871. Prior to that most trade unions were considered to be unlawful bodies because they were 'in restraint of trade'. The Act gave them a special dispensation, or 'immunity', from the liabilities and disabilities to which this had exposed them, and also made it possible for them to register if they wished. Registration imposed obligations upon unions to make returns and to include certain provisions in their rules, but both obligations and advantages were marginal.

If the Act had done nothing more its effect would not only have been to allow the unions access to the courts to protect their funds and property, but also to expose many of their actions to review by the courts. The authors of the Act were anxious to avoid this second potential consequence, and section 4 was intended to exclude the courts. It stated that nothing in the Act was to enable a court 'to entertain any legal proceeding instituted with the object of directly enforcing or recovering damages for the breach of' restrictive practices, trade union rules on subscriptions, benefits and fines, and agreements between unions. However, the consequences of this section were not as sweeping as might have been anticipated. It did not prevent the courts from interpreting trade union constitutions on any point; and in a long series of cases the courts allowed proceedings on matters covered by the section on the grounds that the plaintiffs were not asking for 'direct enforcement'. Cases included requests to the courts to restrain unions from raising money or spending it contrary to their rules, or expelling members contrary to their rules, and to recover damages for wrongful expulsion. The majority of the Donovan Commission felt that the scope of section 4 had been 'very greatly cut down by judicial decisions'.[3] Potentially the most important limitation on unions resulting from the interpretation of section 4 by the courts was the possibility of actions to restrain unions from paying strike benefits in strikes called in violation of their rules. Many unions require a ballot to be held before a major strike is called, but in an emergency the choice may be to call a strike at once or not at all. Almost all of the unions which were in this

[3] *Report*, p. 218.

position at the time of the General Strike in 1926 decided to disregard their rules. However, an action could be brought only by a union member, and in most instances unions were able to rely on their members' loyalty in such emergencies.

Trade union political activities were regulated by the Trade Union Act 1913 which was mainly concerned with the right of trade unions to spend money on political activities. They were allowed to do so provided that a ballot of their members authorized such expenditure; that they established a special fund for the purpose; and that members were able to 'opt out' of contributing to it.

The most important of all areas of industrial relations from which the law has been as far as possible kept out is the strike. The relationship between strikes and the law has already been mentioned in connection with strikes in breach of collective agreements and in breach of union rules, but the most important instrument available to the courts in attempting to regulate strikes has been the doctrine of conspiracy. One aspect of this doctrine is that certain acts which, when performed by a single person, would not be criminal, nor actionable in a civil court, may nevertheless be criminal or actionable when performed by several people acting together—a 'combination'; and a combination which threatens one or more of these acts may also be liable to criminal or civil proceedings. The unions were first brought up against the doctrine in criminal cases. They sought the aid of parliament which enacted, in the Conspiracy and Protection of Property Act 1875, that an agreement or combination to do an act 'in contemplation or furtherance of a trade dispute' could only be indicted as a conspiracy if the act would have been punishable as a crime when committed by one person. Subsequently the courts brought the doctrine of conspiracy into play in civil actions against trade unions. The unions turned to parliament again, and in response the Trade Disputes Act 1906 gave protection from civil proceedings to acts done by agreement or combination 'in contemplation or furtherance of a trade dispute' unless they would have been actionable without any combination.

The 1906 Act also gave trade unions complete immunity from civil actions of this kind by forbidding the courts to entertain 'an action against a trade union . . . in respect of any tortious act alleged to have been committed by or on behalf of the trade union'. This immunity was not confined to actions in contemplation or furtherance of a trade dispute; and it did not give protection to trade union officers and members. But section 3 gave protection to strike leaders, whether official or unofficial, in strikes in which workers left their jobs in breach of their individual contracts of employment. Each individual worker remained liable for breaking his own contract, but the section protected the strike leader who 'induced' workers to do so, provided that it was in contemplation or furtherance of a trade dispute.

In 1965 another Trade Disputes Act was needed to close a loophole in the 1906 Act revealed by the case of *Rookes* v. *Barnard*. This case turned on the tort of intimidation, which is threatening an unlawful act. The unlawful act threatened in this instance was the breach by the workers of their contracts of employment. It is unlawful when committed by a single person so that their leaders were not protected from an action for conspiracy, although there was no doubt that they were acting in contemplation or furtherance of a trade dispute; nor were they protected by section 3 of the 1906 Act for the case against them was not that they had induced their members to break their contracts of employment—no contracts had yet been broken—but that they had intimidated the employer. The union itself was protected from any action for tort and proceedings were therefore brought against individuals; but since one of them was a full-time officer of the union who had acted on its behalf, the union could not easily deny moral responsibility for meeting the damages and costs arising out of the case. The 1965 Act therefore specifically protected a threat that a contract of employment would be broken and a threat to induce others to break their contracts, provided that the threat was made in contemplation or furtherance of a trade dispute.

In most instances in which civil proceedings were brought against a union or union leaders in connection with a strike, the primary object was not to secure damages but to obtain an 'interlocutory injunction' restraining the union or the strike leaders until the substance of the case was settled. The courts were entitled to grant such an injunction where there was reasonable ground for supposing that an action for damages might succeed. Since it is often difficult to renew a strike after it has been called off, an injunction may defeat the strike even if the ultimate decision is in the union's favour, or if—as commonly happens—the case is pursued no further.

The rights of strike pickets were defined in the 1875 Act and extended in 1906. In 1875 picketing was permitted 'in order merely to obtain or communicate information'. Because of restrictive interpretation of this right by the courts the 1906 Act permitted picketing so long as it was 'merely for the purpose of peacefully obtaining or communicating information, or of peacefully persuading any person to work or abstain from working'; and was done 'in contemplation or furtherance of a trade dispute'.

THE PRIMACY OF VOLUNTARY ACTION

In Britain, wrote Kahn-Freund, 'the law seeks to stimulate collective bargaining and the application of collective agreements by indirect inducements in preference to direct compulsion, and, where this fails, to provide substitute standards enforceable by legal sanctions. The principles and procedures which govern the establishment of these standards are intended to assist the industries concerned in developing voluntary bargaining habits. All statutory methods of fixing wages and other conditions of employment are by the law itself considered as a second best.' He went on to assert that 'minimum wage legislation is much the most important substitute for collective bargaining'.[4]

Modern minimum wage legislation in Britain began with the Trade Boards Act 1909. Originally intended to protect workers from the evils of 'sweating', the boards were also made available, following the reports of the Whitley Committee, to industries in which organization was too weak to support effective voluntary collective bargaining. This committee looked forward to a postwar world in which all well-organized industries would regulate their industrial relations by voluntary agreements; elsewhere trade boards would protect the unorganized and foster the habit of collective regulation, so that ultimately voluntary collective bargaining would be universal.

Renamed wages councils after the Second World War, these bodies consisted of equal numbers of persons from such unions and employers' organizations as existed in their industries, together with not more than three independents, all of them government appointees. One of the independents was chairman. The councils were empowered to make proposals for minimum remuneration and holidays in the industries they covered. A proposal went to the minister, who might refer it back, but had to embody it in an order

[4] Flanders and Clegg, *op. cit.*, pp. 65–6.

unless the council changed their minds. Provided that the representatives of the two sides were able to agree, there was little for the independent members to do. Otherwise they tried to bring the two sides closer together and in the end cast their votes with one side or the other to make up a majority. A wages inspectorate was responsible for enforcement.

At their peak the councils covered nearly four million workers. In addition there were two Agricultural Wages Boards, one for England and Wales and one for Scotland. The main difference between their powers and those of the councils was that the proposals of the two boards were not subject to ministerial confirmation. They also had their own inspectorate.

The value of wages councils in developing habits of voluntary bargaining was demonstrated by the abolition of a number of them over the postwar years on the grounds that voluntary arrangements were strong enough to give adequate protection to employees. But most of these were special cases. Furniture manufacture, for example, has a long history of collective organization and bargaining, but their strength was eroded during the interwar years of unemployment, and in 1938 the employers were able to show that 96 per cent of workers employed in cabinet-making in London were paid less than the agreed rates.[5] A council was established in 1940, collective organization and observation of agreed rates improved, and in 1947 both sides of the industry felt sufficiently confident to ask for the council's abolition. In baking, separate councils were established for England and Wales (1938) and Scotland (1939), not for lack of voluntary organization and collective bargaining, but because of the failure of the two sides to agree on the control of nightwork in bakeries. It was thought that a satisfactory arrangement would need statutory support.[6] In 1948 the Scottish section of the industry signed a voluntary agreement on nightwork and the council was abolished in 1963. The council for England and Wales followed in 1971.

Several other manufacturing industries which had not developed effective organization before the Act was applied to them, nevertheless possessed the kind of characteristics which might be expected to lead to collective bargaining, such as relatively large units of production and the domination of the employers' side by a few large firms which were not opposed to collective regulation. They included the Rubber Manufacturing Council, the Sugar, Confectionery and Food

[5] F. J. Bayliss, *British Wages Councils*, pp. 35–6.   [6] *Ibid.*, p. 36.

Preserving Council, the Tin Box Council and the Tobacco Council which were abolished over the years 1953–63.

In most instances in which the abolition of a council has been under discussion the employers have been more reluctant than the unions. They feared that without legal enforcement of minimum standards some smaller firms might resort to undercutting in both wages and prices, and their organization would not be able to stop it. A cynic might suggest that they preferred to be regulated by the state free of charge rather than go to the trouble and expense of regulating themselves. At the beginning of the sixties the main union in the Paper Bag and Paper Box Councils, the Society of Graphical and Allied Trades, took the view that technological change had made these industries virtually a section of the printing industry whose agreements could easily have been extended to cover them. They felt that the councils were being 'used by employers to obstruct the extension of collective bargaining'.[7] Employer obstruction was evident in road haulage where the hauliers refused to allow the Road Haulage Association to enter into agreements which would be binding on them.[8] The unions, on the other hand, could be reasonably confident that voluntary agreements would be upheld in the larger undertakings where their members were to be found, and believed that the knowledge that regulation would henceforth depend on voluntary action might encourage recruitment. They in their turn might be criticized as showing little concern for employees in the small firms and for homeworkers who are generally the lowest paid of all, the most likely to suffer from abolition, and the least likely to join trade unions.

There were other industries in which the councils could be said to have improved organization and bargaining without necessarily reaching the stage when abolition could be recommended. In clothing there were several councils and a number of agreements, the most important between the Clothing Manufacturers' Federation and the Tailors and Garment Workers. It provided that: 'In the absence of any agreement to the contrary no alteration in rates of wages or conditions of employment shall become operative unless and until such alteration shall have become obligatory under Orders of the Ready-made and Wholesale Bespoke Tailoring Wages Council and the Wholesale Mantle and Costume Wages Council'. The councils were therefore instruments for endorsing and enforcing

---

[7] *Ibid.*, p. 147.   [8] See p. 75.

collective agreements and their decisions were closely followed by the other clothing wages councils.[9]

Under the Agricultural Wages Boards the Agricultural and Allied Workers had grown to be a union of some strength. Although overall union density in agriculture is only 22 per cent.[10] the union argues that a large number of employees in agriculture are members of farmers' families and therefore not part of the union's potential. The National Farmers Union is a notably robust organization. Both bodies nevertheless took the view that effective regulation would be impossible without statutory machinery. 'Because employment is spread over a very large number of small and scattered units . . . statutory regulation is needed to secure adequate enforcement.'[11]

Elsewhere councils had achieved less. Many of them were in minor manufacturing trades 'characterised by a large number of small employers, many of whom are hostile to any form of association, by a very high proportion of women employees for factory trades, and by the prevalence of piece-work and home-work'. The unions, in most instances the Transport and General Workers and the General and Municipal Workers, kept the councils going, waiting 'for a general movement of wages to take place before bringing these Councils into line'.[12] By 1970 most of these councils had been in existence for fifty years or more without making a significant contribution to voluntary organization.

The majority of employees covered by the councils were, however, in service industries. Retail distribution, hotels and catering, laundries and hairdressing accounted for over two million of the three and a half million workers in wages council industries at the time of the Donovan Commission's report. Trade union density in retail distribution was estimated by Price and Bain at 15 per cent in 1948 and 11.4 per cent in 1974, the decline being accounted for by the fall in co-operative employment where closed shops are general. Since in 1974 co-operatives accounted for about 5 per cent of 1.2 million employees covered by retail wages councils, trade union density in the rest of the industry cannot have been more than 7 per cent. Nevertheless, in addition to the agreement with the Co-operative Union, there were several agreements negotiated between the Shop Distributive and Allied Workers and multiple retail associa-

---

[9] National Board for Prices and Incomes, *Pay and Conditions in the Clothing Manufacturing Industries*, p. 45.
[10] Price and Bain, *op. cit.*
[11] *Donovan Report*, p. 66.
[12] Bayliss, *op. cit.*, pp. 146–7.

tions. The National Board for Prices and Incomes reported that 'about 90,000 full and part-time workers, over a quarter of those within the scope of the Drapery Wages Council, are covered by voluntarily negotiated wage agreements'.[13]

The figure given by Price and Bain for union density in hotels and catering in 1974 was 5 per cent in a labour force of over 800,000, but these figures do not fully allow for industrial and institutional catering, much of which is included in returns for the industries which it serves. At that time there was relatively little collective bargaining outside industrial catering where about 60 per cent of employees were covered by agreements of one sort or another negotiated in the industries, companies or plants which they served.[14] The British Hotels Restaurants and Caterers Association and the General and Municipal Workers Union had an agreement dating from 1947 which allowed for discussion of pay and conditions of employment but contained no substantive provisions. It is of relatively little significance except to stake out the union's claim to be the appropriate union for hotels and restaurants. In 1947 the union made a colourful attempt to organize the London hotels, and in 1968 the Transport and General Workers made another flamboyant gesture in Torquay, the end result of which was an agreement between the local hotels and their rival general union. The other major sector of catering is pubs and clubs, where the one island of trade unionism was the public house managers whose union, the National Association of Licensed House Managers, achieved an agreement with the Brewers' Society in 1969.

Another test of the success of statutory wage regulation is its effect on pay. In 1964 the wages council inspectorate detected and recovered arrears of wages affecting 10,335 workers, and arrears of holiday pay affecting 5,635 workers, but the average amounts were very small, little more than £4 a head for holiday pay and £13 a head for wages. However, the intention of statutory pay regulation was not merely to enforce a minimum, but to improve standards. The amounts of arrears recovered is of less importance than the minimum level which is thereby enforced. In their survey of retail distribution the Commission on Industrial Relations questioned independent members of the nine retail councils. Only one of them

[13] *Pay of Workers in the Retail Drapery, Outfitting and Footwear Trades*, pp. 10–11.
[14] Commission on Industrial Relations, *The Hotel and Catering Industry*, Part II, p. 5.

saw the statutory minimum as 'a living wage'.[15] The effect of the councils may also be assessed by comparing earnings in wages council industries with those in other industries. Of twenty-two wages council industries for which the Donovan Commission was able to find 'sufficiently relevant figures', four—cutlery, paper bag, paper box, and road haulage (all now abolished)—returned earnings for men which were above the national average. Most of the others were well below and the Commission concluded that pay in wages council industries did not 'seem to have improved significantly in relation to that of other industries'.[16]

Another consideration is the impact of increases in statutory minimum rates. The National Board for Prices and Incomes found that the earnings of male shop assistants and cashiers in drapery, which included very little overtime, were roughly 50 per cent over the statutory minimum, with wide variations from one undertaking to another. Nevertheless, it was customary 'for nearly all employers to pass on an increase agreed by the Wages Council to most, if not all, of their employees'.[17] Thus the consequence of increasing a minimum rate intended to protect the low-paid was to extend an equivalent increase in pay to the relatively high-paid.

Another form of state support for collective bargaining is the official conciliation and arbitration service which, according to Kahn-Freund, has 'been among the most effective methods employed towards the furtherance of collective bargaining and, where this does not succeed, towards the creation of substitutes for collective bargaining'.[18] Following the report of the Royal Commission on Labour in 1894, the Conciliation Act 1896 empowered the Board of Trade to appoint arbitrators at the request of both sides and conciliators at the request of either side, and to inquire into disputes. In fact this merely authorized what the Board's labour department was already doing. In 1919 the Industrial Courts Act established the Industrial Court as a permanent independent tribunal for voluntary arbitration at the request of both parties, and empowered the Minister of Labour, whose Department had taken over the work of the labour department of the Board of Trade, to set up courts of inquiry to investigate the causes and circumstances of industrial disputes.

[15] Commission on Industrial Relations, *Retail Distribution*, p. 59.
[16] *Report*, p. 66.
[17] National Board for Prices and Incomes, *Pay of Workers in the Retail Drapery, Outfitting and Footwear Trades*, p. 18.
[18] Flanders and Clegg, *op. cit.*, p. 87.

The conciliation service operated both at headquarters and in regional offices of the Ministry of Labour. It tried 'to keep in close touch with leading representatives of employers and trade unions', for example by appointing liaison officers to sit on national negotiating bodies. Normally conciliation followed an application from one or both parties, but the Department was entitled to indicate that its services were available. Once the conciliator had informed himself of the facts he might proceed by separate talks with each side or by joint meetings in which he took the chair. Either way, the discussions were intended to be 'a continuation of the process of collective bargaining with outside assistance' in which an 'essential feature' was 'the independence and impartiality of the conciliator'. If he could not persuade the parties into an agreement, he might suggest arbitration.[19]

In 1964 the conciliation service dealt with 408 disputes, the majority of them referred by the unions. Over the years 1960–4 a stoppage of work took place on 'about 20–25 per cent' of the occasions on which the service was used. It follows that there were probably about a hundred strikes in 1964 in disputes referred to the service. The total number of strikes in 1964 was 2,524, but only seventy of these were official and in the remainder 'conciliation has commonly been inhibited by the concern that nothing should be done which might appear to condone or even encourage breaches of agreements. . . . Exceptionally . . . conciliation action is taken while such strikes are in progress', but the Department 'never deals with unofficial strike leaders but only with authorised officers of the trade unions concerned'; and even so it usually intervened only where it appeared that the strike might have 'a seriously damaging effect on the economy'. Accordingly the direct effect of the service on strikes was relatively small. In its evidence to the Donovan Commission, the Department asked whether it 'should intervene more frequently in circumstances of this kind'.[20]

Three members of the Industrial Court took part in each hearing—an independent chairman (usually the full-time president), an employer and a trade unionist. Normally its awards were agreed by all three of them, but exceptionally they were chairman's awards. Awards were not legally binding on the parties, but as 'they result from a joint desire for settlement by arbitration, the question of

---

[19] Donovan Commission, *Written Evidence of the Ministry of Labour*, p. 95.
[20] *Ibid.*, pp. 96–8.

enforcement does not generally arise'.[21] In addition to voluntary arbitration the court took legally enforceable decisions under the fair wages resolution, the Terms and Conditions of Employment Act and other special legislation of that kind. Apart from this special business, the court dealt with an average of forty arbitration cases a year during 1960–4. In addition the Civil Service Arbitration Tribunal was dealing with about sixteen cases a year, several other public industries and services had their own tribunals, and single arbitrators appointed by the department (including independent chairmen of negotiating bodies empowered to act as arbitrators) were handing down an average of twenty-five awards a year.[22] Taking into account the relatively small number of employees concerned in most cases before the court, these figures suggest that arbitration played only a modest role in industrial relations.

The court and other arbitration tribunals shared the anxiety of the conciliation service to maintain a scrupulous independence and to ensure that the outcome should as far as possible be acceptable to the parties. These considerations supported the general practice of not giving reasons for awards. The first president, Sir William Mackenzie (later Lord Amulree), gave reasons and hoped to build up a body of 'case law', but his successors did not share his view. One of them, Sir Roy Wilson, told the Donovan Commission that giving reasons would 'result in prolonging and possibly even exacerbating the differences between the parties, or in transferring the area of controversy from one topic or topics to another'. In addition case law might restrict the court in subsequent awards; there might be occasions on which the members could agree upon an award but not upon the reasons for it; and giving reasons might embarrass the employer and union members of the court.[23] He thought 'it would greatly decrease the popularity of arbitration and the confidence the parties have in arbitration if we had to give reasons';[24] but arbitration was not in great demand as it was.

The only detailed study of the work of an arbitration tribunal in Britain deals with the Industrial Disputes Tribunal which was abolished in 1959. It shows that disproportionate use was made of the tribunal by local authority and health service unions, which at that time rarely contemplated industrial action; and by unions dealing with non-federated firms in private industry 'where the unions

[21] *Ibid.*, p. 104.
[23] *Minutes of Evidence*, pp. 1935–6.
[22] *Ibid.*, p. 111.
[24] *Ibid.*, Q. 7223.

are known to be generally far less well-organised' than in federated firms.[25] Unilateral arbitration therefore had a special attraction for trade unions in weak positions. Most of the tribunal's awards concerned pay, and the study suggests that, although it followed the general practice of not giving reasons, the tribunal nevertheless had a policy in these cases.

> Essentially the Tribunal granted wage increases that did not differ substantially from those obtained by other methods—e.g. negotiation, recourse to the Industrial Court, and so on. . . . Terrington [the chairman] was concerned to settle references according to what appeared to be 'the going rate'.[26]

When a public inquiry into an industrial dispute or problem appeared to be needed, the Department was not limited to a court of inquiry. In addition committees of investigation, normally used for less important disputes, could be set up under the 1896 Act, and committees of inquiry could be appointed under general powers. Nevertheless, over the years the majority of investigations into major disputes were conducted by courts of inquiry.

'A Court is generally appointed only as a last resort when no agreed settlement of a dispute seems possible, and when an unbiased and independent examination of the facts is considered to be in the public interest.'[27] Normally an independent chairman—usually a judge, a lawyer, or an academic—sat with an employer and a trade unionist. There was no need for the consent of the parties to an inquiry; and inquiries could be used in unofficial disputes where arbitration would be out of the question, for example to investigate 'a highly publicised and notorious "trouble spot"', such as 'the 1957 inquiry at Briggs Motor Bodies, and its sequel at Fords in 1963'.[28] Unlike arbitration tribunals which did not summon witnesses, courts of inquiry could interrogate the leaders of unofficial disputes without according them parity of status with full-time union officers.

However, the contrast between arbitration and inquiry must not

---

[25] W. E. J. McCarthy, 'Compulsory Arbitration in Britain: the Work of the Industrial Disputes Tribunal', p. 37.

[26] *Ibid.*, p. 39.

[27] Donovan Commission, *Written Evidence of the Ministry of Labour*, p. 106.

[28] W. E. J. McCarthy and B. A. Clifford, 'The Work of Industrial Courts of Inquiry'.

be exaggerated. Although the consent of the parties to the appointment of a court was not obligatory, careful soundings were usually taken, and the department was 'unlikely to set the machinery in motion if they have reason to believe that either party would regard this as unhelpful'.[29] Nor were courts necessarily expected to do a different job from arbitration tribunals. A court's terms of reference were in most instances to inquire into the causes and circumstances of a dispute and to report, but with rare exceptions courts also made recommendations for a settlement. McCarthy and Clifford explained the 'frequent use of courts to settle national wages and conditions in engineering, shipbuilding and printing' by the dislike of both sides of these industries for arbitration. 'By contrast, both sides have found the court of inquiry machinery more acceptable.'[30] Moreover, courts followed much the same criteria in pay disputes as tribunals did. Many of them justified increases 'by reference to so-called "comparability" arguments'. Some recommended adjustments in line with others doing similar work, and others favoured 'equal increases for groups traditionally linked together in some customary "wage-round" process'.[31]

Nevertheless there were differences. Courts normally gave reasons for their recommendations. Their obligation to comment on the causes and circumstances of disputes often led them to comment on procedures and sometimes to recommend procedural change. On these issues they showed themselves to be 'strong constitutionalists', with an 'uncompromisingly hostile attitude . . . to unconstitutional action of any kind'. McCarthy and Clifford concluded that the courts seemed

> to assume that it cannot really be in the interests of any group to act unconstitutionally. . . . It is arguable that this naive and legalistic approach has militated against attempts to analyse and prescribe for problems such as some of those existing in, say, Fords in 1957, and London Airport in 1958.

Whereas the recommendations of the courts on pay were nearly always accepted, their proposals for procedural change were often ignored.[32]

Wages councils and the conciliation and arbitration service were the chief instruments used by the state to encourage the development

[29] *Ibid.*   [30] *Ibid.*   [31] *Ibid.*   [32] *Ibid.*

of collective bargaining and to provide substitute standards where they were needed. They had been tested over several decades, but by the time the Donovan Commission was appointed they were beginning to show signs of wear. Some wages councils had done their job and been abolished, but the major councils which remained had become mechanisms for transmitting general pay movements to both low-paid and high-paid workers within their scope instead of promoting collective bargaining and raising the relative standards of the low-paid. The conciliation and arbitration services played a marginal part in industrial relations. They were unable to deal with the growing problem of unofficial disputes. The more flexible machinery of the court of inquiry allowed these courts to investigate such disputes, but their rigidly constitutional preconceptions prevented them from effectively analysing their causes or prescribing workable recommendations.

CHANGING ATTITUDES: INCOMES POLICY

From time to time there have been emergencies when the doctrine of voluntarism has had to be set aside, or at least to suffer considerable limitations upon its application. Wartime is the outstanding example. The First World War brought bans on strikes, compulsory arbitration, wage controls, conscription, controls over the mobility of labour, price controls, limitations on profits, and rationing. However, these measures were introduced bit by bit, and the administrators had to learn how to operate them as they went along. Consequently there was a good deal of inefficiency, hardship, a lack of co-ordination, and unrest. With general assent the controls were dismantled rapidly at the end of the war.

In the Second World War the administration of the home front was more successful. The experience of the First World War was available to the administrators and the relatively smooth operation of labour controls, price controls, and rationing showed that they had learned their lessons. Conscription and exemptions for munitions workers and specialists operated with less friction than in 1914–18. Compulsory arbitration and a ban on strikes were accepted more readily, and wage controls were less in evidence. The unions promised to exercise restraint in return for an undertaking by the government to stabilize the cost of living index by price controls and subsidies. There was relatively little large-scale industrial conflict; prices remained remarkably stable after the first year of war; real earnings actually rose, particularly for low-paid workers; and there were widespread if piecemeal extensions of social services.

The administration of industrial relations was in the hands of Ernest Bevin, who was general secretary of the Transport and General Workers and became Minister of Labour in 1940. Union negotiations with the government were handled by Walter Citrine, the ablest secretary Congress has ever had. There were other special circumstances as well. American lend-lease helped to pay for the war; and the cost of living index was manipulated. But it was nevertheless a remarkable achievement, and the memory of their wartime accomplishments has continued to influence the thinking of British unions ever since.

The Labour government elected in 1945 had little difficulty in persuading the unions to continue the wartime controls during the period of demobilization; but, even so, the postwar Labour government was less successful than the wartime coalition. Lend-lease was cut off at the end of the war; there were labour shortages, a convertibility crisis, a fuel crisis, and even an extension of rationing. Exports could not be expanded fast enough to offset the loss of former overseas markets and the running down of overseas investments during the war. In 1948 the government demanded even more rigid restraint in pay settlements than had operated during the war. In their White Paper on *Personal Incomes Costs and Prices* in February 1948 they announced that, with the possible exception of undermanned industries, there was 'no justification for any general increase of individual money incomes'. A conference of trade union executives called by the General Council to discuss the policy gave its grudging approval on the understanding that exception would also be made for claims based on 'increased output', for workers paid 'below a reasonable standard of subsistence' and for increases demanded to safeguard 'essential' differentials. Fortunately for the success of the policy, little attempt was made to exploit these sweeping exceptions, and restraint operated by holding back claims and limiting concessions. Some industries, such as the railways, received no general increase for more than two years and others, such as engineering, received only one. Increases in weekly and hourly earnings were a good deal less than they had been over the previous two years, and than they were to be in 1951.

By the autumn of 1949 the unions began to turn against the policy. No attempt had been made to limit the operation of existing agreements, and industries with agreed cost-of-living sliding scales continued to apply them. Following devaluation at the end of 1949 the Chancellor of the Exchequer, Stafford Cripps, tried to safeguard its advantages by asking the unions to accept a 'wage-freeze' so long as the retail price index did not rise by more than a specified number of points. This would have meant the voluntary suspension of the sliding scales. The General Council gave its approval, but the unions directly concerned did not. At a further conference of union executives the majority for a freeze was so small as to foreshadow the end of the policy which was finally abandoned in the autumn of 1950 after the Trades Union Congress had voted it down at its annual meeting in September.

The Conservative government which took office after the 1951 election was committed to the abandonment of economic controls, including incomes policy, and for the next few years they did little more than indicate from time to time that there was still a need for pay restraint. But after they had been in office for three or four years the basic problem of the postwar British economy began to make itself felt. Economic growth was slower than that of Britain's overseas competitors. British costs therefore tended to rise in comparison with theirs. British exports became less competitive and imports rose. The remedies which were available included deflation, which further depresses economic growth; and devaluation, which pushes up the domestic price level. There is therefore an attraction in an incomes policy which can slow down cost increases without causing unemployment or an increase in prices. Indeed, since rapidly rising wages could offset the advantages of deflation or devaluation, an incomes policy can be seen as part of an overall strategy for economic growth along with other measures such as devaluation, as Stafford Cripps saw it in 1949–50.

In 1956 his Conservative successor, Harold Macmillan, persuaded the Federation of British Industries, the British Employers Confederation, the National Union of Manufacturers, the Associated British Chambers of Commerce, and the nationalized industries to accept a voluntary 'price plateau'. Price stability was intended to bring pay stability, for, with stable prices, employers would be unable to give pay increases much in excess of the growth of productivity. The outcome was the engineering and shipbuilding strikes of

March 1957, in which Macmillan, now Prime Minister, decided that a prolonged strike on this scale was an even greater danger to the economy than wage increases, and prevailed upon the employers to make an offer.

On 21 July 1961 another Conservative Chancellor, Selwyn Lloyd, announced a temporary pause in pay increases in the public sector, and asked private industry to follow suit. The pause came to an end the following March. During those eight months it held up the application of awards and the negotiation of new agreements in the public sector, and probably slowed down the pace of pay increases in private industry. The intention was to allow time for the government to work out a long-term policy which appeared in *Incomes Policy: The Next Step*. It was a more sophisticated document than the White Paper of 1948. Pay increases were to be related to the expected annual increase in productivity with special provision for exceptional circumstances. A National Incomes Commission was appointed to apply the policy to particular circumstances but, outside the public sector, they could only review settlements already made unless the parties agreed to invite them to examine a pay claim. The unions ignored both the Commission and the policy as a whole. In these circumstances the Commission was 'unable to make any effective contribution towards the development of an agreed wages policy'.[33] Almost their only achievement was to recommend a substantial increase in the salaries of university teachers. Moreover, they were overshadowed by the National Economic Development Council, set up in February 1962 with senior ministers and leading trade unionists and employers among its members, and served by a powerful staff of experts. In March 1963 their report on the *Growth of the United Kingdom to 1966* made the assumption that a growth rate of 4 per cent was a feasible objective for Britain and gave grounds for supposing that a more effective incomes policy might emerge from the involvement of the unions in economic planning.

These developments also affected the Labour party, which had been very shy of the whole subject since 1950. It could hardly appear less enthusiastic for economic planning than the Conservatives, and by the time of its narrow victory in the October 1964 election, the party was committed to 'planned wages growth'. The new government demonstrated the seriousness of its intentions by establishing a new Department of Economic Affairs to be responsible for

[33] C. W. Guillebaud, *Wage Determination and Wage Policy*, p. 42.

economic planning, with George Brown, deputy leader of the party, at its head. By the end of the year he had persuaded the General Council and the employers' organizations to sign a *Declaration of Intent*, followed in the spring of 1965 by agreed statements on a new incomes policy not very different from the Conservatives' 1962 policy except that it covered prices as well as pay; but there was to be a National Board for Prices and Incomes with substantially more impressive membership, staffing, and powers than those of the National Incomes Commission. 'Claims, settlements or questions relating to pay or other conditions of service or employment' could be referred by the government to the board without any mention of consent by the parties; and in November, after further consultations, a voluntary warning system was established to make sure that the government was made aware of prospective pay and price increases so that references could be made to the board before they took effect. Nevertheless pay and prices continued to rise more rapidly than the economic planners had allowed for, and it was evident that many pay settlements were not observing the criteria of the policy.

In 1966 a national shipping strike which lasted for two months coincided with another crisis in the balance of payments. One reason for the crisis was an impression overseas that the incomes policy was a failure. Since the short-run solution for the crisis involved borrowing abroad, reinforcement of the policy had an immediate advantage in facilitating loans, quite apart from its ultimate effect on pay and prices. On 20 July the Prime Minister, Harold Wilson, announced a complete standstill on pay increases for six months, and on price increases except for those due to higher import prices or tax changes. A Prices and Incomes Act was hurried through parliament to give statutory force to the early warning system and to the standstill.

The standstill was succeeded by six months of 'severe restraint' and thereafter more White Papers spelled out further variations in the policy. Successive Acts extended the government's power to hold up increases in pay and prices on which the board had reported adversely; and these powers were used. By 1969, however, it was evident that the penalties were no longer effective. Many pay increases were well above the prescribed limits; the number of strikes was rising to unprecedented figures; and the government was anxious to be rid of its embarrassing policy as soon as possible. By the time they were replaced by the Conservatives in June 1970 the policy was in ruins, although the Prices and Incomes Act had not yet been repealed.

Although the victorious Conservative government was committed to economic freedom, they nevertheless showed a lively interest in voluntary pay restraint. In October the Secretary of State for Employment met with representatives of unions and employers to explain the government's policy of decelerating pay increases in the public sector (known as 'N–1') and to express the hope that the private sector would follow their lead. Through 1971 the response was patchy, but the decisive test came in January 1972 with a national coalmining strike, which lasted for seven weeks, extracting increased offers from the Coal Board, then substantially enhanced recommendations from a court of inquiry, and finally additional concessions from the Prime Minister himself at a negotiating session in Downing Street.

The government's policy had achieved more success with the employers than with the unions, for in July 1971 the Confederation of British Industry had initiated a limit of 5 per cent a year on price increases provided the public sector would do the same. A year later it was accepted that voluntary price restraint had been fairly successful, but could not continue much longer unless the rate of pay increases was cut back. The Confederation was not able to persuade its members to renew their support for more than three months. In August 1972 the government began a series of talks with the Confederation and the Trades Union Congress to explore the possibility of an agreed policy on pay and prices. The talks continued through September and October, but broke down on 2 November. The government then rushed a Counter-Inflation Act through parliament imposing a statutory standstill on pay, prices, dividends, and rent, to take effect on 7 November. In March 1973 the standstill was succeeded by a statutory limit on pay increases of £1 per person plus 4 per cent of the existing pay bill excluding overtime. Agreements negotiated on these lines could not take effect until twelve months after the previous main settlement in the relevant negotiating groups. A further stage of the policy began in November 1973 with a general limit of 7 per cent on the group pay bill, but with a number of loopholes which could lead to higher payments. By this time the miners had already imposed a ban on overtime and safety work in support of their claim for an increase above the limits. Having successfully run down stocks of coal, they struck in

February 1974. An election was called, and the government was defeated.

The limits specified in the price and pay codes promulgated under the Counter-Inflation Act were administered by a Pay Board and a Price Commission which had far less room for manoeuvre than the National Board for Prices and Incomes, for these new bodies had no authority to depart from the codes, which were subject to interpretation by the courts. All pay settlements affecting a thousand workers or more had to be reported to the Pay Board for approval before they could be put into effect. Settlements for smaller groups were subject to review. The only loophole was a special power for the Secretary of State to treat particular price and pay increases as exceptions.

This power had to be used by the new Labour Secretary of State to permit the final settlement of the miners' dispute to go through as an exception, for the Act remained in force until July. One of the provisions of the code for the final stage of the policy permitted increases of 40p per person for each rise of 1 per cent in the retail price index over 7 per cent. The Conservatives had hoped to hold price increases below 7 per cent between November 1973 and November 1974; but they reckoned without the fuel crisis. In April 1974 the index passed the threshold and payments started. Eight million workers were already covered by 'threshold' agreements, and many others pressed their employers into hasty settlements. By October the threshold payments amounted to £4.40 a week.

Having turned against incomes policy before leaving office, the Labour party once more changed their minds in opposition. They devised a 'social contract' with the Trades Union Congress, whereby the unions undertook to assist the next Labour government to resolve the country's economic problems in return for the restoration of full employment, further moves towards economic equality, and a programme of legal and social reforms desired by the unions. In September 1974, with Labour in office, Congress approved proposals for implementing the social contract which retained the twelve month rule, and acknowledged that 'the scope for real increases in consumption at present is limited', so that 'a central negotiating objective in the coming period will be to ensure that real incomes are maintained'. By January 1975 the annual rate of increase in the index of retail prices was 20 per cent and still rising.

By the spring it was evident that the social contract in its current form was not yielding the expected results. At the beginning of July, with the annual rate of price increases over 25 per cent, the Chancellor, Denis Healey, announced a number of harsh economic measures to bring inflation under control and to restore confidence in sterling once again; and the General Council proposed that the twelve month rule should continue for pay increases, which should be limited to £6 a week for adult employees over the next year. No formal machinery was instituted to operate the policy, but the Price Commission, which had been retained by the new government, was instructed to disallow any pay increases above the £6 limit in assessing claims for price increases.

The new voluntary limit on pay proved surprisingly successful, but the reduction in the rate of price inflation was slower than anticipated. For 1976–7 the government and the Trades Union Congress agreed on a 5 per cent increase all round with a lower limit of £2.50, and an upper limit of £4. Another run on sterling in the autumn of 1976 sent prices soaring again, but by the summer of 1977 the rate of inflation was once more falling towards the short-term target of 10 per cent a year.

By this time the unions were becoming restive, and the most that the General Council could obtain from Congress for 1977–8 was a reaffirmation of the twelve month rule, with no limit on the amount of increases. But the government announced its own target of a 10 per cent limit on earnings, and promised to use a variety of administrative sanctions against employers who exceeded the limit. A year later the rate of inflation was down to 8 per cent, and the government, again acting on their own, announced a 5 per cent pay limit for the next twelve months, with some scope for flexibility.

For seventeen years, therefore, the country has not been without some form of incomes policy for more than a few months at a time. Such a state of affairs appears to be far removed from a voluntary system of industrial relations. Nevertheless it is not easy to judge what permanent effect all these incomes policies have had on the system of bargaining over pay. A more detailed assessment is attempted in the next chapter.

CHANGING ATTITUDES: THE REFORM OF LABOUR LAW

Voluntarism has been under attack from other directions as well. There have been increasing doubts about the capacity of collective bargaining to deal with a number of other aspects of industrial relations besides wage inflation which are seen as problems; and a rapidly rising volume of bills and statutes designed to provide legal solutions to them has challenged the principles of the abstention of the law and the primacy of collective bargaining, at least as those principles were formerly understood.

The opening of the attack appeared to be intended to restore the primacy of collective bargaining by the removal of wartime restrictions continued after the war. In 1951 the wartime arbitration system had been amended. As a result of trade union protests following the use of the wartime order to take legal proceedings against strikers, the ban on strikes was dropped. Henceforth the former National Arbitration Tribunal was renamed the Industrial Disputes Tribunal. It continued to be available at the request of either party and its awards were still enforceable; but workers and unions were free to strike, and employers to lock out. In 1958 the Minister of Labour, Ian Macleod, decided that compulsory arbitration should go. He believed that in its current form it was biased towards the unions, and promoted inflation. But there was an obstacle. During and after the war it had become an established tenet of voluntarism that any new departures in labour law must have the consent of the unions and employers. Since many employers, although by no means all of them, shared his view of the existing arrangements, he was able to win their consent without too much difficulty; but the majority of the unions considered that compulsory arbitration was of value to them. The minister therefore informed Congress that the existing arrangements rested on wartime powers. The government thought it was time to dispense with these, and compulsory arbitration would therefore disappear unless it was continued by new legislation. New legislation, however, would require the consent of both parties, and the employers would not agree. So compulsory arbitration lapsed, although by general agreement the Terms and Conditions of Employment Act 1959 maintained a means of coercing non-federated employers to observe terms not less favourable than those in the relevant agreements.

The next move was the Contracts of Employment Act 1963. This modest statute required employers to observe minimum periods of notice ranging from one week after six months' continuous employment to four weeks after four years' employment, and also required them, with certain exceptions, to give each employee with three months' service 'written particulars' of certain terms of his employment. This second requirement could be met by referring the employee to a document containing the particulars, which might be a collective agreement. The Act's main distinction was that although both the Trades Union Congress and the British Employers' Confederation opposed its passage as an undesirable interference in industrial relations, the government went ahead nevertheless.

In 1958 the deficiencies of existing arrangements for industrial training led to the formation of the Industrial Training Council with representatives of employers, unions, and the government. The results of this voluntary body fell so far short of what was thought to be needed that, with general approval, the Industrial Training Act 1964 set up statutory training boards financed by compulsory levies in each major group of industries. The Redundancy Payments Act 1965, planned by the Conservatives and passed by Labour, also had the approval of both employers and unions. It was the consequence of a widespread belief that economic growth in Britain was held up by lack of labour mobility. Henceforth a worker with a minimum period of service was entitled to compensation, related to age and service, for loss of job through redundancy. Its passage implied a failure of the two sides of industry to negotiate agreements on compensation for redundancy.

There were also demands for a wholesale review of industrial relations and labour law in Britain. In 1958 the Inns of Court Conservative and Unionist Society launched a wide-ranging attack on the unions in *A Giant's Strength*, castigating the unions as too powerful and seeking legal protection against them for individuals and for society. The onslaught was not wholly partisan for in 1961 Eric Wigham, the respected and liberal-minded industrial correspondent of *The Times*, published *What's Wrong with the Unions* which criticized the unions as inefficient, antiquated, and obstructive bodies; and *Spotlight on the Unions*, published by the *Daily Mirror*, contained a popular account of some of their alleged shortcomings. The Labour government which came to power in 1964 held that there were sufficient grounds to warrant a public inquiry, and the following year they appointed the Royal (Donovan) Commission on Trade Unions and Employers' Associations with wide terms of reference. Three years later the Commission reported.

To many of its critics the Donovan Report seemed to be a defence of voluntarism. The Commission acknowledged many defects in British industrial relations, but did not identify the unions as their main cause. They attributed them primarily to the structure of collective bargaining in private industry with its 'two systems of industrial relations'—the formal and the informal—and to the autonomy and fragmentation of informal bargaining. In their view this state of affairs was primarily due to employers' associations and managers. Employers' associations had lost authority because managers preferred to settle issues within the plant. Where they had the choice, managers showed a marked preference for dealing with shop stewards rather than full-time union officers; but at the same time they were reluctant to acknowledge the stewards' authority in formal agreements, or to negotiate plant-wide settlements with them. Most companies, said the Commission, lacked effective personnel policies; they lived from hand to mouth. Shop stewards drew their power mainly from two sources: the collective power of the work groups they represented and the willingness of managers to deal with them. In general the unions had little control over the developments which had led to a shift in power towards the shop floor, although the shift had been assisted by multi-unionism.

The Commission associated the development of workplace bargaining with the rapid rise in the number of strikes outside coalmining; they believed that heavy reliance on custom and practice fostered inefficiency; and they held that workplace bargaining as it then existed was an obstacle to an effective incomes policy. For, 'so long as workplace bargaining remains informal, autonomous and fragmented the drift of earnings away from rates of pay cannot be brought under control'.[34]

The means to reform of collective bargaining was not primarily through the law. The Commission did not suppose that the legal enforcement of collective agreements would be likely to reduce the number of strikes in breach of agreement. The parties' intention that existing agreements should not be contracts was 'manifest from the style in which the agreements are expressed. To make them enforceable would in the first place require their redrafting.' But even if that were done,

> the root of the evil is in our present methods of collective bargaining and especially in our methods of workshop bargaining. . . .

[34] *Report*, p. 53.

Until this defect is remedied, all attempts to make procedure agreements legally binding are bound to defeat themselves.[35]

Instead the main instrument for reform was to be the 'factory-wide agreement', although, in a multi-plant company, a company agreement might serve the purpose. Such agreements were to replace the existing arrangements with 'comprehensive and authoritative collective bargaining machinery' at plant or company level, which would include joint procedure agreements and 'pay structures which are comprehensive, fair and conducive to efficiency'.[36]

The task to be performed was therefore essentially educational. Existing defects were

> primarily due to widespread ignorance about the most sensible and effective means of conducting industrial relations, and to the very considerable obstacles to the use of sensible and effective methods contained in our present system of industrial relations.[37]

Education was to begin with the report itself, and to be continued by a Commission on Industrial Relations which the report proposed should be established by parliament and given responsibility for the reconstruction of British industrial relations through investigating particular cases and problems. The process should be hastened by a legal obligation on companies, initially those with more than five thousand employees, to register their agreements, or to report that they had none and why. Registration would provide a spur to companies to get on with the job, and direct the attention of the Department of Employment to cases and problems which should be referred to the Commission for inquiry.

These recommendations contained no great threat to voluntarism, but the Donovan Commission proposed a number of other changes in the law as well. Doubts about the legal status of trade unions and employers' associations should be removed by giving them full corporate personality. The requirements of the rulebooks of registered unions should be extended to ensure that the rules were 'clear and unambiguous' and contained 'better safeguards for individual members'.[38] The existing protection from proceedings for inducing a breach of the contract of employment given to actions taken in

---

[35] *Ibid.*, pp. 126–8. [36] *Ibid.*, p. 44. [37] *Ibid.*, p. 51. [38] *Ibid.*, pp. 174–5.

contemplation or furtherance of a trade dispute should extend also to proceedings for inducing a breach of a commercial contract, mainly on the grounds that the law on this point was obscure and capricious.[39] In accordance with the Commission's view that,

> properly conducted, collective bargaining is the most effective means of giving workers the right to representation in decisions affecting their working lives, a right which is or should be the prerogative of every worker in a democratic society[40]

they proposed that a stipulation in a contract of employment that an employee must not belong to a trade union should be void; and that the Commission on Industrial Relations should investigate complaints that employers refused to recognize trade unions. A dismissed employee who believed that his dismissal had been unfair should be entitled to complain to a tribunal empowered to order reinstatement, with compensation as an alternative if either party preferred it. Complaints against disciplinary action by a trade union and against malpractices in union elections should be heard by a review body, of two trade unionists with a lawyer as chairman, which would also deal with disputes between trade unions and the Registrar as to whether their rules met the requirements of the law.

The Commission also suggested changes affecting wages councils and the conciliation service. Wages council legislation should be amended to facilitate the abolition of councils, and to enable councils to encourage 'the development of collective dealings between managers and shop stewards . . . in individual factories'.[41] The Secretary of State for Employment

> should, in appropriate cases, place on an industrial relations officer or officers the duty of obtaining the full facts about unofficial and unconstitutional stoppages in any industry, region or undertaking where they are causing particular difficulties

and the powers granted by the relevant Acts should be widened for this purpose.[42]

[39] At this point the Commission diverged. Seven of them wished both immunities to be limited to registered unions and those acting on their behalf, thus leaving unofficial strike leaders unprotected, and giving unions an incentive to register. The other five proposed that the immunities should apply to all strike leaders, and registration should be compulsory. (*Ibid.*, pp. 214–15.)

[40] *Report*, p. 54.　　　　[41] *Ibid.*, p. 67.　　　　[42] *Ibid.*, pp. 119–20.

The report was published in June 1968. In January 1969 the government brought out its plans for legislation in a White Paper entitled *In Place of Strife*, and meanwhile set up the Commission on Industrial Relations to begin its work without statutory powers. The proposals for legislation were mainly drawn from the report, but the government believed the electorate wanted anti-strike legislation so they made several additions of their own of which the most notable were proposals to empower the Secretary of State to enforce, by means of orders, solutions for inter-union disputes, and conciliation pauses in 'unconstitutional strikes and in strikes where, because there is no agreed procedure or for other reasons, adequate joint discussions have not taken place'. [43] These proposals became known as the 'penal clauses' since failure to comply with the orders would render those concerned liable to fines. In April the government announced that they would go ahead with a brief bill including these two measures but leaving the main body of the Donovan recommendations to the next session. This threw the unions into an uproar, and it became evident that many Labour backbenchers would not vote for the bill. Accordingly in June the government dropped the bill in return for a 'solemn and binding undertaking' from the General Council to secure wider powers from Congress to deal with inter-union disputes and unconstitutional strikes. Thereafter the government set about preparing a new bill, again derived from the Donovan Report, but this time with omissions rather than additions. Almost everything that could be interpreted as in any way offensive to the unions was left out. But this bill was overtaken by the general election of June 1970. The victorious Conservatives set about legislating their own proposals for the statutory reform of industrial relations.

THE INDUSTRIAL RELATIONS ACT

Some of these proposals had been set out in *Fair Deal at Work* which had been published by the Conservative party shortly before the Donovan report appeared; but their Industrial Relations Act also showed the influence of the Donovan Report and borrowed extensively from American legislation. The authors shared many of the concerns of the Donovan Commission, especially over the incidence

[43] p. 28.

of unofficial and unconstitutional strikes, but they differed sharply from the Donovan Commission in their diagnosis of the causes of the defects in British industrial relations, and therefore in the remedies which they prescribed. They believed that the unions must bear the primary responsibility for these defects, and that many of the shortcomings of the unions were due to the traditional abstinence of the law from industrial relations.

The Act relied heavily on two devices to improve standards of trade union conduct. Firstly, a number of forms of industrial relations behaviour were classified as 'unfair industrial practices' with legal remedies for those who felt that they had been unfairly treated. Although some types of action by employers were included in the list, most unfair industrial practices were forms of trade union action. Secondly, trade unions were given several inducements to register, and the rules and conduct of registered trade unions were subject to stringent requirements and the scrutiny of the Registrar.

Like the Donovan Commission, the authors of the Act proposed to create new rights for trade unions and for individual workers. They agreed with the Commission that the law should assist trade unions to secure recognition from employers, but this and several other union rights were limited to registered unions. They gave workers a right to belong to a registered union, or not to belong to any trade union if that was their choice.

Unofficial and unconstitutional strikes were enmeshed in a web of liabilities. Written collective agreements were to be legal contracts unless they contained an express disclaimer. Without it, a strike in breach of a procedure established by a written agreement gave grounds for proceedings against the strike leaders, and against the union itself unless it took 'all such steps as are reasonably practicable' to prevent anyone purporting to act on its behalf from acting contrary to the undertaking given or implied in the agreement. A registered trade union was protected from proceedings for inducing a breach of contract (whether of employment or commercial) if it was acting in contemplation or furtherance of a trade dispute; but an unregistered union had no such protection, nor had an officer or member of a registered union unless he was acting 'within the scope of his authority'. The rules of registered unions had to specify 'any body by which, and any official by whom, instructions may be given to members of the organisation on its behalf for any kind of industrial action, and the circumstances in which any such instructions may be so given'. Consequently unofficial strikes in registered trade unions and all strikes in unregistered trade unions rendered the strike leaders liable whenever they brought their members out without giving due notice to the employer.

Limits were placed on the liability of registered unions before a new National Industrial Relations Court which was to hear cases of alleged unfair industrial practices. The maximum figure for the largest unions was £100,000. There was no limit for unregistered unions. Only registered unions could seek for compulsory arbitration to be imposed on an employer who refused recognition when it had been recommended by the Commission on Industrial Relations (which was retained and given statutory powers under the Act); or who refused to disclose information to their representatives 'in accordance with good industrial relations practice'. Employers could enter into agreements with registered trade unions to establish 'agency shops' in which the only alternatives to union membership were to establish a conscientious objection to joining a trade union and contribute to an agreed charity, or to pay the union the equivalent of union dues without joining. If a ballot of the workers affected favoured an agency shop by either a majority of those eligible to vote, or a two-thirds majority of those voting, the employer was obliged to grant it. Furthermore, an 'approved closed shop' could be lawfully implemented for a registered union provided that the Commission on Industrial Relations was satisfied that certain stringent conditions were met (amounting to their being convinced that effective collective bargaining depended on a closed shop); that a ballot went in favour; and that the Industrial Relations Court approved. Here the only alternative to union membership was to qualify as a conscientious objector. The consequence was that whereas the dismissal of a worker because he did not belong to a union would normally have given him grounds to apply to an industrial tribunal[44] for reinstatement or compensation, in an agency shop or an approved closed shop there was no such remedy, unless the dismissed worker was a conscientious objector or (in an agency shop) contributed to the union. Another advantage of registration was that registered unions did not pay tax on their investment income from funds earmarked for friendly benefits, whereas unregistered unions had to pay. In some unions large sums were at stake.

---

[44] The industrial tribunals were created by the Industrial Training Act 1964, and their scope had been extended by the Redundancy Payments Act.

This was the central structure of the Act, but there was much more besides in its 170 sections and 9 schedules. Noting the Donovan Report's strictures on the state of industrial relations in the plant, its authors had devised their own remedies. The Commission on Industrial Relations were empowered, on a reference from the Industrial Relations Court, to investigate 'units of employment' which lacked procedure agreements, or suitable procedure agreements, or where the procedures did not prevent unconstitutional strikes; and to propose new or revised procedures. Within six months of their report an employer or a registered trade union could ask the Industrial Relations Court for an order giving the proposed procedure the effect of a legally enforceable contract 'as if a contract consisting of these provisions had been made between those parties'.

North American concepts of 'bargaining units' and 'exclusive representation' were borrowed to make the procedure for securing trade union recognition into a device for reducing the undesirable effects of multi-unionism. A 'joint negotiating panel' of unions could be recognized as the 'sole bargaining agent' for a bargaining unit provided that the unions had authorized it to act on their behalf.

The Registrar supervised only registered unions, but there was also a set of principles with which all unions had to comply, with provision for complaints to be heard by industrial tribunals, and, for registered unions, also by the Industrial Relations Court. Certain organizations, such as professional associations, debarred by their charters or by registration under the Companies Act from being trade unions, nevertheless undertook some trade union functions such as bargaining with employers. The Act created a 'special register' to allow them to enjoy the protection and privileges of registered trade unions provided they met the relevant conditions.

Another import from North America was a set of emergency procedures for enforcing a cooling-off period of up to sixty days, and for requiring a strike ballot, intended for use when major strikes or impending strikes threatened the national interest. The Donovan Commission had examined and rejected proposals of this kind on the grounds that compulsory strike ballots in North America almost always favoured strikes and also restricted the negotiators' room for manoeuvre in seeking a settlement.

The Act put relatively little emphasis on the duty of managers to improve industrial relations, but the government promised a code of practice which was published in January 1972. It gave far more space to managerial responsibilities and employment policies than to the duties of trade unions and employers' associations. In spirit, if not always in detail, it had much in common with the Donovan recommendations. Failure to observe the code did not lead to liability to proceedings, but the Industrial Relations Court and the tribunals were to take it into account in their decisions.

The success of the Act depended on three things: the willingness of unions to register—or rather to remain registered, for most significant unions were already registered under the 1871 Act; the willingness of employers to institute proceedings against unions and strike leaders; and the capacity of the new court to enforce its decisions.

The government made no more than perfunctory attempts to consult with union leaders over their legislative proposals, but they confidently expected that the heavy disabilities and disadvantages of unregistered unions would keep the unions on the register. In December 1970 the bill was presented to parliament and in January 1971 the Trades Union Congress opened its campaign of opposition. The mood of trade union activists was manifested by a demonstration of over a hundred thousand in London on 21 February and two one-day strikes of 1.25 million engineering and shipbuilding workers in March. Although not sponsored by Congress, both strikes were supported by the Engineers and the second by the Transport and General Workers as well. On 18 March a special meeting of Congress agreed on a plan of action which included refusal to co-operate with the Commission on Industrial Relations and the Industrial Relations Court; withdrawal of trade unionists serving on industrial tribunals; insistence on disclaimers in all agreements to stop them becoming legally binding contracts; and a strong recommendation against registration. At the annual meeting in September this recommendation was converted into an instruction, against the advice of the General Council.

There were a number of small and middle-sized unions with special reasons for registration. The Seamen and Actors' Equity asserted that they could not operate effectively without industry-wide closed shops. The Bank Employees feared that they could not withstand the competition of the bank staff associations, which had no inhibitions against registration, unless they too were on the register. The National Graphical Association stood to lose heavily on its large investment income. There were also five large unions whose position was in doubt—the General and Municipal Workers, the Electricians, and the National and Local Government Officers, whose leaders were not wholly averse to the Act; the Shop Distributive and Allied Workers who feared that their closed shops in co-operative societies might crumble away unless they could make use of the provisions for agency shops; and the Scientific Technical and Managerial Staffs who were eager to exploit opportunities for growth among white collar employees. The position of the General and Municipal Workers was critical. They compete with the Transport and General Workers over such a broad front that, had they stayed on the register, the Transport and General Workers might have felt obliged to follow them; and the policy of deregistration would have been in ruins.

The issue was not settled until 1972. First the leaders of the General and Municipal Workers decided to come off the register after hearing reports from the regions that the active members would accept nothing else. They were followed by the National and Local Government Officers. The committal of five dockers to prison by the Industrial Relations Court in July helped to convince the remaining three major unions that they could not stay on the register. This left the smaller unions. Thirty-two of them, with about half a million members in all, were suspended by the General Council, and twenty, with 360,000 members, were finally expelled by Congress in 1973, one or two others having resigned in the meantime.

This outcome made it impossible to reform union rules and behaviour through the requirements of registration. In fact the experience of the unions which defied the ruling of Congress suggests that the Registrar's influence would have made itself felt only over a considerable period of years, for he had approved the rules of only two of them by 1974 when his job was brought to a halt by the change of government.

The willingness of employers to operate the Act may be gauged from their treatment of the closed shop. A survey of major companies and nationalized industries found that some or all of the employees in about half of seventy-seven companies and eleven out of fourteen nationalized industries were in closed shops. The research team reported that

> every manager whom we interviewed, who had a direct responsibility for collective bargaining, whether in the private or in the public sector, wanted to preserve the status quo where there were

closed shops. No company at any level issued direct instructions to the contrary.[45]

Their report went on to describe ways in which managers sought to ensure that non-unionists were not recruited into closed shops, and that existing members did not disturb the situation by resigning.[46] These findings indicate that large numbers of managers were engaged in making sure that the statutory right not to belong to a trade union was rendered inoperative for the millions of employees who worked in closed shops. When the respondents were asked whether their companies had used the provisions of the Act on industrial disputes to bring proceedings against trade unions, or had considered doing so, it emerged that not one had used them, and only three had given serious consideration to doing so.[47] There were, however, enough exceptions elsewhere to provide the Industrial Relations Court with a sufficient number of cases to show something of what the Act could achieve.

One of the first important disputes to come before the court was not referred by an employer but by the Secretary of State. In April 1972 he asked for a cooling-off period in a railway dispute after the unions had rejected an arbitration award and instituted working to rule and an overtime ban.[48] When this failed to produce a settlement, he asked for a second cooling-off period and a statutory ballot. The railwaymen voted in favour of their claim by six to one, and sanctions were resumed until further concessions had been made. That was the last that was heard of the emergency procedures.

During 1972 there was a series of disputes in the docks over the threat of containerization to dockers' jobs. Transport and storage companies were picketed to force them to employ dockers to load and unload containers. The Industrial Relations Court issued a number of injunctions in these disputes, some of them against the Transport and General Workers and others against shop stewards. Some were not obeyed. On 16 June three London dockers were arrested for contempt of court. Protest strikes began in several ports,

[45] Weekes *et al.*, *Industrial Relations and the Limits of Law*, p. 42.
[46] *Ibid.*, pp. 43–50.
[47] *Ibid.*, pp. 210–13.
[48] This gave the court the opportunity to decide that these forms of pressure were 'irregular industrial actions' as defined by the Act. These were actions short of strikes, in contemplation or furtherance of trade disputes, in which workers interfered with production *and* broke their contracts.

but next day the Official Solicitor emerged from the obscurity of his normal functions to secure their release, and the strikes were called off. On 22 July the court ordered the imprisonment of five London dockers. This was followed by widespread strikes in the docks and other industries, and the General Council called a one-day protest strike for 31 July.

Meanwhile a Liverpool case had found its way to the House of Lords. The issue was whether the Transport and General Workers or their stewards in the Liverpool docks were responsible for blacking of a firm called Heatons. The Industrial Relations Court held the union responsible. When they refused to attend the hearings the court fined them for contempt. In the end the union paid but appealed. In June the Court of Appeal reversed the decision, holding that the stewards were responsible. On 26 July the House of Lords decided that the stewards had been acting on the union's behalf and the union must be held responsible. The five London dockers were therefore released, and the strikes were called off.

The next major conflict came over the rights of union members. In October 1972 the court found that it was an unfair industrial practice for the Engineers to refuse to allow a member called Goad to attend branch meetings, and ordered them to let him attend. Following the *Heatons case*, the Trades Union Congress had made it clear that its policy did not prevent unions defending themselves before the court, but the Engineers were determined to avoid any contamination. They did not appear; they did not pay a fine of £5,000, nor a further fine of £50,000. The money was sequestered from union funds, and there were more large-scale strikes.

The final battle was also with the Engineers over a strike for union recognition at Con-Mech (Engineers). The court granted an injunction. The union maintained the strike. A fine of £75,000 was taken from sequestered assets, and there were more protest strikes. In March 1974 the court awarded £47,000 compensation to the company. When the union failed to pay, the court decided that all the union's assets should be sequestered to discover whether there was enough to meet the bill. On 8 May three hundred thousand engineering workers struck and a national engineering stoppage seemed inevitable, to the acute embarrassment of the Labour government which had recently taken office pledged to repeal the Act. The situation was saved by a group of anonymous donors who handed over £65,000 which satisfied the sequestrators. In July the Trade

Union and Labour Relations Act put an end to the court and most of the Industrial Relations Act.

One more decision of the court deserves mention. Langston, an employee of Chrysler, had been trying for two years to establish his right to continue in employment although he had left the union and Chrysler was a closed shop. The men would not have him. For months he was suspended on full pay, but in the end he was dismissed. The company admitted his dismissal was legally unfair and offered compensation. In May 1974 the court decided not to make Chrysler take him back on the grounds that the opening words of the Act enjoined that its provisions 'shall have effect for the purpose of promoting good industrial relations'. The Act outlawed the closed shop, but the court could not stop it.

It can be argued that, in rather different circumstances, one major union after another might have decided for registration, and a more diplomatic Industrial Relations Court could have avoided confrontations at least until the new institutions became established. Then, with some amendments, the Act might have survived. On the other hand, it is easy to build up a case that British unions could never be reconciled to the Act, or anything like it. The Act outraged their traditional approach to the function of law in industrial relations and offered them relatively little by way of compensation. In the United States the federal legislation which limits and controls trade unions was built on the Wagner Act of 1935. This Act came at a time when American unions were still trying to establish themselves, and it offered them substantial benefits in recognition and increased membership. They profited handsomely from it, and when, twelve years later, the Taft-Hartley Act exacted a high price for continued enjoyments of the benefits, they decided they could not do without them. By contrast the Industrial Relations Act came at a time when British unions had been firmly established for decades. Many of them could see little advantage in it for themselves, and all could see substantial disadvantages. For the Act was Wagner and Taft-Hartley rolled into one with a good deal more besides.

One of the assumptions made by the authors of the Act was that trade unions are too powerful. They could argue that the experience of the Act confirmed their opinion, although it was not the kind of confirmation that they wanted. In a period of little more than two years the unions had defied, defeated and destroyed one of the most significant Acts of Parliament of the century. The lesson which the

Labour party leaders had learned over *In Place of Strife* was massively confirmed, and the social contract which they were developing with the unions during their period of opposition included a large programme of reforms and additions to labour law which was largely drawn up by the unions and their legal advisers. Much of this programme was carried out when Labour returned to office in 1974. It is the subject of Chapter 10.

THE TRADES UNION CONGRESS

When the Trades Union Congress came into being in the late eighteen-sixties, British unions had already burned their fingers in earlier experiments with central confederations possessing wide powers. The title which they gave to the executive body of Congress—the parliamentary committee—made plain that its function was to lobby parliament to secure support for legislation which Congress wished to promote. Only slowly and with caution did Congress venture into other fields, and, when bold new ventures were demanded, they avoided direct responsibility by calling new agencies into being.

The first of these was the General Federation of Trade Unions, formed in 1899 to provide central strike insurance for those unions which wished to join. For some years it cut a considerable figure in the trade union world, but has long since settled down to provide insurance and common services to a group of small unions. The second was the Labour Representation Committee. By 1900 the unions had been sending representatives to parliament for a quarter of a century, and had made more than one attempt to create their own electoral organization. In that year they joined with three socialist groups to found the new committee which prospered and became the modern Labour party. The marks of its origins are still visible in the powers which the party constitution grants to affiliated unions.

While Labour was replacing the Liberals as the country's major party of the left, Congress was acquiring the confidence to widen its own powers. During and immediately after the war several other bodies were in competition with Congress for recognition as the central representative organization of the unions. In 1921 Congress reasserted its authority as the industrial spokesman of the unions by widening its powers, replacing the parliamentary committee by a General Council, and increasing its resources and staff. In 1924 the General Council was empowered to intervene in disputes in which negotiations broke down and other workers were likely to be involved or affected by the outcome. If such a dispute led to a stoppage and the union concerned had followed the council's advice, the council was to 'take steps to organise on behalf of the union or unions concerned all such moral and material support as the circumstances of the dispute may appear to justify'.

It was under this rule that the General Council arranged an embargo on the transport of coal in 1925, thus forcing the Conservative government to intervene in the current coal dispute by offering a subsidy to maintain miners' wages. The rule provided such authority as the council had to call the general strike nine months later, when the subsidy came to an end.

After 1926 Congress and the council paid less attention to increasing their formal powers than to extending their authority in other fields. Guided by their general secretary, Citrine, they sought to achieve this aim through co-operation with the central employers' organizations following the Mond–Turner talks.[49] Next they turned back to their traditional activities of pressure on legislation and government action. Citrine insisted that governments should deal with the trade union movement only through the council. Access of union leaders to honours and places on government committees was controlled by the council and therefore by Citrine.

Because the nineteen-thirties were a period of gradually extending government intervention in the economy, this policy led to a steady increase in the standing of Congress up to the outbreak of the Second World War. During the war, government intervention reached out to most aspects of economic affairs; consultation with the council and its staff became a central feature of policy-making; the conduct of domestic affairs was remarkably successful; and the standing of Congress rose to a peak. It was almost as high after the return of a Labour government in 1945, but as the government's economic difficulties mounted and they turned to more overt methods of pay restraint, differences developed between the government and the council, and the council's influence over the unions began to slip.

The decline continued after 1951 under Conservative governments, and the influence of Congress reached a low point at the end

[49] See pp. 338–40.

of the fifties, symbolized by the abolition of the Industrial Disputes Tribunal against the wishes of the unions. Within a year or so, however, the Conservatives had become converts to economic planning, and were seeking the support of the General Council for their schemes.

The unions reacted strongly against the pay pause in 1961, and it did not seem to be an auspicious time for a Conservative government to ask for trade union support for a new venture into economic planning. Nevertheless, at the end of the year the government invited the General Council to participate in the proposed National Economic Development Council. The general secretary was now George Woodcock, and he and those of his colleagues who were concerned with the unions' public image and the authority of Congress persuaded the other members of the council that 'they should put to a practical test the question whether participation would give them a genuine opportunity of influencing the Government's policies in ways that would help trade unionists'.[50] Six members of the council were appointed to the National Economic Development Council, and Congress ratified the decision. This was done despite the strong union disapproval of the government's next venture in pay policy, the National Incomes Commission. In 1963 Congress approved a report from the council on *Economic Development and Planning*, which contained several innovations in trade union thinking, although the section on 'prices and incomes' had to be revised to make plain that there was no commitment to 'wage restraint'.[51]

The council had already ventured on one or two initiatives in which Woodcock had had a hand as assistant general secretary. In 1955 the issue of trade union finances was taken up. A limited survey revealed that a 'number of unions spent more than they received in contributions'; that 'the real value of reserves per member today is lower than it was in 1939'; and that 'the increases that have taken place in contributions are inadequate to meet the increased costs of administration'.[52] Next year a wider survey confirmed the findings.[53] Since 1955 was the year in which the rate of increase in union contributions began to accelerate, it may be that the council's surveys helped to hasten the change.

A bolder venture came in 1959 when the council undertook an

[50] Trades Union Congress, *Annual Report*, 1962, p. 254.
[51] *Ibid.*, 1963, pp. 480–95.   [52] *Ibid.*, 1955, pp. 304–5.
[53] *Ibid.*, 1956, p. 305.

investigation into 'the broad problems of disputes, workshop representation and related matters'. Their interim report, published the following year, seemed to promise radical recommendations. It did not burke the difficulties, and went so far as to suggest that 'it would . . . be attractive to recommend direct communication between the secretary of a joint committee of unions nationally and the officers of joint stewards committees in the industry concerned'.[54] However, this suggested invasion of individual union autonomy was too much and next year's report merely informed Congress that the council would continue its discussions.

In 1960 Woodcock succeeded Tewson, who had been general secretary since Citrine left in 1946, and took up the vexed question of union structure. At the 1962 Congress he argued the case for industrial unionism, but in the end the council's report on union structure drew attention to 'the severely practical limits within which . . . it might be possible and desirable for some unions to come more closely to an industrial basis of organisation'.[55]

With the election of a Labour government in 1964, an innovating general secretary at Congress House, signs of a new mood in the council and Congress, and a tripartite agreement on a *Statement of Intent* covering economic planning and incomes policy, there was good reason to expect that the functions and standing of Congress would soon surpass even the wartime achievements; but it was not to be, although Congress did launch its boldest innovation so far.

When a voluntary early warning system for pay and prices was developed in the autumn of 1965 the council undertook to deal with the pay claims of affiliated unions. They asked the unions to inform them of all impending claims, and set up a special committee to review them. If the committee did not wish to comment the union or unions would be informed within a month. Otherwise the committee would make written observations or arrange for a discussion. The council undertook 'to keep the Government informed of developments'.[56]

This arrangement ceased with the standstill in July 1966, after which the law required notification of claims and settlements direct to the Ministry of Labour. However, the council decided to retain its own vetting arrangements, looking forward to a stage in which there would be 'a transition from a largely Government-determined pol-

---

[54] *Ibid.*, 1960, pp. 124–30.   [55] *Ibid.*, 1963, pp. 122–5.
[56] *Prices and Incomes Policy: An "Early Warning" System.*

icy to a policy of which the ingredients were determined by the trade union Movement'.[57] They proposed that the government should cease to rely on statutory powers after August 1967 and trust Congress to 'strengthen its own wage-vetting scheme'; but the government had no faith in the ability of Congress to exercise effective control, and refused.[58]

The General Council therefore devised their own pay policy at the beginning of 1967 and secured the endorsement of a conference of union executives on 2 March by a vote of eight to one. In most respects the council's criteria for pay did not differ materially from those of the government, but they included clear guidance for action on low pay. The council decided 'to aim at progressively raising national minimum rates to a level of £15 a week' and as a first step to allow 'claims for increases of up to £1 a week in national minimum rates which were less than £14 a week, on condition that the full increases were applicable only to those workers who were on or near the existing minimum, with tapering increases to those whose current earnings (excluding overtime) were not more than £15 a week'.[59]

Between November 1966 and the following July, 340 claims were notified, covering just over four million workers. Approval was withheld from 40 per cent of the claims covering 40 per cent of the workers. 'In other cases the committee indicated that they would have no objections to negotiations proceeding on part or all of the claims, but in many instances indicated modifications which they considered should be made.'[60] One observer remarked that the committee had 'been acting with vigour and determination' and had 'shown that it takes seriously the implications of its contention, that voluntary action within the Trade Union movement is capable of exercising an effective measure of control over wage increases which could be detrimental to the national interest'.[61]

However, the council's policy ran into trouble with unions of skilled workers who feared their differentials would be cut back by the preference given to the low-paid. In its place the council proposed uniform money increases for all workers which would yield

---

[57] Trades Union Congress, *Annual Report*, 1967, p. 328.
[58] Leo Panitch, *Social Democracy and Industrial Militancy*, p. 141.
[59] Trades Union Congress, *Annual Report*, 1967, pp. 328–9.
[60] *Ibid.*, pp. 332–3.
[61] C. W. Guillebaud, *Wage Determination and Wage Policy*, p. 54.

higher percentage increases for the lower-paid. These new guidelines were published in the council's *Economic Review 1968*, which was itself an innovation.[62] However, the rapid growth of earnings during 1967 had already revealed the weaknesses of the council's policy as well as the government's. As time passed it became evident that the vetting of claims gave their incomes policy committee little control over actual negotiations, as in those affecting dockers and draughtsmen in 1967 and manual engineering workers in 1968. In developing its own policy the council had in mind the example of the Swedish confederation of unions which exercises considerable control over the claims and settlements of its constituent unions. Its ability to do so, however, is largely due to the centralization of power in the Swedish confederation of employers' associations. Close co-operation between the two confederations enables them to exercise a joint influence on negotiations and settlements. The new Confederation of British Industry was unwilling to accept any responsibility for administering the government's policy so far as it affected prices, and undertook to play only a limited part in the voluntary scheme for notifying pay claims and settlements set up in 1965.[63]

Meanwhile relations between the government and the unions were worsening. Rattled by the meagre results of their economic policies and by the rising number of strikes, the government blamed the unions for many of their failures, and turned their attention to the prospect of anti-strike legislation following the Donovan Report. In the war Ernest Bevin had provided a solid link between the unions and the wartime coalition, and Harold Wilson had probably hoped that Frank Cousins, the general secretary of the Transport and General Workers, could perform the same function when he asked him to join the cabinet in 1964 as Minister of Technology; but Cousins was unpredictable. He accepted the invitation to join the cabinet despite his opposition to its incomes policy, and returned to his union when the policy was given statutory backing. In 1968 one of the government's foremost supporters among union leaders, Lord

---

[62] Looking forward optimistically to an increase of 'five per cent or rather more' in productivity from mid-1968 to mid-1969, the council foresaw a 'tolerable increase of five per cent or somewhat more in earnings per head'. Of this they expected about 1.5 per cent to be absorbed by local productivity bargaining, leaving 3.5 to 4 per cent for general increases. Excluding juveniles and part-time workers, this would yield 70p a week on average (*Economic Review 1968*, pp. 64–70).

[63] *Prices and Incomes Policy: An "Early Warning" System.*

Carron, was replaced as president of the Engineers by Hugh Scanlon, a militant and a powerful critic of the government; and in 1969 Jack Jones became general secretary of the Transport and General Workers, bringing to the office more steadfast support for leftwing principles and a more determined personality than his predecessor. When Woodcock resigned early in that year to become the first chairman of the Commission on Industrial Relations, it was clear that the direction of Congress would be in the hands of Scanlon and Jones.

Along with the new general secretary of Congress, Victor Feather, they took charge of the negotiations with the government over the legislative proposals following on *In Place of Strife*. The resounding defeat of the government helped to restore the authority of the General Council and the process was assisted by the vigorous efforts of the council and their staff to follow up the Donovan Report with a thoroughgoing re-examination of union policies and structure. Among other things, this review led to the development of industry committees,[64] and to a vigorous expansion of Congress provisions for trade union training. On the other hand, the implementation of the 'solemn and binding undertaking' given to the government to amend the rules of Congress made little difference to its authority in practice. Stoppages in inter-union disputes were forbidden until after investigation by the council or its disputes committee. When faced with a dispute which might have 'serious consequences' and where they found that 'there should be no stoppage of work before procedure is exhausted', the council had power to instruct the union or unions concerned to take 'immediate and energetic steps to obtain a resumption of work' and to deal with them under rule 13 (which provides for suspension and ultimate expulsion) if they did not comply. As evidence of the unions' good faith, Feather devoted much of his time over the next few months to acting as a conciliator in strikes; but his efforts had no visible effect on the rapidly accelerating increase in strike figures; and the council made little use of its new powers.

The conflict over the Industrial Relations Act added greatly to the council's standing both in the country and with the unions. Besides proving that the unions could destroy Conservative legislation as well as Labour's legislative proposals, it was the occasion for Congress to use its disciplinary powers far more vigorously than ever

[64] See p. 188.

before. The major previous instance had been the expulsion of the Electricians in 1961. In their investigation of the Electricians' affairs during 1959–60 the council had proceeded with obvious reluctance. Expulsion was recommended only after gross malpractices had been exposed and condemned by the courts, and the Electricians were readmitted with patent relief as soon as they had changed their leaders. It was believed that the expulsion of a major union could harm Congress as much as the union, by diminishing its representative character. In 1972–3, however, Congress threatened thirty-two unions with expulsion and actually expelled twenty. Although none of them had as many members as the Electricians, that could not have been foreseen when the instruction was given to deregister.

The development of the social contract brought the council and their staff into the planning of a whole programme of government legislation and action as never before; and in 1975 the new stature of Congress was demonstrated beyond doubt when the council devised their own incomes policy—which was accepted without significant change by the government—and proceeded to enforce it with remarkable success.

With no major unions left outside its fold, Congress is now the unchallenged representative of British trade unions. At the beginning of the sixties, plans for a separate white collar confederation had been far advanced. It was to include, among others, the National and Local Government Officers, the Teachers, and the major technical and executive unions in the civil service. They hoped to receive the same access to government as Congress, but their hopes were destroyed when the Conservative government rejected their claims, giving all the union places on the National Economic Development Council to Congress. Since then, these unions have been persuaded by their leaders that their only chance to share in the making of economic and industrial policies is through affiliation to Congress, whose 115 affiliated unions now include more than 90 per cent of British union members.

Between them these affiliates send over a thousand delegates to the annual meeting, held in the first full week in September at a major seaside resort. The three main functions of the meeting are to elect the General Council for the forthcoming year; to discuss the report of the retiring council; and to debate resolutions submitted by the council or by constituent unions, most of the latter being composited by the standing orders committee. Although unions are entitled to delegations according to their size, important or controversial issues are decided by 'card votes' in which each union casts the votes of its entire membership for or against the motion. The council dominates Congress, a good deal of time being occupied by its members introducing reports and resolutions, and intervening in, or replying to, debates. Unless the council is divided, it is not easy for Congress to initiate policy, for if it passes a positive resolution contrary to the council's wishes, council can usually ignore it or make only empty gestures towards its fulfilment. On the other hand, Congress can effectively censure the council which is sensitive to a 'reference back' of part of its report. A reference back is almost invariably followed by a modification of the council's line. A favourite device for dealing with potentially dangerous resolutions is to ask for them to be referred to the council for examination.

The council's forty-one members are elected from nineteen groups of unions (eighteen industrial groups and one for women) but by the votes of the whole of Congress. Consequently if the large unions act together, as they usually do, their votes can determine the composition of the council. In 1977–8 each of the five unions with more than 500,000 members was represented by its chief officer, and there were also ten other officers from those five unions on the council. Each of the nine unions with between 200,000 and 500,000 members were also represented by their chief officers. One of them, the Mineworkers, has two chief officers, the president and the general secretary, both on the council; and one of the remaining eight had a second officer on the council. Of the ten unions with between 100,000 and 200,000 members, five were represented by their chief officers; and of the 93 unions with less than 100,000 members, ten had their chief officers on the council.

In addition to the general secretary, and his deputy and two assistants, Congress employs a headquarters staff of about a hundred, organized into seven departments. Most of the officers in these departments are university graduates. They constitute by far the largest group of specialists in the trade union movement. In 1963 the council took over responsibility for trade union education from the National Council of Labour Colleges and the Workers' Educational Trade Union Committee. This takeover gave the council its first full-time regional officers—education 'officers whose main responsibility is to administer a national programme of courses for shop stewards and other workplace representatives. These are mainly day release courses running over a period of weeks, taught by public education bodies, but to a syllabus designed by Congress. In 1976–7 there were 1,540 of these courses, almost a third of them dealing with industrial safety, with 21,372 students in all.

Otherwise the Regional Councils, drawn from full-time officers of affiliated unions, lead a shadowy existence, although there is a vigorous Scottish Trades Union Congress. Local co-ordination of the unions is primarily the job of the trades councils. Trades councils in some major cities can trace their history back before the foundation of Congress, but growing centralization in the unions robbed them of many of their former functions. They have a number of administrative jobs, such as nominating trade unionists to local commitees and tribunals, and they provide a forum for the discussion of issues which local trade unionists wish to air.

The services which Congress can offer to its constituent unions are limited by its income. In 1978 affiliation fees were 20p per member a year, less than 2 per cent of the average contribution per member received by British trade unions, and little more than 0.25 per cent of the average *weekly* pay of British employees. The equivalent figures in many western European countries are significantly higher.

The council meets monthly, mainly to approve the work of its numerous committees, whose members and chairmen are selected with a close regard for seniority—as is the chairman of the council itself. His tenure is limited to one year. The former parliamentary committee's task of influencing legislation and government departments remains an important function of the council, although methods have changed with the times. With the rise of the Labour party there has been less need to cultivate friendly members of parliament to sponsor measures; and as the cabinet has come to dominate parliament, contacts with government departments have become all-important. Deputations are still sent to ministers to present Congress resolutions, but in addition the council now makes nominations to all relevant Royal Commissions and committees of inquiry, and also to a large number of permanent committees which give direct access to government departments. In 1972 a TUC–Labour Party Liaison Committee was set up with representatives from the General Council, the parliamentary party, and the party's national executive. It drew up the social contract and remained in existence after Labour took office to suggest and review government policies.

The constitutional powers of the council are set out in rules 11–13 dealing with industrial disputes, inter-union disputes, and the conduct of affiliated unions. These have already been outlined.[65] However, they are not the chief source of the council's authority. When the moment is ripe, they can commit the movement to a course of action by calling a conference of trade union executives, who have the power to act on behalf of their members, or are willing to assume it. Such a meeting authorized the general strike in 1926; and since 1948 a number of decisions on government incomes policies and on Congress's own incomes policies have been taken by such meetings or by special meetings of Congress.

THE CONFEDERATION OF BRITISH INDUSTRY

Central organization among British employers did not become permanent until the First World War. Government intervention in industry brought, first, the National Union of Manufacturers in 1915, and next the more weighty Federation of British Industry in 1917, both concerned primarily with commercial issues. The National Confederation of Employers' Organizations developed out of the employers' side of the National Industrial Conference summoned by the government in 1919 to discuss postwar industrial relations. Later it changed its name to the British Employers' Confederation.

After the National Industrial Conference came to an end the Confederation played a minor part in interwar industrial relations, although there was an opportunity to make its mark after the General Strike. In September 1927 the president of Congress announced that 'practically nothing has yet been done to establish effective machinery of joint conference between representative organisations entitled to speak for industry as a whole'.[66] At this stage there was no response from the Confederation or from the Federation of British Industries, but Sir Alfred Mond, chairman of ICI, brought together a group of leading industrialists to meet the General Council, whose chairman was now Ben Turner, in the 'Mond–Turner' talks.

The talks led to a series of recommendations under three headings. The first group of proposals were for changes in industry procedures

[65] See pp. 185, 329, 334.
[66] Trades Union Congress, *Annual Report*, 1927, p. 67.

for handling disputes and for a permanent National Industrial Council representing the central bodies on both sides of industry. The second group constituted a reflationary economic policy for government action well in advance of anything that either the Conservative or Labour parties were willing to accept. The third group dealt with what was called 'rationalization'. The unions recognized the need for industrial reorganization and the introduction of new technology; and the employers accepted that consultation was necessary to protect the interests of displaced workers.

The participants in the talks could not initiate action by themselves. Items under the second heading were for government action, and nothing could be done under the first and third headings without the co-operation of the employers' organizations. The Federation responded warmly. Its council were 'wholeheartedly at one with the conference in its prime objective'.[67] But the two central employers' organizations had been constructed to different plans. The Federation included companies as well as trade associations. Representatives of major companies figured largely in its counsels, and many of the group which Mond (by now Lord Melchett) had brought together were present or past officeholders. By contrast only employers' associations could affiliate to the Confederation. The lead was taken by their full-time officers, notably Sir Allan Smith of the engineering employers. His federation had called the meeting which formed the Confederation, and had provided the Confederation's first headquarters. The views of the constituent associations varied. Some were favourable. Others rejected the new disputes machinery, but were prepared to accept a National Industrial Council. The remainder condemned the whole report. There was, said the engineering employers, 'as little justification for discussion with a political Trades Union Congress as with a political Conservative, Liberal or even Communist Party'. Nevertheless, the leaders braced themselves to accept some form of consultation with Congress, 'not', as one of them said, 'in the interests of the Mond–Turner Reports, but in the interests of the unity of employers'.[68]

When the representatives of the three organizations met in April 1929, the employers explained that the difference in responsibilities between the Federation and the Confederation made it impossible

[67] Federation of British Industries, *Grand Council Minutes*, 11 July 1928.
[68] National Confederation of Employers Organizations, *Industrial Peace Files*, 30 November 1928 and 8 February 1929.

for them to come together in a single National Industrial Council. Instead they proposed a permissive arrangement whereby the Federation and Congress could consult, if they wished, on any matter within the competence of the Federation; and there could be consultation with the Confederation on similar terms. But consultation must not 'invade the province and trespass on the function of the individual constituents' of any of the three bodies.[69] This cumbersome machinery was accepted by the General Council for lack of a better offer. It was used once or twice over the next few years, but achieved little and fell into disuse. Whereas the General Council were eager to extend their functions and augment their authority, the Confederation had no such ambition. Had the employers been willing to accept and act on the Mond–Turner proposals, the subsequent course of industrial relations in Britain might have been very different.

As it was, the Confederation's main functions were to make representations to governments on legislative proposals concerning labour matters, and to represent British employers at meetings of the International Labour Organization. After issuing two reports in the 1931 economic crisis, its voice was not heard in public for twenty-four years. During and after the war Confederation representatives sat alongside those of Congress on the many advisory committees set up by the government on industrial matters, but they played a minor and essentially conservative role. Their behaviour suggested that they believed that employers should not normally promote change, for change in industrial relations was likely to be for the worse; they should prevent change if they could; but, if it had to be, they should accept it quietly.

In 1955, however, there were signs of a fresh approach. Under a new director, Sir George Pollock, the Confederation announced its views on inflation in *Britain's Industrial Future*, and began to circulate a fortnightly *Bulletin* whose editorials were plainly intended to mould employer opinion. In 1959 the bulletin was made available to the press. During the next few years the Confederation made two attempts to crystallize the views of organized employers by holding conferences. At the second, in 1961, several academic specialists in industrial relations were present and an officer of Congress gave a talk. The main topic showed a readiness to discuss current realities in industrial relations for it dealt with the question whether 'plant-by-plant negotiation' should be encouraged or countered by more 'cen-

[69] Trades Union Congress, *Annual Report*, 1929, pp. 205–9.

tralisation and co-ordination between industries'.[70] In 1962 the Confederation met with Congress to discuss three issues; the training of shop stewards, dismissal procedure, and payment during sickness. On the first the Confederation undertook to recommend their members to consider releasing shop stewards with pay in order to attend courses.[71] In 1964 the two bodies undertook an 'experimental investigation into strikes in breach of procedure, or called at little notice, as a fact-finding exercise'.[72]

From time to time proposals had been made for an amalgamation between the Confederation and the Federation of British Industries. In 1962 the formation of the National Economic Development Council emphasized the drawbacks of separation. Since the council's work included labour and commercial matters it straddled the spheres of interest of both organizations; and the National Association of British Manufacturers (as the National Union of Manufacturers was now called) might also have a claim to a seat as the representative of the interests of small firms. Accordingly, whereas the General Council nominated the six trade union members, the Chancellor of the Exchequer chose six individual employers to represent private industry. The nationalized industries were represented separately.

Under this spur the central employers' organizations agreed on the objectives of an amalgamated body and appointed a commission of two to advise on a suitable constitution. Their report,[73] which was accepted in 1964, led to the formation of the Confederation of British Industry by Royal Charter in 1965. In addition to the three amalgamating organizations the new body included the main nationalized industries.

The major constitutional problem had been to reconcile the structure of the Confederation, which admitted only employers' associations into membership, with that of the other two bodies, which included both trade associations and individual companies. The new Confederation admits companies, trade associations, employers' associations, and nationalized industries. Its council of four hundred members consists of about 250 representatives of employers' associations and trade associations along with representatives of the

---

[70] British Employers' Confederation, *Bulletin*, 31 May 1961.
[71] *Ibid.*, 8 May 1963.
[72] Donovan Commission, *Selected Written Evidence*, pp. 252–3.
[73] Benson and Brown, *Report on the Formation of a National Industrial Organisation*.

regional councils and elected representatives of individual companies. Industrial relations were originally entrusted to a labour and social affairs committee of representatives of employers' associations, the nationalized industries, and those 'large individual company members which negotiate direct with the unions'.[74] This committee in turn appointed standing committees on industrial relations, wages and conditions of employment, training, and other topics.

A few years later this unwieldy arrangement was replaced by a relatively small employment policy committee which has become the Confederation's main instrument for formulating industrial relations policy. Along with federation directors it included the personnel directors of some of the country's largest companies and nationalized industries, and proved itself a high-powered and well-informed committee. It is, however, subject to the council of the Confederation, which is large, unwieldy, erratic, and includes many members who are not expert in industrial relations; and the authority of the council itself is limited. Like the British Employers' Confederation before it, the Confederation contains in its Charter

> a proviso that [it] should not do anything in pursuance of its object which would interfere with any of its members in the conduct or management of its own affairs or which would be inconsistent with the retention by members of their complete autonomy and independence of action.[75]

The council of the Confederation has no power to intervene in disputes; it has not taken upon itself the vetting of its members' negotiating proposals as the General Council has done; it has no equivalent mechanism to the conference of trade union executives to commit its affiliates to a common course of action; and it held its first national conference in 1977.

In 1975 the machinery of the Confederation was strengthened by setting up a president's committee consisting of about twenty-five leading representatives from the main sections of its membership—large companies, small firms, associations, nationalized industries—and its major committees. The president's committee is not part of the formal constitution, and its official function is to advise the president; but it meets monthly (like the council), reviews policy

---

[74] Donovan Commission, *Selected Written Evidence*, p. 248.   [75] *Ibid.*, p. 247.

documents, and carries considerable weight. It is the Confederation's nearest equivalent to the General Council of Congress.

The Confederation has not achieved the same standing with governments as Congress has. Government incomes policies have been angled mainly at the unions, and the Confederation's representatives have either been very much the third party in joint discussions, as in the Chequers and Downing Street talks in 1972, or absent as in the formulation of the social contract pay policies. Relations between the Confederation and the Conservative party are far less close than those between the unions and the Labour party, both constitutionally and in practice. Although the Confederation had its own distinct views on the Conservative proposals for industrial relations legislation in 1970, and had set up a working party to formulate proposals which were adopted by the council in July 1970, the Conservative government was almost as perfunctory in its consultation with them as it was with Congress; and it made few concessions to the Confederation's opinions in the drafting and passage of the bill. Consequently 'mainly as a result of provisions insisted on by the Conservatives against the wishes of business the effect of the legislation was to damage the interests of business by creating industrial disruption'.[76]

The Confederation's boldest achievement so far was the 5 per cent limit on price increases which accompanied the N–1 pay policy of the Heath administration; although the consequent squeeze on profits was a considerable embarrassment, especially as the policy had no detectable long-term effect in reducing inflation. Under the subsequent Labour government, the Confederation's proposals on taxation appeared to gain considerable influence, and its campaign against the Bullock Report was highly effective.[77] Moreover, its leaders have regular discussions with members of the General Council and with ministers, and their advice and suggestions have helped to shape other aspects of policy under both Conservative and Labour governments.

To rival the influence of Congress, there would need to be a radical reform in the structure of the Confederation and a radical change in the attitude of British employers towards collective action. A review of structure was undertaken in 1971 by a committee commissioned by both the Confederation and the Associated British Chambers of Commerce and chaired by Lord Devlin. Its report[78] had little effect at

[76] Michael Moran, *The Politics of Industrial Relations*, p. 152.   [77] See p. 443.
[78] *Report of Commission of Inquiry into Industrial and Commercial Representation.*

the time, but since 1976 the Confederation has had some success in extending its coverage in finance and business as well as in industry to approach nearer to the goal of the Confederation of British Business proposed in the Devlin report. For industrial relations, however, a change in attitudes is more critical than structural reform. 'In the past', noted a consultative document published by the Confederation in 1977,

> employers have usually preferred independence to collective action so as to avoid involvement in issues with which they are not directly concerned and to retain independence over their own affairs. . . . Change will not succeed unless employers are determined and committed, and are prepared to act, both individually and together. . . . Given our industrial relations history, greater employer strength will not be easy to achieve; self-fulfilling expectations about trade union power and employer weakness will be hard to change. Nevertheless, increased employer solidarity and determination is crucial to our pay bargaining system.[79]

At least the diagnosis has been made.

[79] *The Future of Pay Determination*, pp. 32–3.

Chapter 9

INCOMES POLICY

OBJECTIVES AND CRITERIA

An incomes policy may be defined as an attempt—usually by a government—to alter the national level of wages and salaries, or to alter the rate at which they change; and one of these objectives cannot be achieved without affecting the other. There have been occasions when governments have made a conscious effort to raise money wages as did Roosevelt's New Deal administration when it tried to reduce unemployment in the United States in the thirties. Such policies are, however, far less common than attempts to hold back the rate of increase in money incomes; and that has been the over-riding objective of British incomes policies.

Some economists argue that incomes policies are either useless, because the level of pay is determined by influences such as the level of employment, the supply of money, and the balance of payments; or self-defeating, in that their effect is likely to be a higher level of pay than might have been expected without interference.[1] Whatever the rights or wrongs of the argument—and it is not easy to find conclusive empirical evidence on the effect of incomes policies—these economists have so far had remarkably little influence on the politicians, administrators, trade unionists, and employers who from time to time involve themselves in attempts to hold back the rate of money pay increases. Sooner or later every British postwar government has decided to make such an attempt, in most instances with the co-operation of either unions or employers, and sometimes both. Faced with the impossibility of achieving their economic aims due to the rate of price inflation, and aware that costs are overwhelmingly the major element in prices, with wages and salaries by far the largest

[1] A recent lively and readable statement of these views is contained in Brittan and Lilley, *The Delusion of Incomes Policy*.

element in costs, they have allowed themselves to be persuaded that there must be some way of arresting the rate of increase in wages and salaries. The most striking example of this conversion was in the early summer of 1975 when British trade union leaders faced the prospect of the annual rate of increases racing past the 25 per cent mark with no obvious likelihood of decelaration unless pay increases abated. They decided that pay increases must and could be abated, although many of them had been arguing for the previous few years that pay was not a major cause of inflation, and incomes policies were either ineffective or positively harmful. Some of them feared for the future of the British democracy unless something was done to arrest inflation, and no one offered them a convincing alternative to pay restraint. Indeed, pay restraint was widely perceived as a necessary complement to curtailing the supply of money, cutting back public expenditure, and putting limits on public sector borrowing in a general policy to counter inflation.

Every postwar incomes policy has spelled out limits to pay increases. In 1948–50 there was held to be 'no justification for any general increase of individual money incomes', although in exceptional instances increases might be justified.[2] Accordingly the policy would have been wholly successful only if all pay increases had been justified on the grounds of an acknowledged exception. The 'price plateau' policy of 1956 aimed at stable prices and the limit on pay increases was therefore whatever could be attained without increasing prices.

The pay pause of 1961–2 aimed to stop all increases in pay for a limited period, as did the standstills of 1966 and 1972–3, but the post-standstill 1962 policy proposed that pay increases overall should not exceed the expected annual increase in productivity which was originally set at 2 to 2.5 per cent, and later revised to 3 to 3.5 per cent. If this target had been achieved, and there had been no marked alteration in the level of import prices, the domestic price level ought to have been stable. However, the White Paper on *Incomes Policy: The Next Step* did not propose that all pay settlements should be within the proposed limit. On the contrary, 'in many cases there may indeed be no justification at present for any increases at all. In others there may be particular circumstances which point the other way.' Examples of these circumstances were given, but

---

[2] White Paper on *Personal Incomes Costs and Prices*.

nothing more was said about instances in which no increase would be justified.

This statement of Conservative policy was taken over with relatively minor changes in the Labour government's White Paper on *Prices and Incomes Policy* in 1965. After the 1966 standstill, however, the 3 to 3.5 per cent target was replaced by a zero norm with more stringent requirements for exceptional treatment—but no suggestions of reduction in money wages to balance exceptional increases.[3] In *Prices and Incomes Policy After 30 June 1967* the government asserted that 'no-one can be entitled to a minimum increase' in pay, and that 'any proposed increase (or other significant improvement) will need to be justified against the criteria' for exceptional treatment, now once more defined as in 1965, and therefore less stringent than in the previous six months. For 1968 and 1969 there was a 'ceiling' of 3.5 per cent within which all increases had 'to be justified against the criteria and considerations of the policy' (still defined as in 1965); however, the ceiling might be exceeded by certain productivity agreements, and in that case no limit was specified.[4] In the last stages of the policy's decline, towards the end of 1969, a further White Paper held that pay increases within a range of 2.5 to 4.5 per cent could be tolerated, with further discussion of criteria for exceptional treatment.[5] A further complication is that from 1967 onwards the Trades Union Congress had been issuing their own criteria for pay increases which diverged from the government's norms and ceilings.

Apart from the pay pause and the standstills, none of the policies mentioned so far gave precise guidance to negotiators. All of them allowed some exceptions, defined in such a way as to leave room for interpretation, and in most instances without any guidance as to the increase which might be granted once a claim was held to warrant exceptional treatment. Some of them stated that there would be cases where less than the 'norm' would be justified without indicating how these instances should be identified. The policy for 1968–9 imposed a ceiling within which pay claims would have to be justified by the criteria, without guidance on how to determine what increase within the ceiling might be appropriate where a particular claim was found to be justified. Percentage increases were clearly intended to

---

[3] *Prices and Incomes Standstill: Period of Severe Restraint.*
[4] *Productivity, Prices and Incomes Policy in 1968 and 1969.*
[5] *Productivity, Prices and Incomes Policy After 1969.*

apply to overall earnings, but until 1973 there were no instructions as to how negotiators should achieve this result. Where employees customarily received cash payments over and above their basic rates, an addition of x per cent to basic rates would yield less than x per cent on earnings. On the other hand, if x per cent of earnings was added to the basic rate, then earnings would be increased by more than that amount for workers with regular overtime or incentive payments related to the basic rate.

Stages two and three of the statutory Conservative policy in 1972–4 were designed to a different pattern. The amount available for pay increases was to be worked out for each group of employees; a group in most instances meaning those covered by the previous settlement. During stage two the total available was £1 a week per employee *plus* 4 per cent of the existing wage bill excluding overtime. Within this total there was room for variation in the distribution of the increase between individuals and grades within the group, so long as the total increase in the pay bill did not exceed the permitted maximum; but no individual could receive a pay increase of more than £250 a year. Negotiations over the division of the total sum available were known as 'kitty' bargaining. The principle remained the same for stage three, although the calculations were a good deal more complicated than in stage two. The general ceiling was 7 per cent on the group pay bill excluding overtime, or alternatively (to benefit the lower-paid) £2.25 per person; with a further 1 per cent for reducing anomalies or obstacles to the effective use of manpower, and an individual limit of £350 a year. There were also several loopholes which could lead to higher payments, but, in contrast to the provisions for exceptional treatment in earlier policies, the circumstances in which they could be used were carefully defined, and a precise limit specified for each of them.

The Conservative stage three was therefore precise but complicated. The Labour policy of 1975 was precise and simple. The Trades Union Congress proposed that the limit should be '£6 a week to all full-time adults (aged 18 and above) up to a cut-off point, with pro rata payments for part-timers and juveniles'.[6] The increases were to paid to individuals as separate supplements to their weekly pay, so that they did not affect basic rates, nor overtime, shift allowances or any other payment related to the basic rate. The sole exception was for additional increases to women as a final step to equal pay by the

[6] Trades Union Congress, *Development of the Social Contract*, p. 15.

end of 1975, when the Equal Pay Act was to take effect. The only disagreement between the General Council and the government was over the individual cut-off point. The General Council proposed £7,000, whereas the government settled for £8,500. The formula for 1976–7 was a supplement of 5 per cent, with a lower limit of £2.50 and an upper limit of £4, but no cut-off. Complications returned in the following year, when the General Council decided that for 1977–8 they could not ask Congress to support more than a strict observance of the twelve month rule. The government nevertheless decided that they must offer guidance on the general level of pay settlements. Their target for prices was that the rate of increase should fall below 10 per cent early in 1978. They judged that this objective might be achieved if the rate of increase in earnings over 1977–8 was not more than 10 per cent; and observed that the '£6 policy, which represented an average increase in wage settlements of nearly 11 per cent, produced an increase in earnings for the year of about 14 per cent'. This meant 'that the general level of settlements must be well within single figures'.[7]

This formulation of aims indicated that the government foresaw the possibility of an increase in living standards during the year. Generally speaking, all designers of incomes policies have claimed that their long-run effect would be to raise real wages faster than they would have risen otherwise, by removing obstacles to economic growth and avoiding the use of such severe restrictions on money supply, investment and public expenditure as would otherwise be necessary. However, although this has always been the long-term objective, under some of the policies it was not expected to be achieved in the short run. These policies were aimed at a future increase in living standards through an improvement in Britain's competitive position. To achieve this, domestic consumption had to be curtailed in order to promote investment and exports. Such policies include Cripps' 'wage freeze' after the devaluation of the pound at the end of 1949, and both the 1975–6 and the 1976–7 stages of the social contract.

Standstills have generally been regarded as harsh but fair, since 'everyone is treated the same'. However, where the policy permits a general increase in pay, union opinion—at least initially—has some-times favoured flat-rate cash increases rather than percentage increases, because 'the higher your income, the more you can afford

[7] *The Attack on Inflation after 31 July 1977.*

to pay the higher prices'. When prices are rising, these two forms of pay policy yield differing results. In a standstill all real incomes are reduced proportionately to the increase in prices. By contrast a flat-rate cash increase may raise the real incomes of the low-paid by increasing their pay by a larger percentage figure than the increase in prices; whereas at some higher level of pay the two cancel out; and above that real incomes fall.

Flat-rate pay increases were in vogue during both World Wars, with consequent compression of differentials. Percentage increases were restored afterwards, although on the second occasion not until about 1950. On both occasions some of the higher paid went on to secure an advantage in percentage terms so that some, but not all, of the lost ground was restored. Similar fluctuations in fashion have occurred more rapidly in recent incomes policies.

In 1967 the General Council designed its separate policy to give an even greater advantage to the low-paid than flat-rate increases would have done. They proposed to confine general increases to the low-paid. Such increases were to be allowed only to those earning less than £15 a week, excluding overtime. Objections from unions of skilled workers forced them to retreat to flat-rate increases in 1968. The Conservative policy of 1972–4 combined percentage and flat-rate increases, with £1 + 4 per cent in stage two, and 7 per cent with a £2.25 minimum and flat-rate threshold payments in stage three. They also placed limits, of £250 and £350 respectively, on the amount that anyone could receive by way of a pay increase. Next came the flat-rate £6 under the social contract, with no increase at all for those earning over £8,500 a year, followed by a 5 per cent increase with cut-off points at each end, of £2.50 and £4. In 1977 the social contract reverted to a percentage figure—10 per cent. There were few trade union objections. Indeed, by this time there was widespread discussion among both trade unionists and employers of the need for a 'restoration of differentials', which meant reverting to the differentials which had existed before the social contract, or even earlier.

Another method of providing special treatment for the low-paid, employed by the policies of 1948–50, 1962 and 1965–70, is to announce that pay claims on their behalf can be given special consideration. These three policies also permitted special consideration to be given to claims for the restoration of differentials. It is evident that a policy which permits exceptional treatment of the low-paid and the restoration of differentials offers a justification for a never-ending spiral of pay increases. The policy-makers therefore tried to ensure that there was no general licence to preserve differentials, but only certain special differentials. In 1948 the Trades Union Congress asked that 'essential' differentials should be maintained; and in 1965 the rubric read: 'where there is widespread recognition that the pay of a certain group of workers has fallen seriously out of line with the level of remuneration for similar work and needs in the national interest to be improved'. For the period of 'severe restraint' in 1967 an increase on these grounds was to be allowed only where it was 'imperative to correct a gross anomaly'. The 1972–4 policies originally contained no similar loopholes but, at the insistence of the government, the Pay Board produced a report on *Anomalies Arising out of the Pay Standstill of November 1972*, and another on *Relativities*. The first dealt with a number of specific cases which received special treatment under the pay code of stage three; and the second proposed permanent machinery 'for considering claims by groups for an improvement of their relative position within the community or in relation to other parts of the same industry'. It was under this second formula that the Conservative government asked the Pay Board to investigate the pay claim of the coalminers who went on strike on 10 February 1974, but the report appeared after the election and Labour's return to power. There were no provisions for the maintenance or restoration of differentials in the social contract up to July 1977, but thereafter differentials could be varied within the overall pay limit for the negotiating group.

A third permissible ground for an exceptional pay increase included in the policies for 1948–50, 1962, and 1965–70 was labour shortage. The 1965 formulation was:

> where it is essential in the national interest to secure a change in the distribution of manpower (or to prevent a change which would otherwise take place) and a pay increase would be both necessary and effective for this purpose.

Labour shortage was the one exception proposed by the government in 1948, the other exceptions at the time having been put forward by Congress. Little use was made of this loophole in 1965–70; and it has found no place in any policy since then. Declining concern with labour shortage may reflect changes in the labour market since the war. Immediately after the war there were acute shortages; by the sixties the situation had eased; and in the seventies the level of unemployment was consistently higher than at any time since 1940.

The fourth justification for exceptional pay increases which figured in the policies for 1948–50, 1962, and 1965–70 was improved productivity. In 1948 Congress held that claims based upon 'the fact of increased output' should be permitted. In 1962 the test was a 'direct contribution . . . to an increase of productivity and a reduction of costs'. In 1965 the wording reflected the experience of productivity bargaining which was then becoming available:

> where the employees concerned, for example by accepting more exacting work or a major change in working practices, make a direct contribution towards increasing productivity in the particular firm or industry. Even in such cases some of the benefits should accrue to the community as a whole in the form of lower prices.

Without question this exception was worked far harder than the others during 1965–70. According to the government, 'over 6 million workers' had 'been involved in over 3,500 productivity agreements' by the end of 1969.[8] However, by that time it had also been brought into disrepute. Estimates of the number of bogus productivity deals vary considerably, but no one doubts that a substantial proportion of them were little more than devices to circumvent the policy.[9]

The productivity exception reappeared in 1973 in stage three of the Conservative policy, as 'efficiency payment schemes' and 'restructuring schemes'. Elaborate precautions were included in the pay code to ensure against abuse. No increases were payable until the results of the first three months had been examined by the Pay Board to make certain that the expected net savings had in fact been achieved. Payments were to be reduced if the expected targets had not been met. Schemes were to be kept under review by means of 'regular management control information' which had to include specified statistics. During the remaining few months of the policy's life nearly five hundred schemes were reported to the board, but less than a hundred had time to submit three-month results. Before its

---

[8] *Productivity, Prices and Incomes Policy After 1969.*
[9] See McKersie and Hunter, *Pay, Productivity and Collective Bargaining,* pp. 247–55.

expiry the board had time to approve fifty-four of these; seven were not approved.[10]

Nothing more was heard of the productivity exception until 1977. When the General Council announced their continued support for the twelve-month rule during the year 1977–8, they added that 'self-financing productivity agreements and improvements in occupational pension schemes should however be negotiable at any time after July 31'. In their White Paper issued a few days later the government gave their blessing to this ruling by announcing that they attached 'the greatest importance to this guidance by the TUC'.[11] Productivity agreements were not included in the 10 per cent limit on earnings which the government added to the guidance of the General Council.

The labour shortage and productivity exceptions were both intended to help a government to meet their economic objectives, but the first could do no more than prevent the policy holding back economic performance, whereas the second was used in 1965–70 as a spur to progress. In the absence of an incomes policy it could be assumed that a company or industry would be likely to increase the rate of pay of grades of employee in such short supply that performance was likely to suffer seriously unless their numbers were increased. If an incomes policy prevented the increase in pay, performance would therefore suffer. So a loophole in the policy was needed to permit an increase in pay. The same argument would apply to the productivity criterion where it could be assumed that in the absence of the policy, the company or firm would have negotiated a productivity agreement. Before 1965, however, productivity agreements had been uncommon. Most companies, public undertakings, and trade unions had given little attention to them. The imposition of narrow limits on general pay increases might therefore be expected to turn the minds of trade unionists to exploring the avenues to exceptional treatment, and to alert managers to the possibility of meeting trade union demands by offering to discuss a productivity agreement. There is no doubt that this is what happened. Had the majority of the productivity agreements which emerged under this pressure been genuine, the national output should have been noticeably higher than it would have been without a productivity exception.

[10] Pay Board, *Sixth Report*.
[11] *The Attack on Inflation After 31st July 1977*.

During 1966–8 the reports of the National Board for Prices and Incomes and the actions of the government both helped to step up the pressure for productivity bargaining. In their report on the *Pay of Busmen* (1966), the board asserted 'the most effective remedy for an undertaking suffering from a shortage of labour is to make better use of the labour which it already has'. In other words, the employer was advised to forget the labour shortage criterion and to concentrate on the productivity exception which would not only solve the labour shortage by increasing the output of the existing labour force, but also justify an exceptional pay increase which would protect him from further loss of labour in the future. In their report on the *Pay and Conditions of Merchant Navy Officers* (1967) the board allowed an exceptional increase in pay to the officers to restore their differential following the substantial increase to ratings at the end of the 1966 shipping strike. They added, however, that it was 'incumbent on the industry to search for ways in which this increase can be used to develop more effective teams of officers and thus lead to ultimate reductions in cost'; and made suggestions about what might be done. In other words, the best justification for a restoration of a differential is an increase in efficiency. In reporting on the pay of manual employees of local authorities and the health service in the same year, the board had no doubt that they were 'among the lowest paid in the country', but diagnosed the 'root cause' of low pay as low productivity. They therefore recommended schemes for linking pay increases with improved efficiency which would justify the pay increases.[12] Wherever they started the board seemed to end up with the productivity criterion.

At the beginning of 1968 the government spelled out the same message in the new version of their policy which required all pay increases to be justified by reference to the criteria, and even then to be limited within a ceiling of 3.5 per cent except for 'agreements which genuinely raise productivity and increase efficiency sufficiently to justify a pay increase above 3½ per cent' and 'major reorganisations of wage and salary structures which can be justified on productivity and efficiency grounds'.[13] The Ministry of Labour was renamed the Department of Employment and Productivity with Barbara Castle as Secretary of State. She left no one in doubt that the

---

[12] *Pay and Conditions of Manual Workers in Local Authorities, the National Health Service, Gas and Water Supply.*

[13] *Productivity, Prices and Incomes Policy in 1968 and 1969.*

promotion of increased productivity through incomes policy had become a central feature of the government's programme.

One other provision for exceptional treatment deserves mention. In devising the third stage of their policy in 1973 the Conservative government were aware that they could expect trouble from the coalminers, who, following their resounding victory over Mr Heath in 1972, had settled within the policy at the beginning of that year, but could hardly be expected to do so for a second year running. They therefore looked about them for a means to offer the miners a special inducement to settle. At the end of 1972 an arbitration award had led to the introduction of shift pay for busmen to take account of their early and late turns. Most underground miners also worked shifts without any special payment for it. The pay code for stage three therefore provided that premium payments could be introduced for hours worked between 2000 hours and 0600 hours on weekdays and for any hours worked on Saturday and Sunday provided the total premium payment did not exceed one-fifth of the basic hourly rate. This clause offered substantial increases in pay to most underground mineworkers and little or nothing to workers in most other industries. Nevertheless this 'unsocial hours' allowance did not serve the purpose that the government had intended. The Mineworkers held out for concessions beyond the limits set out in the pay code, and the policy was overturned with the government.

The unsocial hours exception could be seen as part of a general concern for equity. If most manual workers receive premium payments for working during these hours, is it not fair that busmen and miners should receive them too? Fair treatment, however, was not the main objective in writing the exception into the stage three code. The main objective was to placate a powerful union in the hope of persuading it to abide by the code.

There are no other examples of designing an incomes policy to suit an individual union, but the desire to win trade union support generally has played a considerable part in most policies. Three of the four exceptions to the 1948 'norm' came from the Trades Union Congress, and were repeated with variations of wording in 1962 and 1965. The White Paper of 1965 had been approved by Congress, and by the employers' organizations. Subsequent versions of the 1965–70 policy had less clear-cut trade union support, but throughout the period (except for the standstill) the government retained the approved exceptions in some shape or form. Although Heath failed to secure a tripartite policy in 1972, stages two and three of the policy which he later imposed were carefully designed to be as attractive as possible to trade unionists, with their bias towards the low-paid, their guarantee of threshold payments, and their provision of loopholes which unions might be able to exploit. Labour's incomes policies from 1974 to 1977 were designed by Congress and accepted with minor modifications by the government, and even in 1977 the first statement of policy came from the General Council, although on this occasion the government's addition—the 10 per cent earnings limit—was more than a minor modification.

In their dealings with the unions over incomes policy, governments were not confronted by a consistent set of union requirements. The trade union approach to incomes policy varied over time. In particular the view of Congress changed with their degree of responsibility for the administration of the policy. When the main responsibility lay with the government, as it did in 1948 and 1965, the General Council argued for a set of exceptions which would allow considerable scope for astute union negotiators. The unions roared their disapproval of the first guidelines for productivity agreements brought out by the National Board for Prices and Incomes in December 1966[14] because they believed that too few of them would be able to satisfy these requirements. On the other hand, when the council brought out their own criteria early the following year they included a much more rigid cut-off for special payments for the low-paid than had ever been suggested before. In 1975, when the council accepted primary responsibility for designing the policy, the only exception which they would countenance was to permit the attainment of equal pay for women.

Trade union and employer attitudes also varied over the course of each incomes policy. As time passed the restrictions of any policy which had a real effect began to chafe. Demands for greater flexibility became louder and attempts were made to meet them. The complexities of the stage three Conservative policy in 1973 were intended to offer flexibility to negotiators; and the specially favoured treatment for productivity agreements in 1968 had the effect of providing a good deal of flexibility to any negotiator who was prepared to find a link between pay and efficiency, thus confounding the gloomy forecasts which followed the publication of the first guidelines on productivity agreements. In 1977, after two years

[14] *Productivity and Pay During the Period of Severe Restraint.*

without recognized loopholes, and considerable 'distortions' in pay structure due to the narrowing of differentials and the payment of increases as 'supplements' instead of additions to basic rates, both unions and employers were clamouring for flexibility. The General Council could find no better means of providing it than a reintroduction of the productivity exception; and the government concurred.

Incomes are derived from other sources besides employment, and the impact of an incomes policy depends partly on changes in direct taxation and the movement of prices while it is in force. Trade unionists have views on these aspects of incomes policy as well as on the criteria for pay increases, and most policies have taken account of their views. Price control, profit control, dividend control, rent control, price subsidies and other devices have been included in one or more of the policies in order to win trade union support. With the success of wartime policies in mind, trade unionists have attached great importance to price control, although the evidence seems to be that it can contribute relatively little to the abatement of inflation without curtailing profitability, and therefore investment, and therefore economic growth. In 1974 the new Labour government retained the statutory price controls which had been introduced by their Conservative predecessors, and also reverted to the wartime policy of subsidizing food prices. However, with rapid inflation of prices of imported foodstuffs, the subsidies had to be scaled down, and the criteria for price increases were subsequently revised to provide more encouragement for investment.

One of the causes of the disintegration of Labour's incomes policy in 1968–70, according to Jackson and his colleagues, was the crossing of the income tax threshold for the first time by large numbers of relatively low-paid wage-earners with dependent families whose real earnings therefore fell at a time when average earnings were rising a little faster than prices.[15] In 1977 and 1978 the Chancellor of the Exchequer, Healey, introduced cuts in income tax in his budget as an inducement to the unions to accept his proposals for pay restraint.

The overt objectives of incomes policy—restraining increases in money wages and salaries; promoting fair treatment; and encouraging economic growth—have therefore been intermingled with covert political motives of securing acceptance of the policy from those whose support is needed; and support may be needed abroad as

[15] Jackson *et al.*, *Do Trade Unions Cause Inflation?*, chapter 3.

well as at home. During the postwar period Britain's economic
problems have led to heavy borrowing from abroad. Lenders often
impose conditions. One of them may be that repayment is guaranteed by financial and economic probity on the part of the borrower.
Some of Britain's postwar incomes policies might not have been
introduced, or might not have been so stringent, without the need to
satisfy overseas creditors and potential creditors.

MACHINERY

No policy takes effect unless someone puts it into practice. Incomes
policy is no exception, but there is a choice of administrators. In 1948
the Labour government relied, as the wartime coalition had done, on
unions and employers to apply the principles which the government
had announced, and, where they failed to agree, on compulsory
arbitration through the National Arbitration Tribunal. The 1956
price plateau relied on the action of employers alone. The pay pause
of 1961 was applied in the public sector by the various powers
available to ministers. The application of the 1962 policy was
entrusted to the National Incomes Commission, which failed
because, among other things, it had no powers. Nevertheless, the
setting up of this new body introduced an important quasi-judicial
element into incomes policy. Previously, independent bodies had
shared in the settlement of pay only where the parties failed to agree.
Now such a body was empowered to test the merits of an agreement
reached between them against a national incomes policy, and to
announce its verdict.

The achievement of the National Board for Prices and Incomes
contrasted sharply with the failure of the National Incomes Commission. This was partly because the board had greater powers, and
partly because the Labour government which took office in 1964 was
more serious about its incomes policy than the outgoing Conservative administration had been about theirs; but it was also due to the
character of the chairman of the board, Aubrey Jones. He was
determined that the board should make its mark, and he succeeded;
although his success cost him his career as a Conservative politician
without endearing him to the Labour party, which used him and
forgot him. His achievement was the more remarkable in that the
powers of the board, although greater than those of the National

Incomes Commission, were nevertheless restricted. They could investigate only those cases which were referred to them by a minister—as regards pay, by the Minister of Labour (subsequently Secretary of State for Employment). Consequently, once vetting became established—first voluntarily and then by statute—there was more than one route through the policy. The Ministry of Labour could decide whether a proposed increase in pay was in accordance with the policy, or to refer it to the board. Besides that, if the issue was considered too important for a departmental decision, it could be sent to the cabinet instead of the board. If there was a claim in which the strict application of the policy might have led to a major strike, there was a clear advantage in reference to the cabinet rather than the board. The board were bound to justify their decisions publicly by reference to the criteria set out in the government's White Papers, and the cabinet were not. In 1966 the board allowed through the increase in pay contained in the first stage of a three-stage agreement in electrical contracting,[16] but proposed that the remaining stages should be renegotiated 'nearer the date of implementation in the light of progress made in ensuring increases in productivity', and that it should not apply to electricians outside the contracting industry.[17] The government, however, decided that it should apply to hospital electricians; and let through the second and third stages of the agreement without renegotiation. The 1967 'Devlin' agreement in the docks included a 'modernization' payment of 5p an hour which had no credible justification under the incomes policy. It was approved by the government without reference to the board. Nevertheless when the agreement came into force there was a prolonged unofficial strike in Liverpool which was only resolved after the intervention of the Prime Minister—but not the board. A further 10p an hour was guaranteed with no greater justification under the policy than the earlier payment. In October 1968 a general strike in the engineering industry was averted by a settlement which offered a three-stage increase in pay far in excess of the current 'ceiling'. There were some clauses in the agreement which made obeisance to productivity, but it is difficult to believe that the board would have accepted them as justification for the increase had they been asked to

[16] The board held that the provision in *Prices and Incomes Standstill: Period of Severe Restraint* which delayed for six months the operative date of increases agreed, but not paid, before 20 July 1966 made it obligatory to allow them at the end of six months.
[17] *Wages and Conditions in the Electrical Contracting Industry.*

do so. Airline pilots struck in March 1969. The settlement increased the salaries of senior pilots by 11 per cent, and overtime provisions offered even higher increases in earnings. The settlement went through without reference to the board.

The board was therefore not in control of the interpretation of the pay policy. For every decision made by the board there were dozens made by the Department, and the Department was not bound to follow the precedents established in the board's reports. Moreover, the Department

> retained its traditional task of conciliation. In the regions the manpower advisers were responsible for both conciliation and the application of incomes policy. Inevitably there were instances in which the two obligations conflicted, and the preservation of industrial peace was often the victor, especially after the example set by the cabinet with the docks. During 1969 and 1970 the senior officials at St. James's Square lost interest in rigorous enforcement, and their attitude was communicated to the regions. By then it was enough if the formalities were observed.[18]

The board therefore concentrated on seeking out 'problems' for which it could prescribe 'solutions'—productivity agreements, new pay structures, revised bargaining arrangements, company agreements, and so on—which could have some beneficial effect on the company and on the economy, and could also appear to justify an increase of pay beyond the current norm or ceiling. To some extent they provided a consultancy service—free, but, once a reference was made, obligatory—and, given their circumstances and the general standards of consultancy, they did not make a bad job of it.

Occasionally, however, they disallowed a proposed pay increase. In December 1967 they reported adversely on a pay increase for provincial busmen reached the week before under the auspices of the conciliation service. Because of the Prices and Incomes Acts—the first of which had given statutory backing to the standstill of July 1966—the pay increase was therefore delayed for twelve months in all. The Transport and General Workers debated a strike, but in the end contented themselves with extracting undertakings from local employers to backdate the increases for twelve months when they became payable. In 1968 the board found that a general pay increase

---

[18] H. A. Clegg, *How to Run an Incomes Policy*, p. 52.

in the building industry was in excess of the 3.5 per cent ceiling and the Department was able to persuade the building industry to pare down their increase to an acceptable figure—at least in the national agreement, whatever may have happened on sites.

Nevertheless the standing of the board remained high throughout most of the period, not only with the public, but even with the unions. The board's reports were good reading; many of them had intelligent comments and suggestions to make; and the board were clearly nobody's stooge. The government continued to place considerable reliance on it and the number of references rose through 1966 and 1967 to a peak in 1968. By 1969, however, the rapidly growing unpopularity of the policy inevitably affected the standing of the board.

The Conservatives believed that they had learned from the mistakes of this period. In 1973 they did not entrust the control of pay and prices to one single body, but established two separate institutions—a Price Commission and a Pay Board. The obligation to report proposed pay settlements led direct to the Pay Board, which not only vetted them, but also investigated complaints that unauthorized payments were being made, and conducted spot checks elsewhere—over 2,600 during the sixteen months of their life. In most instances where investigations or spot checks uncovered infringements of the code, the board were able to persuade the employers and unions to make appropriate alterations. Otherwise 'warning notices' were issued, followed if need be by restricting orders. The board issued 133 notices and thirty orders. The only escape route was the power of the Secretary of State to 'consent' to exceptional increases; but this was not used under the Conservatives. On the one occasion on which its use might have been expected—the coalmining strike of 1974—the government chose to refer the matter back to the board for their reconsideration in the light of their report on *Relativities*.

The board were therefore not bypassed, but that did not give them a free hand. They, and the Price Commission, were obliged to follow codes which were defined far more tightly than previous pay and prices policies, and were also statutory instruments open to interpretation by the courts. The pay codes strove to close or limit every possible loophole. New recruits could not be taken on at rates of pay higher than those of the former employees whom they replaced. Rates on new work were to be no higher than was paid for similar work in the same locality. Unless increased earnings under systems of payment by results were due to 'direct and measurable contributions by the employees to increased output' they were to be offset against the next pay increase. Efficiency schemes were subject to tight restrictions.

There was, however, some room for flexibility. One example was the settlement of a dispute in the gas industry. This industry normally settles at much the same time as the electricity supply industry and for a similar increase in pay. On this occasion electricity supply had settled shortly before the standstill, but negotiations in the gas industry were not then completed, and the stage two code did not permit a pay increase as large as that granted by the electricity supply settlement. In February 1973 the General and Municipal Workers instituted an overtime ban and selective strikes which lasted for several weeks until an improved offer, including a reduction in pension contributions and concessions on redundancy, brought a settlement without infringing the code. There is a similar traditional relationship between the pay of local authority manual workers and 'ancillary' workers in hospitals; and these two groups were also split apart by the standstill. In March the ancillary workers began selective strikes which at one time affected up to 750 hospitals. Once more room for settlement was found within the code—this time by means of concessions in the rate of advance towards equal pay.

There was also a conflict over the arrangements for adjusting civil service pay by 'fair comparisons'. The review of civil service pay was caught by the standstill, and the increases it indicated would have been in excess of the provisions of the stage two code. In March 1973, three civil service unions called a one-day strike, followed by selective stoppages. The solution was for the Secretary of State to request the Pay Board to inquire into anomalies arising out of the standstill. In September the board reported that, where there were close, clear and predictable links between the pay settlements of two groups of workers which had been broken by the standstill, there was an anomaly which ought to be rectified. In general, groups of workers who thought that they qualified under this rubric would have to demonstrate their case, but the board had no doubt that the non-industrial civil servants 'should rank as an anomaly'.[19] The civil servants received their increases.

[19] *Anomalies Arising out of the Pay Standstill of November 1972.*

In the view of the Pay Board

it was most important that the policy should be seen to be responsive to feelings of injustice in order to maintain acceptability of,
and acquiescence in the policy. The anomalies and relativities
references were of immense value in holding out hopes of future
remedy to many who regarded their current relative position, in
terms of remuneration, as intolerably—or almost intolerably—inequitable.[20]

Nevertheless the General Council would have nothing to do with
flexible arrangements of this kind when they constructed their £6
policy in 1975.

The General Council had no wish for a statutory policy. Their
experience of the Prices and Incomes Acts 1966–70 and the
Counter-Inflation Acts 1972–4 had confirmed the unions in their
dislike of such instruments, and the General Council were able to
draw some credit from the 'voluntary' status of their proposals.
They might be strict, but at least there was no danger of trade
unionists being subject to fines for failure to comply, or, if the fines
were not paid, to imprisonment. Success would depend on self-
discipline by trade unions and employers. The General Council were
equally opposed to the creation of yet another independent body to
administer the policy. If most of the unions had tolerated the
National Board for Prices and Incomes for a while, they had always
resented the detailed surveillance of the Pay Board. Moreover, they
hoped there would be far less need for interpretation and inspection
with a simple £6 limit than with the complicated criteria that those
two boards had been called on to interpret. Nevertheless, the council
foresaw that there might 'be isolated instances of negotiators
experiencing difficulties in applying or observing the pay limit'.
Their solution, 'where unions and employers both agree that there is
a serious difficulty', was for them to 'make a joint submission to the
TUC and the CBI, who will jointly examine the problem and
determine whether this should be submitted to ACAS for arbitration'.[21]

The government voiced no disagreement with this proposal for
resolving difficulties over the application of the limit, but they were
unhappy over the absence of statutory powers. They could, and did,

[20] *Experience of Operating a Statutory Incomes Policy.*
[21] *The Development of the Social Contract.*

undertake that the limit would be observed in the public sector; and that, where a private employer broke the pay-limit, the Price Commission would disallow the whole pay increase when considering an application for an increase in prices. Probably with foreign creditors in mind, they went on to say that if they found that 'the policy needs to be enforced by applying a legal power of compulsion they will not hesitate to do this'. They had, they said, prepared legislation 'which, if applied in particular cases, would make it illegal for the employer to exceed the pay limit', and, if need be, they would ask parliament to approve it.[22] In fact, it seems that it was impossible to draft legislation which would penalize employers without any risk of proceedings against employees, and nothing more was heard of this proposal.

Experience showed that the General Council had been correct in anticipating difficulties in applying the £6 limit. There were many more than the council had foreseen. Nevertheless the machinery suggested by the council was not called into being. There were no joint submissions to Congress and the Confederation of British Industry, and no references to the Advisory Conciliation and Arbitration Service for arbitration.[23] Instead Congress and the Confederation undertook to advise their own members, and the Department of Employment instituted an advisory service. The General Council circulated affiliated unions with a paper containing 'a number of points of interpretation of the pay guidelines', and 'over the course of the year some 500 requests for advice were dealt with mainly by telephone and correspondence'. In some instances union representatives met officers of Congress, and 'in a few cases more formal discussions were held between panels of the General Council and representatives of union sides of joint negotiating bodies'.[24] The Confederation of British Industry published *The New Anti-Inflation Policy: Practical Guidance for Employers*, in which various points of interpretation had been 'cleared' with the Department of Employ-

[22] *The Attack on Inflation.*

[23] The Service considered their attitude and 'decided that conciliation should be available as before to help parties in their negotiations and, as an independent body, ACAS should not act as an interpreter or as an enforcement agency for the incomes policy. Nevertheless it was accepted that it would be realistic to inquire whether in any particular dispute the parties had taken account of the policy. If doubts arose it could be suggested to them that they should consult, where appropriate, the CBI or the TUC or seek an interpretation from the Department of Employment.' *First Annual Report*, 1975, p. 10.

[24] Trades Union Congress, *Annual Report*, 1976, pp. 300, 308–9.

ment. They suggested that further queries could be discussed with their employment advisory service, or with the Department which carried the main burden of interpretation, for it was usually the employers who were most anxious for guidance on whether a proposed pay increase conflicted with the policy, and for them the government interpretation was authoritative. Thus the first step was in most instances an approach by the employer, or a joint approach, to the Department, which has gradually elaborated a lengthy list of points of guidance for successive stages of the policy. Subsequently, if the union were dissatisfied, they might take the issue up with the economic department of Congress.

Disagreements between the Department and the General Council's staff had to be resolved by informal discussions. In these negotiations the General Council's staff were in a strong position because of the government's anxiety for continued union support for incomes policy; but it must not be supposed that the policy was substantially diluted at their insistence. On the contrary, the most notable controversies over the application of the policy were when individual trade unions challenged interpretations which had been accepted by both the Department and the General Council. There was a difference of opinion about the application of the twelve-month rule to the Seamen because their 1975 increase had been paid in three stages. The Seamen held they were due for a £6 increase in July 1976, but the government and the General Council both held that the due date was January 1977 when the amount would be 5 per cent with an upper limit of £4 as provided for stage two of the policy beginning in August 1976. Early in September 1976 a ballot returned a marginal majority in favour of industrial action and the union executive gave notice of a strike; but further talks with the economic committee of the General Council led to negotiations over improved fringe benefits and a settlement which was held to be within the policy. Another crisis occurred in January 1977 when the Mineworkers' executive, authorized by a ballot to call a strike if necessary, asked for an improved offer on early retirement. Agreement was reached after both sides had met the economic committee. It included the crucial provision that the new scheme should come into operation on 1 August 1977, incomes policy permitting. As it turned out, improvement in occupational pension schemes were one of the two exceptions included in the General Council's statement on policy for 1977–8 and accepted by the government.

After July 1977 the responsibility for administration, apart from the twelve-month rule, was the government's alone. They undertook an active campaign to secure compliance with their 10 per cent limit, announcing a number of administrative sanctions for private employers who exceeded it, such as the loss of financial guarantees for export orders; and included an obligation to observe the policy in government contracts. However, the main problem was not in the private sector where employers who wished, as many of them now did, to pay more than a 10 per cent increase could nearly always find some productivity formula to excuse their action. It was in the public sector. The first major test came in November 1977 with a national strike by firemen for an increase well in excess of the limit. The firemen appealed to the General Council for help, but the council were not prepared to interpret their commitment not to support the 10 per cent limit as an obligation to do battle to overthrow it. They refused support of any kind, and when the government offered a compromise of a guaranteed advance in relative pay and improvement in conditions after the end of July 1978, the council advised the firemen to accept it.

RESULTS

It is impossible to make any worthwhile estimate of the overall effects of British incomes policies. It has been the intention of those who designed them to allow a faster rate of growth than would otherwise have been possible. In fact the rate of growth has not improved as incomes policies have become more frequent and in the seventies, with almost continuous incomes policies, it has fallen off. Another intention has been to avoid the use of other economic curbs which would have increased unemployment. During the sixties and seventies the trend in unemployment has been upwards. This is not to say that incomes policies have hampered growth and caused unemployment, although some economists assert that they have. The whole subject is too complex for that. All that can be said with certainty is that no one has yet devised a convincing method of assessing the results.

This conclusion remains valid even if the task is limited to evaluating the effect on overall movements in pay. To do that it is necessary to pick out the other factors which might be expected to affect movements in pay—employment, the terms of trade, the money supply, investment, and so on—and estimate what their effects would have been in the absence of the policies. The difference between what might have been and what actually happened is then a measure of the effect of the policies. Various economic 'models' have been devised for this purpose; but different models yield different results. One model shows that the Labour government's policy 1967–9 was reducing the rate of increase in pay by about 1 per cent a year,[25] and another indicates that pay was rising as fast as it would have done without the policy.[26]

In any case the effect of a policy cannot be judged only by what happened while it was in force. It is a fairly common experience that the rate of increase in pay rises sharply at the end of an incomes policy, as it did in 1951, 1969–70 and 1974. Since they may plausibly be regarded as consequences of the policies, these pay 'explosions' must also be brought into the account. It is for this reason that assessment cannot be carried out by a straight comparison of pay movements during the policy with those immediately before and after. By that test the policy of 1948–50 would appear to have had a considerable effect, but it may have been only a short-run effect which would be reduced or wiped out if the longer-term consequences were included. For the same reason it is not yet time to assess the effect of the social contract. We do not know what will happen when it is finally terminated.

Assessment remains problematic even if the test is narrowed down to a comparison between the requirements of the policy for a given period and what actually happened to pay over that period. The earlier policies were too loosely specified for a comparison of this kind to be made except on a very rough and ready basis. The 1948–50 policy laid down that there was no justification for general pay increases, although there might be exceptions. Since the great majority of manual workers received at least one increase in pay over the period, it may be presumed that the policy cannot have been rigidly applied. The policy for 1968 and 1969 prescribed a ceiling of

[25] In 1968 the National Board for Prices and Incomes (*Third Annual Report*) published the 'first results' of calculations done for them which indicated 'that the average increase in earnings . . . may have been just under 1 per cent less than it otherwise would have been' (p. 12 and Appendix A).

[26] Lipsey and Parkin found that 'only one period of incomes policy exert[ed] a significant average downward pressure on wages'. It was 1948–50. ('Incomes Policy: A Reappraisal'.)

3.5 per cent a year with certain productivity agreements as the sole exception. The increase in the index of monthly earnings[27] from January 1968 to January 1970 was at an annual rate of 8.5 per cent. It is not likely that the difference between the ceiling and the earnings figures can be accounted for entirely by approved productivity agreements.

The Conservative statutory policy for 1972–4 and the social contract from July 1975 to July 1977 were both more closely specified than their predecessors, but, even so, there are difficulties over comparisons between their requirements and the actual results. In both instances there were agreements entered into before the policy began which provided for staged increases which fell during the period of the policy; they were allowed to take effect (in some cases after a delay) even where they exceeded the limits of the policy. In 1972–4 they included agreements for the country's two largest industries, engineering and construction. Since no one knows how many engineering workers were affected by the industry agreement on minimum rates at that time, and how many by their plant agreements only, it is impossible to calculate the effect of this exception. In addition both policies permitted incremental payments, promotions and upgrading even though they entailed increases over the limit. In 1962–4 the Pay Board reported that, although the limits were determined by reference to the pay bill of each bargaining group, industry negotiating bodies generally did not know the pay bill of the undertakings covered by their agreements. The board therefore allowed the increase to be applied to the basic rate, or in some instances to weekly earnings excluding overtime.[28] The results might have diverged considerably from the intention of the policy. Moves towards equal pay were exempted from the limits on both occasions. Overtime earnings and payment by results were effectively neglected by both policies,[29] and there was an average increase of over half an hour a week in overtime worked by men in 1973. These are only a selection of the factors which would have to be

[27] This series, which is available since 1967, covers all employees.

[28] Pay Board, *Second Report*.

[29] Although the pay codes of the 1972–4 policy tried to bring payment by results within the limits, the application of the provision required information which most employers had not got. Accordingly, 'PBR workers were largely insulated from the rigours of the policy, during a period of rising activity, and . . . the more decayed the scheme, the greater the immunity from the policy'. (Pay Board, *Experience of Operating a Statutory Incomes Policy*.)

taken into account in a precise comparison between the expected effects of the two policies and the actual movements in pay.

However, even if all the relevant allowances were to be made, it is not easy to see that they could explain all the differences between the requirements of the 1972–4 policy and the movements in earnings over that period.[30] The overall target for November 1972 to November 1973 was about 7.5 per cent and the increase in the monthly earnings index was about 12 per cent (about 60 per cent above target). The figures for the following twelve months are hardly relevant since by April the policy was in the hands of a government which had no sympathy with it, and it was wound up in June.

After July 1975 the social contract fared somewhat better. The target for 1975–6 was about 11 per cent and the increase in the monthly earnings index from August 1975 to August 1976 was 14 per cent (27 per cent higher). In 1976–7 the target was something more than 5 per cent and the increase in earnings was about 8 per cent, which probably works out at an excess of less than 50 per cent. If allowance could be made for everything that should be taken into account in assessing the policies for 1975–7 it is quite likely that the remainder would be relatively small, probably well under 20 per cent of the target.

These problems apply, however, to the overall assessment of the two policies. Because of their simplicity it is possible to work out their expected effect on particular groups of workers much more precisely. Where detailed earnings figures are available for the period of the policy, a reliable estimate can therefore be made of their effect on each group. Detailed pay records from forty midlands engineering plants permitted comparisons to be made between the increases allowed under the codes (including moves towards equal pay and threshold payments) and the actual earnings of a number of grades of engineering workers—manual and white collar, male and female—for the three stages of the 1972–4 policy up to June 1974. They indicate a high degree of conformity for most grades, even for those in which piecework was common, and a dramatic narrowing of differentials, although there was undershooting as well as over-

[30] 'Even allowing for the effect of improving labour demand on overtime earnings, . . . there remains a substantial discrepancy between the rate of increase in average earnings and the targets of Stages 2 and 3.' (L. C. Hunter, 'British Incomes Policy 1972–1974'.)

shooting of the policy targets.[31] The evidence is too limited to allow general conclusions to be drawn, but it emphasizes that inferences drawn from the movement of global averages should be treated with caution; and it is possible that the correspondence between prescription and performance under Heath's statutory policy may have been closer than has been supposed. This observation could only be tested if detailed evidence of the earnings of each grade of employee was available for all industries and areas or at least for a representative sample.

It is generally believed that post-1972 incomes policies have led to a substantial compression of pay differentials. However, the only marked change which can be discovered from global earnings figures is in the differential between men and women. For many decades the average weekly earnings of women wage-earners had stood at about 50 per cent of those of men. In October 1970 the proportion was almost exactly 50 per cent; by 1976 it was just over 60 per cent. The major cause of this remarkable shift was almost certainly the Equal Pay Act. Sixty per cent is not equality, but the Act affects only those jobs which are performed by both men and women, or included in a common job evaluation scheme; women are effectively excluded from most high-paid jobs; and they work little overtime whereas male wage-earners average several hours overtime a week. For all these reasons the Equal Pay Act cannot be expected to bring equal earnings.

This reduction in the sex differential was not matched by an equivalent change in the distribution of men's earnings, or, for that matter, in the distribution of earnings among women. The bottom decile for adult manual men in the *New Earnings Survey 1972* was 67.6 per cent of the median weekly earnings, and in 1977 it was 70.6 per cent. The comparable figures for adult manual women were 68.9 per cent and 70.3 per cent.

Once more there is a conflict between global earnings figures and more detailed information from individual industries. In 1972 the margin between the earnings of an engineering fitter and an engineering labourer was 37 per cent. By 1976 the figure had fallen to 27 per cent. Brown's figures for engineering in the midlands tell the same story. The margin between the skilled male machinist and the male labourer fell from 65 per cent to 49 per cent; and that between the skilled electrician and the labourer from 53 per cent to 35 per cent.

[31] William Brown, 'Incomes Policy and Pay Differentials'.

To explain how differentials can be compressed within industries while the overall distribution of earnings remains almost unaltered would require a detailed study of movements in earnings within and between industries. Whatever the explanation, the change in differentials between grades in individual industries is a matter of importance for those industries, as was demonstrated by major strikes of toolmakers in British Leyland and other engineering firms in 1977.

However, even this shift in the differential for skill cannot be attributed entirely to incomes policy, for it had started before incomes policies began to offer more than empty promises to the lower-paid. In 1969 the earnings of the engineering fitter were 42 per cent above those of the labourer, compared with a margin of 37 per cent in 1972; and Brown's figures indicate a similar trend. They also show that the compression after 1972 did not occur primarily under tight incomes policy, but under the relatively free collective bargaining of the first period of the social contract in 1974–5. He points out that 'this experience was common throughout the British engineering industry', and contends that the most satisfactory explanation is 'the rapid increase in price inflation'[32] which accelerated in 1969 and 1970 and again in 1974, reaching its peak in 1975. Confirmation of this hypothesis is provided by the coincidence of earlier periods of sharp reductions in differentials with periods of wartime inflation after 1914 and 1939; and the findings of a subsequent article by Brown, as yet unpublished, examining the experiences of the same midlands plants under the social contract from 1975 to 1977. This demonstrates that the social contract's policy was closely followed in the plant as Heath's statutory policy had been, although once more the correspondence was greater in the overall figures than in the earnings of individual grades. This time, however, divergences from the policy favoured the higher-paid grades at the expense of the lower-paid. Differentials began to open out despite the directives of the social contract and in sympathy with the reduction in the rate of price inflation.

The effects of incomes policy are not confined to movements in earnings. Incomes policies can also play a part in altering the structure of collective bargaining. Without much doubt the most important of these alterations in Britain has been the growth of plant-wide pay agreements. There were other factors at work, and it is impossible to quantify the contribution of incomes policy, but the rapid

[32] *Ibid.*

spread of productivity bargaining under the pressure of the 1965–70 policy certainly made a contribution to the change; and the insistence of the 1972–4 policy on the identification of bargaining groups helped to confirm it and to divorce plant pay bargaining from industry bargaining. Although it was possible for a company or plant to follow the relevant industry agreement and negotiate an agreement of its own, so long as the limit was not exceeded over the twelve-month period, this did not leave much room for a plant or company agreement in most industries, and it was therefore easier for a company which wanted to have some control over its own pay structure to negotiate on its own, divorcing itself entirely from the industry pay agreement. The social contract may have exercised further pressure in the same direction, but probably most of the changes had already been completed. Since the detailed control of pay structures in the plant was one essential element in both the 1972–4 policy and the social contract, the development of plant-wide pay agreements was an instrument as well as a consequence of incomes policy. If the social contract has controlled pay more successfully than Heath's policy did, one of the reasons may be that he handed over to the Labour government a system of pay bargaining more amenable to control than the system which they had bequeathed to him in 1970.

Chapter 7 suggested that incomes policies have influenced the pattern of strikes. Relatively strict incomes policies have sharply reduced the number of strikes over pay, and have therefore led to a considerable decline in the total number of strikes, with a corresponding rise when the policy comes to an end or slackens off. In the long run these fluctuations may not seem to have great significance, but it is also arguable that incomes policy has altered the long-term trend in the size of strikes by its effect on industrial action in the public sector. For more than twenty years after the war the public sector, apart from coalmining, regularly returned relatively low figures for strikes per employee, with very occasional large-scale strikes. This record may be attributed to the centralization of bargaining in the public sector which made it difficult for the unions to secure significant concessions by local stoppages; and to the desire of both unions and managers to avoid major conflicts because of their belief that the public sector should be capable of more rational behaviour and more orderly relationships than the private sector. Centralization has remained, but the desire to avoid trials of strength lost its potency with the wave of major official public sector strikes which began in 1970, preceded by large-scale unofficial public sector strikes in the previous year. The immediate cause was the failure of pay offers to meet the expectations of public sector employees in one service after another, and the hard line adopted by their employers as a result of government pressure; but the government approach was strongly influenced by incomes policy, especially in the period of the N–1 policy, when Heath's administration tried to hold the public sector within the limits prescribed by their policy as an example to the private sector. The outcome was not a reduction in pay in the public sector relative to private employment, but a series of major conflicts and strikes which took public sector pay ahead.[33]

The firemen's strike in 1977–8 was the first major official stoppage in the public sector to arise under the social contract, but the public sector elsewhere has caused the government, and the General Council, at least as much anxiety as has private industry. It is likely that it will take a number of years to restore the former attitudes of the public sector towards industrial conflict, if indeed that ever happens. This is not a change in the structure of collective bargaining; it is the exploitation of a potentiality which has always existed within the structure of bargaining in the public sector; but the consequence has been an important shift in collective bargaining behaviour.

Incomes policies have also had an effect upon some of the devices used to regulate pay in collective agreements, including 'fair pay' comparisons, cost of living sliding scales, and incremental scales. Following the guidance of the 1965 White Paper on *Prices and Incomes Policy* which stated that 'less weight than hitherto will have to be given' to, among other things, 'comparisons with levels or trends of incomes in other employments', the National Board for Prices and Incomes condemned all the formulas for automatic pay comparisons which were brought to their attention. Such devices, they argued, 'provide a mechanism for spreading increases in wage rates from one group to another, regardless of the reasons for which the original increases were given'. Because of this, 'the doctrine of comparisons

[33] In 'Earnings in the Public and Private Sectors 1950–75', A. J. H. Dean constructed separate series of earnings figures for manual employees in the two sectors and concluded that: '(1) public and private earnings moved closely together throughout the 1950s and 1960s; (2) in the 1970s the two series ceased to move as closely together and in 1974 they diverged considerably with public sector earnings moving a long way ahead of private sector earnings in an unprecedented fashion'.

. . . can in fact frustrate the social case for special treatment for particular groups'.[34] As a result of reports by the board, the Guillebaud formula for railway pay, the Phelps Brown formula for London busmen, and the system for adjusting the pay of industrial civil servants were all terminated. The one formula to survive was the civil service system of fair pay comparisons, which was never referred to the board, although its operation was delayed in 1968–9 by the government, and again in 1972–3 under the Conservative statutory incomes policy.[35] In 1975 the social contract went further. In *The Development of the Social Contract*, the General Council stated that their £6 limit would 'entail the temporary suspension of systems of pay determination based on traditional links in the private and public sector, and the suspension in particular of civil service comparability exercises'. The government not only accepted this decision, but also went on to disband the Civil Service Pay Research Unit, although it was reconstituted and recommenced its work in 1978.

The 1965 White Paper also included changes in the cost of living among the factors affecting pay which would have to be accorded 'less weight than hitherto'. In 1965 some two million employees were covered by cost of living sliding scales which provided for automatic adjustment of wage rates on some prearranged basis in accordance with changes in the official retail price index. These arrangements had enjoyed an even wider coverage shortly after the First World War, but in the long period of declining prices which began in 1921 the successive wage cuts which they brought made them unpopular with the unions and many of them were terminated. In 1965 the largest single group of employees affected by them were manual workers in the building industry.

Some of the agreements provided for periodic adjustments according to the movement of the retail price index, for example every six months. Others prescribed adjustments whenever the index shifted by a given number of points. Few of them yielded an increase in pay proportionately as large as the increase in the price index; and, even if the increases had been in proportion to price movements, they would not have kept up with increases in pay in other industries which, taking one year with another, normally rise more rapidly than prices. In order to keep up, therefore, the industries with sliding scales had from time to time to negotiate advances

[34] *General Report April 1965 to July 1966.*   [35] See p. 113.

in pay in addition to those which arose from the scales. Adjustments outside the scale were settled every two years in printing and in footwear, leaving the scale to do its work in the interval.

Accordingly, although the unions concerned had refused to suspend their sliding scales at Stafford Cripps's request in 1950, the scales were cumbersome and did not avoid conflict in pay negotiations. The National Board for Prices and Incomes recommended their termination where they came across them;[36] they were not exempted from standstills and ceilings on the statutory policies which began in 1966; and by 1970 the two largest industries with sliding scales—construction and printing—had abandoned them, as had several smaller industries. The threshold payments included in stage three of Heath's statutory policy constituted a temporary cost of living sliding scale for the whole country, but, in view of the substantial contribution which they made to the frightening inflation of 1974–5, it is unlikely that the experiment will be repeated, at least for some time.

One contentious issue in incomes policies, and especially those which impose standstills or ceilings, is incremental scales of pay which provide automatic or semi-automatic increments at regular intervals, usually annually. These scales are relatively rare among manual workers who generally emphasize 'the rate for the job'; but they are common among white collar employees in the public sector; whereas in many private industries there is an annual review of white collar salaries at which the granting of an increase is given or withheld according to 'merit', and merit also determines the amount. Incremental scales have invariably been exempted from standstills and ceilings on the grounds that they are part of the contractual salary for the job, and that they do not normally add to the costs because the additional payments made to employees advancing up the scale are cancelled by employees at the top of the scale retiring, or leaving for other employment, or being promoted to a higher grade, and being replaced by new entrants at the bottom of the scale. Counter arguments are also available. The claim that incremental scales do not add to costs depends on the structure of the labour force and rates of recruitment and retirement, and proves in many instances to be ill-founded; and the justice of an incomes policy

[36] In their report on *Wages, Costs and Prices in the Printing Industry*, the board proposed that the industry's scale should be terminated in the next round of pay negotiations.

which says that no manual worker is entitled to an increase, or to more than 3.5 per cent, or more than £6, while most white collar employees in the public service are entitled to a substantial increment in addition to whatever the policy prescribes, is not self-evident, at least to manual workers. Nevertheless the arguments in favour of allowing the incremental scales to continue have always carried the day. It might be supposed that one of the reasons for their retention has been the large part which civil servants, who benefit from them, usually play in the design of incomes policies; but the General Council has also accepted the merits of the case. *The Development of the Social Contract* stated that: 'Already established incremental and wage-for-age scales are payable provided that this does not raise the overall wage bill by more than £6 per head'. In practice this proviso was not rigorously enforced. To do so would have been to penalize employees whose undertakings keep accurate records. Moreover, companies in the private sector were allowed to reconstruct their systems of annual review to the point where they could be accepted as amounting to incremental scales. There has therefore been a considerable shift towards more systematized schemes of annual pay review for salaried employees in the private sector.

If incomes policy has led to important changes in the structure of collective bargaining, in collective bargaining behaviour, and in the devices used to regulate pay, then it might be expected that it would also have brought about substantial changes in the organization of the parties to collective bargaining. Restructuring within the unions to take account of workplace organization occurred at much the same time as the shift to plant-wide pay agreements, which was encouraged by incomes policy, but the unions were reacting to the growth in shop steward power which was already far advanced before the change in bargaining arrangements; so the restructuring probably owes little to incomes policy. Another notable development in the unions at that time was an increase in the status and authority of Congress and its General Council within the trade union movement. However, this was mainly due to the defeat over labour legislation of successive governments by the unions under the leadership of the General Council. These achievements persuaded the Labour party leaders to offer the unions a social contract, and gave the council sufficient authority over the unions to carry their support for its incomes policies from 1975 to 1977 and even into 1978.

On the employers' side the shift to safety-net pay agreements at industry level has followed on the spread of plant-wide bargaining which has in turn been encouraged by incomes policy; and as a result employers' associations have put more resources into their advisory services. But incomes policy has not made much impression on the structure of the Confederation of British Industry. Apart from the 5 per cent price limit of 1971–2, the Confederation has generally avoided taking a large share in the operation of incomes policy.

It is impossible to offer an accurate overall assessment of the organizational effects of incomes policy, largely because the most important of them is the reconstruction of plant bargaining, and the contribution of incomes policy to this development cannot be separated out from those of the other influences at work. Unquestionably its share has been significant. On the other hand, it might have been expected that a period of seventeen years in which there have been only brief intervals between pay policies would have brought about even greater changes.

THE FUTURE

Things might have been different if there had been a continuous incomes policy over a considerable period—if the Prices and Incomes Board had been continued, with union consent, by successive governments; or if, in the future, the General Council were to continue to develop the social contract with Conservative as well as Labour governments. Then there would have to be lasting changes in the relationship between the General Council and affiliated unions; the Confederation of British Industry would have to accept overt responsibility for administering the contract, and alter its structure to suit; trade union officers, shop stewards, and managers would learn new habits which could not be sloughed off in a few weeks. One of the most important questions which has to be answered by anyone who would forecast the future of British industrial relations, therefore, is: what is going to happen to incomes policy?

If there were no more incomes policies there would be no further influence of incomes policy on industrial relations to be considered. North sea oil will reduce the risk of balance-of-payments crises over the next twenty years, and it could be argued that there will be far less need for pay restraint than there has been since the war. However, a rapidly increasing flow of oil has not so far eased our economic difficulties very much; and everyone acknowledges the need to 'modernize' British industry so that Britain will be competitive when the oil runs out. Governments will therefore be under pressure to demonstrate that the country is devoting adequate resources to the task of modernization, and therefore to limit resources used on other items, including pay. This pressure is likely to turn their mind to incomes policy, since monetary restraint would check the process of modernization as well as the rate of increase in pay and prices—if indeed the degree of monetary restraint which is politically acceptable would have a sufficient impact on pay settlements to hold back prices.

The relevant question therefore is not whether Britain will soon see the last of incomes policy, but whether the future will bring another series of short-lived policies or one lasting policy. The answer depends in part on whether lessons drawn from past experiences can show how incomes policy might be operated more successfully in the future. At first sight past policies seem to be a source of confusion rather than enlightenment. They have displayed a wide variety of formulas, administrative arrangements, and legal and social supports. Some have been resounding failures; none has achieved unchallenged success; and the criteria of success are themselves debatable. Each policy seems to have generated mounting pressure which has finally burst through to destroy it. In some of them this pressure has come from differential increases in wage drift;[37] in others from the compression of differentials between grades; and in others from differences in treatment between public and private sectors. During 1977 and 1978 pressure from all three sources appeared to be building up against the social contract. Policy-makers who have tried to learn from earlier policies have not necessarily met with more success than those who have disregarded the past. Heath's Pay Board and pay code were carefully designed to retain what seemed to be the good features of the previous Labour government's policies, and to avoid their defects; and his was perhaps the most disastrous failure of them all.

Nevertheless it can be argued that something has been learned about the procedures whereby incomes policies are formulated and administered. The main theme of this book is that collective bargain-

[37] The major study of the 1948–50 policy, unfortunately still unpublished, argues cogently that this was the main cause of its downfall. (John Corina, *The British Experiment in Wage Restraint.*)

ing is the central process in industrial relations. Perhaps incomes policies should therefore be seen as exercises in bargaining. At times the formulation of policy has amounted to a negotiated settlement although the negotiators have normally been curiously shy of acknowledging it. When the government announced their policy in 1948, the unions protested that they had not been consulted, but gave their support subject to qualifications which were thereafter understood to apply. Under the social contract the General Council have announced their policy each year up to 1977, and the government has accepted, with additions of varying importance. In 1964–6 the policy and machinery for its application were actually agreed in discussions between the government, the unions, and the employers, but from July 1966 onwards the government had to be content with 'reluctant acquiescence' from the unions.

The Conservative policies of 1972–4 make an interesting case. Outstanding among the reasons for the failure of the N–1 formula was union opposition. Accordingly the prime minister made a valiant attempt to reach agreement with the unions (and the employers) on a new policy. He failed partly because he insisted that there were certain items of 'government policy' which were not negotiable. According to the General Council, 'there had been a willingness on the part of the TUC to negotiate but negotiation had now been ruled out by the Government'.[38] Thereafter a unilateral government policy was enforced by statute, but the prime minister continued to seek the co-operation of the unions. He met the General Council and individual union leaders, and the pay codes were formulated with their wishes and problems very much in mind. If the broad definition of collective bargaining suggested in Chapter 1 is accepted, these dealings have a good claim to be classed as a form of collective bargaining.

Bargaining has not stopped with the formulation of incomes policy. Earlier chapters have argued that the administration of collective agreements is a major, and certainly the most time-consuming, aspect of collective bargaining. If incomes policies are seen as a form of collective agreement, then this comment applies to their administration also. However, with the setting up of the National Incomes Commission in 1962 a semi-judicial element was introduced into their administration. The Commission was an independent body whose job it was to say how the policy of the 1962 White Paper

[38] Trades Union Congress, *The Chequers and Downing Street Talks*, p. 20.

applied to particular claims, or even to settlements which had already been reached. Such a task is far removed from the business of a disputes procedure in which representatives of the two sides apply their agreements to particular circumstances, perhaps adjusting them a little to fit; and even from the work of an arbitration tribunal which is brought in to settle an issue on which the parties cannot agree.

Without powers, and with a policy to which almost no one paid attention, the Commission made little impact, but their semi-judicial function was handed on to the Prices and Incomes Board which had both powers and prestige. The job of the board was to investigate each case referred to them and to report on how the proposed pay increase matched up to the criteria of the policy. This left the board little scope to bargain. However, under the early warning system, proposed pay settlements did not go direct to the board. Notification was to the Department of Employment which decided in the great majority of cases that they did not need to go to the board, and could refer difficult cases to the government instead of the board. The Department and the government were in a position to bargain if they wanted, and in some instances it was suspected that their objective in refraining from a reference to the board was to circumvent their own policies in order to placate some powerful group. The existence of two sets of standards helped to undermine the policy.

To avoid this, when they set up their Pay Board, the Conservatives provided that notification should be direct to the board, and gave the board a legally enforceable pay code so that their decisions were subject to review in the courts. Suspicion of double-dealing therefore played little part in the downfall of the policy, which owed more to the extreme inflexibility of these arrangements. The general reports of the board on *Anomalies arising out of the Pay Standstill* and *Relativities* attempted to reintroduce scope for special treatment for hard cases, but even so it was impossible to find room for a deal with the miners before it was too late.

With the Pay Board, the semi-judicial system of incomes policy administration had been pushed to the limit. A radically different method was chosen for the social contract, closely akin to the normal British method of administering collective agreements. The task of administration was played down, and what had to be done was carried out by the parties to the contract. Up to July 1977 the General Council and the government shared the onus of applying their policies. The system was not inflexible. They could make minor adjustments to meet difficulties which might otherwise have developed into major conflicts. On the other hand there was not a high risk of overgenerous concessions which would have eroded the policy because both parties had staked their reputations on its success, and each was watching the other. This manner of running an incomes policy seemed to work more smoothly than any of the semi-judicial arrangements; and it still appeared to have the advantage of them after July 1977 when the General Council's undertaking was limited to seeing that the unions observed those parts of the policy which had the council's assent.

Bargainers need inducements or sanctions to persuade the other side. For their part the unions can rely on their capacity to give or withhold consent for pay restraint. Governments have had to make use of a wider range of bargaining counters. The greatest inducement which they could offer might be to produce results in terms of stable prices and rising living standards, but unexpected misfortunes have played havoc with economic forecasting in postwar Britain, and governments have almost always taken an optimistic view of what can be achieved. Patriotism and loyalty have been extensively exploited, but they are wasting assets. The unions have offered preference for the lower-paid and other avenues to exceptional treatment under pay policies, along with price, rent, dividend and profit controls. Since 1975 the threat that, without a policy, retail prices might rise by 25 per cent a year or more has been a powerful sanction. In addition, the social contract has widened the scope for bargaining to include the whole of government economic and social policy, and in particular legislative measures favourable to the unions and concessions on income tax. These two counters have the advantage that they can be used again. With some ingenuity, new legislative proposals can be designed and, in most years, some room can be found for tax adjustments which favour the majority of employees.

Probably the best guess that can be made about the future of incomes policy in Britain is that a succession of relatively short-lived incomes policies may be expected over the next two decades to match those of the last twenty years, separated by similar short intervals without an overt policy. It would, after all, be a bold prophet who would predict a social contract between the unions and a Conservative government. Nevertheless, the argument of the last few paragraphs has been that governments and unions are becoming more expert at negotiating and administering incomes policies. There is therefore a prospect that policies may be rather more lasting and successful in the future than in the past. If that were to happen, it is likely that they will work greater changes in British industrial relations than past policies have done.

Chapter 10

LABOUR LAW

THE 'REPEAL' OF THE INDUSTRIAL RELATIONS ACT

The first commitment of the Labour government which came to power in March 1974 under their social contract with the unions was the repeal of the Industrial Relations Act. This obligation was formally discharged by the passage of the Trade Union and Labour Relations Act the following July. The first subsection of the first section reads: 'The Industrial Relations Act 1971 is hereby repealed'; but in any normal sense repeal was out of the question. The next subsection begins: 'Nevertheless . . .', and the whole Act, with 31 sections, and five schedules occupying more space than the 31 sections, is a substantial piece of legislation.

Total repeal of the Industrial Relations Act was impossible because that Act had repealed most of the legislation on trade unions and trade disputes since 1871. The effect of repeal would therefore have been to revert to the situation as it existed before the Trade Union Act 1871 which might have been a good deal more unwelcome to the unions than the Industrial Relations Act itself. It might have been possible to cobble together a statute which would have restored the law more or less as it had been in 1970, but this was impracticable for two reasons. Firstly, even if the law as it existed in 1970 had been wholly acceptable to the unions, the opportunity which re-enactment would have presented for clarification, amendment, and modernization would have been irresistible. Secondly, there were parts of the Industrial Relations Act which both the unions and the government wished to retain, notably the procedures for dealing with unfair dismissal, and a good deal of the 1974 Act was taken up with re-enacting sections of the Act which it had just repealed.

However, the 1974 Act was only the beginning of the government's obligations. The social contract provided for an addition to the body of labour legislation which, when and if it is all enacted, will comfortably exceed in volume the total corpus of British labour legislation as it existed in 1970, or even in June 1974. The centrepiece of this programme was the Employment Protection Act 1975 which created a whole series of new individual rights for employees and new collective rights for trade unions; but there was much more besides. Among other measures of importance for industrial relations are the Health and Safety at Work Act 1974, the Social Security Pensions Act 1975, the Industry Act 1975, the Sex Discrimination Act 1975 (complementing the Equal Pay Act 1970 which came into force at the end of 1975), and the Race Relations Act 1976 which substantially amended the 1968 Act. In addition, the social contract included proposals for a major extension of industrial democracy by means of supervisory boards for large companies, half of whose members were to be trade union nominees. Although this proposal has been much discussed, a bill has not yet been presented to parliament.

The Trade Union and Labour Relations Act 1974 did not entirely fulfil the intentions of government or unions. Both of them were extremely anxious to get a bill through but the government did not command a majority in the Commons. A number of amendments had therefore to be accepted. After a second election, in October, had given the government an overall majority of one, an amending bill was introduced to remove the most objectionable changes and to restore most of the original provisions. The House of Lords, which had been responsible for many of the amendments, reintroduced most of them, and it was not until early in 1976 that the Trade Union and Labour Relations (Amendment) Act was passed.

Taken together, the two statutes restore the law on strikes and picketing much as it was in 1970 except that further protection is given to strikers in several respects. The protection against proceedings for inducing a breach of contract 'in contemplation or furtherance of a trade dispute' has been extended to commercial contracts as well as contracts of employment, and now also covers inducing another person to interfere or to induce any other person to interfere with the performance of the contract. No court is empowered to 'compel an employee to do any work or attend at any place for the doing of any work'. The use of injunctions in strikes has been limited by requiring the court to satisfy itself that the party against whom the injunction is directed has been given a reasonable opportunity to state his case. The definition of a 'trade dispute' has been revised to remove some uncertainties, for example as to whether a recognition dispute is included, and extended to include disputes overseas. The status of collective agreements has been clarified by specifically stating that no agreement is to be treated as a legally enforceable contract unless it is in writing and 'contains a provision which (however expressed) states that the parties intended that the agreement shall be a legally enforceable contract'.

Trade union objections to corporate status were met by restoring their status as unincorporated bodies, but retaining the right to sue and be sued in their own names which the 1971 Act had given them through incorporation. Pre-1971 confusion over the status of employers' associations was cleared up by giving them an option between incorporation and unincorporated status. Trade unions and employers' associations were given separate definitions, and the definition of a trade union was changed. Before 1971 it had been, in essence,

> any combination . . . the principal objects of which are . . . the regulation of relations between workmen and masters, or between workmen and workmen, . . . or the imposing of restrictive conditions on the conduct of any trade or business. . . .[1]

Now it became 'an organisation' of workers 'whose principal purposes include the regulation of relations between workers . . . and employers or employers' associations'. Besides bringing the wording up to date, the definition allowed organizations such as professional associations to be trade unions so long as they took part in collective bargaining.

The 1974 Act also introduced the category of an 'independent trade union' which is a trade union 'not under the domination or control of an employer' or an employers' association, and 'not liable to interference by an employer . . . or association . . . tending towards such control'. The full significance of this new category did not become apparent until the Employment Protection Act came into force. Nearly all the new rights which this Act gave to unions were limited to independent trade unions, and a Certification Officer was to be appointed. Under the 1974 Act the registration of trade

[1] *Donovan Report*, p. 205.

unions had been replaced by the maintenance of a list of trade unions. Together with certain other duties carried out by the Registrar of Friendly Societies in relation to trade unions, this function was transferred to the new officer who was also to issue a certificate of independence to a union on the list provided that application was made and that he had 'determined' that it was independent.

In proposing these arrangements the intention of the General Council had been to deny access to the various collective rights established by the Employment Protection Act to those unions which were not affiliated to Congress or recognized by Congress as *bona fide* trade unions—which roughly means organizations which do not compete with affiliated unions and which observe other principles of what the General Council regards as good trade union behaviour. But that is not what the Act says, and that is not how it turned out. The Certification Officer issued certificates to a number of 'staff associations' and other bodies which are in competition with affiliated unions. They met the definition of a trade union and he could find no evidence of employer domination or interference tending towards it. The Employment Protection Act also created a statutory right to recognition, which was of course limited to independent unions. Armed with their certificates, therefore, these staff associations and other unwelcome bodies were entitled to seek the support of the law to secure recognition even in an area which an affiliated union claimed as its province. Moreover, its certificate would allow any of these bodies to proclaim its status as a certificated independent union in approaching workers with a view to recruitment, and employers with a view to voluntary recognition.

Outraged by these developments, the General Council and the affiliated unions debated what was to be done. They considered various ways of tightening the requirements of independent status, but could find no form of words which was likely to exclude most of the organizations to which they objected. Furthermore, the more restrictive the requirements, the higher the status which would be conferred on these organizations by their certificates of independence. The General Council might have been happy for the legislation to be amended to substitute 'affiliated union' for 'independent union', but it did not seem likely that parliament would be willing to grant such a monopoly to the Trades Union Congress. The other possibility was to acknowledge that the whole business of restricting rights to certificated unions had been misconceived, and to open them to all the unions on the list, thus disposing of certificates of independence and the cachet that they conferred; and leaving it to the Advisory Conciliation and Arbitration Service to decide whether any question of independence should affect their recommendation concerning trade union recognition in a particular case. This confession of failure had a good deal of support, but it was not a sufficiently urgent amendment to have a pressing claim on parliamentary time, so the matter was left as it stood.

One omission from the Trade Union and Labour Relations Act should be noted. The unions had hoped that it would modernize the law on picketing. The provisions of the 1906 Act predated the large-scale development of motorized transport. Pickets cannot peacefully persuade drivers or passengers in cars, trucks or buses without first stopping the vehicles. As things stood, pickets who stopped vehicles were committing the offence of obstructing free passage on the highway. On the other hand, to give pickets the right to halt vehicles would be a substantial extension of their powers which might enable them to block the highway for hours on end in some disputes. No suitable form of words could be found to resolve this dilemma, and the Act merely restored the rights of pickets as they had stood before the Industrial Relations Act.

In most strikes picketing is of little importance. It is unlikely that any employees affected will report for work where unions are strongly organized, and their managers might be embarrassed if they did so. However, 'blacklegs' are of importance in some stoppages, as in the Grunwick dispute of 1976–8, where only a minority of the workers struck for recognition; and there are other strikes, like that of the miners in 1972, where the movement of supplies is of crucial importance. On that occasion the miners wanted to stop supplies of coal to power stations, and in some cases oil deliveries as well. The Grunwick pickets wanted to prevent their colleagues, who were brought to work in buses, from entering the plant. In both strikes the pickets had to stop vehicles in order to achieve their objective. Their method was 'mass picketing', used with success by the miners, but without avail at Grunwick. In these and similar instances the law was frequently broken, and arrests were made; but the control of the pickets rested on what the police decided to be politic in the circumstances rather than on the wording of statutes.[2]

[2] Otto Kahn-Freund, *Labour and the Law*, pp. 261–5.

NEW LAWS AND AGENCIES

Having restored and rationalized the legal status of trade unions, employers' associations, and trade disputes as they had existed before 1971, the second obligation which the social contract imposed on the new government in relation to labour legislation was to give employers, trade unionists and trade unions the kind of positive rights under the law which the unions believed should be theirs.

The centrepiece of this 'new deal' was the Employment Protection Act, which might be regarded in some ways as Labour's counterpart to the Industrial Relations Act. However, in their construction the two statutes contrasted strongly. For all its faults, the Industrial Relations Act was carefully designed and drafted to form an integrated whole. Each part of it fitted into and supported the others. By contrast the Employment Protection Act is the outcome of stringing together a 'shopping list' of disparate proposals for legislation which the General Council presented to the government. There was little overall design to this very substantial piece of legislation[3] and the draftsmen had to do the best with it that they could. Moreover, it did not constitute by any means the whole of the 'new deal'.

In comparing the Employment Protection Act with the Industrial Relations Act it should also be noted that the former is a far less original piece of legislation than the latter. The two parts of the Employment Protection Act which have attracted most attention and caused the largest volume of business are those dealing with unfair dismissal and trade union recognition. The new government and the unions were so much in agreement with what the Conservatives had done on unfair dismissal that a good deal of the Trade Union and Labour Relations Act was a re-enactment of the provisions of the earlier Act on this subject (with some extensions) so that it could continue in operation without interruption. The Employment Protection Act merely added further extensions. The Conservative provisions on union recognition were not retained, but, when the Labour proposals appeared, they could be seen to have borrowed extensively from the Conservative statute; and the same could be

---

[3] The bulk of the Act exceeds that of the Industrial Relations Act. Its 129 sections fall short of the 170 sections of the earlier Act, but it makes up for this with no less than 18 schedules (which constitute almost half its bulk) compared with 9 in the Industrial Relations Act.

said of several other parts of the Employment Protection Act, such as its provisions on disclosure of information.

Several new agencies were established to interpret and administer the new rights. The most novel and important of them was the Advisory Conciliation and Arbitration Service, set up by administrative action in September 1974, and given statutory status by the Employment Protection Act. Its origins go back to the N–1 incomes policy of the Conservatives. Both unions and employers had been disturbed by the decision of the government in 1970 to refuse access to the Department of Employment's conciliation service in certain cases where it was evident that the settlement would exceed the level of pay increase allowed under the policy. Accordingly in 1972 the Trades Union Congress and the Confederation of British Industry signed their first, and so far their only, agreement setting out arrangements of their own for supplying conciliators and arbitrators to fill the gap in the official services. The agreement had been used only once when it was overtaken by the statutory incomes policy of November 1972. Continued operation would have been possible only if Congress and the Confederation had been prepared to take responsibility for conciliated settlements and arbitration awards which might have been in conflict with the law. But the notion of an independent service for which Congress and the Confederation would share responsibility had won a good deal of support. It could be argued that the official service would be more likely to enjoy the goodwill of the parties, and therefore to resolve disputes more effectively, if it was transferred from the Department to an independent body. Moreover, the argument ran, the multiplication of public bodies in the industrial relations field had led to confusion and duplication. Why not, therefore, combine conciliation and arbitration with the investigatory and advisory functions of the Commission on Industrial Relations in a single independent service? The most appropriate time to offer advice to companies and unions on improving their industrial relations performance is when they realize they have a problem, and the reference of a dispute or difficulty to the conciliation service is clear indication that they know they have trouble. It was already accepted practice for the service, in appropriate instances, to move on from conciliation to offer advice on how relations might be improved in the future, and a combined service including the resources then separately employed by the Commission on Industrial Relations would be able to exploit opportunities for reform even more effectively.[4] Following this line of reasoning, the Labour government transferred the existing service and some of the staff of the Commission (which was wound up) to a Council consisting of a chairman and three other independent members, three General Council nominees and three nominees from the Confederation. When the Act was passed the following year the general duty of the Service became one

of promoting the improvement of industrial relations, and in particular of encouraging the extension of collective bargaining and the development and, where necessary, reform of collective bargaining machinery.

One of the tasks which the Service took over from the Department was to conciliate between the dismissed employee and the employer in complaints of unfair dismissal in the hope that the matter could be settled without a hearing by an industrial tribunal. Work of this kind grew rapidly with the extension of the scope of unfair dismissal, and with the creation of a number of new rights for employees. The Service also acquired new conciliation duties in several types of industrial disputes in which legislation provided for statutory intervention with the possibility of enforceable settlements. The most important of these was the new procedure for trade union recognition. The Employment Protection Act also retained the device of a code of industrial relations practice which had been introduced by the 1971 Act, and entrusted the drafting of codes to the Service.

Where the new legislation provided for the enforceable settlement of an industrial dispute, it was in most instances provided by an award of the Central Arbitration Committee which became an implied term in the employment contracts of the employees concerned. This committee took over from the Conservatives' Industrial Arbitration Board which had in turn replaced the Industrial Court. Along with the Certification Officer, the committee is formally part of the Advisory Conciliation and Arbitration Service, whose Council has to be consulted about appointments, but the three bodies operate entirely independently.

Regarded more generally, the creation of the Service can be seen as part of a wholesale retreat of the Department of Employment from

[4] This argument was set out by McCarthy and Ellis in *Management by Agreement*, chapter 7.

its former administrative functions, in which the Manpower Services Commission and the Health and Safety Commission have taken over other large areas of the Department's responsibilities. As a result the Department has become a relatively small organization with supervision and policy-making as its main duties.

The extension of existing individual employment rights, and the creation of new ones, have added considerably to the work of the industrial tribunals as well as to that of the Service. The abolition of the National Industrial Relations Court in 1974 left them without a specialized appeal tribunal, so that more and more inconsistency was apparent in their decisions until the Employment Protection Act established the Employment Appeal Tribunal to hear appeals from decisions of industrial tribunals on points of law, and from decisions of the Certification Officer on both fact and law. In a series of leading cases it has established greater uniformity in tribunal decisions.

Finally, the Equal Opportunities Commission and the Racial Equality Commission were set up by the Sex Discrimination Act and the Race Relations Act 1976. The Racial Equality Commission took over the functions of both the former Race Relations Board and the Community Relations Commission. Much of the work of these two new bodies is of no direct concern to industrial relations, but they also deal with discrimination in employment.

The substance of the new rights is examined in the following sections, dealing first with individual employment rights, and separating out rights to protection against discrimination in employment from the rest. Next come the rights of trade unionists and trade unions, with a separate section for trade union recognition. Thirdly, consideration is given to new developments in more traditional areas of state intervention—support for and substitutes for collective bargaining. Finally, an attempt is made to assess the overall impact of the new labour legislation.

INDIVIDUAL EMPLOYMENT RIGHTS

As things now stand it is open to a dismissed employee with six months' service or more to complain to an industrial tribunal that his dismissal was unfair. When the tribunal hear the case it is for the employer to show them that the dismissal was fair and reasonable. Dismissal is normally justified where the employer can show that the

decision was taken after proper inquiries, and was due to the conduct
of the employee or his inability to perform the job he was employed
to fill. If the employer fails to establish his case, the tribunal normally
awards compensation to the dismissed employee. The amount
awarded is in the first instance determined by the complainant's
length of service and the loss suffered, but there are also several other
considerations which affect it. The tribunal may reduce the amount
where the complainant's conduct has contributed to his dismissal,
although not justifying it. They are entitled to make an additional
award where the employer fails to reinstate or re-engage an employee after they have ordered him to do so; and the amount of
this additional award is increased where the dismissal was unfair
because it discriminated against the employee on grounds of trade
union membership or activity, or sex, or race.[5] Taking all these
factors into account it is possible for compensation to total over
£10,000.

In 1977 a total of 35,389 complaints of unfair dismissal were
lodged, and 36.3 per cent of these reached tribunal hearings. Compensation was awarded in 25.7 per cent of the cases heard, reinstatement in 0.8 per cent, and re-engagement in 0.6 per cent.[6] It is evident
that the law does not offer much protection to workers against losing
their jobs through unfair dismissal, but for the most part offers
compensation where a tribunal accepts that the dismissal was unfair.
During 1977 the amount was below £300 in 44.2 per cent of the cases
in which compensation was awarded, and less than £500 in two-
thirds; it exceeded £1,000 in 13.9 per cent of them. These figures can
be compared with the experience of 1975, before the Employment
Protection Act had introduced a 'basic award' and increased the scale
of compensation. In that year 65.3 per cent of the awards were below
£300, 80.5 per cent below £500 and 7.9 per cent over £1,000. There is
not very much difference between the two years when inflation is
taken into account.

The small proportion of cases in which reinstatement or re-
engagement are awarded has been observed from the start, and the
Employment Protection Act attempted to give employees greater
protection by introducing an 'order' to reinstate or re-engage,
backed by additional compensation where the employer failed to

---

[5] Protection against unfair dismissal under these headings is not limited to employees with six months' service or more.
[6] *Department of Employment Gazette*, May 1978.

comply. However, this provision seems to have had no effect. The proportion of cases in which the tribunals decided in favour of reinstatement or re-engagement has not increased. To do the tribunals justice, it appears to be the case that most complainants do not want their jobs back. Having quarrelled with his employer, the complainant normally does not wish to work for him again, but, since he believes that his dismissal was wrong, he wants to see the employer before a tribunal and to watch the tribunal award against him and make him pay compensation.

When a complaint is received by an industrial tribunal, a copy is sent to the Advisory Conciliation and Arbitration Service. An officer of the Service then offers to settle the complaint by conciliation between the complainant and the employer. It is heard by the tribunal only if it is not settled by the Service, nor settled privately, nor withdrawn without a settlement. In 1977 not far short of two-thirds of all complaints were disposed of without troubling a tribunal. Of these 44 per cent were withdrawn without a settlement for one reason or another, and some form of settlement was achieved in the remaining 56 per cent. A settlement in conciliation is therefore considerably more likely than an award to the complainant by a tribunal, for in 1977 just short of 70 per cent of complaints which reached tribunals were dismissed. On the other hand the amount of compensation received through settlements was less than from the tribunals. The figure was below £300 in 77.8 per cent of the conciliated compensation settlements in 1977, compared with 44.2 per cent of compensation awards by tribunals. One reason for the greater likelihood of a settlement than of an award to the complainant is that employers may not wish to go to a tribunal unless they are sure that they are in the right. Another is the 'nuisance value' settlement. Even if the employer is confident that the tribunal will find in his favour, the cost of employing a solicitor[7] and of the attendance of perhaps two or three managers or foremen as witnesses may run into hundreds of pounds. It is therefore cheaper to settle at £50 or thereabouts which was at that time the 'going rate' for cases of this kind. Such settlements help to explain the lower level of compensation in settlements than in awards, although there are other reasons as well. For example the complainant may have been out of work longer by the time his case is heard than if he had settled, and his loss will therefore

---

[7] Representation by a solicitor is not required before the tribunals but is becoming increasingly common, especially for employers.

have been greater. Reinstatement and re-engagement are about as rare in settlements as in tribunal decisions.

One consequence of a statutory remedy for unfair dismissal demonstrates that individual employment rights and trade union rights cannot be wholly separated; for it is now necessary to consider whether the dismissal of non-unionists or lapsed unionists or expelled unionists is fair or unfair if it is done in accordance with a closed shop agreement. The Trade Union and Labour Relations Act, as amended by the 1976 Act, states that such a dismissal is to be regarded as fair 'unless the employee genuinely objects on grounds of religious belief to being a member of any trade union whatsoever'. It is not easy to see that any other course was open in a country which decides to provide a statutory remedy for unfair dismissal, and in which the closed shop is widespread and has long been regarded (apart from the Industrial Relations Act) as a legitimate objective for trade unions. The next step, therefore, was to provide a legal definition of what the Act calls a 'union membership agreement'.

In the 1974 Act such an agreement could be made only by an independent trade union and it had to require every one of an 'identifiable class of employees' to be or to become 'a member of the union or one of the unions which is or are parties to the agreement or arrangement or of another appropriate independent trade union'. A case arose at the Ferrybridge power station in Yorkshire. A closed shop agreement exists between the Electricity Council and the unions which represent the manual employees in electricity supply. A number of disaffected union members had established a breakaway union, the Electricity Supply Union. This body failed to secure recognition and its membership melted away, but a handful at Ferrybridge refused to accept defeat. Under the agreement they were therefore dismissed. They appealed to the tribunal which upheld their complaints and awarded compensation. Their dismissals were unfair because the tribunal found there was no union membership agreement at Ferrybridge. Besides these malcontents, there were other manual employees there who were not members of one of the signatory unions or of another appropriate union but were nevertheless tolerated. The agreement did not therefore have 'the effect of requiring' every employee to be a member of an appropriate union.

These other employees were not non-unionists. They were members of the Boilermakers' union. In the British trade union movement a holder of a Boilermakers' card is not normally required to transfer to another union merely because his union is not formally recognized in the industry or plant concerned. That would be likely to cause unnecessary trouble, like prodding a sleeping Alsatian with a pointed stick; and in any case when trouble arises, or a need for collective action, the holder of a Boilermakers' card is likely to respect trade union principles with meticulous care. However, the then law made no allowance for a practice of this kind.

The Ferrybridge case was decided shortly before the 1976 amending Act took effect. This altered the definition of a union membership agreement by replacing the words 'appropriate trade union' by 'specified trade union', so that the Electricity Council and the recognized unions could 'specify' the Boilermakers if they chose; and by dropping the requirement that everyone in the relevant class of employee belong to the union. The test is now whether 'it is the practice . . . for employees to belong'.

This instance illustrates a general characteristic of closed shops in Britain as they are administered by trade unions. Where prospective employees must belong to one or more unions in order to get a job (pre-entry closed shop) there is usually a strict limitation of entry to those who hold the cards of the union or unions. For here the intention is to reserve the jobs for members only. However, where the agreement merely requires the new employee to join one of the signatory unions within a specified time, the intention is to ensure that he will observe union decisions, take part in collective action and pay union dues. Consequently a paid-up card of any *bona fide* union may fairly easily be taken to provide the necessary guarantee; and holders of printers' or building workers' or shop assistants' or coalminers' or agricultural workers' cards may be found working unmolested in car plants or shipyards. Indeed, in some instances even non-unionists may be tolerated if their sincerity is respected and they do not take advantage of their position to propagate anti-union views or to weaken collective action. In other words, trade unionists on the shop floor regard a closed shop as giving them the right to decide whom they will work with. This kind of practice is not readily amenable to definition by the law or regulation by the courts. Since there is no reason to suppose that Ferrybridge was the last occasion on which a tribunal may be called on to handle a complaint concerning dismissal under a union membership agreement, there could be trouble ahead. Meanwhile there are indications that employers are tightening their administration of closed shop agreements.

The closed shop is an emotive issue, above all for Conservative politicians. In 1974 the Labour government had been forced to accept an amendment adding to the grounds for regarding a dismissal as unfair even though carried out under a union membership agreement. In addition to genuine objection on religious grounds to being a member of any trade union were added the words 'or on any reasonable grounds to being a member of a particular trade union'. This left a gaping and ill-defined hole—from the legal point of view—in the closed shop. It was a qualification which the Conservatives had not introduced into the 'approved closed shop' permitted under the Industrial Relations Act. The government proposed to delete it in the amending Act. At this point the opposition raised a storm about the freedom of the press, on the grounds that, if newspaper editors were required to be members of a trade union, the union might use its power to interfere with their editorial freedom. The controversy led to one of the periodic battles between Labour governments and the House of Lords. It was finally resolved by providing for the preparation of a 'charter containing practical guidance for employers, trade unions and editors and other journalists on matters relating to the freedom of the press'. This charter was to be agreed between the parties, or, failing agreement, devised by a representative committee appointed by the Secretary of State, and approved by parliament. It was to provide for a body to hear and determine complaints. The charter is still awaited.

It was often asserted in this controversy that the Act was establishing 'legally enforceable closed shops'. Accordingly it is worth repeating that (apart from the Industrial Relations Act) the closed shop has been a lawful objective of trade union action in Britain since the nineteenth century; and that the current law on unfair dismissals merely provides that a dismissal under a union membership agreement is not to be regarded as unfair. A closed shop is coercive, and is intended to be so, but the coercion lies in the agreement or understanding or arrangement which imposes a closed shop, and not in the law on unfair dismissal.

Another point at which the individual right to a remedy for unfair dismissal impinges on the collective rights of trade unions is the potential competition between the statutory procedure for dealing with complaints of unfair dismissal and the right under agreements, or custom and practice, for unions to take up the case of a dismissed member directly with the employer. However, surveys of employees who make use of the statutory procedure indicate that they are not a representative sample of the employed population.

> Unfair dismissal claims. . . stemmed disproportionately from the private rather then the public sector and within the private sector they came disproportionately from small firms. Three in four claims came either from manual workers in small private firms or from white-collar workers generally. This may reflect the . . . greater likelihood of a public sector employee being covered by a formal, joint dismissal procedure. Moreover, it may reflect the relative insecurity of small as compared with large firms. All the indices suggest that those areas where unions were well organised produced few applications of unfair dismissal.[8]

This survey was carried out under the Industrial Relations Act when a number of unions refused to represent their members before industrial tribunals, but a similar bias towards employees in small private firms has been found in later investigations.[9] Accordingly it appears that well-organized unions can offer their members a fair degree of security against unfair dismissal through voluntary procedures or the threat of industrial action; and that the statutory procedure mainly provides unorganized or ill-organized workers with an opportunity to secure some financial compensation after they have been unfairly dismissed. Nevertheless unions do use the tribunals, and representation of members at tribunal hearings has become a substantial part of the job of many trade union officers.

Competition between statutory procedures and voluntary practices can occur in relation to other individual employment rights which have been created in recent years. The statutory right of redundant workers to compensation has to some extent undermined the resistance of those unions which traditionally dealt with redundancy by refusing to countenance it. Their members may prefer compensation to resistance. On the other hand, in many instances the statutory provisions have assisted union action by establishing a minimum from which unions can start to negotiate higher levels of compensation. In any event, industrial tribunals are not often called upon to take decisions on those matters which mainly concern the unions in redundancy disputes. The unions are interested in whether

[8] Weekes *et al.*, *op. cit.*, p. 15.
[9] For example, projects conducted by Warwick students as part of the MA Industrial Relations degree.

there is to be a redundancy, how many workers should go, how they should be chosen, and whether the level of compensation should exceed the statutory minimum. The tribunals are called upon in those relatively rare cases where there is a difference of opinion as to whether a dismissal is a redundancy or not, or how the rules for determining the statutory compensation apply to particular employees.

The new individual employment rights established by the Employment Protection Act are: an entitlement to a modest guarantee payment of up to £6 a week for up to five days in three months; an entitlement to payment during medical suspension; rights not to be dismissed because of pregnancy and to be reinstated after maternity; a right to time off to look for work or arrange training in the event of redundancy; a right to a written statement of reasons for dismissal; and an entitlement to an itemized pay statement. While they may be important to the individuals they affect, most of these rights have little impact on the traditional areas of trade union action. The level of guarantee payment suggests that it is intended to encourage unions to do better, not to establish a norm. The most significant of them in practice have been the rights concerning pregnancy and maternity which can present employers with tricky problems of manpower planning in keeping posts open for employees who may decide in the end not to return to work.

Complaints under these headings are handled in the same way as complaints of unfair dismissal. They are lodged with the industrial tribunals which pass them on to the Service for conciliation. If they are not settled by the Service, or settled privately, or withdrawn without a settlement, they are heard by the tribunals. So far they have not created anything like the volume of business that has come from unfair dismissal. Together with the rights granted to trade unionists by the Act they accounted for about 9 per cent of the cases referred to the Service by industrial tribunals in 1977.

Although legislation on racial discrimination came first, it is convenient to start an account of statutory action against discrimination in employment with the Equal Pay Act which covers a limited area of discrimination and deals with it in a very different manner from that of the Race Relations Act and the Sex Discrimination Act. It was passed in 1970 to give equality in pay and other contractual terms of employment by the end of 1975 to a woman who performs the 'same or broadly similar work' as a man working for the same employer, or whose work has been assessed at an equivalent value to his under a job evaluation scheme. It was not intended to give all women equal pay with men, but only the minority of women who can meet the conditions laid down in the Act. Given that limitation, the considerable increase in the relative pay of women since 1975[10] indicates that it has had a fair success.

There are two channels of enforcement. Individual complaints are passed by the industrial tribunals to the Service whose officers offer to conciliate. If they fail, the case is heard by a tribunal. Alternatively, trade unions, employers or the Secretary of State may report discriminatory collective agreements, pay structures and wage regulation orders to the Central Arbitration Committee for amendment. Initially the interpretations of the 'same or broadly similar work' by industrial tribunals were often narrow and inconsistent, but subsequently a number of decisions handed down by the Employment Appeal Tribunal widened and standardized the interpretation given to these words, although not all its decisions have favoured women. Meanwhile the Central Arbitration Committee has adopted a flexible approach in order to identify discrimination which 'does not always appear on the face of the agreement' and 'to ensure that discrimination has been truly removed'.[11]

The Act has also helped to galvanize trade unions and the Trades Union Congress into greater activity to secure relative improvements in women's pay, and to increase participation by women trade unionists in the affairs of their unions. The original legislation was sped on its way by a famous strike of women at Ford's Dagenham factory, and in 1976 a prolonged strike at Trico helped to publicize the demand for equal pay. With the backing of the Act, some trade unions have been able to negotiate a number of relative pay increases for women.[12] The main criticism of the Act does not relate to the effectiveness of the machinery for its administration and enforcement, or to the impetus it has given to action by trade unions, but to the limitation of its scope.

The verdict on the Race Relations and Sex Discrimination Acts is less encouraging. The first Race Relations Act was passed in 1965. It was a modest measure which did not touch on employment issues. By 1968 it was judged to have provided sufficient evidence that the

[10] See p. 370.
[11] Central Arbitration Committee, *Annual Report 1977*, p. 16.
[12] Jean Coussins, *The Equality Report*, pp. 73–9.

law can deal with racial discrimination for a second Act to be passed to strengthen the provisions of the first and to extend them to cover employment. Racial discrimination in selection, promotion, dismissal, and terms and conditions of employment became unlawful, as also did discrimination by trade unions against members or potential members on grounds of race. The normal procedure was by means of an individual complaint of discrimination handled by one of the Race Relation Board's regional conciliation committees; but complaints were rare. Many victims of discrimination were unaware of the existence of the Act. Many of those who knew that discrimination was unlawful had no idea of how to make a complaint. Many of those who knew how to complain feared reprisals at work if they made use of their rights. Others regarded the likelihood of success as too small to make it worth their while to complain; and experience showed that discrimination in employment is not easily proved. If conciliation failed, it was for the board to initiate proceedings, not the complainant. Until 1975 the board did not win any of the cases of employment discrimination which they took to court, and, over the whole period of the 1968 Act's operation, the success rate of such cases was far below that in other areas of discrimination. There were also other instances of employment discrimination where there were no grounds for a complaint under the law. Where a company, or a plant, or a grade of employee included no black workers, it was often the case that there were no black applicants for jobs. They did not believe that it was worth their while to try. No individual therefore had grounds to complain.

As a result of this experience the Sex Discrimination Act and the third Race Relations Act did not give the responsibility for administering conciliation procedures to the Equal Opportunities Commission and the Racial Equality Commission. Complaints of discrimination on grounds of race or sex go to the tribunals which send them to the Advisory Conciliation and Arbitration Service for conciliation. If conciliation fails or is rejected, the complainant has the right to be heard by the tribunal. Where they think it is appropriate to assist a complainant, either Commission may do so. They also have powers to conduct formal investigations into areas where discrimination is suspected and to issue non-discrimination notices where they find that the law has been broken. If a notice is not obeyed, the Commission concerned can apply to the court for an injunction to compel obedience. The two Commissions are therefore entitled to step in where individuals are unable or unwilling to complain, and their investigatory powers can help to overcome the difficulty of proving discrimination.

Although it is too early to attempt any but the most tentative assessment of this new machinery, experience so far does not suggest that it provides a reliable remedy for discrimination in employment. Both racial and sex discrimination are widespread in Britain, in employment as in other spheres. The evidence on racial discrimination is contained in the reports of Political and Economic Planning on the subject,[13] and is apparent to anyone who pays attention to the treatment of black employees. The evidence on sex discrimination is there for everyone to see. One of the severest limitations on the Equal Pay Act is the exclusion of women from many high-paid occupations, or the existence of narrow limitations on their entry. These could be challenged under the Sex Discrimination Act. For these reasons it seems likely that instances of racial and sex discrimination outnumber by far instances of dismissals which are unfair on grounds other than race and sex. Nevertheless in 1977 the Service received over 38,000 complaints of unfair dismissal, nearly a thousand complaints under the Equal Pay Act, only 367 complaints of sex discrimination, and a mere 206 complaints of racial discrimination in the six months that the new Race Relations Act was in operation. So far the powers of the two Commissions to investigate and to issue non-discrimination notices have not replaced individual complaints as the main instrument for combating discrimination in employment.

Nor does it seem likely that trade union action will make serious inroads into discrimination at work, apart from equal pay. Several strikes in recent years, of which the Mansfield Hosiery dispute was the most notorious example,[14] have drawn attention to discrimination at work. Generally unions of skilled workers and unions with skilled sections are particularly prone to both racial and sex discrimination. There are, however, some signs of change. The Trades Union Congress and some individual unions have taken steps towards removing discriminatory practices and encouraging black workers and women workers to join unions and to participate fully in their work. There are even one or two black full-time trade union officers, just as some unions with large—or even majority—women

---

[13] The most recent is D. J. Smith, *Racial Disadvantage in Employment*.
[14] Commission on Industrial Relations, *Mansfield Hosiery Mills Limited*.

membership have had one or two women full-time officers for many years. But unions are still too riddled with discriminatory beliefs and practices to be effective instruments for the removal of discrimination in employment.

RIGHTS FOR TRADE UNIONISTS AND TRADE UNIONS

By comparison with other countries, Britain was late in giving legal protection to employees against discrimination on the ground of union membership. It was not until 1971 that the 'yellow dog' contract banning union membership was made illegal. Currently the Trade Union and Labour Relations Act and the Employment Protection Act between them protect the right of an employee to be or seek to be a member of an independent trade union, and to take part in its activities 'at any appropriate time'. Protection is given against dismissal and action short of dismissal; and, with certain exceptions, it extends to activities on the employer's premises (although not in working hours without his consent), thus creating a 'right to organize' where unions are unrecognized. If an employee complains that he has been dismissed on one of these grounds, and has the backing of his union, an industrial tribunal can compel his employer to keep him on until the complaint is settled.

Other rights are confined to members of recognized trade unions. The Employment Protection Act obliges employers to allow those of their employees who are officials of recognized independent trade unions (and that includes shop stewards) to take time off with pay to carry out collective bargaining and related duties, and to attend relevant training courses which have trade union approval. Employers must also grant time off (with nothing said about payment) to members of such unions to take part in approved trade union activities. It is doubtful whether these provisions will have much effect in the public sector or in most well-organized private companies, where facilities are already fairly generous, although they may make it easier in some of them for shop stewards to secure release for training. The main intention of the authors was probably to strengthen trade unions in plants where, although recognized, they are as yet relatively weak.

It is already evident that the provisions of the Health and Safety at Work Act concerning safety representatives will have a more widespread impact. As amended by the Employment Protection Act, they require employers to accept and provide facilities for safety representatives and safety committees appointed by recognized independent trade unions. Their intention is to increase trade union participation in the formulation and application of safety policies and standards at work, as well as securing greater compliance with statutory standards. Although health and safety are long-standing concerns of trade unions and subjects of bargaining in the plant, and safety committees are already fairly common, the job of safety representative is relatively novel outside coalmining. Time off with pay for him to carry out his duties and undergo relevant training will entail additional expenditure by employers almost everywhere.

Another group of rights apply not to individual trade unionists or trade union representatives, but to trade unions as such. They are all intended to strengthen or extend collective bargaining. The provisions of the Social Security Pensions Act on consultation with trade unions over occupational pension schemes have already been mentioned.[15] They have proved highly effective in promoting what amounts to bargaining between companies and recognized trade unions over pensions, and therefore in developing collective bargaining at company level.

Another endeavour to promote collective bargaining—by negotiating procedures on dismissal—has so far come to nothing. The Trade Union and Labour Relations Act maintained the exemption granted by the Industrial Relations Act from its provisions on unfair dismissal for a 'dismissal procedures agreement' provided it satisfied certain requirements. It had to include an appeal to an independent body as the final stage, and its remedies had to be 'on the whole as beneficial as (but not necessarily identical with)' those in the Act. These requirements proved too exacting, and there are no exemptions. Where unions are strong, they are generally content to rely on existing procedures and their own strength; and employers generally prefer the industrial tribunals to the possibility of an independent umpire. In practice tribunals have no authority to enforce reinstatement. Employers might feel obliged to accept an award of reinstatement from an umpire under agreements to which they were parties.

The Employment Protection Act gives recognized trade unions

[15] p. 4.

the right to be consulted about redundancy proposals. Unless 'special circumstances' make it 'not reasonably practicable' for him, an employer has to give notice of redundancy proposals to them (the minimum period of notice depending on the numbers affected), with reasons and detailed information on a number of relevant points. He must consider any representations which the unions make, and reply to them. If he rejects them he must give reasons for his decision. This is as far as the law can go towards encouraging bargaining over redundancy without specifically requiring employers to bargain about it, but it may not lead to a rapid growth in the number of standing agreements on redundancy in private companies. Employers may not be anxious to go beyond the minimum requirements of the law, and the fear that such agreements could increase the likelihood and extent of redundancies is still widespread in British unions. Perhaps the main benefit to the unions will be to ensure that they receive fuller information on proposed redundancies.

The Act also imposes a general duty on employers to disclose information to representatives of recognized independent trade unions. The information to be disclosed is information without which their conduct of bargaining would be impeded, and which 'it would be in accordance with good industrial relations practice that he [the employer] should disclose to them for the purposes of collective bargaining'. A similar provision in the Industrial Relations Act was not used, and cases are only now coming forward under the present Act. It is therefore impossible to assess the outcome of such a novel requirement. There are those who doubt whether, even with the law behind them, unions can extract much information of use to them out of employers who are determined to conceal it.

Where the law imposes obligations, it has to provide penalties for those who fail to comply, and novel obligations may require unusual penalties. Where individuals are concerned, the Employment Protection Act provides for complaints to be made to an industrial tribunal which is entitled to award compensation to them. Where the employer fails to allow time off work as required by the Act, compensation is to be

of such amount as the tribunal considers just and equitable in all the circumstances having regard to the employer's default in failing to permit time off . . . and to any loss sustained by the employee which is attributable to the matters complained of.

This may not appear to be entirely appropriate when time off is refused to a shop steward, for the loss which results from a steward being prevented from carrying out his duties may be sustained by his members or his union more than by the steward himself; but it provides a deterrent for the employer, and it avoids the use of an injunction to force the employer to comply with his obligation. An injunction would be backed by proceedings for contempt which could lead to imprisonment, and that is a sanction for which British industrial relations practitioners have a strong dislike.

A similarly devious device is used to enforce the obligation upon an employer to consult over redundancy. The trade union is entitled to complain to the industrial tribunal, but the penalty is the payment of compensation, called a 'protective award', to the employees who have been or are to be dismissed. Such a penalty is not applicable where an employer fails to fulfil his obligation to disclose information. In this instance the union's complaint goes to the Central Arbitration Committee. If the committee finds that the complaint is well-founded, and the employer persists in refusing to disclose, the union is entitled to submit a claim for an improvement in the terms and conditions of employment of the workers concerned, on which the committee may make a binding award. This sanction was taken over from the Industrial Relations Act whose authors derived it from the Donovan Report where it was proposed as appropriate for use against employers who refused to accept a recommendation to recognize a trade union. It is clearly a cumbersome method of avoiding the direct enforcement of a duty to disclose information; but no occasion has so far arisen for it to be tested.

The authors of the Employment Protection Act recognized that some of the rights which it created were expressed in general terms. To give them greater specificity, they turned to the Industrial Relations Act's device of a code of industrial relations practice. One of the amendments to the Trade Union and Labour Relations Act which had been accepted by the government was the retention of their predecessors' code of practice. The Employment Protection Act provided for it to be replaced subsequently by codes on particular aspects of industrial relations drafted by the Service, and in particular required the Service to prepare codes on disclosure of information and time off for trade union duties and activities. Like their predecessor, these codes were to be submitted to parliament for approval, and failure to comply with them was not to lead to liability to proceedings, but they were to be taken into account in relevant cases.

As it happened, the Service's first code was on *Disciplinary Practice and Procedures in Employment*. It revised and expanded a section of the previous code, and was relatively non-controversial. Since industrial tribunals had already taken account of the former code in deciding what procedures employers should be expected to follow in dismissing an employee, it had little impact on the conduct of unfair dismissal cases. The next two codes were more controversial.

The attempt to clarify the obligation to disclose information for collective bargaining purposes already had a considerable history when the Service acquired responsibility for it. The consultative document which preceded the Industrial Relations Bill promised that the bill itself would be more informative on this obligation, but, when the bill emerged, the task of explaining what was involved was entrusted to the authors of the code. They in turn passed it on to the Commission on Industrial Relations which issued one of their least enlightening reports.[16] Since the tribunals heard no complaints under this section of the Act the Service had relatively little to guide them when they took over responsibility.

What trade unionists would like to see is a list of topics on which employers are obliged to give them information. For their part, employers would like to see a list of those topics on which they are not required to disclose information because, in the words of the Act, it 'would cause substantial injury to the employer's undertaking for reasons other than its effect on collective bargaining'. The question which faces everyone who has tried to elucidate the obligation to disclose is whether it is possible to draw up lists which would be valid regardless of the circumstances of the undertaking. So far the official answer has invariably been that it is not possible. The Service have done their best by drawing up an illustrative list of topics on which, subject to the circumstances of the case, it might normally be expected that an employer should disclose information, and examples of circumstances in which he should normally not be required to disclose. This formulation inevitably leaves a great deal of discretion to the Central Arbitration Committee in dealing with complaints. Meanwhile, the history of attempts to define the obligation to disclose information in collective bargaining must call into question the appropriateness of statutory enforcement.

[16] *Disclosure of Information.*

The Service faced a less baffling problem in listing the duties for which an employee who is a trade union official should be allowed time off with pay, for the tasks in which shop stewards are involved when conducting collective bargaining in the plant are tolerably well-established in well-organized undertakings. Many of the criticisms of this draft code when it appeared should in fact have been directed at the Act rather than the code. For example, it was said that the code did not distinguish between time off with pay for trade union duties in the plant and unpaid time off for trade union activities. There is, however, no such distinction in the Act. It makes no reference, one way or the other, to whether time off for union activities should be paid or not. Similarly the code gives the employers no voice in the conduct of the training courses for which they are obliged to give paid leave of absence, because the Act's only requirement is that a course should be 'approved by the Trades Union Congress or by the independent trade union of which he [the prospective trainee] is an official'. The Service also ran into criticism over the wording of their guidance on 'the occasions on which and any conditions subject to which' time off should be taken. Evidently the safety and the efficiency of the undertaking are very important considerations, but the Act creates a duty for the employer to give time off for certain activities; it does not give him a right to refuse because the circumstances are unsuitable; and the Service cannot create such a right.

When drafting their codes the Service conduct inquiries to inform themselves of current practice and the views of interested bodies. The publication of drafts is followed by a period for the submission of views, after which a revised version is submitted to the Secretary of State to be laid before parliament. Sixty thousand copies of the draft report on disclosure of information were issued and 140 written submissions were received. Nevertheless the most significant evidence comes from Congress and the Confederation which are consulted informally while the draft is in preparation and formally after it has been issued. It could be said that a good deal of the draft of any code has been negotiated between the Service and the staffs of those two bodies. This practice is, of course, highly desirable if the codes are to be respected and observed. Only if they appeal to employers and trade unionists as reasonable and helpful are they likely to be followed by the majority and enforced, if need be, on the minority. It is a matter for argument whether it might not have been better to lay the responsibility for drafting codes directly on Congress and the Confederation rather than on the Service. Codes which had been directly negotiated between them would command wider respect, but there would be the risk of the two bodies failing to agree.

RECOGNITION

As it has turned out, by far the most controversial of the rights created for trade unions by the Employment Protection Act has been the right to seek statutory support for claims for recognition by employers. The recognition procedure of the Employment Protection Act is less complicated than that of the Industrial Relations Act. In most respects it goes back to the proposals of the Donovan Commission. A new feature is that the procedure cannot be initiated by employers as could that of the Industrial Relations Act;[17] but only by an independent trade union. Once a reference is made, it is the duty of the Service to consult all parties concerned and to try to settle the recognition issue by conciliation. If that fails, the Service is bound to conduct an inquiry during which 'the Service shall ascertain the opinions of workers to whom the issue relates by any means it thinks fit'. However, the Act lays down formal rules which must be followed if the Service chooses to use a ballot. If the issue is still not settled or withdrawn, the Service must either recommend recognition and give reasons for their recommendation, or give reasons for not making a recommendation. If the employer does not comply with a recommendation, and further conciliation fails, the union may complain to the Central Arbitration Committee. Where the committee find the complaint well-founded, they proceed to hear a claim for improvements in the terms of employment of the employees covered by the recommendation and to issue an award which is binding on the employer unless it is superseded by an agreement between him and the employees concerned which improves on the terms of the award. The union is entitled to return twelve months later with another claim if the recommendation has still not been accepted. Here again direct enforcement is avoided, and the assumption is that employers will prefer to recognize trade unions rather than to be subject to periodic compulsory arbitration.

[17] Employers are entitled to ask for the help of the Service over a problem of recognition. They are debarred only from using the *statutory* procedure.

Table 13 shows that, after pay, recognition is also the most frequent cause of disputes handled by the Service through *voluntary* conciliation. In 1975 there were 416 such disputes. Next year, despite the availability of the statutory procedure from February onwards, the number had risen to 697, and in 1977 it was 635. Most of these were settled, a majority by the granting of recognition or representation rights, and a minority by the withdrawal of the claim. A fair number of the cases which were not settled reappeared as statutory references, but in addition a number of new claims were referred directly under that section. Altogether there were 461 statutory references in 1976 and 577 in 1977.

By comparison the workload of the Commission on Industrial Relations had been minute. They dealt with less than fifty recognition cases over four years. Consequently, although the experience of the Commission gave the Service guidance on the conduct of investigations and some of the problems involved in recognition,[18] the Service has to work at a much smarter pace. The majority of the cases are local and concern relatively small numbers of workers. They are handled by the regional staff of the Service who have no previous experience of operating a conciliation procedure with a sanction against the employer who fails to settle. Many of them fear that this new duty could tarnish their prized reputation for impartiality. Because of the novelty of the procedure, and the need to develop acceptable and uniform practices, the Service took some time in catching up with the growth of their workload, and it was not until the last quarter of 1977 that they disposed of as many cases as were referred to them during the quarter.

Problems have occurred under four main headings: the determination of the bargaining group; the support among the workers concerned which is necessary to justify recognition; competition between trade unions for recognition; and obstruction by employers.

The reference must specify the group of employees which the union seeks to represent, but it may be amended during the course of conciliation. Even then the Service may decide that the grouping which the union proposes is inappropriate. They may recommend a smaller group, but they cannot enlarge the bargaining group. If they recommend recognition and think that other employees should be included within its scope, they are limited to giving advice on the point.

[18] Commission on Industrial Relations, *Trade Union Recognition: CIR Experience.*

It is not uncommon for the union and the employer to disagree over the appropriate bargaining group. In these cases the employer almost invariably argues for a wider group than the union proposes, 'for example, where union support is concentrated and relatively strong in one area and the employer argues that this area should be regarded as only part of a larger area where union support may be proportionately much less'.[19] In a number of instances the employer has argued that recognition should not be granted in one plant alone since the terms and conditions of the grades of employees concerned are standardized throughout the company, and recognition in one plant would bring undesirable fragmentation. Alternatively, where the union claims to represent a relatively small group of employees within a plant, say fitters or draughtsmen, the employer may argue that all manual workers, or all white collar employees, should form a single group. In several instances an employer has asserted that all the employees in a plant, including managers, form a single integral group and should be so considered for the purpose of judging the recognition issue. No firm rules have emerged from the recommendations issued so far. Nevertheless, the Service has indicated that it has regard for current practice in the industry concerned, and, generally speaking, British practice in private employment favours recognition plant by plant, with two or more bargaining groups in plants of any size. In making a recommendation for recognition the Service is required to state 'whether the recommendation is for recognition generally, or in respect of one or more specified matters'. In several instances where some conditions of employment are standardized throughout a company, whereas others are left to the discretion of local managers, the Service has recommended recognition in one plant to negotiate over matters which are settled locally.

To 'ascertain the opinions of workers to whom the issue relates', the Service normally sends them a questionnaire in which they are asked about their union membership, if any, whether they wish to be represented by a union in negotiation with their employer, and whether it should be the union or unions making the reference. In most cases those who are not members of the union or unions making the reference are asked whether they would join if recognition was granted. It has been decided by the courts that these questionnaires are formal ballots. Where the response rate is high and the majority wish to be represented in collective bargaining by the union

[19] Advisory Conciliation and Arbitration Service, *Annual Report*, 1976, p. 48.

or unions making the reference, and there is already a substantial union membership, recognition is always recommended, unless a question of inter-union competition arises. Where well over half the respondents do not wish for collective bargaining, no recommendation is made. Most references come into one or other of these categories, but there remains a sizable minority of cases which are less straightforward. In several cases recognition has been recommended although less than half the respondents wanted collective bargaining; and it has also been recommended in a few cases in which a majority has favoured collective bargaining but the union making the reference has not received the support of a majority. A very low union membership has led to a decision not to recommend recognition in one or two cases, and a low response rate has had the same effect in one or two others.

The most difficult cases of inter-union competition occur where collective bargaining arrangements are already established but an outside union claims recognition and proves majority support in the group concerned. The outstanding case so far has been the claim of the United Kingdom Association of Professional Engineers to represent senior staff employed by W. H. Allen, an engineering firm in Bedford.[20] The application was opposed not only by the employer, but also by the Engineering Employers Federation and the Confederation of Shipbuilding and Engineering Unions on the grounds that adequate bargaining arrangements already exist and that the intrusion of an additional union would harm industrial relations in the industry. The firm is federated, and although the federation's agreements with the five unions already recognized to represent staff in the industry do not cover senior staff, the principle of local recognition for them on the basis of union membership was agreed in 1976. The Service decided to make no recommendation, but this decision was nullified by the High Court, a verdict which is discussed later.

The United Kingdom Association of Professional Engineers is not affiliated to the Trades Union Congress. Affiliated unions are advised by Congress that they

> should not . . . invoke the Act's procedures on recognition without consultation and agreement with any other affiliated union

---

[20] Advisory Conciliation and Arbitration Service, *W. H. Allen Sons and Company Limited and the United Kingdom Association of Professional Engineers.*

with an interest in the matter. Where there is disagreement between affiliated unions about a claim for recognition the matter
should be resolved through the TUC disputes procedure.[21]

Where their consultations reveal that more than one affiliated union
may be interested in a reference, the Service draw the attention of the
unions to this advice, and the matter is usually settled between them.
However, in a few instances a reference has been pressed despite the
claims of another affiliated union to represent the employees concerned. In the General Accident case[22] the Service recommended that
both unions should be recognized.

In 1977 an affiliated union, the Electrical Power Engineers
Association, changed its name to the Engineers and Managers
Association and set about recruiting managers in engineering and
elsewhere. References have been made to the Service, who have so
far made no recommendation.

Because some of the necessary information may not otherwise be
obtainable, the Service needs the co-operation of the employer in
order to make its inquiries. In particular it is usually impossible for
the Service to 'ascertain the opinions of workers to whom the issue
relates' without his help. Where relatively few employees are concerned, the Service may be able to contact them through the union,
but otherwise the employer's co-operation is necessary to conduct a
ballot, or to obtain the names and addresses of the employees concerned so as to distribute questionnaires by post. Some employers
have refused to co-operate, while others have delayed so long in
giving consent that the Service have decided to go ahead with their
inquiries as best they can without their help. Prolonged delay can be
particularly unfair to the union. When they have been persuaded to
join a union for the benefits that it can bring them, employees expect
to see results. Without recognition there can be no results, and if
recognition is delayed for many months they may lose heart and
drop out of the union. Employees who have promised support for
the union may turn against it when they find that the expected
investigation by the Service does not materialize, especially if it is
made clear to them that their employer is actively opposing recogni-

[21] Advisory Conciliation and Arbitration Service, *Annual Report*, 1977, p. 48.

[22] Advisory Conciliation and Arbitration Service, *General Accident Fire and Life
Assurance Corporation Limited, the Association of Scientific Technical and Managerial Staffs
and the Association of Professional Executive Clerical and Computer Staff*.

tion. Consequently an employer who opposes recognition may destroy the union's support by prevarication.

Some of these problems were illustrated by the notorious Grunwick dispute. In this instance a minority of employees struck and subsequently joined a union. The employer dismissed all the strikers.[23] The union submitted a statutory reference. The Service decided that the employer was taking too much time over their request for his co-operation, and went ahead without it. They discovered that the strikers, who had now been out for some months, were unanimously in favour of recognition, and, believing that they had done all they could to fulfil their statutory duty, they reported in favour of recognition. The employer challenged the recommendation in the courts. The case eventually reached the House of Lords.

This was not the first case brought against the Service. Their discretion had already been shown to be limited in *Powley* v. *ACAS* which turned on the question whether the name of an uncertificated staff association should have been included in a questionnaire. The judge held that, in exercising their discretion, the Service must not 'take into account irrelevant considerations' nor fail 'to take into account relevant considerations'. It was for the court to say what was relevant and what was irrelevant. By not including the name of the association, the Service was 'proposing to issue a questionnaire which is unsuitable to inform them of the relevant facts', and he therefore gave judgement against them.

The main issue in the Grunwick case was whether the Service were entitled to proceed without ascertaining the opinions of those who had remained at work when the employer had delayed giving the Service access to them. The House of Lords decided that they were not. In the judgement of Lord Diplock, which was accepted without qualification by two of his four colleagues, it was the duty of the Service to

> ascertain and take into consideration the opinions on that issue of the work force as a whole, and, where there is a reasonable possibility that there may be conflict of opinions, . . . [to] ascertain and take into consideration those that are held by every group of workers of any significant size that forms part of the work force that would be affected by the recommendation.

[23] He said that he would have preferred to dismiss only some of them, but the Trade Union and Labour Relations Act makes it unfair to dismiss a striker unless all those on strike are dismissed.

From the Service's point of view, the most restrictive decision came in *UKAPE* v. *ACAS* (the Allen case). The crucial point here was the interpretation of their 'general duty of promoting the improvement of industrial relations, and in particular of encouraging the extension of collective bargaining'. The Service decided that the damage which would be done to industrial relations in engineering by the recognition of the United Kingdom Association of Professional Engineers outweighed the benefit from according the senior staff at W. H. Allen the right to be represented in collective bargaining by the union of their choice. Mr Justice May held that they were not entitled to come to this decision. The duty of encouraging the extension of collective bargaining was not subject to the general duty of promoting the improvement of industrial relations. The Service had 'misdirected' themselves in supposing that a recommendation on trade union recognition 'must be consistent with established collective bargaining arrangements'. If this verdict is upheld on appeal it will overturn a number of other important decisions by the Service, and dismay both Congress and the Confederation—and many of their constituents. Besides that, other writs have been issued or are pending, and they might lead to further limitations upon the discretion of the Service.

The effect on the work of the Service has been considerable. They can do little in relation to a statutory reference on trade union recognition without looking over both shoulders in search of possible legal implications. Even then they have to reckon that the legal implications may turn out to be different from what they surmise or are advised.

However, the consequences go a good deal wider than that. Trends in judicial decisions usually reflect social attitudes. It is significant that the Grunwick dispute was a *cause célèbre* for other reasons besides the court case. As the strike ran on into 1977 it began to attract widespread sympathy and support among trade unionists. Mass picketing began in the spring and continued, with intermissions, into the autumn—by far the most sustained campaign of mass picketing on record in Britain. Injuries to police and pickets, and arrests of pickets, were almost daily occurrences. Pressure mounted for government intervention. A court of inquiry was appointed by the government (not by the Service) under Lord Scarman and mass picketing was called off while the inquiry proceeded. The report was published towards the end of August. Because of the case which was then before the House of Lords the court of inquiry made no positive recommendation on recognition; but they had 'no doubt that union representation, if properly encouraged and responsibly exercised, could in future help the company as well as its employees'. In addition, they recommended the company should, if practicable, 'offer re-employment to all those strikers who before the dispute were full-time employees of the company who wish to be taken back', with *ex gratia* payments related to service for those for whom there were no vacancies.[24] There was no legal obligation on the company to accept the court's recommendations and suggestions, and they decided to do nothing until the House of Lords verdict was known. Mass picketing was resumed for a few weeks, and the dispute dragged on for almost another year. The Service recommenced their investigation, but they were still refused the facilities which they believed they needed, and in the end they decided that they were unable to carry out their statutory duties.

The Grunwick dispute made it evident, if evidence was needed, that trade union recognition, like the closed shop, is a highly contentious issue. There are at least two major issues in dispute. The first is whether collective bargaining is a superior method of regulating industrial relations in comparison with unilateral managerial control; and the second is whether each individual employee should have a right to an equal say in a decision concerning the introduction of collective bargaining, or a change in the bargaining representative, for the group to which he belongs.

On the first point British public policy has favoured collective bargaining at least since the final report of the Royal Commission of Labour in 1894, and its general acceptance by parliament. Their views on the merits of collective bargaining were reinforced and expanded by the reports of the Whitley Committee in 1917–18 and the report of the Donovan Commission in 1968. A general commitment to collective bargaining was written into the first section of the Conservative Industrial Relations Act and into Labour's Employment Protection Act. Nevertheless the superiority of collective bargaining is by no means universally accepted. In the opinions which they have expressed to the Service during recognition inquiries, some large and many small employers have asserted that collective bargaining is undesirable in their particular circumstances. They believe that they have relationships with their employees, or with the

[24] *Scarman Report*, p. 23.

grades of employees concerned in the reference, which are to the advantage of the undertaking and the workers, and which would be destroyed by the intervention of a trade union. In many small companies the employer believes that he is directly acquainted with the wishes and interests of his employees and that he looks after them better than any trade union could do. In some instances the employer claims that his company has constructed a non-union representative system which is accomplishing everything of value that a union can offer, without the defects of union representation to the company.

In many cases the employer goes on to say that he would be happy to accept trade union recognition if it was established that a clear majority of his employees, or those in the grades in question, wanted it; but the test of the employees' wishes differ from one employer to another. One employer may want to see more than half of them in the union; another may be prepared to accept a majority in a ballot. There are other variations. Some employers concerned in recognition references wish to stipulate that abstentions should be counted with votes against recognition, so that those who vote for recognition must constitute a majority of the employees concerned for recognition to be granted.

Setting these variations aside, many people find an inherent attraction in leaving the question of union recognition to be settled by a majority decision of the employees concerned; but many trade unionists do not agree. They hold that a union should be entitled to represent and bargain on behalf of its *members* regardless of their numbers and what proportion of the employees they constitute. They admit that the employer may feel obliged to extend the terms and conditions of employment negotiated with the union to the remainder of his employees, and that the consequence of this may be that the terms of employment of a majority who do not wish for collective bargaining are determined by an agreement negotiated on behalf of a minority; but they take the view that this consequence is not their affair. It is the concern of the employer and the non-unionists. They point out that it is the tradition of the engineering and some other industries that unions should be recognized to represent their members—a tradition embodied in the agreements of the Engineering Employers Federation and accepted by at least some non-federated employers.

Furthermore, trade unionists argue that the influence of the employer must not be neglected in recognition disputes. Where workers are not protected by a trade union, the employer may have considerable influence over them through his control over the distribution of jobs and favours, over promotion and even over dismissal. White collar employees are especially vulnerable to fear of being passed over for promotion. This can affect union recruitment and canvassing support for the union before a ballot, if not the ballot itself; and, even then, employees may not be absolutely convinced of its secrecy.

These differences of opinion are not new, but they did not command much attention so long as recognition disputes were left to the parties to settle. They acquired a novel importance with the Donovan Commission's proposal for a statutory recognition procedure. In the view of the Donovan Commission 'collective bargaining is the best method of conducting industrial relations' and,

> since collective bargaining depends on the existence, strength and recognition of trade unions, the test in dealing with any dispute over recognition—other than a dispute between unions over recognition—should be whether the union or unions in question can reasonably be expected to develop and sustain adequate representation for the purpose of collective bargaining among workers in the company or factory concerned, or among a distinct section of those workers. A ballot may be useful in applying the test, but could rarely determine the issue by itself.[25]

On this view, the test is not what the majority wants, but whether the union can sustain effective collective bargaining. Majority support for collective bargaining before recognition has been granted is of help in achieving that end, but it is not a necessary condition of successful collective bargaining. The Donovan Commission's reasoning provides the justification for the question asked of non-unionists by the Service (and by the Commission on Industrial Relations before it): whether they would join the union if it was recognized by the company. Such a hypothetical question may be irrelevant to eliciting the wishes of employees for and against collective bargaining, but it is relevant to the prospects for the success of collective bargaining once the union is recognized.

Behind the differences of opinion over recognition which are commonly found between employers and trade unions lies another which is less frequently brought into the open. Many employers

---

[25] *Report*, p. 50.

concerned in recognition disputes show by their words and behaviour that they believe they have a right to share in determining the matter—a right to make up their minds whether recognition would be in the interest of their employees, a right to say whether the union should have access to the employees to put its case, and a right to settle the conditions under which the opinions of their employees should be elicited, and what questions should be asked. Trade unions admit that the employer may have the power to determine some or all of these things, but they deny that he has any moral right to do so; morally, it is not his business.

There is one point on which many employers believe theirs are the only opinions which count, and that is the bargaining group. If an employer has standard terms and conditions of employment throughout his company, then, they assert, recognition must be company-wide if there is to be recognition at all; if he chooses to treat all the employees within the plant—manual, white collar and managerial—as a single group, then they must be a single group for the purpose of collective bargaining. For their part, trade unions might allow that this was a matter on which the employer's opinion should be heard; but equal or greater weight should be given to their own views. It is illogical, they would argue, that the first step in a collective bargaining relationship should be a unilateral decision by the employer; and in many instances, they would add, the employer's choice of group is designed to frustrate the union's claim to recognition by gerrymandering a majority against it.

Substantial differences exist between the Trades Union Congress and the Confederation of British Industry over the criteria for settling recognition disputes. Congress's approach is much the same as that of the Donovan report. The Confederation's position was put to their first national conference in November 1977. It contained four points. The first was that 'the overriding purpose of any ACAS recommendation will be to improve industrial relations', so that the Service's duty to extend collective bargaining must take second place. The second was that 'account will be taken of the size and structure of the company, its personnel policies and the need to avoid the fragmentation of bargaining units', so that the choice of bargaining unit is to be guided by the employer's existing organization and policy, decided before recognition. The third was that 'an indication will be given of what number or proportion of those employees who want a union to represent them and of those who are already in union membership that will be regarded as significant', so that the decision is not to be taken solely on the evidence concerning the prospects for effective collective bargaining in the particular case. The fourth and final point was that 'no hypothetical questions will be asked in any survey of employee attitudes', so as to get rid of the question to non-unionists asking them whether they will join the union if it is recognized.[26]

With these wide differences in approach between Congress and the Confederation, it seems unlikely that the Service will be able to issue a code of practice on trade union recognition for some time to come. However, the conflict over recognition should not be seen primarily as one between organized workers and organized employers. After all, trade unions, employers' associations, and most large companies in Britain all support collective bargaining, which depends on trade union recognition. Their differences on the subject can hardly be fundamental. But there are other views. A great many people in Britain resent the developments in labour legislation and labour policy over recent years. They see the country, and especially the small employer, as overburdened with Acts, regulations, and form-filling concerning employment. Much of it appears to them to derive from legislation imposed by the trade unions under the social contract. With short memories, they see incomes policy as a socialistic device for curtailing the rewards of enterprise and hard work, again arising from the social contract. They resent the growing power of unions in the workplace, as well as in Whitehall and Westminster, and they attribute to it much of Britain's poor economic performance. In short, most of their troubles are due to the unions. The Grunwick dispute presented them with a symbol of their grievances, for here was a bureaucratic agency, bent on using its powers to impose trade unionism on an enterprising and profitable small firm, whose managers and workers were at one in wishing to have nothing to do with it. Sentiments of this kind permitted Mr Ward of Grunwick to become a hero for many people, and may have pushed the Confederation towards hard-line attitudes on the criteria required for trade union recognition which many of its members might have preferred to avoid.

Nevertheless, it should not be imagined that every statutory reference on trade union recognition is a battle ground for conflicting views. Of the 1,038 references made to the Service up to the end of

[26] Confederation of British Industry, *Britain Means Business 1977*, p. 34.

1977, about 40 per cent (408) were settled voluntarily. In more than half of these there had been an agreement on recognition: 178 giving full recognition, and 35 either partial recognition or representation rights. In twelve cases the application was withdrawn to allow further negotiations on recognition between the parties. A further 183 applications had been withdrawn by the unions, 122 of them because their membership had been found to be low. Some of the settlements and withdrawals had occurred during the conciliation or inquiry stage of the Service's work, and some of them as a result of the draft report which the Service always issues to the parties. Only 92 references had reached the stage of a final report.[27] Recognition had not been recommended in 21 of these; and in 71 cases the recommendation had been for recognition. In eight of these full recognition had been granted and in five more of them recognition was still under discussion. In some of the remainder the employer had lodged an application under section 13 of the Act which permits either party to seek a variation or revocation of a recommendation on the grounds that 'circumstances have changed or further information has become available'; and in others the unions had lodged formal complaints that the employer was not complying with the recommendation. Two of them had reached the Central Arbitration Committee which had upheld both of them. However, the committee had not issued awards which were likely to put pressure on the employer to recognize. The first was a case in which the Service had recommended recognition in one unit of a multi-plant company, for the purpose of bargaining over matters which were within the discretion of the unit manager. The union claimed an improvement in shift allowances which was not awarded because they were not within his discretion.[28] In the second case the union asked the committee to award an amendment to the terms of the contracts of employment of the workers concerned to include the recognition of the union to bargain on their behalf. The committee, 'whilst sympathetic to the view of the Union', held that they had no power to do so.[29] Subsequent cases have not shown any greater inclination on the part of the committee to issue 'penal' awards against employers who fail to carry out recommendations to recognize.

These figures indicate, as might have been expected, that it is the difficult cases which reach the stage of a final report. So far the total

[27] Advisory Conciliation and Arbitration Service, *Annual Report*, 1977, p. 76.
[28] Award No. 189.　　　　　　　　[29] Award No. 272.

number of employees covered by final reports is little more than twenty thousand. It is debatable whether that outcome is worth the bitter social conflict which has arisen around the operation of the statutory recognition procedure.

CONCILIATION, ARBITRATION AND INQUIRY

In contrast to statutory recognition references, there are other aspects of the Service's work in which they have undoubtedly been successful. One of them is the traditional task of supporting collective bargaining by conciliation, arbitration and inquiry. The annual number of requests for voluntary conciliation in industrial disputes has grown from about a thousand in 1973 to well over three thousand in both 1976 and 1977, and there has been an even larger increase in the cases referred to arbitration or mediation. In 1973 the figure was fifty-four, compared with 323 in 1976 and 327 in 1977. It is not possible to make a similar comparison for advisory work because, prior to the establishment of the Service, this was split between the Commission and the Department and because statistics were not then kept in the same form as they are now; but there is no doubt that there has been a considerable increase here as well. In 1977 the number of 'short advisory visits', many of them to explain the new legislation which had recently come into force, was not far short of nine thousand, and the number of 'diagnostic surveys' and 'advisory projects' came to over two hundred and fifty.

Conciliation and advisory work is carried out by the staff of the Service. The great majority of them work from one or other of the nine regional offices; but conciliation in national disputes is carried out from head office which also provides teams to undertake long-term inquiries into industrial relations problems in major companies or industries. In 1976, for example, the Service conducted an inquiry into industrial relations in the printing industry at the request of the Royal Commission on the Press.

The staff of the Service arrange for arbitration where that is the wish of the parties, but the arbitrators are drawn from outside the Service, from lists of suitable persons kept by the Service. The majority of cases are heard by single arbitrators, but in about 10–15 per cent of them the parties prefer a board of arbitration with three members—a chairman and one member nominated by each of the two sides. Alternatively cases can be referred to the Central Arbitration Committee. In some disputes in which parties are not prepared to accept the moral commitment to abide by the award which is implicit in a reference to arbitration, they are nevertheless prepared to accept a mediator (also from outside the Service) who tries to find an agreed solution, and, if he fails, normally makes a recommendation which the parties are not committed to accept. In 1977 the Service appointed 27 mediators, and four boards of mediation. Finally, an alternative to an inquiry by the Service is the appointment of an ad hoc court or committee of investigation where that is more acceptable to the parties, but so far this device has been used sparingly. In 1976 a committee of inquiry was appointed to investigate industrial relations in the London Fire Service, and in 1978 another investigated a bus dispute in Leeds.

The rapid growth in the Service's business should probably be attributed to the fact that the parties are more committed to it than they were to the departmental service. This is particularly true of the trade unions from whom the majority of references come. In 1977 the unions initiated 54 per cent of voluntary conciliation cases compared with 20 per cent from employers and 23 per cent of joint applications. (The remaining 3 per cent were initiated by the Service itself.) Since the Service was established, full-time officers in some unions have been under instructions to refer disputes to the Service before any question of industrial action can be considered. However, the continued increase in references in 1976 and the maintenance of the 1976 total in 1977 suggest that, in addition to their original commitment, the unions were reasonably satisfied with the service they received. The same inference may be made about the employers, since the number of employer references and joint references have kept pace with the increase in union references.

In 1976 the Service reported that 'conciliated settlements were reached or arrangements to make progress towards a settlement were agreed between the parties' in 74 per cent of the conciliation cases.[30] But it would be necessary to establish what would be an appropriate standard before that figure could be rated a success or a failure. The increased usage of conciliation is therefore probably the best test of the performance of the Service.

More information is available about arbitration, for in 1976 the Council instituted a study of thirty arbitration cases. 'In all cases the

[30] Advisory Conciliation and Arbitration Service, *Annual Report*, 1977, p. 9.

awards had been accepted and implemented and the parties stated that they would be prepared to use arbitration again. In two-thirds of the cases the parties agreed that arbitration had resolved the dispute to their mutual satisfaction.'[31]

Although requests for information on current legislation owe more to the productivity of parliament than the excellence of the Service, continued requests for assistance with procedures, payment systems, job evaluation, labour turnover, and similar matters may be taken as some indication of consumer satisfaction. But in this branch of the Service's activities the number of visits or projects is not an adequate measure of consumer demand. The Service must deal with the individual complaints and collective disputes referred to it, and the growth of those aspects of their work necessarily limits their ability to handle requests for advice and information, at least until new staff is recruited and trained to deal with them. The volume of advisory work might have risen faster if the demand for conciliation had grown less rapidly.

One interesting feature of the growth of the Service's collective conciliation and arbitration is that it has taken place during a period of strict incomes policy. It might have been supposed that there would not be much to dispute about at such a time. Table 13 sets out completed conciliation cases referred to arbitration in 1975 and 1977 according to the issue in dispute. It shows that not far short of half of conciliation cases concerned issues which have no direct relevance to pay or terms and conditions of service, whereas about four-fifths of arbitration cases dealt with these issues. Moreover, the Service divides the pay disputes referred to arbitration into general pay claims and others. In 1975, with five months of incomes policy, general pay claims accounted for 36 per cent of all pay claims, whereas in 1976, with continuous incomes policy, they had fallen to 7 per cent. Incomes policy, therefore, had a pronounced effect on the disputes coming to arbitration, and presumably also to conciliation; but the number of disputes over other pay issues and other terms of employment rose to compensate for the shortfall in general pay claim disputes. It seems that when trade unionists are prevented from bargaining about general pay increases they look for other issues on which to base a claim.

It might also have been supposed that doubts about the independence of the Service under a government incomes policy would have

[31] Advisory Conciliation and Arbitration Service, *Annual Report*, 1976, pp. 16–17.

Table 13

*Conciliation and Arbitration Cases
Handled by the Advisory Conciliation and
Arbitration Service in 1975 and 1977, Analysed
by Issue in Dispute*[32]

Cause of Dispute	Completed Conciliation Cases		Cases Referred to Arbitration Mediation and Investigation	
	1975 (%)	1977 (%)	1975 (%)	1977 (%)
General Pay Claim	57	55.4	29.1	5.2
Other Pay Matters and Terms and Conditions of Employment			50.0	71.2
Recognition	21	22.0	1.0	–
Demarcation	1	1.1	1.3	2.1
Other Trade Union Matters	2.5	4.9	1.3	1.5
Redundancy	5	4.6	0.3	1.2
Dismissal and Discipline	10	8.3	15.0	14.0
Others	3.5	3.7	2.0	4.8

curtailed demand for their assistance. It is, after all, staffed by civil servants. In fact there is no evidence of a decline in demand, nor of a loss of confidence in the independence of the Service. The Service's decision that it was not their job to interpret or enforce the policy (although they would enquire whether the parties had taken it into account)[33] apparently convinced unions and employers that the Service was making its own decisions, and was not subject to government dictation.

Another interesting feature of collective conciliation under the Service is that the problem of conciliation in unofficial strikes, which seemed to be a severe restriction on the work of the Department's service at the time of the Donovan Commission, has now disappeared without trace. This is not because the volume of unofficial strikes has notably diminished, nor because the Service has taken a radically new approach to the problem . It seems to reflect a change in trade union attitudes to unofficial strikes. It is now rare for such

[32] Advisory Conciliation and Arbitration Service, *Annual Reports*, 1976 and 1977.
[33] See footnote, p. 364.

strikes to be regarded as set-piece battles between the official union leaders and subversive malcontents; instead they are seen as a natural and inevitable aspect of trade union behaviour. The union leaders are anxious for them to be settled and therefore ready to welcome the help of the Service.

WAGES COUNCILS AND LOW PAY

Another traditional function of the state in industrial relations is to supplement collective bargaining by establishing wages councils. Following criticism of wages councils in the Donovan report and in several reports of the National Board for Prices and Incomes, both the Industrial Relations Act and the Employment Protection Act made new arrangements for their review and abolition. Under the Industrial Relations Act the responsibility for review was entrusted to the Commission on Industrial Relations, and it now rests with the Service.

Together with the Donovan report itself, these changes appear to have had some effect. Ten wages councils were abolished in the twenty-four years from 1945 to 1968. In total they covered about four hundred thousand employees at the time of their abolition. Over the ten years following the Donovan report, the number of councils abolished rose to fourteen, covering over six hundred thousand employees. Five of them were abolished following reports of the Commission on Industrial Relations; one, the Road Haulage Wages Council, following a report by the Service; and another, the Industrial Catering Council, following a report by a Commission of Inquiry, appointed shortly before the Service had acquired statutory responsibility in this area, which included two members of the Council of the Service.

Most councils have given way to industry-wide voluntary bargaining bodies which had been established in the industries for which they were responsible. A few of them have been replaced by the agreements of another major industry into which they have been absorbed. The engineering industry's agreement had, for example, come to be accepted in most of the plants covered by the Stamped or Pressed Metal-Wares Wages Council, and provided the grounds for its abolition in 1974.[34] By contrast the Road Haulage Wages Council

[34] Commission on Industrial Relations, *Stamped or Pressed Metal-Wares Wages Council.*

made way for regional agreements. The employers had argued the need to maintain the council in order to have some national machinery for the settlement of pay which, they said, was needed 'to prevent leapfrogging of wage claims, between individual employers or between regions'. The Service were not impressed, for they could find no evidence that the council had this effect, but they recognized 'a need in what is a national industry for a forum wherein matters of common interest to all parties concerned in the functioning of the industry could be discussed'. They also noted that most of the regional agreements were thin on procedural arrangements and hoped that they would soon 'be extended by the inclusion of suitable procedures which strengthen them as collective bargaining arrangements'. However, the continuation of the council would not have done anything to meet these needs.[35]

Industrial catering provided a more complex problem. The Commission on Industrial Relations reviewed the operations of its council in 1972. The majority of the workers in the scope of the council were directly employed by the undertakings for which they catered, but just over a quarter were employed by catering contractors. Nearly two-thirds of the workers in directly-run units were covered by collective bargaining arrangements of one sort or another: some by industry agreements which provided 'a special rate for catering workers or they may be covered by a rate for general or auxiliary workers'; and some by a company agreement which included specific provision for catering workers or dealt with catering workers alone. Agreements of this kind might also be extended to cover a contractor's staff; otherwise some catering contractors had their own agreements with the unions. Altogether about 48 per cent of contractors' employees were covered by collective agreements.[36] Since some form of industrial catering is to be found in almost every sizable industry and service in the country, the consequence is that industrial catering employees come under a uniquely numerous and varied collection of agreements. The Commission found that 'the median rate paid in the industry in the London area is almost 75 per cent higher than the statutory minimum rate and in other areas is almost 50 per cent higher'. They also found that instances of under-

[35] Advisory Conciliation and Arbitration Service, *Road Haulage Wages Council*, pp. 47–9.
[36] Commission on Industrial Relations, *Industrial Catering*, p. 5.

payment were relatively rare. For these reasons they decided that there was 'a strong case for abolition'.[37]

Because of objections by the employers a further Commission of Inquiry was needed before action could be taken. The unions 'were strongly opposed to retaining the Council'. The chairman of the council thought that it was 'a ritualistic and inefficient way of establishing minimum rates', but 'felt that the position of the vulnerable minority must be safeguarded'—perhaps by a national minimum rate for all catering workers. The Low Pay Unit also gave evidence and argued that the council 'should continue for the time being to provide . . . protection for the lower paid, whose position would deteriorate still further if the Council were abolished'. Finally, the employers believed that abolition might lead to

a danger of wage cutting and consequential lowering of standards in the industry. Given the nature of industrial catering there was no central body that could replace the Council on an industry-wide basis. A significant minority of workers would be left without any protection.[38]

The Commission had no authority to propose a minimum wage for all catering workers, and there was general agreement that there was no satisfactory way of 'excluding those areas of the industry in which collective bargaining is relatively well developed, while retaining the protection of the Council for employees in the remainder of the industry'.[39] The choice was therefore between retention or total abolition. The Commission believed that there were good prospects for a further extension of collective bargaining in directly-run units. In the contracting sector the employers were strongly organized by the catering advisory panel of the British Hotels Restaurants and Caterers Association. The Commission suggested that the panel had it within their power to maintain the centralized regulation of pay which they said they wanted, by establishing negotiating machinery with the unions. They therefore decided for abolition.

There now remain three main groups of wages councils. One of them is a manufacturing industry, clothing, with nine separate coun-

---

[37] *Ibid.*, pp. 9, 14.
[38] *Report of the Commission of Inquiry on the Draft Order to abolish the Industrial and Staff Canteen Undertakings Wages Council*, pp. 11–18.
[39] *Ibid.*, p. 22.

cils for different sections of the industry. They were investigated by
the National Board for Prices and Incomes in 1969. The board found
that collective agreements covered much of the industry, and that the
councils were mainly bodies for endorsing these agreements and
enforcing them on unfederated employers. They recommended a
phased programme of abolition over the next four years, starting
with the most strongly organized sections of the industry.[40] The
Tailors and Garment Workers, however, did not accept the recommendation. Like the employers, they were afraid that in this fiercely
competitive industry the withdrawal of statutory minimum rates
would lead to rate-cutting which would ultimately undermine standards even in the larger and well-organized undertakings. With both
union and employers in favour of retaining the councils, nothing has
been done, although the rapid decline in the industry's labour
force—from about 440,000 at the time of the board's report to little
more than three hundred thousand today—has been accompanied by
a substantial rise in trade union density, so that the case for retention
must be weaker now than it was in 1969. On the other hand the case
for abolition may not be strong. Provided that there is no great harm
in using wages councils as rubber stamps, there may be a positive
advantage in giving statutory force to the industry's voluntary
agreements in this way if the view of the two sides on the effect of
competition is correct. There would be a disadvantage in retention if
it impeded the further growth of collective bargaining as the
National Board for Prices and Incomes feared. In their view collective bargaining at plant level

> outside a few large firms is non-existent. . . . In the present situa-
> tion the workers have no effective voice in the establishment of
> payment systems, wages structures and conditions of work.
> Normally the only course open to workers who fail to obtain
> redress for their grievances is to leave their jobs and go else-
> where. . . . Shop stewards, where they exist at all, . . . are often
> merely collectors of union subscriptions.[41]

But the growth in union density suggests that the situation is changing.

The largest of the three groups of wages councils is in retail

[40] National Board for Prices and Incomes, *Pay and Conditions in the Clothing
Manufacturing Industries*, chapter 6.
[41] *Ibid.*, pp. 17–18.

distribution. The Commission on Industrial Relations reported on them in 1974.[42] They found encouraging developments in collective bargaining. A few years before, the main coverage had been provided by the co-operative society agreement and 'trade' agreements with groups of multiple shops. In 1968 the multiple tailors' agreement was terminated and replaced by company agreements with individual undertakings, and other trades began to follow their example. By 1974 about a third of the employees within the scope of the councils were covered by collective agreements of one sort or another. Almost three-quarters of these employees were under company agreements (although some of them were also subject to trade agreements). Most of the trade agreements provided rates which were only marginally above the statutory rates, and only the co-operative agreement included a grievance procedure, whereas most company agreements set rates 20 to 30 per cent above the statutory rates, and frequently included long-service pay, increments, pensions, recognition, facilities for workplace representatives, and the check-off; all of them contained grievance procedures. Since pay was nevertheless relatively low, no one suggested that the wages councils could be abolished. However, the evidence was that the existing councils established trade by trade (drapery, furnishing, food, newsagents, etc.) no longer fitted the organization of the industry, and the Union of Shop Distributive and Allied Workers suggested that the nine existing councils should be amalgamated into two councils, one for durable goods and the other for non-durables. The Commission itself favoured one council for the whole of the retailing trades. After further examination and a reference to the Service, the union's proposal was accepted, and there are now two retail wages councils. The Commission on Industrial Relations felt that it would be unwise to exclude the sectors of the industry in which collective bargaining was relatively well-developed from the scope of the statutory machinery, but, since company bargaining is continuing to develop, the councils' job will more and more be to look after employees in small shops whose interest and concerns may diverge considerably from those of workers in the larger undertakings.

The third group is hotels and catering, now excluding industrial catering. Here the only development in collective bargaining which the Commission could report was the start of a move from a

[42] Commission on Industrial Relations, *Retail Distribution*.

national agreement for public house managers to company agreements with individual brewing companies. Otherwise in pubs and clubs there was little organization and actual pay was closely influenced by the statutory rates. In hotels and restaurants the minimum rates 'were said to have little direct relevance', but 'unit management is granted a great deal of autonomy in establishing individual wage rates in hotels'; staff answered questions concerning their working hours 'with a great deal of uncertainty'; and the proceeds of service charges (which were taking the place of tips) were distributed at the discretion of the manager. [43] The main obstacle to the development of collective bargaining appeared to be the shortcomings of the unions since most workers who were surveyed did not know there was a union for hotel workers, or could not name it; and about half said they would join a union if invited. The Commission reported that 'in the past, trade union growth in hotels, albeit on a very small scale, has come about mainly through the use of industrial action'; but they did not draw the obvious moral. [44] They could not suggest any change in the catering wages councils—aside from industrial catering—which would promise improvements, and their recommendations were pious rather than practical. Nevertheless it appears that there has been a fairly rapid growth in trade union membership and recognition in hotels during 1977 and 1978. [45]

In 1978 a report by the Service on the Button Manufacturing Wages Council drew attention to another important problem. They found that collective bargaining had developed sufficiently to make the council unnecessary for factory employees, but there were also homeworkers who were in serious need of protection. They recommended that the scope of the council should be changed accordingly. [46] There are, however, only a few hundred homeworking buttonmakers, whereas the best available estimate of the total number of homeworkers in the country is at least a quarter of a million. [47] Scattered evidence suggests that they are generally badly paid, and almost universally without trade union protection. Some of them come within the scope of wages councils, but the machinery of the councils and the wages inspectorate is not suited to their needs;

[43] Commission on Industrial Relations, *Hotels and Restaurants*, pp. 22–5.
[44] *Ibid.*, pp. 40–1.
[45] *Industrial Relations Review and Report*, No. 179, July 1978.
[46] Advisory Conciliation and Arbitration Service, *Button Manufacturing Wages Council*.
[47] Marie Brown, *Sweated Labour: A Study of Homework*, p. 3.

and the statutory arrangements for local authority inspection are woefully inadequate.

In 1977 the number of workers in wages councils industries to whom arrears were paid as a result of inspection (26,920) was about 60 per cent higher than in 1964, although the number of workers covered by councils had declined. The amount of arrears (£1,588,248) was ten times higher than in 1964, and more than double the 1964 figure when inflation is taken into account. These figures may indicate that the inspectorate is more effective than it was. In 1976 a programme of 'saturation' inspections was introduced to give greater publicity to their work, and eleven towns were included in the programme for 1977.[48] But the figures demonstrate that there is still a considerable problem of underpayment.

This brief survey suggests that, unless the Tailors and Garment Workers change their minds on the value of the clothing councils, the rate of abolition of wages councils is likely to fall off. It follows that wages councils may be less effective means of encouraging the development of collective bargaining in the industries now covered by councils than they were in industries where councils have been abolished; and the evidence also indicates that there are many workers both inside and outside wages councils who need protection which the councils are not appropriately constructed to provide. There is need therefore for alternative means of protecting the low-paid and ill-organized.

One possible alternative is a national minimum wage such as exists in the United States, France and other countries. In 1969 a report issued by the Department of Employment drew attention to a number of disadvantages of such an arrangement. It would involve a considerable administration burden. It would be necessary to decide whether the minimum should apply on an hourly or weekly basis, whether or not overtime earnings should be included, and whether the minimum should apply to rates or earnings. The cost of applying the same minimum to men and women would be considerable (and that remains true even after the Equal Pay Act); and the cost would also be affected by the attitude of higher-paid workers to the maintenance of their differentials. 'The higher the level of the minimum at its introduction, the greater the risk seems of its setting off pressures for the maintenance of differentials.'[49] The social contract would

---

[48] *Department of Employment Gazette*, May 1978.
[49] *A National Minimum Wage (Report of an Inter-Departmental Working Party)*, p. 53.

have provided an ideal opportunity for introducing a national minimum wage if the unions had wanted it.

The Employment Protection Act introduced a number of changes in the constitution and powers of wages councils. Workers' and employers' representatives are now appointed directly by unions and employers' associations. Councils can now settle any terms and conditions of employment. They no longer submit proposals to the Secretary of State for him to embody in an order; they make their own orders, and they can backdate application to the date on which they made the original decision (i.e. before giving notice and considering representations). However, these alterations do not seem likely to affect the ability of the councils to fulfil their main objectives, and they certainly have not done so yet.

The Act also created a new institution—the Statutory Joint Industrial Council. This may be briefly described as a wages council without the independent members. In other words it is closely akin to a voluntary collective bargaining body whose agreements are enforceable, but with one important difference. Where the two sides of such a council cannot reach agreement, and conciliation fails, the dispute must be submitted to binding arbitration. No such council has yet been set up. It is available only to industries which currently have wages councils, and in an industry in which the union or unions have advanced so far as to be able to dispense with the independent members on their wages councils they may not want to commit themselves to submit to compulsory and binding arbitration.

Still another provision of the Act was represented as a remedy for low pay. This was schedule 11, which took the place of the Terms and Conditions of Employment Act 1959. Part I of the schedule repeats and redefines the entitlement of workers to claim that the provisions of relevant industry or district collective agreements should be applied to them even though their employer is not a party to the agreements; but it then goes on to create a new entitlement, 'where, or so far as, there are no recognised terms and conditions', to claim the 'general level of terms and conditions' applied in companies in the same industry, in the same district and in similar circumstances. These provisions appear to do no more than extend to all employees an entitlement which the fair wages resolution gave to the employees of government contractors long ago. But there is an important difference. The fair wages resolution does not give the workers who are not employed by government contractors the right to claim the terms and conditions of the contractors, so that the improvements which come out of the application of the resolution do not raise the standard of comparison. But, under the Act, everyone is entitled to claim the general level of terms and conditions wherever there are no recognized conditions, and an improvement for one group of employees affects the general level for the next group of employees who make use of the schedule; and so on. This may not be of much significance among manual workers, the majority of whom are covered by recognized terms and cannot therefore use the 'general level' provision—although many employees in wages council industries are entitled to do so; but it is of much greater interest to white collar workers in private employment, for there are few industry or district agreements to provide them with recognized terms. Consequently employers feared that the schedule would lead to endless leapfrogging claims from groups of white collar employees.

The new schedule brought a sharp increase in the workload of the Central Arbitration Committee. The procedure is for claims to be referred to the Service. They take what steps seem convenient to settle the claim, but by conciliation only. They do not make recommendations as with statutory recognition references. If conciliation fails, the claim goes back to the committee for arbitration. In 1976 the committee received 132 references for arbitration, 54 of them arising under the Terms and Conditions of Employment Act; in 1977 there were 1,030 references, 742 of them under schedule 11, and 230 under the fair wages resolution.[50] To cope with rising business, a number of additional vice-chairmen and members were appointed to the committee so that it could sit in several divisions. However, since the schedule presents a number of novel issues and since there is no superior tribunal of appeal—except on matters of law—these administrative changes add to the task of securing uniformity in the committee's decisions.

The first year's experience of schedule 11 is not an adequate guide to what may happen in the future. Once the structure of the committee's decisions is established, it is possible that fewer claims will come forward, and more of them will be settled by the Service, which will be able to give firmer guidance on the awards which the committee had made on similar claims. Furthermore, schedule 11 has so far operated under the social contract, and awards of the committee

[50] Central Arbitration Committee, *Annual Reports*, 1976 and 1977.

under schedule 11 and under the fair wages resolution are not required to conform to the limits laid down for pay increases by the contract, or since July 1977 by the government. Many of the claims reported under the schedule and the resolution have been intended to beat the pay policy, and would not have arisen under other circumstances. In a considerable proportion of them unions and employers are effectively in collusion.

It is too early to attempt any assessment of the economic impact of schedule 11 or of its effect on low pay; but it is already evident that awards issued under the schedule are not confined to raising the relative pay of low-paid employees as those words are normally interpreted. Awards have been issued in favour of skilled workers as well as unskilled, and of managerial staff as well as clerical workers. It is true that, if their case is to succeed, the terms and conditions of the employees concerned, taken as a whole, must be less favourable than the general level *for that class of employee*; but in principle the schedule is as applicable to professors and judges as to farmworkers and cleaners.

Part II of the schedule allows an independent trade union to report a claim to the Service, on behalf of one or more members employed within the scope of the wages council, for 'the lowest current rate of remuneration' paid under a collective agreement covering 'a significant number of establishments within' the council's 'field of operation'. During 1977 seven such claims were reported.

LEGISLATION UNDER THE SOCIAL CONTRACT: A PRELIMINARY ASSESSMENT

Legislation under the social contract has already proved itself more durable than the Industrial Relations Act. Some of it has lasted longer than that Act did, and there is no evidence that a future Conservative government will sweep it away, whereas it was clear long before 1974 that the Industrial Relations Act was doomed under a Labour Government. It has already achieved substantial results. The services of the Advisory Conciliation and Arbitration Service are in demand as those of the former departmental service never were; the statutory procedure for trade union recognition has been widely used and has led to the recognition of trade unions, or rights of representation, in almost half of the cases which have so far been completed; there is now widespread bargaining over occupational pensions; women's pay has increased relative to men's pay (although under an Act passed in 1970); schedule 11 of the Employment Protection Act has brought a spate of claims for increases in pay to bring workers up to the 'general level'; and the number of employees entitled to compensation for unfair dismissal has been greatly increased.

On the other hand the authors of the Act have several grounds for disappointment. Despite their amendments to the law on unfair dismissal intended to give greater security of employment, it continues, with rare exceptions, to be a means of providing compensation for those who establish that they have been unfairly dismissed. Equal pay apart, new legislation on discrimination in employment has so far proved pitifully inadequate. Changes in the law on wages councils have made no more than a modest contribution to the problems of low pay and lack of collective bargaining in the industries concerned. The widespread use of schedule 11 is due to the loophole which it provides through incomes policy, and not to its efficacy as a means of aiding the low-paid.

Above all, the only one among the new rights which has been seriously tested, the statutory procedure for trade union recognition, has brought a series of court cases which have interpreted the law in ways which have astounded the authors of the social contract and threaten to constrict the discretion of the Advisory Conciliation and Arbitration Service within narrow limits. If it is upheld, the decision in the Allen case could undermine established machinery of collective bargaining in a number of industries. Moreover, the certification of independent unions has not yielded the benefits that the unions expected, and the closed shop has become a subject for judicial definition.

Finally, the Donovan Commission, to whom a number of these reforms can be traced, envisaged a far-reaching reform of the structures and procedures of collective bargaining, especially in private industry, which they expected to lead to substantial changes in the pattern of strikes and in manpower utilization. The Commission on Industrial Relations was charged with the task and set about it energetically, although it was soon hampered by incorporation in the Industrial Relations Act. Its responsibilities, along with some of its staff, were inherited by the Advisory Conciliation and Arbitration Service, but for the Service this was only one among a wide range of duties. By this time, moreover, the reform of plant bargaining recommended by the Donovan report had to a considerable extent been carried through by the spread of plant-wide pay agreements and procedures, although the consequential changes sought by the Commission had been by no means fully realized.

The Service's achievements must be judged in the light of these developments. They have handled a large volume of advisory work and investigations, many of which have led to changes in industrial relations procedures and practices, but the great majority of these assignments have been concerned with improving industrial relations performance to an acceptable standard rather than introducing novel and sweeping reforms. Perhaps that is what is required at this stage. Alternatively British industrial relations may still be in need of reform, on a different plane to that of the Donovan recommendations, and the Service has so far failed to grasp what is required. But, if that is so, no one has yet told the Service what it should be doing.

It is, of course, far too soon to venture a definitive judgement on the social contract legislation, but if the balance had to be struck at this point, it would not necessarily be favourable. That may or may not be surprising, but what really requires explanation is why, with their traditional distrust of the law, British trade unions had ever expected anything different. They inherited the belief that, outside the provision of certain minimum standards of safety and health, of minimum rates of pay in low-paid industries, and of optional services of conciliation and arbitration, the proper task of labour legislation was to minimize the jurisdiction of the courts in trade disputes, trade union affairs, and collective bargaining. It is in accordance with this inheritance that the unions should have recreated and strengthened their traditional immunities when they got rid of the Industrial Relations Act; but why did they suppose there was no risk in going on to legislate extensively, not only on individual employment rights, but also to create new rights for trade unionists and trade unions which open up large areas of trade union action to judicial interpretation?

One reason is the changing composition of the trade union movement. The source of uncompromising opposition to further legal intervention was in the unions dominated by skilled manual workers, notably the Engineers. In their evidence to the Donovan Commission, the general unions and many white collar unions showed that they believed they could gain from an extension of labour law, for example into support for trade union recognition, and into protection of workers from unfair dismissal; and their combined membership now accounts for a majority of votes at the Trades Union Congress. But there is also another explanation.

Part of it lies in the nature of the social contract itself. The leaders of the Labour party wanted the unions to commit themselves to support the economic policies of a future Labour government, including an agreed policy on pay, and they offered the unions *carte blanche* to write their own labour laws. The General Council were anxious to help the Labour party. Accordingly they tried to win the support of their members for the contract by convincing them that it was to their advantage. They therefore took up the party's offer on labour legislation. All were agreed that the Industrial Relations Act must go, but they also wanted new legislation. Any suggestion was welcome; the time for critical review could come later when they were discussing draft legislation with a Labour government. In this way there emerged the proposals set out in the *Annual Report* of Congress for 1974.[51]

The second part of the explanation lies in the reception of the General Council's proposals by the new Secretary of State in 1974. With minor exceptions, he welcomed them so warmly that a search began for even more suggestions to add to the list, and a few were found, for example on wages councils. There was no detailed and searching scrutiny of the merits or practicability of the proposals.

The third part of the explanation lies in the drafting. The General Council has good legal advice, but at this time their advisers were mainly concerned with the Trade Union and Labour Relations Act and the subsequent amending Act. Consequently the Employment Protection Bill lacked sufficient attention from go-betweens who understood both the intentions of the authors of the Act and the language of the parliamentary draftsmen.

It is only fair to add that trade union leaders were not alone in finding their expectations confounded. The recommendations of the Donovan Commission on trade union recognition were closely followed by the authors of the Employment Protection Act. The Commission said of them that 'they avoid the difficulty of detailed intervention by the courts in the processes of industrial relations which appear to us to be a consequence of enforcing recognition by law as in the USA'.[52] It should be added that, besides a judge as

[51] pp. 74–80.   [52] *Report*, p. 65.

chairman, the Commission included an eminent solicitor, a Q.C., and the world's most eminent labour lawyer.

INDUSTRIAL DEMOCRACY

One major item in the social contract's programme of labour legislation has not yet found its way into an Act, or even into a draft of a bill. It is the proposal that legislation should provide for the introduction of supervisory boards in British companies employing more than a given number of workers and for half of their members to be trade union nominees.

This proposal is the consequence of a remarkable reversal in the attitude of the Trades Union Congress. Until recently British trade unions had never favoured trade union representation on company boards. For a period between the wars Congress was committed to a proposal that half the members of the boards of nationalized industries should be appointed by the unions, but this demand had been abandoned by the time the postwar Labour government set about implementing its programme of nationalization. However, in their evidence to the Donovan Commission the General Council suggested that there should be experiments in trade union representation on company boards. Further changes followed in 1972, when Britain was in the process of joining the European Community and the Commission of the Community published draft proposals for a 'fifth directive' on company law. All companies with over five hundred employees were to have supervisory boards with one-third of their members representing employees; they were also to have works councils elected to represent all the workers. It therefore seemed inevitable that the General Council would soon face a proposal for legislation on these lines in Britain, and they had to consider their response. They were certainly not in favour of the proposals as they stood, but a blank rejection seemed politically unwise. Those who favoured worker representation on boards, including Jack Jones, therefore had an opportunity to persuade the council to counter the proposals with a far more radical plan of their own, rejecting workers' councils outright, demanding half the seats on the supervisory boards and insisting that the employee representatives should be chosen by the unions. It seemed certain that the Heath administration would find this plan wholly unacceptable, and, perhaps lightheartedly, Congress in September 1973 approved the General Council's report on *Industrial Democracy* which embodied these proposals. It also reverted to the interwar demand that half the members of the boards of nationalized industries should be trade union nominees; and included a number of suggestions for extending and enriching collective bargaining. A year later the debate was more serious. By now a Labour government was in office, committed to the social contract which included a proposal for legislation on Congress's scheme for industrial democracy. Two propositions were before the delegates. The General Council's report, presented as an interim document the year before, was now put forward, with a few amendments, for confirmation; but there was also a resolution, which might well have been read as a wrecking amendment, supported by the Engineers, the General and Municipal Workers, the Electricians and other unions. It proclaimed collective bargaining as the primary function of trade unions, and drew attention to the dangers of compromising trade union independence by participation in management.[53] Not wishing to test opinions by a vote which would certainly have been close-run, the council put up their general secretary to inform Congress that the two propositions were in fact complementary and to point out that the report proposed that worker representatives should be on company boards only where the unions concerned wanted it.

This compromise avoided a showdown, but it was not a good basis for legislation, and in July 1975 the government decided to set up a committee to look into the matter. Its terms of reference were carefully designed to win the assent of the General Council to the delay which was entailed in reference to a committee. They began:

Accepting the need for a radical extension of industrial democracy in the control of companies by means of representation on boards of directors, and accepting the essential role of trade union organisations in this process, to consider how such an extension can best be achieved, taking into account in particular the proposals of the

---

[53] The first part of the resolution reads: 'Congress reaffirms that the overriding role of the unions is the advancement of the interests of their members. It therefore requires that any extension of trade union participation in industrial management shall be, and be seen to be, an extension of collective bargaining and shall in no sense compromise the unions' role as here defined.' (Trades Union Congress, *Annual Report*, 1974, pp. 521–30.)

Trades Union Congress report on industrial democracy as well as experience in Britain, the EEC and other countries.

The membership was announced in December. Sir Alan (now Lord) Bullock was chairman. The three representatives of Congress were all supporters of the General Council's proposals, and a fourth member was the council's legal adviser. The committee were asked to report in twelve months and did so. Majority and minority reports were completed in December 1976 and published the next month. The majority report was signed by the five members already mentioned and two others, one of whom entered substantial reservations in a note of dissent. The three employers on the committee (a fourth having resigned) signed the minority report.

The majority report moved away from the original position of the General Council in two important respects. Firstly, there were to be no supervisory boards. They thought that the importation of this continental device into Britain in order to accommodate worker representatives

> could have one of two main consequences: either it would . . . so delimit the powers of the board on which employees are represented that employee participation in decision-making would be very restricted; or it would impose strains and tensions on decision-making at top level, by requiring the adoption of an alien and rigid board structure.[54]

Secondly, while accepting the principle of parity of representation on the board for employees and shareholders, they proposed that their representatives should jointly co-opt a third group of members. They suggested that this arrangement should operate in companies with two thousand or more employees in the United Kingdom, estimating that this included 'some 738 enterprises employing in all 6 or 7 million people in the United Kingdom'[55]—provided that the employees voted in favour, and that the affirmative voters constituted at least a third of all eligible employees.

Most of their proposals formed a carefully designed plan for making such an arrangement workable in the circumstances of British industrial relations. To deal with multi-unionism, they proposed that, after an affirmative ballot, a Joint Representation Committee,

---

[54] *Report of the Committee of Inquiry on Industrial Democracy*, p. 77.
[55] *Ibid.*, p. 129.

of all the recognized independent unions in the company which wished to be included, should be established to negotiate with the shareholders' representatives on the size of the board, to decide how the workers' representatives were to be selected, and to form the link between the employees and the board members. They held that there was no reason for introducing works councils in Britain, since shop stewards already provided an adequate 'sub-structure' of employee representatives. They devised a complicated but essential set of expedients for applying the proposals to British companies with overseas employees, and to British subsidiaries of overseas companies. They proposed an Industrial Democracy Commission to supervise elections, and deal with deadlocks which might arise, for example in the establishment of Joint Representation Committees and appointments to the boards.

Had the majority finished their report at this stage, they would have been able to claim, with justice, that they had devised a workable arrangement for instituting a system of worker directors which met the narrow requirements imposed on them by their terms of reference. They went on, however, to argue that a system on these lines *ought* to be established. 'During our inquiry', they said, 'we found a widespread conviction, which we share, that the problem of Britain as an industrialised nation is not a lack of native capacity in its working population so much as a failure to draw out their energies and skill to anything like their full potential.' The remedy was to put 'the relationship between capital and labour on to a new basis which will involve not just management but the whole workforce in sharing responsibility for the success and profitability of the enterprise'. This new basis, they believed, could be constructed by carrying through their proposals, and the evidence for their belief was the 'success in improving industrial relations which neighbouring countries in Europe . . . have had in following this path of development'.[56] They quoted particularly West Germany and Sweden.

At this point the majority overreached themselves. The form of representation which they proposed was radically different from anything that exists anywhere in Europe, and its consequences cannot therefore be predicted from European experience. Moreover, they themselves found all the forms of worker representation in Europe which they examined, with the possible exception of that which operates in the West German coal and steel industries, to be

[56] *Ibid.*, p. 160.

unsatisfactory, and the German coal and steel system is representation on a supervisory board which the committee considered to be inappropriate in Britain. Thirdly, systems of worker representation in use in western Europe have had relatively little effect on industrial relations or economic performance, as was made clear in a report specially commissioned by the Bullock Committee.[57] The excellent postwar industrial relations records of Sweden and West Germany are due to other features of the industrial relations systems in those two countries, especially the works councils of West Germany and the centralization of power in the confederations of both unions and employers in Sweden.[58] There is little or no relevant evidence to judge the consequences of implementing the proposals of the majority of the Bullock Committee. It would be a step in the dark.

The minority preferred supervisory boards as vehicles for worker representation. Worker representatives should constitute less than half the board and should be elected by all employees. There should be no representatives on the board unless the majority of employees voted in favour of representation of this kind, and until an Employee Council had been chosen by an electorate consisting of all employees and had 'operated effectively for a specified number of years'.[59] However, their proposals were probably not as significant as their rejection of the majority report in which they expressed the opinion of the great majority of managers in Britain. The most important contribution to the debate from the employers' side was the evidence offered to the Bullock Committee from the Confederation of British Industry which argued for a flexible approach, in which 'participative arrangements must be designed to fit a company structure, and not vice versa'. Companies should therefore be obliged to reach participation agreements 'with their employees (and/or their representatives, where appropriate)'. These agreements should aim to achieve a number of objectives, concerned with improving communications on a wide range of matters and with promoting the 'involvement of the employee in the content and purpose of his job'.[60] Where a company with more than two thousand employees failed to reach an agreement on these lines over a four-year period, a system of participation should be imposed by arbitration, provided

---

[57] Batstone and Davies, *Industrial Democracy: European Experience.*
[58] Clegg, *Trade Unionism under Collective Bargaining.*
[59] *Report of the Committee of Inquiry on Industrial Democracy*, p. 183.
[60] Confederation of British Industry, *Evidence to the Bullock Committee.*

that the scheme received 'affirmation in a secret ballot by a majority of employees'. Worker representation on the board was an appropriate subject for a participation agreement, but was not to be imposed by arbitration. An arbitrated scheme was to be designed by an independent Participation Agency.[61] Following the report of the Bullock Committee, these proposals were reiterated in a further publication, *In Place of Bullock*. They should probably not be regarded as proposals which had the warm support of the majority of British managers, but as the least damaging alternative to the Bullock report which could command any political credibility.

The majority report of the Bullock Committee was received with a roar of condemnation in which British managers were able to express their chagrin at what they perceived as years of growing union power and increasing legislative intervention in the running of private undertakings. There was relatively little favourable comment.

In September 1977 Congress welcomed the analysis of the Bullock Committee, but asked for

> statutory backing to all unions wishing to establish joint control of strategic planning decisions via trade union machinery. This legislation would include the option of parity representation on the board, but would also link up with more flexible forms of joint regulation more clearly based on collective bargaining.

Meanwhile the government had promised to publish its legislative proposals in a White Paper which eventually appeared in May 1978. Companies employing more than five hundred workers were to be obliged 'to discuss with representatives of employees all major proposals affecting the employees of the business before decisions are made'. Representation was to be arranged through joint representation committees of recognized unions. After three or four years there was to be a further obligation on companies employing two thousand or more, if asked by their joint representation committees, to include employee representatives on their boards; but supervisory boards were to be instituted for the purpose and, initially at least, employee representation was not to exceed one-third.[62] This selection of items from the majority and minority reports of the Bullock Committee and the evidence of the Confederation of British Industry may not yet be the last word on the subject.

[61] *Ibid.*   [62] *Industrial Democracy*.

Chapter 11

THEORIES AND DEFINITIONS

The central theme of this book has been the importance of the structure of collective bargaining to an understanding of industrial relations in Britain. The argument begins with the considerable degree of unilateral control over the terms and conditions of their employment established by many unions of skilled workers during the nineteenth century, partly because at that time employers and their associations were reluctant to engage in collective bargaining. Two legacies of this unilateral regulation to the period when collective bargaining became general were that bargaining had to accommodate a large volume of workplace custom and practice, especially in matters of work organization; and that shop stewards became fairly widely established even before 1914. Although obscured, these legacies survived the interwar years of centralized bargaining and unemployment. Under the pressure of conditions during and after the Second World War plant managers in manufacturing found they needed to supplement centralized agreements with more detailed regulation of payment systems and work organization in the plant. In doing so they had to deal with shop stewards, and there grew up an informal but effective system of bargaining and union organization in the workplace. This development owed little to the trade unions outside the plant whose attitudes and structures had been adapted to centralized bargaining.

During the postwar years managers adopted a series of new techniques in an attempt to secure greater control over the deployment of manpower and the organization of work in the plant. Eventually, with government encouragement, the use of these techniques led to the widespread introduction of plant-wide pay agreements and the formalization of plant bargaining, with a consequent centralization of trade union organization in the workplace, which nevertheless retained a high degree of independence from outside union control.

By and large the history of industrial relations in those few private service industries with substantial trade union organization has been much the same.

Although wedded to centralized agreements and disputes procedures, which they had in many instances forced on the unions, employers' associations had in the end to recognize the growth of plant bargaining by diversifying their functions and reconstructing their pay agreements. Eventually trade unions outside the plant were also driven to make adjustments to take account of the changed structure of bargaining, especially by reforming their systems of government to accommodate shop stewards and workplace organization.

Meanwhile the public sector was growing fast. Because of its highly centralized methods of management, its collective bargaining was also centralized. Nevertheless some public industries and services inherited trade union workplace representation with considerable control over work organization; and, with growing economic stringency, all of them experienced the same need for greater managerial control as had manufacturing industry, and made use of many of the same techniques in order to achieve it. In local government, education and the health service, the use of these techniques led to the conscious introduction by management and unions of shop steward organization where it did not exist before.

Despite the formalization of plant bargaining, there is still much informality in styles of bargaining in the workplace. There must be if plant bargainers are to negotiate effectively on the resolution of industrial disputes and problems. Such formalization as there has been has not generally diminished the power of trade union workplace organizations or their control over work arrangements.

In order to achieve their bargaining objectives, managers and trade union representatives appeal to values which depend on comparisons. The art of bargaining consists in selecting and highlighting advantageous comparisons. Changes in the structure of collective bargaining emphasize some comparisons at the expense of others.

The pattern of strikes in postwar Britain and, insofar as it can be discerned, the pattern of other forms of industrial action as well can be partly explained by differences in the structure of collective bargaining between sectors of employment and over time.

Wartime apart, the accepted approach of the British state to industrial relations was to abstain from intervention in strikes and trade union affairs; and also from intervention in collective bargaining where it was well-established, but to offer supports for collective bargaining where they were welcomed, and to find substitutes for it where it was ineffective, or did not exist. Since 1945, however, state intervention has grown for two reasons.

Firstly, economic circumstances have driven both Labour and Conservative administrations into a series of incomes policies. The more rigorous of these have had a considerable effect on collective bargaining while they have lasted—for example, by altering the criteria of acceptable settlements and the pattern of strikes—and have also given an impetus to the long-term development of plant-wide pay agreements. However, their overall impact has been restricted by their discontinuity. In the intervals, bargaining has relapsed towards the starting-point. Nevertheless, the authors of the social contract seem to have appreciated that the operation of an incomes policy is an exercise in collective bargaining at national level and to show greater skill in bargaining of this kind than did their predecessors.

There have also been energetic attempts to control collective bargaining and trade unions by direct legislative intervention. The ambitious bid of the Industrial Relations Act 1971 to curb strikes and reform trade unions proved a spectacular failure and it was largely repealed. The social contract legislation was intended to support collective bargaining rather than to control it, but in order to provide more than traditional support it crossed over the traditional frontiers of state intervention. The long-run consequence might be a gradual extension of judicial control over collective bargaining. However, the eagerness of the courts to advance into this new territory has scared the unions and placed the future of some of the new legislation in doubt.

Does all this amount to a theory of industrial relations with the structure of collective bargaining as the main explanatory variable? It certainly does not do so as it has been presented here. The first task of the foregoing chapters has been to describe what appear to be the main elements of, and developments in, British industrial relations; only after that have explanations been offered—where they were available, and as they seemed to fit in. It is now possible to show that many of them can be brought together to form something of a common theme, and that may make the presentation of the material sufficiently systematic to justify the title of this book; but the exposition and verification of a theory would have to proceed on very different lines.

Since no theory of industrial relations has emerged, at least so far, from this line of inquiry, perhaps it should be sought elsewhere, for example in the established social sciences. Economics is the most senior and developed of the social sciences; and, generally speaking, at least in Anglo-Saxon countries, the study of industrial relations has grown up as an aspect of applied economics. Is it not reasonable to suppose that economic theory should play a major part in interpreting industrial relations?

The relevant part of economics is the theory of the labour market, but this has fallen into disrepute because it cannot explain the behaviour of labour markets. The most notable empirical investigation of labour markets in Britain concluded that 'there were a number of important issues, particularly in the field of wage determination, which have not been satisfactorily resolved and will remain unresolved until we admit the influence of non-economic forces'.[1] There is not much to be gained by looking to economics for a theory of industrial relations if economists have to go outside economics to find an explanation for wage determination.

It does not follow that the student of industrial relations should disregard economics. The disintegration of their central theory has driven labour economists to engage in an ever more extensive search for subordinate theories which, they hope, can be shown to hold good for some limited area of labour market behaviour; and many of these studies are of direct relevance to industrial relations. The theory of the dual labour market,[2] for example, should be called to the attention of anyone who seeks to explore the differences in collective bargaining behaviour between manufacturing and the service sector; but neither this nor other subordinate labour market theories hold out any promise of a general theory of industrial relations.

Subordinate theorizing by sociologists has been of even greater value to students of industrial relations than the contributions of economists. Earlier chapters in this book reveal a larger debt to sociologists than to economists—for example to studies of shop stewards,[3] of union government,[4] and of collective bargaining;[5] and

---

[1] MacKay *et al.*, *Labour Markets under Different Market Conditions*, p. 388.
[2] Doeringer and Piore, *Internal Labor Markets and Manpower Analysis*.
[3] pp. 60–1.   [4] pp. 205, 208.   [5] pp. 238–44.

such sociological studies as Joan Woodward's *The Dock Worker* and
David Lockwood's *The Black-coated Worker* have had a substantial
influence on the study of industrial relations in Britain for more than
twenty years. But these studies have gone no further than the work
of labour economists to provide a theory of industrial relations.

There has, however, been an attempt to derive a general theory of
industrial relations from sociology. Its author, John Dunlop, is a
distinguished labour economist, who was keen to give to the study
of industrial relations (to which he himself has contributed liberally)
the same status as economics enjoys. Drawing upon the analytical
scheme developed by the eminent sociologist Talcott Parsons, he
proclaimed that:

> An industrial-relations system is to be viewed as an analytical
> subsystem of an industrial society on the same logical plane as an
> economic subsystem. The industrial-relations system is not
> coterminus with the economic system; in some respects the two
> overlap and in other respects both have different scopes. The
> procurement of a work force and the setting of compensation for
> labour services are common centres of interest. A systematic
> explanation of production, however, is within economics but
> outside the scope of industrial relations. The full range of rule-
> making governing the work place is outside the scope of an
> economic system but central to an industrial-relations system.[6]

For him an industrial relations system comprised: the actors
(hierarchies of managers and workers and specialized government
agencies); certain contexts (technology, the market and 'the locus
and distribution of power in the larger society'); 'an ideology which
binds the industrial-relations system together'; 'and a body of rules
created to govern the actors at the work place and work community'.[7] The actors make the rules within the constraints imposed by
the contexts and their ideology. He goes on to examine substantive
and procedural rules of industrial relations in coalmining and construction in a number of countries to show that the similarity of
many of the rules can be explained by technologies and market
conditions which transcend national boundaries, and that dis-
similarities of rules on other matters are due to 'special features of the
several national industrial-relations systems'.[8]

[6] John Dunlop, *Industrial Relations Systems*, p. 5.
[7] *Ibid.*, p. 7.   [8] *Ibid.*, p. 195.

In this way, Dunlop asserted, he had developed 'a systematic body of ideas for arranging and interpreting the known facts of worker–manager–government interactions'[9] which provided 'a genuine discipline'.[10] The claim to have offered a systematic method of arranging at least some elements of the subject matter of industrial relations must be granted, but to be accepted as a theory of industrial relations, it has to interpret the 'known facts'. Technology and the market are without question important explanatory variables in industrial relations. But they do not constitute a general theory by themselves. Wide differences between the industrial relations systems persist in developed 'western' democratic countries despite a considerable convergence of technologies and market conditions. For Dunlop these divergences are explained by 'the locus and distribution of power'[11] within each country. This phrase, however, reads like a 'catch-all' expression to cover every relevant influence that does not come under the headings of technology and market conditions. If so, it is not much of a theory unless the relevant elements in the locus and distribution of power are picked out and their relationship with patterns of employment rules demonstrated. Dunlop does not do this, and his claim to have established a general theory is not established.

There is still another suggested source for a theory of industrial relations—Marxism. Its advocates would probably take the view that the agnostic attitude to theory in industrial relations which has been adopted in this chapter so far is disingenuous and misleading. One of them has written of an earlier version of this book that its 'author's theoretical presuppositions—which reflect the empiricist–pluralist school long predominant in British academic writing on industrial relations—are not explicitly stated'; and that, where 'theoretical assumptions' are not made explicit, they

are not excluded, they are merely hidden below the surface. . . . Criteria of selection . . . are not made explicit and are therefore shielded from criticism. Such a situation is unhealthy for the writer, and unhelpful for the introductory student.[12]

It is therefore convenient at this point to examine the relevance of Marxist and pluralist theory to industrial relations and in doing so to

---

[9] *Ibid.*, p. 380.   [10] *Ibid.*, p. 6.   [11] *Ibid.*, p. 11.
[12] Richard Hyman, *Industrial Relations, A Marxist Introduction*, pp. 10, 205.

honour the undertaking, given at the beginning of the first chapter, to deal in the last chapter with the definition of the subject.

How do Marxism and pluralism differ in their analyses of industrial relations? Richard Hyman argues that they diverge from the start—in their definitions of its subject-matter. As examples of pluralist definitions he takes that of Allan Flanders—'the institutions of job regulation';[13] and John Dunlop's notion of an 'industrial-relations system' which analyses 'the rules of the work place and the work community'.[14] Hyman criticizes Flanders' definition because 'the interest is in how existing patterns of social relations are stabilised, rather than in the significance in their own right of challenges to the prevailing social structure'; and detects this conservative tendency at three points. Firstly, the word 'institutions' directs attention to formal organizations rather than to the informal organizations which are more likely to be the source of challenges to the system. Secondly, the word 'regulation is far too restrictive. . . . The focus is on how any conflict is contained and controlled, rather than on the processes through which disagreements and disputes are generated.' Thirdly, Dunlop's notion of a *system* of rules, which Flanders quoted with approval although he did not incorporate it in his definition, also puts undue emphasis on the maintenance of stability. Consequently, Hyman offers an amended definition—'the process of control over work relations'—which, he claims, is free from these defects.[15]

For some people the word 'institutions' may signify formal rather than informal organizations; but it does not have to do so. It can be used to cover both types of organization equally, and in fact most sociologists and students of industrial relations use it that way. Certainly that was Flanders' usage. His major work, *The Fawley Productivity Agreements*, was very largely a study of informal organization in workplace industrial relations. While noting that, at one time, writers on industrial relations concentrated on formal organizations (perhaps because informal organizations in industrial relations were then inadequately researched, rather than from a desire to mislead), Hyman himself acknowledges that they no longer do so. There does not seem to be much to argue about here.

It must be admitted that the word 'process' calls up notions of change and development more readily than does 'institution'. On the

[13] *Industrial Relations: What is Wrong with the System*, p. 10.
[14] *Op. cit.*, pp. 380–9.　　　[15] *Op. cit.*, pp. 10–12.

other hand, it is narrower than 'institution'. Collective bargaining can be described either as an institution or as a process, but it is stretching language to call a trade union or an employers' association—or a shop stewards' committee—a process. Flanders' definition therefore explicitly includes a number of important aspects of industrial relations which Hyman's words do not readily cover. If the point had been put to Flanders, he might very well have been willing to compromise on 'the institutions and processes of job regulation'. But there is also a more radical solution. Neither word is essential to the definition. Job regulation cannot be studied in the abstract. It must be observed embodied in institutions and operating through processes. Consequently, the student of job regulation must study both institutions and processes. Nothing therefore is lost if Flanders' definition is reduced to two words—'job regulation';[16] and any limitation implied by the word 'institutions' is thereby removed.

It is also true that the word 'control' has a wider significance than 'regulation'. The behaviour of strikers, for example, may be influenced by the treatment of strikes on the media. Those who control the media could therefore be said to have 'control' over the strikers. If so, a study of the reporting of strikes is relevant to industrial relations, although it is not part of 'job regulation'. However, on this definition almost anything might be relevant to industrial relations. If, as Hyman accepts,

> rules of various kinds clearly do pervade the world of work and employment, and the institutions which devise and implement this network of rules are of central importance to the study of industrial relations,[17]

then there is advantage in a definition which directs attention to the central features of the subject, even at the expense of some loss of coverage.

It cannot be denied that the words 'regulation' and 'system' have conservative implications. Both imply stability, for without order there can be neither rules nor systems. But the definition is not necessarily the worse for that. It becomes disadvantageous only if it directs attention away from the causes of disagreement and conflict in industrial relations. But a definition which lays stress upon the

---

[16] This has always been my definition. See *The System of Industrial Relations in Great Britain*, 1970 edn., p. 1.   [17] *Op. cit.*, p. 11.

mechanisms which limit conflict and restore stability must also direct attention to sources of dispute and disorder without which those mechanisms would be unnecessary. It is certainly possible for a student of industrial relations to ignore conflict, or to understimate its importance. But if he does, the blame cannot be ascribed to Flanders' definition. It belongs to his own lack of comprehension.

There remains Hyman's substitution of 'work relations' for 'job'. He does not set out the case for it at length, but it appears to derive from his belief that Flanders' definition gives too much weight to formal organizations. Once that belief is shown to be erroneous, the substitution can be seen to be disadvantageous. There is no doubt that the employment relationship is central to industrial relations. 'Job' therefore gives much greater precision to the definition than the vague phrase 'work relations' would do.

Flanders' definition can therefore be defended against Hyman's criticisms, but it is even more important to note that there is no chasm between the two definitions. 'Job regulation' is to be preferred for its greater elegance and precision, but if students of industrial relations had to rub along with 'processes of control over work relations' they would probably manage fairly well; and come to much the same conclusions at the end of the day.

To say that there is not much to choose between Marxist and pluralist definitions of industrial relations is not to say that Marxism and pluralism are the same. That would be nonsense. Even so, the difference between their analyses of industrial relations should not be exaggerated. There is much in common between the accounts which they give of both 'western' societies in general and industrial relations in particular. Both Marxists and pluralists are concerned with conflict, and both are concerned with stability. Both regard conflict as inevitable in industrial relations as in other aspects of social life. Both face the problem of explaining how social conflict can persist for long periods without destroying society—the record of industrial conflict in Britain goes back for two centuries or more, but so far it has been contained. And there is much common ground in their answers.

One essential element in the Marxist account of industrial relations is that trade unions become enmeshed in the institutions and operations of capitalist society. Different terms have been used for this entanglement—economism, incorporation, institutionalization—and fine distinctions may be made between them, but the general process affects all union representatives who come into contact with managers and employers' associations. So long as both sides would prefer a settlement reasonably near their own objectives to a trial of strength, they must explore the possibility of such a settlement, usually through a series of meetings. Even when they have decided how far they can push each other, there are other things to be considered before deciding whether to risk a stoppage. They have to live together. They will be negotiating with each other next year, the year after, and maybe ten years hence. It may therefore be unwise to extract the last ounce on every favourable occasion for fear of reprisal when circumstances are unfavourable. Then there is the administration of the agreement, which brings the two sides together day after day. Thus unions become involved in operating and elaborating the system of industrial relations within capitalist society.

It is not a matter of treachery or crossing over to the other side. There may, of course, be 'bent' trade union officers, just as corruption is found in other walks of life, but this process affects *all* union representatives who take collective bargaining seriously. Communist and other left-wing officers and shop stewards cultivate their contacts with managers and their sources of information in order to be able to 'deliver the goods' to their members. They, like their colleagues, are well aware that their effectiveness in their job depends on good professional relations with management negotiators. Equally, economism or incorporation does not meant that union officers always refrain from using the pressures that they command. They know that their ability to 'deliver the goods' depends in the last resort on the damage they can do to the business of the firms with which they deal. If challenged, they must demonstrate their strength. But competent negotiators on both sides will want to be sure that the occasion and the benefits to be gained really justify open conflicts.

Institutionalization reduces the potentiality of the unions as instruments of radical protest and revolt. For the great majority of trade unionists who are not revolutionaries this may not be a matter of regret. Indeed it is quite wrong to suppose that trade unions were once revolutionary organizations which have subsequently been tamed. Most unions have never been revolutionary organizations. From the point of view of the revolutionary, however, the consequences are to be deplored. For in most countries the trade unions are the largest and most important organizations of workers. Where they are allied to a political party they provide the party with wider support, greater funds and more activists than it could ever hope to find for itself. Consequently, no revolutionary movement has much chance of success without widespread support among the unions. It is true that in most unions the revolutionary trade unionists has the opportunity to canvass his beliefs in the attempt to win support against the day of the revolution. But that is not enough for the Marxist. He demands that workers should be politicized by action; that they should learn to use the collective power of the union as an instrument of revolt in the day-to-day business of dealing with shop floor problems so that they will be ready to use it for the revolution when the occasion arises. And this preparation is hampered by the assimilation of unions into the capitalist system, which may give the workers the best deal that they can hope for under a capitalist system, but hinders the use of the unions as instruments of class warfare.

Assimilation is not inevitable. Unions may choose to resist it. For three-quarters of a century the syndicalist doctrine has preached resistance and spelled out how it is to be organized. Unions must enter into no commitments. By all means let the union terminate a strike when the employer grants an improvement, but it must not promise to honour the new arrangement as a binding agreement. If the opportunity is there, a new strike should be called the following week. The union should not accumulate funds, for union officers are reluctant to risk large investments. Without funds there is nothing to risk. The union should call short sharp strikes so as not to strain the workers' resources too much or, better still, employ sabotage which permits workers to hurt their employers without sacrificing their pay. The union should not bother too much about mass membership. The members should be a class-conscious elite who will naturally take the lead in any conflict with management, but whose militant decisions and policies cannot be overridden by the votes of a non-militant majority.

Syndicalism and kindred doctrines have had an influence in Britain, but few unions have acted upon them, and then only for short periods. But things are different in France. For many years before 1914 syndicalism was the predominant philosophy of the French unions, and it has continued to have a considerable influence in the major union federations there, including the largest of them, the Communist-dominated C.G.T. The benefits of this state of affairs for the revolutionary are obvious. The major federations are committed to revolution, although they do not always make the best use of their opportunities. The drawbacks are equally evident. In the private sector the unions are woefully weak in membership and in resources. Collective bargaining is ill-developed, and the actual earnings of French workers in the private sector owe more to the uncovenanted concessions by their employers than to the efforts of their unions.

This is the Marxist theory of economism, or incorporation, or institutionalization. The pluralist can accept every word of it. Indeed, without using these words, Chapter 6 has already described its main features. The terminology may differ. The pluralist may prefer to talk of social democracies (where the term applies) rather than capitalist socieites. He may describe as 'conflict between pressure groups' what the Marxist calls class conflict (although many Marxists admit that class conflict is frequently obscured by 'sectionalism'). The pluralist term for economism or incorporation might be 'a process of concession and compromise which helps to bind society together'. But translation is easy.

The two philosophies do not necessarily differ even when they turn from analysis to prediction. Many modern Marxists do not regard the proletarian revolution as inevitable. The contradictions in capitalist society create the conditions for it, but whether it occurs and whether it is successful depend on how men choose to act. For their part, pluralists cannot demonstrate that existing plural societies will be permanent. Concession and compromise may contain conflict, but they cannot be guaranteed to do so for ever.

The divergence between Marxists and pluralists is therefore to be found mainly in their attitudes. Marxists regret the process of assimilation because it postpones the revolution, and they argue that trade unionists should beware of it. Pluralists welcome it as a means to social stability, and they advise trade unionists to make the best of it. For the Marxist, the revolution will bring a new social order freeing men and women to achieve their full potential. For the pluralist, the Marxist social order will suppress and iron out sectional interests and beliefs in deference to a monolithic and monotonous creed. These are differences of enormous significance, but they are remote from the analysis of contemporary British industrial relations.

Another common feature of the analyses of industrial relations offered by the two philosophies is their generality. Marxism sets out to explain the whole of social development. Pluralism claims to account for the operation of all plural societies. Consequently neither of them provides ready answers to questions with which this book has been concerned: why has workplace organization played such a large part in British industrial relations? why have employers' associations failed to regulate pay in postwar Britain? how can the complex structure of British trade unions be explained? or what accounts for the varied success of British incomes policies? There is often little to choose between the answers which Marxists and pluralists give to these questions;[18] and it not infrequently happens that there are wide differences among Marxists and among pluralists. For both philosophies are so general that they are compatible with a wide range of answers to subordinate questions of this kind.

Students of industrial relations should therefore be aware that Marxist industrial relations and pluralist industrial relations are not two different subjects, and that Marxist and pluralist examiners of their work are not likely to award radically different marks to the same student. They may make more progress by concentrating on the relative cogency of various answers to questions in industrial relations than by trying to devise Marxist or pluralist answers, or by trying to discern the precise philosophical presuppositions of each author or teacher. However, those who have read this chapter will now be aware, if they were not before, of the philosophical presuppositions of its author. They can judge for themselves how far these presuppositions affect his treatment of British industrial relations in earlier chapters; and whether or not they render it suspect.

[18] The reader can, for example, compare the accounts of British union structure and of the significance of workplace organization in British industrial relations given in Chapters 1 and 4 with those in Chapters 2 and 6 of *Industrial Relations, A Marxist Introduction* by Richard Hyman.

INDEX OF REFERENCES

Acton Society Trust. *Management Succession: the Recruitment, Selection, Training and Promotion of Managers*. London: the Trust, 1956, 157

Advisory Conciliation and Arbitration Service. *Disciplinary Practice and Procedures in Employment*. Code of Practice 1. London: HMSO, n.d., 406

———. *Disclosure of Information to Trade Unions for Collective Bargaining Purposes*. Code of Practice 2. London: HMSO, n.d., 406

———. *First Annual Report*. London: ACAS, 1976, 364

———. *Annual Report 1976*. London: ACAS, 1977, 410, 422, 424

———. *Annual Report 1977*. London: ACAS, 1978, 412, 420, 422, 424

———. *General Accident Fire and Life Assurance Corporation Limited, the Association of Scientific, Technical and Managerial Staffs and the Association of Professional, Executive, Clerical and Computer Staff*. Trade Union Recognition, Employment Protection Act 1975 Section 12-Report No 16. London: ACAS, 1977, 412

———. *W. H. Allen Sons and Company Limited and the United Kingdom Association of Professional Engineers*. Trade Union Recognition, Employment Protection Act Section 12-Report No 68. London: ACAS, 1977, 411

———. *Road Haulage Wages Council*. Report No 6. London: ACAS, 1976, 75, 78, 79, 426

———. *Button Manufacturing Wages Council*. Report No 11. London: ACAS, 1978, 430

Allen, V. L. *Trade Union Leadership, Based on a Study of Arthur Deakin*. London: Longmans, Green, 1957, 222, 223

Associated British Chambers of Commerce and Confederation of British Industry. *Report of the Commission of Inquiry into Industrial and Commercial Representation*. London: ABCC,CBI, 1972. Chairman: Lord Devlin, 343

Bain, G.S. *The Growth of White-Collar Unionism*. Oxford: Clarendon P, 1970, 183

———, and F. Elsheikh, *Union Growth and the Business Cycle*. Oxford: Blackwell, 1976, 178

Baldwin, G. B. *Beyond Nationalisation: the Labor Problems of British Coal*. Cambridge, Mass.: Harvard U.P., 1955, 272

Batstone, Eric, Ian Boraston and Stephen Frenkel. *Shop Stewards in Action: the Organisation of Workplace Conflict and Accommodation*. Oxford: Blackwell, 1977, 12, 43, 44, 60, 61, 239, 241, 252

———. *The Social Organisation of Strikes*. Oxford: Blackwell, 1978, 261, 271, 286

Batstone, Eric and P. L. Davies. *Industrial Democracy: European Experience*. Two Reports prepared for the Industrial Democracy Committee. London: HMSO, 1976, 442

Bayliss, F. J. *British Wages Councils*. Oxford: Blackwell, 1962, 297, 298, 299

Bealey, Frank. 'The Political System of the Post Office Engineering Union'. *British Journal of Industrial Relations*, xv (November 1977), 211

Benson, Henry, and Sam Brown. *Report on the Formation of a National Industrial Organisation*. London: National Association of British Manufacturers, Federation of British Industries, British Employers Confederation, 1964, 341

Board of Trade. *Earnings and Hours of Labour of Workpeople of the United Kingdom*, vi. *Metal, Engineering and Shipbuilding Trades in 1906*. London: HMSO, 1911 (Cd. 5184), 130

Boraston, Ian, H. A. Clegg and Malcolm Rimmer. *Workplace and Union: a Study of Local Relationships in Fourteen Unions*. London: Heinemann, 1975, 10, 33, 34, 50, 53, 57, 199, 200, 215

Braverman, Harry. *Labor and Monopoly Capital: the Degradation of Work in the Twentieth Century*, New York and London: Monthly Review Press, 1974, 132

British Employers Confederation. *Bulletin*, 341

——. *Britain's Industrial Future*. London: BEC, 1955, 340

British Standards Institution. *Glossary of Terms in Work Study*. London: BSI, 1959, 132

Brittan, Samuel, and Peter Lilley. *The Delusion of Incomes Policy*. London: Temple Smith, 1977, 343

Brown, Marie. *Sweated Labour: a Study of Homework*. London: Low Pay Unit, 1974, 430

Brown, William. A Consideration of "Custom and Practice". *British Journal of Industrial Relations*, x (March 1972), 27

——. *Piecework Bargaining*. London: Heinemann, 1973, 4, 27, 28, 29, 134

——. 'Incomes Policy and Pay Differentials'. *Oxford Bulletin of Economics and Statistics*, 58 (February 1976), 370, 371

——. and Margaret Lawson. 'The Training of Trade Union Officers'. *British Journal of Industrial Relations*, xi (November 1973), 231

——. and Keith Sisson. 'The Use of Comparisons in Workplace Wage Determination'. *British Journal of Industrial Relations*, xiii (March 1975), 251

——, and Michael Terry. 'The Changing Nature of National Wage Agreements'. *Scottish Journal of Political Economy*, 25 (June 1978), 18

——, Robert Ebsworth and Michael Terry. 'Factors Shaping Shop Steward Organisation in Britain'. *British Journal of Industrial Relations*, xvi (July 1978), 37, 42, 44, 45, 46, 48, 53, 191

Business Statistics Office, *Business Monitor*. London: HMSO, 6

——. *Census of Distribution*. London: HMSO, 6

Cameron, G. C. 'Post-War Strikes in the North-East Shipbuilding and Shiprepairing Industry'. *British Journal of Industrial Relations*, ii (March 1964), 15, 276

Carey, Alex. 'The Hawthorne Studies: a Radical Criticism'. *American Sociological Review* (June 1967), 153

Cassier's Magazine, 20

Central Arbitration Committee. *Annual Report 1976*. London: HMSO, 1977, 433

——. Annual Report 1977. London: HMSO, 1978, 399, 433

——. *Avis Rent-a-Car Limited and Transport and General Workers Union*. Award 189, 1977. (typescript), 420

——. *Phoenix Timber Company Limited and Transport and General Workers Union*. Award 272, 1977. (typescript), 420

Central Policy Review Staff. *The Future of the British Car Industry*. London: HMSO, 1975, 147

Central Statistical Office. *Annual Abstract of Statistics*. London: HMSO, 7

Chemicals Economic Development Committee, *Chemical Manpower in Europe*. London: HMSO, 1973, 193, 194

Clegg, H. A. *Labour Relations in London Transport*. Oxford: Blackwell, 1950, 222, 223

——. *General Union: a Study of the National Union of General and Municipal Workers.* Oxford: Blackwell, 1954, 35, 222

——. *General Union in a Changing Society: a Short History of the National Union of General and Municipal Workers, 1889–1964.* Oxford: Blackwell, 1964, 22

——. *The System of Industrial Relations in Great Britain.* Oxford: Blackwell, 1970, 451

——. *How to Run an Incomes Policy, and Why We Made Such a Mess of the Last One.* London: Heinemann, 1971, 143, 144, 360

——. *Trade Unionism under Collective Bargaining: a Theory Based on Comparisons of Six Countries.* Oxford: Blackwell, 1976, 442

——, and R. Adams. *The Employers' Challenge: a Study of the National Shipbuilding and Engineering Disputes of 1957.* Oxford: Blackwell, 1957, 187

——, and T. E. Chester. *Wages Policy and the Health Service.* Oxford: Blackwell, 1957, 106

——, A. Fox and A. F. Thompson. *A History of British Trade Unions Since 1889.* Vol. 1. Oxford: Clarendon P, 1964, 22

——, A. J. Killick and R. Adams. *Trade Union Officers: a Study of Full-time Officers, Branch Secretaries and Shop Stewards in British Trade Unions.* Oxford: Blackwell, 1961, 44, 56, 58

Cliff, Tony. *The Employers' Offensive.* London: Pluto P., 1970, 253

Cole, G. D. H. *Workshop Organisation.* Oxford: Clarendon P, 1923, 21

——. *Attempts at General Union: a Study in British Trade Union History,* London: Macmillan, 1953, 26

Cole, W. J. 'Research Note. The Financing of the Individual Striker: A Case Study in the Building Industry'. *British Journal of Industrial Relations,* xiii (March 1975), 283

Commission on Industrial Relations. *The Hotel and Catering Industry.* London: HMSO. Part i. *Hotels and Restaurants.* Report 23, 1971. (Cmnd 4789), 430

Part ii *Industrial Catering.* Report 27. London: HMSO, 1972, 300, 426,427

——. *Disclosure of Information.* Report 31. London: HMSO, 1972, 406

——. *Industrial Relations Training.* Report 33. London: HMSO, 1972, 93

——. *Stamped or Pressed Metal-Wares Wages Council.* Report 50. London: HMSO, 1973, 425

——. *Mansfield Hosiery Mills Limited.* Report 76, London: HMSO, 1974, 401

——. *Industrial Relations in Multi-plant Undertakings.* Report 85. London: HMSO, 1974, 12

——. *Retail Distribution.* Report 89. London: HMSO, 1974, 75, 301, 429

——. *Employers Organisations and Industrial Relations.* Study No 1. London: HMSO, 1972, 77, 79, 91, 92, 94, 99

——. *Industrial Relations at Establishment Level: a Statistical Survey.* Study No 2. London: HMSO, 1973, 41, 51

——. *Trade Union Recognition; CIR Experience.* Study No 5. London: HMSO, 1974, 409

Commissions, Committees and Courts of Inquiry:-

Report of the Commission of Inquiry on the Draft Order to Abolish the Industrial and Staff Canteen Undertakings Wages Council. London: HMSO, 1975. Chairman: H. A. Clegg, 427

Report of the Committee of Inquiry on Industrial Democracy. London: HMSO, 1977. (Cmnd 6706).Chairman: Lord Bullock, 10, 440, 441, 442

Final Report of the Committee of Inquiry into Certain Matters Concerning the Port Transport Industry. London: HMSO, 1965. (Cmnd 2523). Chairman: Lord Devlin, 40, 77, 142, 215, 275

Report of a Court of Inquiry into Trade Disputes at the Barbican and Horseferry Road Construction Sites in London. London: HMSO, 1967 (Cmnd 3396). Chairman: Sir John Cameron, 39

Final Report of the Court of Inquiry into Certain Matters Concerning the Shipping Industry. London: HMSO, 1967, (Cmnd 3211). Chairman: Lord Pearson, 41, 73, 74

Report of a Court of Inquiry under Lord Pearson into the Dispute between the British Steel Corporation and Certain of their Employees. London: HMSO, 1968. (Cmnd 3754), 184

Report of the Court of Inquiry under Lord Scarman into the Dispute between Grunwick Processing Laboratories Limited and Members of the Association of Professional, Executive, Clerical and Computer Staff. London: HMSO, 1977. (Cmnd 6922), 102, 415

Report of a Court of Inquiry into a Dispute between the National Union of Blastfurnacemen and the British Steel Corporation. London: ACAS, 1975. Chairman: Sir Richard Way, 189

Report of a Court of Inquiry into a Dispute between the Parties represented on the National Joint Council for the Electricity Supply Industry. London: HMSO, 1971. (Cmnd 4594). Chairman: Lord Wilberforce, 114, 259

Confederation of British Industry. *The New Anti-Inflation Policy: Practical Guidance for Employers,* London: CBI, 1975, 364

———. *Evidence to the Bullock Committee.* London: CBI, 1976 (typescript), 442, 443

———. *Britain Means Business 1977.* CBI First National Conference. London: CBI, 1977, 419

———. *In Place of Bullock.* London: CBI, 1977, 156, 443

———. *The Future of Pay Determination: a Discussion Document.* London: CBI, 1977, 344

Conservative Party. *Fair Deal at Work.* London: Conservative Political Centre, 1968, 319

Corina, John. *The British Experiment in Wage Restraint with Special Reference to 1948–50.* D.Phil. thesis, University of Oxford, 1961, 378

Coventry and District Engineering Employers Association. *Annual Report* 1976. Coventry: the Association, 1976, 88

Coussins, Jean. *The Equality Report.* London: National Council for Civil Liberties, 1977, 399

Crichton, Anne, 'The IPM in 1950 and 1960.' *Personnel Management,* December 1961, 127

Daniel, W. W. *Wage Determination in Industry.* London: PEP Report 563, 1976, 9–10

———. *The Next Stage of Incomes Policy.* London: PEP Report 568, 1977, 10, 249, 250

Davies, R. J. *An Economic Analysis of Quarterly Strike Activity in the United Kingdom 1966–75.* M. A. dissertation, University of Warwick, 1976, 278

Dean, A. J. H. 'Earnings in the Public and Private Sectors 1950–75'. *National Institute Economic Review* (November 1975), 373

Department of Employment. *The Reform of Collective Bargaining at Plant and Company Level.* London: HMSO, 1971 (Manpower Paper 5), 17, 50, 129

Department of Employment Gazette, 85, 266, 277, 392, 431

Department of Employment and Productivity. *A National Minimum Wage: Report of an Inter-Departmental Working Party.* London: HMSO, 1969, 431

Doeringer, Peter and Michael Piore. *Internal Labor Markets and Manpower Analysis.* Lexington, Mass: Heath, 1971, 447

Dunlop, John. *Industrial Relations Systems.* Southern Illinois U.P.: Feffer and Simons, 1971, 448, 449

Durcan, J. and W. E. J. McCarthy. 'The State Subsidy Theory of Strikes: An Examination of Statistical Data for the Period 1956–1970'. *British Journal of Industrial Relations,* XII (March 1974), 283

Edelstein, J. D. and Malcolm Warner. *Comparative Union Democracy: Organisation and Opposition in British and American Unions.* London: Allen and Unwin, 1975, 208

Edwards, Christine. 'Measuring Union Power; a Comparison of Two Methods applied to the Study of Local Union Power in the Coal Industry'. *British Journal of Industrial Relations*, xvi (March 1978), 242, 256

Eldridge, J. E. T. *Industrial Disputes: Essays in the Sociology of Industrial Relations*. London: Routledge, 1968, 192

Elliott, R. F. 'The National Wage Round in the United Kingdom: a Sceptical View'. *Oxford Bulletin of Economics and Statistics*, 38 (August 1976), 247

Engineering Employers Federation. *Annual Review 1976–7*. London: EEF, 1977, 268

Federation of British Industry. *Grand Council Minutes* (typescript) 339

Flanders, Allan, *The Fawley Productivity Agreements: a Case Study of Management and Collective Bargaining*. London: Faber, 1964, 16, 128, 140, 142, 158

——. *Industrial Relations: What is Wrong with the System? An Essay on its Theory and Future* London: Faber, 1965, 450

——, and H. A. Clegg. *The System of Industrial Relations in Great Britain*. Oxford: Blackwell, 1954, 290, 296, 301

Fox, Alan. *Industrial Sociology and Industrial Relations*. London: HMSO, 1966. (Donovan Commission Research Paper 3), 162, 163

Friedmann, Georges. *Industrial Society: the Emergence of the Human Problems of Automation*. Glencoe, IL: Free P., 1955, 132

Fryer, Bob, Andy Fairclough and Tom Manson. *Organisation and Change in the National Union of Public Employees*. University of Warwick: Department of Sociology, 1974, 218

Gallie, Duncan. *In Search of the New Working Class: Automation and Social Integration within the Capitalist Enterprise*. Cambridge: Cambridge U.P., 1978, 254

Gennard, John. *Financing Strikers*. London: Macmillan, 1977, 281, 283

——, and Roger Lasko. 'The Individual and Strike'. *British Journal of Industrial Relations*, xiii (November 1975), 283

Goodman, J. F. B., E. G. A. Armstrong, J. E. Davis and A. Wagner, *Rule-Making and Industrial Peace: Industrial Relations in the Footwear Industry*. London: Croom Helm, 1977, 81

Goodman, J. F. B. and T. G. Whittingham. *Shop Stewards in British Industry*. New York: McGraw Hill, 1969, 43

Gospel, Howard. 'The Development of Managerial Organisation in Industrial Relations – a Historical Perspective' (unpublished typescript), 126

Government Social Survey. *Workplace Industrial Relations*. London: HMSO, 1968, 13, 45, 52, 56, 87, 94, 160, 224, 258

Grant, Wyn, and David Marsh. *The Confederation of British Industry*. London: Hodder and Stoughton, 1977, 95

Guillebaud, C. W. *Determination and Wage Policy: a Lecture and a Postscript*. Welwyn: Nisbet, 1967 ed., 309, 332

H. M. Treasury. *Staff Relations in the Civil Service*. London: HMSO 1975, 104

Hansard, 69

Hemingway, John, *Conflict and Democracy: Studies in Trade Union Government*. Oxford: Clarendon P. 223

——, and I. Keyser. *Who's in Charge? Worker Sit-ins in Britain Today*. Metra Consulting Group, 1975, 269

Hill, Stephen. *The Dockers: Class and Tradition in London*. London: Heinemann, 1976, 40

Howe, Ellic. *The London Compositor: Documents relating to Wages, Working Conditions and Customs of the London Printing Trade 1785–1900*, London. Bibliographical Society, 1947, 63

Hughes, John. *Trade Union Structure and Goverment*. London: HMSO, 1967–8. (Donovan Commission Research Paper 5).
Part 1. *Structure and Development*, 165, 185
Part 2. *Membership Participation and Trade Union Government*, 200
Hunter, Laurence. 'British Incomes Policy 1972–1974'. *Industrial and Labor Relations Review*, 29 (October 1975), 369
Hyman, Richard. *Disputes Procedure in Action: a Study of the Engineering Disputes Procedure in Coventry*. London: Heinemann, 1972, 243, 244
——. *Strikes*. London: Fontana, 1972, 262, 269
——. *Industrial Relations: a Marxist Introduction*. London: Macmillan, 1975, 449, 450, 451, 456
——, and Ian Brough. *Social Values and Industrial Relations*. Oxford: Blackwell, 1975, 249

Industrial Council: Inquiry into Industrial Agreements. *Minutes of Evidence, etc.* London: HMSO, 1913 (Cd 6953) Chairman: G. Askwith, 64
Industrial Relations Review and Report, 225, 430
Inns of Court Conservative and Unionist Society. *A Giant's Strength: Some Thoughts on the Constitutional and Legal Position of Trade Unions in England*. London: the Society, Johnson, 1958, 315
Institute of Personnel Management, (Manab Thakur and Deirdre Gill). *Job Evaluation in Practice: A Survey of 213 Organisations in the UK*. London: IPM, 1976, 139
International Labour Office, *British Joint Production Machinery*. Montreal: I.L.O., 1944, 152

Jackson, Dudley, H. A. Turner and Frank Wilkinson. *Do Trade Unions Cause Inflation? Two Studies: with a Theoretical Introduction and Policy Conclusion*. Cambridge: Cambridge U.P., 1972, 357
Jacobson, Sydney, and William Connor. *The Daily Mirror Spotlight on Trade Unions*. London: Daily Mirror, n.d., 315

Kahn-Freund, Otto. 'Intergroup Conflicts and their Settlement'. *British Journal of Sociology*, 5 (September 1954), 117
——. *Labour and the Law*. London: Stevens, 1977, ed., 387.
Keohane, D. J. *An Account and Assessment of two Employers Associations in Building and Civil Engineering*. M.A. dissertation, University of Warwick, 1976, 89, 90
Knowles, K. G. J. C., and D. Robinson. 'Wage Rounds and Wage Policy'. *Bulletin of the Oxford University Institute of Statistics*, 24 (May 1962), 247

Lane, Tony, and Kenneth Roberts. *Strike at Pilkingtons*. London: Collins/Fontana, 1971, 224
Lerner, Shirley. *Breakaway Unions and the Small Trade Union*. London: Allen and Unwin, 48, 185
——, and John Bescoby. 'Shop Steward Combine Committees in the British Engineering Industry'. *British Journal of Industrial Relations*, IV (July 1966), 48
Lipset, S. M., M. Trow and J. Coleman. *Union Democracy: the Internal Politics of the International Typographical Union*. Glencoe, Ill.: Free Press, 1956, 205
Lipsey, R. G. and J. M. Parkin. 'Incomes Policy: a Reappraisal'. *Economica*, XXXVII (May 1970), 367
Lockwood, David. *The Blackcoated Worker: a Study in Class Consciousness*. London: Allen and Unwin, 1958, 448

McCarthy, W. E. J. *The Closed Shop in Britain*. Oxford: Blackwell, 1964, 25, 204

——. *The Role of Shop Stewards in British Industrial Relations: a Survey of Existing Information and Research*. London: HMSO, 1966 (Donovan Commission Research Paper 1), 16, 31, 44, 155, 235, 236, 237, 288

——. 'Compulsory Arbitration in Great Britain: the Work of the Industrial Disputes Tribunal, *Three Studies in Collective Bargaining*. London: HMSO, 1968 (Donovan Commission Research Paper 8), 304

——, and B. A. Clifford. 'The Work of Industrial Courts of Inquiry'. *British Journal of Industrial Relations*, IV (March 1966), 304, 305

——, and N. D. Ellis. *Management by Agreement: an Alternative to the Industrial Relations Act*. London: Hutchinson, 1973, 390

——, and S. R. Parker. *Shop Stewards and Workshop Relations: the Results of a Study undertaken by the Government Social Survey for the Royal Commission on Trade Unions and Employers Associations*. London: HMSO, 1968 (Donovan Commission Research Paper 10), 51

MacKay, D. I., D. Boddy, J. Brack, J. A. Diack, N. Jones. *Labour Markets under Different Employment Conditions*. London: Allen and Unwin, 1971, 447

McKersie, Robert and Laurence Hunter. *Pay, Productivity and Collective Bargaining*. London: Macmillan, 1973, 143, 151, 352

Marsh, A. I. *Industrial Relations in Engineering*. Oxford, London: Pergamon P., 1965, 93

——, and E. E. Coker. 'Shop Steward Organisation in the Engineering Industry'. *British Journal of Industrial Relations*, I (June 1963), 52, 155

——, and W. E. J. McCarthy. *Disputes Procedure in Britain*. London: HMSO, 1968 (Donovan Commission Research Paper 2, part 2), 89

Mayo, Elton. *The Human Problems of an Industrial Civilisation*. New York: Macmillan, 1933, 153

Mellish, Michael. *The Docks after Devlin: a Study of the Effects of the Recommendations of the Devlin Committee on Industrial Relations in the London Docks*. London: Heinemann, 1972, 40, 279

Michels, Robert. *Political Parties*. Glencoe, Ill.: Free Press, 1949, 200

Ministry of Labour. Motor Industry Joint Labour Council. *Report by Mr A. J. Scamp on the Activities of the Council*. London: HMSO, 1966, 261

Ministry of Labour Gazette, 14

Ministry of Labour and National Service. *Industrial Relations Handbook*, 1944. Supplement No 3. *Joint Consultation in Industry*. London: HMSO, 1949, 154

——. *Annual Report 1949*. London: HMSO, 1950 (Cmd 8017), 154

Ministry of Munitions. *History of the Ministry of Munitions*. [London] 1918–22, 133

Moran, Michael. *The Union of Post Office Workers: a Study in Political Sociology*. London: Macmillan, 1974, 219

——. *The Politics of Industrial Relations: The Origins, Life and Death of the 1971 Industrial Relations Act*. London: Macmillan, 1977, 343

Morrison, Herbert. *Socialisation and Transport: the Organisation of Socialised Industries with particular reference to the London Passenger Transport Bill*. London: Constable, 1933, 153

Moxon, G. R. 'The Growth of Personnel Management in Great Britain during the War, 1939–1944'. *International Labour Review*, L (December 1944), 126

Moxon J. *Mechanick Exercises, or the Doctrine of Handy-works*. London: Joseph Moxon, 1677–83, 19

Munns, V. G. and W. E. J. McCarthy. *Employers' Associations: the Results of Two Studies*. London: HMSO, 1967 (Donovan Commission Research Paper 7), 74, 93, 96, 97, 99

Myers, C. S. *Industrial Psychology in Great Britain*. London: Cape, 1926, 133

National Association for the Promotion of Social Science (Committee on Trade Societies). *Trade Societies and Strikes*. London: John W. Parker, 1860, 63, 64

National Board for Prices and Incomes. *Reports*. London: HMSO:-

No 1. *Wages, Costs and Prices in the Printing Industry*, 1965 (Cmnd 2750) 15, 375

No 2. *Pay and Conditions of Service of British Railways Staff*, 1966 (Cmnd 2873), 112

No 11. *Pay of Higher Civil Servants*, 1966 (Cmnd 2882), 111

No 16. *Pay and Conditions of Busmen*, 1966 (Cmnd 3012), 112, 354

No 18. *Pay of Industrial Civil Servants*, 1966 (Cmnd 3034), 111

No 19. *General Report April 1965 to July 1966*, (Cmnd 3087), 374

No. 23. *Productivity and Pay During the Period of Severe Restraint*, 1966 (Cmnd 3167), 356

No 24. *Wages and Conditions in the Electrical Contracting Industry*, 1966 (Cmnd 3172), 359

No 27. *Pay of Workers in the Retail Drapery, Outfitting and Footwear Trades*, 1967 (Cmnd 3224), 300, 301

No 29. *Pay and Conditions of Manual Workers in Local Authorities, the National Health Service, Gas and Water Supply*, 1967 (Cmnd 3230), 36, 354

No 35. *Pay and Conditions of Merchant Navy Officers*, 1967 (Cmnd 3302), 78, 354

No 36. *Productivity Agreements* (1), 1967 (Cmnd 3311), 72, 103, 113, 140, 143

No 65. *Payment by Results Systems*, 1968 (Cmnd 3627), 15, 16, 131, 133, 134, 135, 136, 144

———. (Supplement). (Cmnd 3627–1), 134, 136, 144

No 77. *Third General Report*, 1968 (Cmnd 3715), 367

No 83. *Job Evaluation*, 1968 (Cmnd 3772), 18, 139

No 92. *Pay and Conditions in the Building Industry*, 1968 (Cmnd 3837), 75, 136

No 98. *Standing Reference on the Pay of University Teachers in Great Britain*, 1968 (Cmnd 3866), 113

No 104. *Pay and Conditions of Service of Engineering Workers (Second Report on the Engineering Industry)*, 1969 (Cmnd 3931), 71

No 110. *Pay and Conditions in the Clothing Manufacturing Industries*, 1969 (Cmnd 4002), 299, 428

No 123. *Productivity Agreements* (2), 1969 (Cmnd 4136), 143

National Confederation of Employers Organisations, *Industrial Peace Files*, 1927–9. (typescript), 339

National Institute of Industrial Psychology, *The Foreman: a Study of Supervision in British Industry*. London: Staples, 1951, 157, 160

National Economic Development Council, *Growth of the United Kingdom to 1966*. London: HMSO, 1963, 309

National Union of Seamen. *Union General Meeting, May 1976: Report of Proceedings*. London: NUS, 1976, 41

Nichols, Theo, and Peter Armstrong. *Workers Divided: a Study in Shopfloor Politics*. London: Fontana, Collins, 1976, 50, 241, 254

Nichols, Theo, and Huw Beynon. *Living with Capitalism: Class Relations in the Modern Factory*. London: Routledge, 1977, 50

Niven, M. M. *Personnel Management 1913–63*. London: Institute of Personnel Management, 1967, 126

Office of Manpower Economics. *Measured Daywork*. London: HMSO, 1973, 146, 147, 158

Office of Population Censuses and Surveys, Social Survey Division (Stanley Parker). *Workplace Industrial Relations 1972: an enquiry carried out on behalf of the Department of Employment*. London: HMSO, 1974, 13, 56

——. *Workplace Industrial Relations 1973: an enquiry carried out on behalf of the Department of Employment.* London: HMSO, 1975, 13, 24, 42, 43, 44, 52, 56, 61, 159, 258, 260

Panitch, Leo. *Social Democracy and Industrial Militancy: the Labour Party, the Trade Unions and Incomes Policy, 1945–1974.* Cambridge U.P., 1976, 332

Pay Board, *Second Report.* House of Commons Paper, 6 October 1973, 368

——. *Sixth Report,* 1974. London: HMSO, 1974 (Cmnd 5723), 353

——. *Anomalies arising out of the Pay Standstill of November 1972.* London: HMSO, 1973 (Cmnd 5429), 351, 362, 380

——. *Problems of Pay Relativities.* London: HMSO, 1974 (Cmnd 5535), 351, 361, 380

——. *Experience of Operating a Statutory Incomes Policy.* London: Pay Board, 1974 (typescript – Crown Copyright), 362, 368

Paynter, Will. *British Trade Unions and the Problems of Change.* London: Allen and Unwin, 1970, 255, 256–7

Personnel Management, 220

Powell, L. H. *The Shipping Federation: a History of the First Sixty Years, 1890–1950.* London: Shipping Federation, 1950, 65

Pratten, C. F. *Labour Productivity within International Companies.* Cambridge: Cambridge U.P., 1976, 193

Price, Robert, and G. S. Bain. 'Union Growth Revisited: 1948–1974 in Perspective', *British Journal of Industrial Relations,* xiv (November 1976), 6, 11, 179, 299

Reconstruction Committee: Sub-Committee on Relations between Employers and Employed. Chairman: J. H. Whitley. *Interim Report on Joint Standing Industrial Councils.* London: HMSO, 1917 (Cd 8606), 31

——. Supplementary Report on Works Committees. London: HMSO, 1968 (Cd 9001), 31

Roberts, B. C. *Trade Union Government and Administration in Great Britain.* London: LSE, Bell, 1956, 205

Roberts, G. *Demarcation Rules in Shipbuilding and Shiprepairing.* Cambridge: Cambridge U.P., 1967, 192

Robertson, E. J. *Productivity Bargaining and the Engineering Industry.* London: Engineering Employers Federation, 1968, 73

Robinson, B. *The Nature and Extent of Employers Organisation: The British Chemical Industry and its Multi-Nationals.* M.A. dissertation, University of Warwick, 1976, 89

Robson, W. A. *Nationalised Industry and Public Ownership.* London: Allen and Unwin, 1960, 109

Roeber, Joe. *Social Change at Work: the ICI Weekly Staff Agreement.* London: Duckworth, 1975, 151, 159, 160

Roethlisberger, F. J. and William J. Dickson. *Management and the Worker: an Account of a Research Program Conducted by the Western Electric Company, Hawthorne Works, Chicago.* New York: Wiley, 1964, 54

Routh, Guy. *Occupation and Pay in Great Britain 1906–60.* Cambridge: Cambridge U.P., 1965, 110, 247, 248

Royal Commission on the Civil Service. Chairman: Lord Tomlin. *Report.* London: HMSO, 1931 (Cmd 3909), 109

Royal Commission on the Civil Service. Chairman: Sir Raymond Priestley. *Report.* London: HMSO, 1955 (Cmd 9631), 109, 110

Royal Commission on Labour 1891–4. Chairman: Duke of Devonshire. *Fifth and Final Report.* London: HMSO, 1894 (C 7421), 124

Royal Commission on the Police. Chairman: H. Willink. *Report.* London: HMSO, 1960 (Cmnd 1222), 112

Royal Commission on the Organisation and Rules of Trade Unions and Other

Associations 1867–9. Chairman: Sir William Erle. *Fifth Report*. London: HMSO, 1867–68 (3980–1), 64
——. *Minutes of Evidence*. London HMSO 1867 (3952–1), 1867–8 (3980), 62, 63, 65
Royal Commission on Trade Unions and Employers Associations 1965–8. Chairman: Lord Donovan. *Report*. London: HMSO, 1968 (Cmnd 3623), 13, 53, 73, 87, 93, 131, 192, 205, 222, 224, 232, 233, 235, 267, 291, 293, 299, 301, 316, 317, 318, 385, 417, 431
——. *Written Evidence of the Ministry of Labour*. London: HMSO, 1965, 302, 303, 304
——. *Minutes of Evidence*. London: HMSO, 1966–8, 87, 115, 303
——. (secretariat). (1) *Productivity Bargaining*; (2) *Restrictive Labour Practices*. London: HMSO, 1967 (Donovan Research Paper 4), 143
—— *Selected Written Evidence*. London: HMSO, 1968, 16, 73, 93, 96, 98, 341, 342
Runciman, W. G. *Relative Deprivation and Social Justice: a Study of Attitudes to Social Equality in Twentieth Century England*. London; Routledge, 1966, 248

Sayles, Leonard. *Behavior of Industrial Work Groups: Prediction and Control*. New York: Wiley, 1963, 55
Scott, W. H., Enid Mumford, I. C. McGivering, J. M. Kirby. *Coal and Conflict: a Study of Industrial Relations at Colleries*. Liverpool: Liverpool U.P., 1963, 54, 273
Shadwell, Arthur. *The Engineering Industry and the Crisis of 1922: a Chapter in Industrial History*. London: John Murray, 1922, 69
Singleton, Norman. *Industrial Relations Procedures*. London: HMSO, 1975, 30, 268
Smith, D. L. *Racial Disadvantage in Employment*. London: PEP Report 544, 1974, 401

Taylor, F. W. *The Principles of Scientific Management*. New York: Harper, 1911, 132
Terry, Michael. 'The Inevitable Growth of Informality', *British Journal of Industrial Relations*, xv (March 1977), 238, 253
Thomson, A. W. J., and V. V. Murray, *Grievance Procedures*. Farnborough, Hants: Saxon House, 1976, 234, 235
Trades Union Congress. *Interim Report on Post-War Reconstruction*. London: TUC, 1944, 153, 154
——. *Economic Development and Planning*. London: TUC, 1963, 330
——. *An Outline of Job Evaluation and Merit Rating*. London: TUC, 1964, 18
——. *Economic Review 1968*. London: TUC, 1968, 333
——. *The Chequers and Downing Street Talks July to November 1972: Report by the TUC*. London: TUC, n.d., 379
——. *Industrial Democracy: Interim Report by the General Council*. London: TUC, 1973, 439
——. *The Development of the Social Contract*. London: TUC, 1975, 348, 363, 376
——. *Annual Reports*. London: TUC:-
1927, 338
1929, 340
1955, 330
1956, 330
1960, 51, 331
1962, 330
1963, 186, 330, 331
1967, 332
1974, 437, 439
1976, 365

Trist, E. L., G. W. Higgin, H. Murray, A. B. Pollock. *Organisational Choice: Capabilities of Groups at the Coal Face under Changing Technologies*. London: Tavistock, 1963, 149

Turner, H. A. *Trade Union Growth Structure and Policy: a Comparative Study of the Cotton Unions*. London: Allen and Unwin, 1962, 165

——, Garfield Clack and Geoffrey Roberts. *Labour Relations in the Motor Industry: a Study of Industrial Unrest and an International Comparison*. London: Allen and Unwin, 1967, 222, 275

——, Geoffrey Roberts, David Roberts. *Management Characteristics and Labour Conflict: a Study of Managerial Organisation, Attitudes and Industrial Relations*. Cambridge: Cambridge U.P., 1977, 56, 128, 279

University of Liverpool, Department of Social Science (Joan Woodward). *The Dock Worker: an Analysis of Employment Conditions in the Port of Manchester*. Liverpool: Liverpool U.P., 1954, 448

Vernon, H.M., *Industrial Fatigue and Efficiency*. London: Routledge, 1921, 133

Walton, Richard, and Robert McKersie. *A Behavioral Theory of Labor Negotiations: an Analysis of a Social Interaction System*. New York: McGraw Hill, 1965, 242, 244, 246

Webb, Sidney and Beatrice. *The History of Trade Unionism 1666–1920*. London: Longman, 1920, 182

Weekes, B. C. M. *The Amalgamated Society of Engineers 1880–1914: a Study of Trade Union Goverment, Politics, and Industrial Policy*. Ph.D. thesis, University of Warwick, 1970, 20

——, Michael Mellish, Linda Dickens, John Lloyd. *Industrial Relations and the Limits of Law: the Industrial Relations Effects of the Industrial Relations Act, 1971*. Oxford: Blackwell, 1975, 30, 325, 397

Wellisz, Stanislas. 'Strikes in Coal-Mining'. *British Journal of Sociology*, 4 (December 1953), 269

White Papers. London: HMSO:-

Personal Incomes, Costs and Prices, 1948 (Cmd 7321), 307, 346

Incomes Policy: the Next Step, 1962 (Cmnd 1626), 309, 346

Prices and Incomes Policy, 1965 (Cmnd 2639), 347, 373

Prices and Incomes Policy: an 'Early Warning' System, 1965 (Cmnd 2808), 331, 333

Prices and Incomes Standstill: Period of Severe Restraint, 1966 (Cmnd 3150), 347, 359

Prices and Incomes Policy after 30 June 1967 (Cmnd 3235), 347

Productivity, Prices and Incomes Policy in 1968 and 1969, 1968 (Cmnd 3590), 347, 354

In Place of Strife, 1969 (Cmnd 3888), 319, 334

Productivity, Prices and Incomes Policy after 1969, 1969 (Cmnd 4237), 347, 352

The Attack on Inflation, 1975 (Cmnd 6151), 364

The Attack on Inflation after 31st July 1977, 1977 (Cmnd 6882), 349, 353

Industrial Democracy, 1978 (Cmnd 7231), 443

Whybrew, E. G. *Overtime Working in Britain: a Study of its Origins, Functions and Methods of Control*. London: HMSO, 1968 (Donovan Research Paper 9), 16, 142

Wigham, Eric. *What's Wrong with the Unions?* London: Penguin, 1961, 315

Woodward, Joan. *Industrial Organisation: Theory and Practice*. London: Oxford U.P., 1965, 161

——, ed., *Industrial Organisation: Behaviour and Control*. London: Oxford U.P., 1970, 162

Wootton, Barbara. *The Social Foundations of Wage Policy: a Study of Contemporary British Wage and Salary Structure*. London: Allen and Unwin, 1955, 246

Wootton, Graham. 'Parties in Union Government, the Association of Shipbuilding and Engineering Draughtsmen'. *Political Studies*, (June 1961), 210
Workers' Union Record, 22

Yates, M. L. *Wages and Labour Conditions in British Engineering*. London: MacDonald and Evans, 1937, 130

GENERAL INDEX